From *Uncle Tom's Cabin* to *The Help*

From *Uncle Tom's Cabin* to *The Help*

Critical Perspectives on White-Authored Narratives of Black Life

Edited by

Claire Oberon Garcia

Vershawn Ashanti Young

Charise Pimentel

palgrave
macmillan

FROM *UNCLE TOM'S CABIN* TO *THE HELP*

Copyright © 2014, Claire Oberon Garcia, Vershawn Ashanti Young, and Charise Pimentel

First published in 2014 by PALGRAVE MACMILLAN® in the United States—a division of St. Martin's Press LLC, 175 Fifth Avenue, New York, NY 10010

Where this book is distributed in the UK, Europe and the rest of the world, this is by Palgrave Macmillan, a division of Macmillan Publishers Limited, registered in England, company number 785998, of Houndmills, Basingstoke, Hampshire RG21 6XS.

Palgrave Macmillan is the global academic imprint of the above companies and has companies and representatives throughout the world.

Palgrave® and Macmillan® are registered trademarks in the United States, the United Kingdom, Europe and other countries.

ISBN: 978-1-137-44625-1

Library of Congress Cataloging-in-Publication Data
   From Uncle Tom's Cabin to The Help : Critical Perspectives on White-Authored Narratives of Black Life / edited by Claire Oberon Garcia, Vershawn Ashanti Young, Charise Pimentel.
      pages cm
   Includes bibliographical references and index.
   ISBN 978-1-137-44625-1 (hardback : alk. paper) 1. African Americans in literature. 2. American literature—White authors—History and criticism. I. Garcia, Claire Oberon, 1956– editor of compilation. II. Young, Vershawn Ashanti, editor of compilation. III. Pimentel, Charise, 1969– editor of compilation.

   PS173.N4F76 2014
   810.9'3520396073—dc23   2014007771

A catalogue record of the book is available from the British Library.

Design by Scribe Inc.

First edition: August 2014

10 9 8 7 6 5 4 3 2 1

To my children, Dolores, Mateo, Joaquin,
and José and my students at Colorado College
who inspire and guide my work for a just and fair society

—Claire Oberon Garcia (COG)

To the foreseeable future when the history of black
servitude will no longer be the expected and most valued
lens through which to see and achieve black American progress

—Vershawn Ashanti Young (VAY)

To my three beautiful children: Quetzin, Quetzalli,
and Maya. I am inspired by the way you continue to challenge
dominant conceptions of race and language.

—Charise Pimentel (CP)

Contents

Acknowledgments

To my husband, José, for his years of love, patience, and support, and to the marvelous scholars who contributed to this volume

—COG

My loving mother once advised that I should become a postal worker, an occupation that she felt wouldn't require that I work around a bunch of people. You have to understand the context. Momma's from the South: Mississippi. And I was a hotheaded high school senior trying to decide on a college. All the schools on my list were predominantly white. So Momma was trying to protect me from being hurt by a world that doesn't want to deal with a smart, outspoken, no-nonsense, won't-take-no-for-an-answer black man. Although I obviously did not take her advice and have achieved a measure of success, I'm not sure she's changed her mind. She's still warning me about being too black around whites. I know other blacks who feel as Momma does. So I first want to acknowledge a different set of folks in this book than I have in my previous ones: Those blacks for whom double consciousness is still a way of dealing with American antiblack values. Those who—sometimes wittingly, sometimes unknowingly—accede to the fallacy of white superiority in a day and age when it's clear that the racist history of America has warped the very fabric of a nation. Those blacks who'd rather cope than fight. Those who'd have their words placed in the mouths of whites to speak rather than to yell from the mountaintop themselves. These folks have a story to tell, too: a story that explains why they accept the norm of American narration geared toward making skittish whites feel better, a story about racial progress that puts the struggle of blacks only in the mouths of black servants. These stories will not, must not, and indeed cannot be told by whites. So I acknowledge those folks who I hope will get to writin'.

I must also give dap to my collaborators, Claire and Charise. To work with you two, with your grace and erudition, was a lesson and a pleasure. Muah! And thanks as always to my supportive family (yes, including Momma): they are listed by name elsewhere, and they should know I love them.

And last, I have to say "Hey, She-pee-pee" to my eight-month-old daughter, Ari Zhah. She's crawling over my feet as I write. And I must say "I love you, Sweetie" to my wife, Yulanda, who is letting Ari do it so that I can stop and get back to the more important things.

—VAY

I would like to acknowledge my academic and life partner, Octavio Pimentel. Thank you for your guidance in academics and in life. I also want to acknowledge my collaborators, Dr. Claire Garcia and Dr. VAY. It was a pleasure to work with you and to collaborate on such an important topic.

—CP

INTRODUCTION

What's at Stake When White Writes Black?

Claire Oberon Garcia, Vershawn Ashanti Young, and Charise Pimentel

Who Gets to Tell the Story?: Racial Ventriloquism Past and Present

Stories shape our identities on both individual and national levels, so it follows that our understandings of US history, the articulation of American values, and how citizens structure social relations are all created and given meaning by and through narratives. However, the stories that educational institutions authorize and that infiltrate our consciousness through popular culture arise from hegemonic power that remains, unto this day, primarily white. To illustrate, consider what *Slate* writer Jessica Roake uncovers about recent high school assignments designed to teach American history and diversity: "In September [2013], 10th-grade students at a Maryland private school were asked to write a historical essay about the black experience in the South during the Jim Crow era with 'specific examples of prejudice' taken from their summer reading text. The three books the students could choose from were presented as equally valid sources for an American history essay on Jim Crow. The books: *I Know Why the Caged Bird Sings, The Secret Life of Bees*, and *The Help*."

Roake underscores the opening point we wish to make: the dominant narrative lens through which Americans are instructed to view race relations has always been a white one. And when it comes to this fact and the assignment given to the tenth-grade Maryland students, Roake expresses her unequivocal opinion: "The idea of introducing students to the history of America's own violent, terror-driven apartheid era through a reading list that is two-thirds books written from the white perspective by white authors is absurd."

Whether one is inclined to debate or agree with Roake is not the point. What's undeniable is that white-authored narratives are consistently used to structure perceptions of American race relations, particularly black racial experiences. Roake illustrates just how routine this practice is by citing several examples centered on Kathryn Stockett's recent novel about black life, *The Help* (2009). These include assignments and posts on The Learning Network, the *New York Times*' esteemed educator's resource website. When implementing such assignments, "one high school in Ohio," Roake writes, "assigned the book as the lone summer reading for *every* English class, from ninth-grade language arts through 12th-grade British literature" (emphasis in original; Roake).

It's not Roake's point, nor ours, to suggest that there are no powerfully influential narratives that originate with and are promoted by blacks and other people of color or that black-authored narratives of black life are not routinely taught from the elementary school to the university level. The point is this: while black writers, filmmakers, television producers, and scriptwriters have attempted to convey both white and black experiences in mainstream media, their works rarely achieve the large-scale market penetration and financial success of white-authored works and thus do not figure greatly in Americans' understanding of race in general and black experiences in particular.

Consider, for instance, the fact that students are much more likely to encounter Harriet Beecher Stowe's nineteenth-century antislavery novel *Uncle Tom's Cabin: Life among the Lowly* (1852)—whether in book, film, music, or stage form—rather than Martin Delaney's liberation manifesto *The Condition, Elevation, Emigration and Destiny of the Colored People of the United States, Politically Considered*, also published in 1852. Consider also that viewers are more likely to take in the melodramatic passing experiences of Fannie Hurst's tragic mulatta in one of the film adaptations of her novel, *Imitation of Life* (1933), than Jessie Fauset's *Plum Bun* (1928), which depicts a white-skinned black woman's experiments in racial passing as part of, in our opinion, a more nuanced and realistic depiction of emotional and artistic self-definition.

Even in the aftermath of the modern civil rights movement, when blacks gained unprecedented access to various institutions and arenas to speak for themselves and there was an increase of popular interest in black-authored narratives, white perspectives on black life still dominated black representations in the mainstream. John Griffin's bestseller *Black Like Me* (1961), for example, which recounts the experiences of a white journalist who goes South to live as a black man in order to address that ever elusive question, "What does it means to be black in America?" prompted complaints from black writers who argued that they themselves had been responding to this question for many years. This was clear in a fifty-year retrospective on the book: "When Griffin was invited to troubled cities, he said exactly the same thing local black people had been saying," notes Nell Irvin Painter, the black historian and the author of *The History of White People*. "But the powers that were could not hear the black people. Black speakers in America had little credibility until 'yesterday.' Some CNN correspondents who are black now get to comment on America, but that's a very recent phenomenon" (Watson 2011). In addition, several influential black critics assailed novelist William Styron's award-winning novel, *The Confessions of Nat*

Turner (1967), as portraying negative stereotypes about blacks, while the lionized white author insisted that he shed light on the black struggle during the troublesome years of the 1960s (see Clarke).

Concerns about the abundant attention given to white-authored stories of black life in relation to the anemic attention paid to the words of blacks continue into the twenty-first century. Despite the critical and commercial success of a few contemporary writers such as Toni Morrison, the independent films of Spike Lee, and the occasional—and usually short-lived (with the exception of *The Cosby Show* and *Scandal*)—television programs written and produced by African Americans, the most influential and widely disseminated narratives of black life are created by white people through institutions and discourses dominated by white money, decision-making power, and interests. Thus the essays included in this collection explore the aesthetic, cultural, social, political, and ideological implications of the continuing phenomenon of white-authored constructions of black experiences. In this collection of essays, the authors are concerned about how white-authored narratives of black life perpetuate racial power relations—namely, whiteness. As will be illustrated throughout this book, the white-authored narratives being examined do not serve the exclusive purpose of depicting black lives and reality. They reproduce whiteness. As Toni Morrison eloquently states in *Playing in the Dark*, "The subject of the dream is the dreamer."

With this critical lens, each author in this volume addresses one or more of the following critical questions in their chapters: What do white-authored narratives of black life—and their appeal—have to tell us about US culture? How are notions of authorial "expertise and experience" inflected by crossing racial lines? How are the history and presence of African-descended people in America being revised and rewritten by whites to address contemporary concerns? Is the more recent popularity of white-authored books and films about blacks a sign of how far "we" have come—or how much farther we have to go in the quest for racial equality and justice?

Surely in the twenty-first century, some may say, after the reelection of the United States' first black president and widespread acknowledgment that artistic freedom remains a necessary characteristic of a democratic society, the act of racial ventriloquism, especially from a sympathetic point of view, needn't be harmful or insulting in itself. Doesn't every artist, writer, producer, or director have the right to tell stories as he or she sees fit? And if people don't like particular representations, couldn't they employ the powerful tactic of counterstorytelling to combat what might be perceived to be limiting and stereotypical? Yet in a recent review of the white writer Margaret Wrinkle's novel *Wash* (2013), which is told in part through a slave's voice, the poet Major Jackson acknowledges that a white writer's decision to appropriate black voices in fiction is still to enter a minefield: "If cultural appropriation must take place, the thinking goes, then authors should treat Black narratives—often the products of U.S. history, and thus as sacred as the Constitution itself—with kid gloves. If they fail even in the slightest, readers are sure to voice criticism and, maybe justifiably, rain down judgment and reckoning" (Jackson 10).

Racial ventriloquism, as Jackson points out, raises a host of issues more complex than those of representations and negative stereotypes. Thus *From* Uncle Tom's Cabin *to* The Help: *Critical Perspectives on White-Authored Narratives of Black Life* also offers analyses of the costs and dangers of what bell hooks calls "fictive ethnography": films and texts that purport to offer insights into the realities of black life and history. Such texts, however well intentioned, are generated within discourses of inequality and vested interests that might not converge. Even white authors who claim to be sympathetic if not empathetic to black concerns, such as Kathryn Stockett and filmmaker Quentin Tarantino, participate in a long history of constructing "blackness" to serve hegemonic concerns; and as much as these writers are praised, they are also criticized for denying and usurping black people's authority and agency over their own experiences and interpretations.

Therefore, while racial ventriloquism has been a major but persistent thread in US literature and film since *Uncle Tom's Cabin*, the turn into the twenty-first century has seen many very popular depictions of African American life created by white writers and directors, including well-known novels and memoirs such as *The No. 1 Ladies' Detective Agency* series (1998), *The Secret Life of Bees* (2002), *The Help* (2009), and *The Blind Side* (2009). While these narratives achieved popular acclaim, they also faced criticism, demonstrating that the much-touted "postracial America" has yet to come to terms with the power of race in our imaginative and social lives. This book, then, also seeks to contextualize these more recent works in a historical landscape that includes Eudora Welty's fiction, Mark Twain's *Adventures of Huckleberry Finn*, and Grace Halsell's *Soul Sister* (1969), as well as mass-market films such as *The Blind Side* (2009), *The Help* (2011), and *Django Unchained* (2012).

Placing these contemporary texts in conversation with canonical texts plays a significant role in our understanding of how the United States seeks to reconcile its racial past with its multiracial present and future. The legacy of the United States' racial history of exploitation and terrorism remains painful, of course, for its black citizens, who still live with its psychic, economic, and social effects; but it is also painful and perplexing for white people. Still benefitting from the laws, social conventions, and narratives that generate and perpetuate white privilege, many white citizen-consumers find it hard to square the often brutal and omnipresent ideology of white supremacy that lies at the heart of American identities and values with notions of the United States as a land of democratic equality and opportunity. The younger generations, including many students at all educational levels, might be especially eager to disassociate themselves from the overt racism of the past as they accept reductive stories of Martin Luther King Jr.'s victories during Black History Month. In an attempt to shed some light on this complexity, our book examines how race is taken up in white-authored narratives that shape a collective American social consciousness.

Troubling *The Help*

> The mammy . . . the pickaninny . . . the coon . . . the Sambo . . . the
> uncle: Well into the middle of the twentieth century, these were some
> of the most popular depictions of black Americans [in the media] . . .
> Today there's little doubt that they shaped the most gut-level feelings
> about race.
>
> —Narrated by Ester Rolle in Marlon Riggs, *Ethnic Notions*

Kathryn Stockett's *The Help* exemplifies the issues we examine in white-authored narratives of black life and thus serves as the anchor narrative of this volume. The novel features a young, college-educated white woman who helps a community of black maids find their voices during the civil rights era in Jackson, Mississippi. Tate Taylor, a white Mississippian, adapted the bestselling novel and directed the film (see IMDb on *The Help*), which became one of the most commercially successful films so far in the twenty-first century. It prominently features several African American characters portrayed by black actors who received critical acclaim for stellar performances, winning Academy and Golden Globe awards. This film, however, while wildly popular, was not unequivocally esteemed. Media mogul Oprah Winfrey may have praised and promoted the film during her speech at the Academy Awards, saying that "When I saw [the film], that is my story" (Winfrey), but writer Touré blasted the film and called it "the most loathsome movie in America." While white audiences tended to respond positively to the movie, reactions among black audiences remain sharply divided.

For black viewers like Winfrey, the film represented familial history: "My grandmother was a maid," she recalls, "her mother was a maid, her mother before her was a slave. My mother was a maid. My grandmother's greatest dream for me was that I would grow up in a family and have a career [as a maid] where she used to say, 'I hope you get some good white folks'" (Winfrey). While Winfrey positively maps the film onto her memory of matrilineal expectations, revealing that she herself was destined for domestic service and is only one great-grandmother past slavery, for Touré this same representation is one of the film's many problems. He complains that it depicts an uncomplicated "world where Blacks are basically a step away from slaves" (Touré). His take is different from Winfrey's assessment that slavery is a too-recent part of her past. He perceives the film's black characters as being portrayed as structurally and culturally inferior to the white characters, resembling slaves themselves, despite the film's setting during a time when blacks were fervently asserting their claims to political and social equality. He criticizes the film's narrative logic, explaining that "the happy ending we get—[actress] Viola Davis' [who plays the lead maid] Aibileen walking home unharmed as the screen fades to Black—is fraudulent and so surreally absurd as to be Dalí-esque" (Touré).

The Help links us to questions that are not only literary or cinematic but also deeply social and political. For example, Stockett initially had trouble publishing her novel on the basis of racial concerns. Before the book saw print, prospective agents and publishers questioned whether in the twenty-first century a white author could, or even ethically should, attempt to create a narrative from the perspective of a black maid—writing the maid's many internal monologues in the first-person and in an awkward and, according to linguists, inept attempt to transcribe Ebonics, no less (see Young, Barrett, and Lovejoy). Yet Stockett found not only a publisher but also fame and great fortune. *The Help* became a *New York Times* bestseller. The Academy Awards, the Golden Globes, and other awards recognized Viola Davis and Octavia Spencer with best lead actress and best supporting actress nominations, respectively, for playing the featured maids. However, just prior to the 2012 Academy Awards ceremony from which Spencer took home the prize, cultural critic and talk-show host Tavis Smiley interviewed the two actresses and raised several critical questions. He raised questions about racial authenticity and representations and about what he sees as Hollywood's power and complicity in limiting black access to and thus presence in influential mass media and culture. Smiley is not alone in challenging the cultural values perpetuated by the film industry's persistent failure to recognize "strong Black heroes" like Denzel Washington's ignored performances of the boxer Hurricane or black activist Malcolm X. Yet Hollywood constantly rewards black actors and actresses for playing subservient, violent, or hypersexual roles often created by whites. Referring to Davis's and Spencer's Oscar nominations, Smiley states, "Something sticks in my craw about celebrating Hattie McDaniel for playing a maid so many years ago and celebrating Black actresses for playing a maid all these years later" (Smiley).

Smiley's critique is only one of several that criticize the novel and film for ignoring the realities and richness of black life in favor of narrowly defined roles that arguably perpetuate white supremacy—especially those of the black maid and mammy. Despite ongoing critiques of the lack of repertoire and depth in black roles in Hollywood films and even in the face of Meryl Streep's public plea at the 2009 Screen Actors Guild Awards—"My God, somebody give her [Viola Davis] a movie" (Waldowski)—Hollywood continues to offer and successfully sell more of the same. Even after Streep's plea, Hollywood offered Davis mammy roles in both *The Help* and *Beautiful Creatures* (2013). In a similar fashion, after her 2009 Oscar nomination for portraying Precious in the movie of the same name, Gabourey Sidibe found herself portraying a maid in Ben Stiller's *Tower Heist* (2011).

The fixation on the black maid and mammy in Hollywood films brings some of the writers in this volume to important questions: Why has the mammy character and her appeal to white audiences endured since before the Civil War through the turbulent 1960s and on to today, in our so-called postracial era? Why is it that so many white Americans are comforted by and long for the idea of the black maid long after the United Daughters of the Confederacy unsuccessfully lobbied Congress to erect a statue of mammy in 1923? Why was the 1960s TV show *Beulah*, featuring the Academy Award–winning Hattie McDaniel as a black maid of the same name, so popular that in 1992 one white TV producer said that "*Beulah* was so successful because everyone wanted a *Beulah* in their home" (Riggs)? Why, after the 9/11 attacks, did Kathryn Stockett get so "homesick" that the voice, comfort, and touch she most longed for was "Demetrie, the African-American maid who worked for Ms. Stockett's grandmother in Jackson in the 1970s and '80s" (Motoko)? Why, under the leadership of the first black president and first black First Lady, did Stockett write a novel to help her bring her Southern past to her Northern present? And why do so many people—white, black, and other—share her feelings of being at "home" with *The Help*? In addition to addressing white America's fetish for the black maid, the essays that focus on *The Help* in this volume are also concerned about white authority of knowledge, narrative authenticity, white nostalgia for the segregated South, the sanitization of the civil rights struggle, the omission of black agency and activism, the persistence of the white savior/hero trope, and the simplification of the pervasive yet elusive workings of racism by positing that some "exceptional" whites can transcend the trappings of race, while other "badly behaved" whites are to be held responsible for racism.

Such timely critiques of *The Help* take on a particular import when we consider other controversial white-authored narratives of black life, such as Stowe's *Uncle Tom's Cabin* (1852) and Styron's *Confessions of Nat Turner* (1967). Both narratives received praise and criticism from both blacks and whites. But unlike Stowe, who wrote *Uncle Tom's Cabin* in the midst of the national controversy over slavery, and Styron, who wrote *Confessions of Nat Turner* during the civil rights movement and at the height of the Black Power movement, Stockett's narrative does not appear at a crisis point in US race relations—or does it? Why does this story of white women and the black women who serve them, depicted against a Southern civil rights–era backdrop and devoid of civil rights struggles, continue to fascinate post-Obama America? Could the success of *The Help* and other twenty-first-century white narratives of black life indeed be a sign of our own racial crisis, one we are slow to recognize and have difficulty naming?

Given the large-scale consumption and cultural impact of Stockett's narrative, we find it imperative to undertake a considerable investigation of the novel and film. The novel continues to gain international attention, with translations in more than forty languages. Public schools and universities around the world regularly teach the film and the book. In record time, *The Help* has become an institutionalized, even a canonized, representation of (African) American culture. It has undoubtedly struck enough of a sympathetic chord in the American psyche that despite its garnering myriad grievances—from the author's celebration of mammy images and erasure of black men to a failed lawsuit by the very real woman who bears a name and other details similar to the novel's protagonist—the book's renown ensures a long publication life and strong influence to American culture. It may well become the *To Kill a Mockingbird* of the twenty-first century. *The Help* already holds an enduring status in our cultural memory, a status that allows contemporary critics to examine *its* similarity to other racially iconic American films and novels.

Critical Perspectives on White-Authored Narratives of Black Life

While *The Help* offers us a departure point for our transhistorical study of white-authored black narratives, contributors to this edited book examine several other texts. These multifarious narratives vary by historical period, genre, and form, including short stories, plays, films, and television shows. The historical works include such classics as *Uncle Tom's Cabin* (1852), the NewSouth edition of *Huckleberry Finn* (2011), *Gone with the Wind* (1939), *Confessions of Nat Turner* (1967), Eudora Welty's short stories, *Black Like Me* (1961), and *Soul Sister* (1969). Recent renditions of white-authored narratives are also analyzed, such as *The Secret Life of Bees* (2002), *The Blind Side* (2009), *Crash* (2004), *Freedom Writers* (2007), *Enemy of the State* (1998), HBO's *The Wire*, and *Django Unchained* (2012).

By contextualizing the featured narratives in the sociohistorical and sociopolitical context in which they were produced, the analyses in this collection are less about author intention and more about narrative subtleties that unwittingly reinforce white ideological frames of knowing. Many of the essays pay attention to how white-authored narratives resonate with and appeal to black audiences. It would be a mistake to ignore the fact that films such as *The Blind Side* and *Django Unchained*; the book and television series *The No. 1 Ladies' Detective Agency*, which starred the singer Jill Scott; and others don't also speak to black anxieties, desires, and tastes.

The essays also point out that the white-authored narratives provide solace to white racial anxiety. Researchers from many different disciplines have duly noted the avoidance and anxiety that whites often exhibit when confronted with the issue of race, which often manifests in white guilt, denial, self-defense, and positioning the self as a "good white." We find that some of the white-authored narratives console racial anxiety with plots that omit white involvement in the production of racism by either conceptualizing racism as something that just simply happens with no agents whatsoever—what Bonilla-Silva refers to as racism without racists—or as something that black people manufacture through bad decision making and/or a lack of desire to improve their circumstances. Both constructions position white people as helpers or saviors to deserving or, in some cases, undeserving black people. Other narratives categorize racism in horrific, historical events that we all can now put behind us, while still others harness the concept of racism to only include those distasteful performances that "racist" individuals enact. These specific constructions excuse white viewers and readers from even remotely considering how they themselves might help reinforce the concept of race, produce racial inequities, or benefit from whiteness and ultimately excuse them from having to do anything to challenge racism.

The essays in this volume challenge the comfort of white privilege and dare to engage the complexities and nuances of racial ventriloquism while avoiding simplistic, essentialist analyses of this powerful yet perplexing aspect of American national consciousness. The first essay, Luminita Dragulescu's "Bearing Witness? The Problem with the White Cross-Racial (Mis)Portrayals of History," establishes a philosophical-historical critical framework for racial ventriloquism. She shows how *The Help* inadvertently reactualizes long-standing concerns with white cross-racial representations of black life and history that flared in the sixties. Ebony Lumumba takes up the issue in her essay, "Must the Novelist Ask Permission?," which considers how Stockett departs from Welty in methods of considering and penning cultural communities outside of her own and probes the question of what constitutes the proper knowledge or license to write black voices. Elizabeth West's chapter, "Blackness as Medium: Envisioning White Southern Womanhood in Eudora Welty's 'A Worn Path' and *Delta Wedding* and Kathryn Stockett's *The Help*," likewise sees literary historical resonances in the popular novel. Comparing Stockett's work to that of another white woman Mississippian, Eudora Welty, West offers a nuanced reading that considers Stockett's link to a legacy of white female writing that employs black women's voices as markers of normative humanity against a backdrop of Southern cruelty. Katrina Thompson, in "Taking Care of White Babies, That's What I Do: *The Help* and Americans' Obsession with the Mammy," offers a historical review of the continual manifestations of the mammy figure that analyzes parallels to Stowe's *Uncle Tom's Cabin* and meditates on the psychic, cultural, and political needs that the mammy figure has fulfilled for over three centuries. Shana Russell explores other psychic and political needs in her chapter, "'When Folks Is Real Friends, There Ain't No Such Thing as Place': Feminist Sisterhood and the Politics of Social Hierarchy in *The Help*." "Black Girlhood and *The Help*: Constructing Black Girlhood in a 'Post'-Racial, -Gender, and -Welfare State" brings a sociological perspective to the literary conversations surrounding *The Help*. Julia Jordan-Zachery shows how the discursive practices deployed in the novel reinscribe racialized and gender tropes that reflect and create societal expectations about girls and the women they become. Mecca Jamilah Sullivan, in "Second (and Third, and Fourth . . .) Helpings," concludes the discussions on *The Help* by examining how the mammy and other stock images of black womanhood in film, books, and other media feed America's addiction to racial, gender, sexual, class, and body othering and its devastating effects on black women's voices and lives.

Paula Marie Seniors takes on the problematics of tropes of black and white Southern womanhood in her examination of the functions of the Southern Belle Fantasy trope and the mammy in the context of May Mallory's political activism during the civil rights struggle of the 1960s. Widening the lens from its focus on Stockett's novel, the next essay in the volume, Robert T. Tally Jr.'s "'Bleeping Mark Twain?' Censorship, *Huckleberry Finn*, and the Functions of Literature" discusses the recent controversy over NewSouth Books' publication of an edition of *Adventures of Huckleberry Finn* as part of a larger debate over the role of literature in education and the world. Tally argues that the debate about censorship discloses a narrowly political program for literature itself, which in turn says much about the role and function of literary texts in education more generally. Josephine Metcalf's essay, "White Lies and Black Consequences," also complicates questions of stereotypes and racial anxieties in her chapter on the controversy surrounding Margaret B. Jones's memoir, which purported to describe black urban gang life, after it was revealed that the author was a white university student who had grown up in affluent, predominantly white suburbia rather than the black neighborhoods that she claimed to experience. Alisha Gaines's chapter, "'A Secondhand Kind of Terror': Grace Halsell, Kathryn Stockett, and the Ironies of Empathy," also takes up the question of a white woman writer's racial passing. Detailing the widely unknown relationship between Halsell and her mentor, the author of the bestselling *Black Like Me*, John Howard Griffin, this chapter reveals how the erasure of the experiences and narratives of black women enables Halsell's racial drag and indexes the imbalanced power dynamics of the empathetic gesture. Shifting our attention to film, the next two essays offer analyses of *The Blind Side*. Pearlie Strother-Adams's chapter, "'Savior,' Good Mother, Jezebel, Tom, Trickster: *The Blind Side* Myth," focuses on mythological and stereotypical images, while Charise Pimentel and Sarah Santíllanes focus on how the apparent racelessness of the film's story actually gives further life to racial ideologies of white supremacy in "Blindsided by Racism: A Critical Racial Analysis of *The Blind Side*." Karen Johnson's analysis of *Django Unchained* examines its relationship to other Hollywood depictions of slavery and argues that while Quentin Tarantino provides a counterhegemonic cultural revisionist narrative of slavery, he also draws on a gallery of stereotypical popular depictions of enslaved people that ultimately doesn't challenge white supremacy. And finally, Jenise Hudson's look at the film *The Kids Are All Right* troubles the postracial backdrop of this 2010 film with an eye to drawing out the film's illustration of the ways in which race and class privilege are mobilized to leverage the same-sex marriage of the film's white main characters at the expense of its nonwhite characters.

The Personal and the Political

What brings you to read this book? And what will you gain from it intellectually and personally? We end with these two interconnected questions in order to spur readers not only to consider the important academic components of the racial issues raised and examined in the ensuing pages but to unearth the individual implications as well. So, as a way to encourage the personal, we want to briefly share what brings each of us to this project—that is, we answer the question, why did I decide to coedit this volume?

Claire Oberon Garcia comes to this project as a professor of American literature and a race and ethnic studies scholar who has become convinced through her work over many years that stories, as our opening line states, create our realities, identities, and collective histories. As she observed the popularity and the growing role of *The Help* in literature instruction, she saw it as yet another chapter in the familiar practice of white power telling black people who they are with presumed racial authority. This worries Claire because *The Help* has received such global prominence in American literature and history curricula. Teachers all over the world are using it as a primary text to teach the American civil rights movement and race relations of that era. And what's more, at the time of this writing, only *The Da Vinci Code* has remained longer on the *New York Times* bestseller list. It's important, then, for Claire in particular, that the popularity and ubiquity of *The Help* and texts like it be consistently challenged and placed in their larger historical and political contexts. She wants to encourage readers, students, and teachers to be more aware of how works such as these perpetuate the racism that so many of us are committed to eradicating.

In his work as a teacher and scholar of African American masculinity, language, and performance, Vershawn Ashanti Young routinely investigates the enduring impact of racial stereotypes on the way blacks perform their genders and the way those performances are perceived in everyday life. At the time of the release of the film version of *The Help*, he was teaching a course on race and gender in contemporary documentary film, with a focus on filmmaker Marlon Riggs. When viewing Riggs's award-winning documentary *Ethnic Notions*, which details the history behind iconography of black gendered caricatures such as the mammy and Sambo, he asked students to place debates about *The Help* within the tradition that Riggs's 1980s film elucidates. Vershawn was surprised by the extent to which both black and white students either refused or were unable to articulate any connection between the two. These kinds of oft-occurring pedagogical experiences, as well as his daily experience as a black man working in predominantly white environments, where he is hyperaware of constructions of his own gender performance, led him to pursue a project that looks at the multiple dynamics of narrative influence on American identities and gendered experiences.

But what led him to consider *The Help* as central to this discussion was his own complicated personal response to the book and movie. He read the book at his mother's suggestion and quibbled with some of the characterizations of black masculinity and the inaccurate representation of African American English. But when he saw the film in an artsy theater that caters to senior citizens, he stunned himself as tears rolled down his cheeks during the closing scene, where the white female toddler cries for her just-fired black mammy to come back. He realized how successfully the film had manipulated his emotions in a direction he was hell-bent on defying. The film's neosentimental approach to the representation of race worked on Vershawn, an African American male critic who wanted to "hate" the film. But he didn't. Therefore, for him, what's most important is analyzing the film's emotional impact within the framework of black folks' everyday realities, both contemporary and historical.

But perhaps Charise Pimentel offers the most striking motivation for editing this book. She describes herself as a white, bilingual, bicultural, academic mother of Mexican children. Even though she grew up in an English-speaking household, she was raised in Spanish-speaking, agricultural, Mexican migrant communities in Northern California. In this environment, she grew up realizing the need to speak Spanish, and when she married her Mexican husband, this need became even more pressing. They wanted their children to speak Spanish and consequently raised them as Spanish monolinguals. They learned English only as it was exposed to them in a schooling context.

Despite her cross-cultural and linguistic experiences, and even being called a race traitor, one thing she has learned is that she can never give up her racial identity. Charise contends that in a racialized society such as the United States, race is a construct ascribed onto a person, regardless of one's actions or desires to forfeit his or her race. With that being said, her work as an antiracist white is not to ignore her whiteness but rather to bring attention to and interrupt the ever-evolving, ubiquitous, and elusive aspects of racism.

Charise comes to this project as a critical scholar of race with a background in critical discourse analysis and critical media literacy, with a specific focus on film. As such, she believes that the white-authored narratives' inattention to race as a persistent social construct offers white redemption and consoles white racial anxiety in a social context where it is taboo to admit complicity in or benefiting from systems of racism. Charise is also troubled by the continual portrayal of enlightened whites "saving" people of color from their racial plight, without a sociopolitical context that brings to light how racism is historically, structurally, and systematically produced or whites' own involvement and investment in systems of racism. Charise believes that the white-authored narratives of black life that are under investigation in this book not only displace white complicity and investments in racism but undermine black agency by omitting narratives of black people who have challenged racism and made tremendous strides in the fight for social justice.

Taking all three of the editors' personal stakes together, we want to encourage readers to look at how, across all the narratives examined in this book, audiences are overly exposed to the narrowly conceived variety of racism that is performed by erratic individuals. Racism defined exclusively by individual performances not only obscures structural, systematic, and discursive forms of racism but also creates the false dichotomy of white racial identity that includes "bad whites" (those who perform racism) and "good whites" (those who do not). Interestingly enough, rarely do Americans ever admit to being racist or bad whites. So, as Leonardo explains, "since very few whites exist who actually believe they are racist, then basically no one is racist and racism disappears more quickly than we can describe it" (82). In the white-authored narratives, there are many examples of this dichotomy of whites. In *Django Unchained*, it is the slaveholders, particularly Calvin Candie (but not Dr. King Schultz), who are portrayed as racists. In *The Help*, we see this contrast in Hilly and her friends in comparison to Skeeter or Celia. Similarly, in *The Blind Side*, audience members see clearly racist individuals, such as Leigh Anne's white country club friends or the proclaimed "rednecks" who call Michael "blue gums" and "a piece of black crap" and even kick him in the head at a football game. These characters can be compared to the seemingly nonracist Tuohy family. The portrayal of white characters as "not racist" serves to assure audience members that whites can transcend the trappings of race. On the other hand, the racist characters and their racist remarks and performances often result in audience members being appalled at these individuals' ill spirits yet at the same time comforted by the notion that racism is contained to "these" people. And as long as Americans are comforted in the myth that racism is somehow contained to the individual performances of racist people, they do not have to consider the far-reaching and devastating institutional and discursive forms of oppression that result in everyday inequities in education, housing, the job market, health care, social services, and the judicial system that such films and novels tend to teach us that only "bad" whites and "bad" people of color sustain.

With this, then, we hope our two questions have more context and import. So we ask them again: Why read this book? And what might you learn intellectually and personally in the process?

Works Cited

Bonilla-Silva, Eduardo. *Racism without Racists: Color-Blind Racism and the Persistence of Racial Inequality in the United States.* Lanham: Rowman and Littlefield, 2014. Print.

Clarke, John Henrik, ed. *William Styron's Nat Turner: Ten Black Writers Respond.* Boston: Beacon Press, 1968. Print.

hooks, bell. *Reel to Real: Race, Sex, and Class at the Movies.* New York: Routledge, 1996. Print.

IMDb Online Resource. *The Help.* Web. December 2013. http://www.imdb.com/title/tt1454029/?ref_=sr_1.

Jackson, Major. "Peculiar Institutions." *New York Times Book Review*, March 24, 2013: 10. Print.

Leonardo, Zeus. *Race, Whiteness, and Education.* New York: Routledge, 2009. Print.

Morrison, Toni. *Playing in the Dark: Whiteness and the Literary Imagination.* New York: Vintage Books, 1993. Print.

Motoko, Rich. "A Southern Mirrored Window." Books. *The New York Times*, November 2, 1992. Web. http://www.nytimes.com/2009/11/03/books/03help.html?pagewanted=all.

Riggs, Marlon. "Interview with Hal Kanter." *Color Adjustment.* 1991. Documentary film.

Roake, Jessica. "Not Helpful: Making Kids Read *The Help* Is *Not* the way to Teach Them about the Civil Rights Struggle." *Slate*, December 2013. Web. January 2, 2014. http://www.slate.com/articles/life/education/2013/12/teachers_assigning_the_help_to_teach_jim_crow_and_civil_rights_aren_t_teaching.single.html.

Smiley, Tavis. "Actresses Viola Davis and Octavia Spencer." *Tavis Smiley.* February 9, 2012. Web. http://www.pbs.org/wnet/tavissmiley/interviews/actresses-viola-davis-octavia-spencer.

Touré. "Is *The Help* the Most Loathsome Movie in America?" *Time Ideas*, February 2, 2012. Web. http://ideas.time.com/2012/02/02/is-the-help-the-most-loathsome-movie-in-america.

Waldowski, Adam. "Will Being a Gracious Loser Keep Meryl Streep from Winning an Oscar?" *Blog: News and Views.* n.d. Web. October 6, 2011. http://www.goldderby.com/news/1998/will-being-a-gracious-loser-keep-meryl-streep-from-winning-an-oscar.html.

Watson, Bruce. "*Black Like Me*, 50 Years Later: John Howard Griffin Gave Readers an Unflinching View of the Jim Crow South. How Has His Book Held Up?" Smithsonian.com, October 2011. Web. December 2013. http://www.smithsonianmag.com/arts-culture/Black-Like-Me-50-Years-Later.html.

Winfrey, Oprah. Speech of Acceptance for the Jean Hersholt Humanitarian Award. Academy Awards Show 2011. n.d. Web. November 13, 2011. http://www.youtube.com/watch?v=zGWLw_E8IM0.

Young, Vershawn Ashanti, Rusty Barrett, and Kim Brian Lovejoy. *Other People's English: Code-Meshing, Code-Switching, and African American Literacy.* New York: Teachers College Press, 2013. Print.

CHAPTER 1

Bearing Witness?

The Problem with the White Cross-Racial (Mis)Portrayals of History

Luminita M. Dragulescu

Within the racial anxieties fixed in the black-white paradigm, cross-racial representations of the Other—to wit, a white author assuming an African American persona or an African American author assuming a white persona—are relevant for either race's beliefs and views on the American racial status quo. Throughout the United States' racial history, whites and nonwhites have negotiated a complicated rapport, constantly challenging their respective power positions. The Baconian principle *scientia potentia est* applies in one race's effort to understand and portray the Other as a means either to control and manipulate or to preclude and defend against the Other more efficiently. More recently, white authors' interest in knowing and representing black life and history stems from their need to lay bare the complexities of racial interactions and to negotiate their many points of discord. Literary imagination, as always, works at the forefront of change when it comes to the appreciation and the readjustment of one racial group's perspective over another, and of racial relations in general. Writers that venture to imagine intimately the racial Other's individual and group consciousness illustrate the sensitive process of rising above racial stereotypes in order to address a conflicted and largely unresolved common history. But, as Kathryn Stockett's *The Help* (2009) has demonstrated more recently, such ventures could subtly reify the racist status quo and only pay lip service to the cause of accurately and honestly representing black history.

With certain important caveats, I uphold the value of cross-racial penning. It suggests a desire to get to know the Other, and thus it could contribute to interracial understanding and reconciliation. However, this chapter identifies some of the concerns with white cross-racial portrayals of history that *The Help*, as one of the latest enterprises of this nature, exemplifies. The novel displays an insufficient, if not perfunctory, knowledge of black history and life. This appears in the author's stereotypical depiction of mid-twentieth-century black life and psyche, according to a twenty-first-century "politically correct" white construction of "blackness."[1] For this reason, *The Help* bears witness to the contemporary racial status quo rather than the status quo ante. There is a conspicuous vilification of most white characters in contrast to the beatification of the black ones. Yet the whites' offenses are quite minor, considering the historic background of the Jim Crow laws and of the civil rights movement's brutal racial clashes. Frustratingly, Stockett portrays the white protagonist as the "savior," confidante, and, most worryingly, the spokesperson for the black characters: a problematic stance in the context of the much-beleaguered black historiography. As such, *The Help* does not depart much from a long tradition of white misrepresentations of the common racial history.

Historically, white imagination has consistently spoken for the racial Other and took it upon itself to "bear witness" to racial history. Writing with a "black" voice is neither new nor exceptional in American literature. Toni Morrison notes that the very characteristics of American literature are in fact responses to the dark, abiding, signing "Africanist presence" that has affected and shaped the development of the American literary canon (5). But beyond the more subtle, all-pervading Africanist presence, there are instances of direct white voicing (white writers undertaking a black persona by writing a first-person narrative) of the black psyche and history that have increased over time. It is well known that runaway slaves' lack of literacy skills often necessitated direct white intervention, and their stories were written by amanuenses. White collectors of folklore, such as Joel Chandler Harris at the end of the nineteenth century, also used a black persona—Uncle Remus—to relay stories. Most noticeably, in 1967, William Styron published *The Confessions of Nat Turner*, a first-person fictional narrative of the 1831 leader of the Virginia slave rebellion. At the time, Styron was one of the first white writers who attempted to undertake an event in American history with a more reverently constructed voice of the racial Other. Albeit well intended, his enterprise met with a critical response that reflected the passionate and incompatible standpoints of whites and African Americans on their common history, particularly interracial clashes such as the Turner Insurrection. The critical upheaval generated by Styron's novel brought to the forefront the chaotic history of race relations in the United States, as well as the precarious racial compromise after the Civil Rights Act of 1964. The black audiences' protest of Styron's take on a most significant event in black history defined certain irreconcilable positions whites and blacks have on appraising their shared past. In regard to ethics of representation, John Henrik Clarke's collection *William Styron's Nat Turner: Ten Black Writers Respond* (1968) was the first of many acerbic reactions to *Confessions* and to reckless, white-authored representations of the black psyche and history. The Styron controversy became the cause célèbre by which we measure the cross-racial politics and ethics of representing the past. Stockett's *The Help* continues to emphasize the problem with white cross-racial representations of US history.

Writing racial history in the "postracial" era implies a complex negotiation between past and present—that is, present views on multifarious and contending representations of a shared history. In effect, it results in the effort to preserve rather than the attempt to obliterate or revise the often competing narratives of blacks and whites. Although contemporary literature that undertakes cross-racial representations of the Other is wary of racial sensitivities and mostly attempts to smooth the asperities of the racial divide when writing US history, it does not succeed in erasing them altogether. The social dynamics of US race relations postulates that it is the burden of racial minorities to navigate, survive, and prosper in a system controlled by whites and not vice versa. Charles Mills is one of the scholars who dismantles the "racial contract" by which the Western world is structured, which favors whites' privilege, whether the beneficiaries acknowledge it or not. Pertinently, Mills observes that "the only people who can find it psychologically possible to deny the centrality of race are those who are racially privileged, for whom race is invisible precisely because the world is structured around them, whiteness as the ground against which the figures of other races . . . appear" (76). Colorblindness and postracialism undeniably serve whites when, pretending to look beyond race in order to overcome racism, they implicitly attempt to erase historical memory. David Theo Goldberg distinguishes between antiracism and what he calls "antiracialism"—a trend that argues for an erasure of racial terms of reference and promotes colorblindness under the pretense of joining the antiracist movement. Goldberg notes that antiracism, on the one hand, "requires historical memory, recalling the conditions of racial degradation and relating contemporary to historical and local to global conditions." Antiracialism, on the other hand, "suggests forgetting, getting over, moving on, wiping away the terms of reference, at best (or worst) a commercial memorialization rather than a recounting and redressing of the terms of humiliation and devaluation" (21). Needless to say, antiracialism is associated with whites or, as Goldberg remarks, "for the most part . . . is whiteness by another name" (21). "Conciliatory" literature such as *The Help* appears as a revisionist, "commercial memorialization" rather than an educated, restorative depiction of race relations in Mississippi at the beginning of the sixties. The promotion of the book and its film adaptation despite disgruntled voices in the black community hints at the hierarchies of racial power that still linger in postracial America. This calls to mind historian Fitzhugh Brundage's assessment that the racial competition for "historical 'truth' cannot be separated from an appraisal of the unequal power that competing groups and individuals exercise over the interpretation of the past." Consequently, we need "to acknowledge that history cannot be separated from practices of domination" (344).

Like *Confessions*, which amid a storm of black criticism enjoyed surprising endorsements from James Baldwin, John Hope Franklin, and J. Saunders Redding, *The Help* got accolades from influential black personalities such as Oprah

Winfrey and the movie adaptation was screened at the Obama White House. The Pulitzer Prize with which *Confessions* was awarded in 1968 and the commercial success *The Help* enjoys more than forty years later signal that white America still welcomes a white-authored black history that validates stereotypes of blackness and sugarcoats the painful common past. But among black audiences, the book, as well as the movie, mostly found detractors who were concerned with Stockett's ethics of representation. Stockett's novel displays the long-standing white misapprehension of the Other despite a declared intent to understand and do justice to blacks. To Styron, writing Nat Turner was "at least partially the accomplishment of a moral duty: to get to know the blacks" (Rewald 81). Like Styron, Stockett declares that she wrote her book because she wanted to grasp the life of her maid, Demetrie. However, black audiences' reaction to both books testifies to the authors' failure in "knowing" the blacks and in relevantly portraying a black view of history. Stockett's novel brought to the forefront several sensitive issues with representing the racial Other.

When writers draw from white conventions of race identity to personify the racial Other, they inevitably vex those who are targeted by these representations. The white author's effort to depict the past by vicariously identifying with the racial Other through narrative imagination is a problematic undertaking that reflects competing, irreconcilable stances on race relations and a disputed history. American literary history displays a long-standing practice of white censorship and of misrepresenting racial minorities' histories. The problem is not one of principle (i.e., that whites should not write across race); rather, the problem lies in white authors' displaying shallow knowledge of other races' culture and history. It is relevant to mention here Wayne J. Urban's experience as a white author writing a biography of the African American educational historian and college president Horace Mann Bond. In 1998, more than a decade before the publication of *The Help*, Urban advises that "any White American writing about an African-American in the late twentieth century must do so with some trepidation. It is a time when African-Americans are reclaiming themselves in a variety of ways from the shackles of their White oppressors. One of the sites of this reclamation project is the scholarly arena where Whites who study Blacks run an increased risk of alienating Black audiences by misunderstanding and misrepresenting their subjects" (105).

Nevertheless, there are a great number of white scholars in black studies, race theory, historical studies, anthropology, sociology, and so on who pertinently and successfully assess and represent black life and history, while white fiction authors who have attempted to delve into black consciousness and represent black perspectives on history and society usually generate controversy.[2] Writing across race is a necessary step in getting to know the Other, but such sensitive ventures require extensive and rigorous research and, most importantly, respectful portrayals. From this point of view, Stockett appears insufficiently fluent in black life, culture, and history to give justice to the community she attempts to represent. Her knowledge of the setting, characters, and history she plots seems perfunctory, and her portrayal is, at times, patronizing.[3]

As the critical and popular response to Styron's *Confessions* demonstrated, even when well intended, a white author assuming a black voice runs the risk of misrepresenting it. More often than not, the white author exhibits conscious and unconscious habits of white privilege, and his or her racial consciousness has been (mis)shaped by a white-constructed "blackness." *The Help* is unsatisfying because it does not deliver either the narrative's premise or the title's promise (unless the title mainly suggests that Stockett's narrative persona, Miss Eugenia "Skeeter" Phelan, is helping the maids voices be heard?). The novel merely skates through the social turmoil of the civil rights era to nitpick on petty domestic fights and society gossip. The author's insistence on portraying whites as inordinately flawed and blacks as saintly resonates with a manipulation of decorum, which, by way of exaggerated racial self-deprecation, subtly reinforces white preeminence. The white party is only guilty of petty crimes in *The Help*; the movement's landmark tragedies, such as the brutal killings of Emmett Till and Medgar Evers, are remote occurrences from the novel's white community. Embarrassingly oblivious to historical record, Stockett mentions Evers being "bludgeoned in [his] front yard" (277). By way of analogy, Stockett subtly declares her allegiance to her race and the Southern racial status quo when she states, "Mississippi is like my mother. I am allowed to complain about her all I want, but God help the person who raises an ill word about her around me, unless she is their mother too" (450). The book's surprisingly mild criticism of white brutality in the time and place it claims to portray indicates the author's loyalty to her race rather than an attempt to reach across the color line. Stockett presents black domestic life through the synecdochal chicken-frying mammy, the angry black woman, and the hackneyed archetype of the absent or drunkard and abusive black man (most notable, Leroy Jackson, Minny's husband) and describes an overall chaotic, terrified black community. Whites, on the other hand, are self-sufficient, catty suburban wives, and white men are benevolent but mostly absent figures in the narrative (like Johnny Foote, Miss Celia's husband and Minny's unknowing employer). Miss Leefolt's desire to conform to the Home Health Sanitation Initiative and build a separate bathroom for the "colored help" looks more like a social climbing maneuver and an attempt to please her bridge buddies than a real concern that blacks are a danger to her health. Disturbingly, the racism of the Jim Crow era appears individualized—a result of peer pressure—rather than systemic; one would wonder what the civil rights activists were fighting for. Stockett certainly "came to bury Caesar, not to praise him."

The hybridized voice that Stockett devises prompts racial dissension, since she defines life experiences and literature along racial lines—an endeavor that is both impractical and damaging. Stockett's enterprise to delve into black consciousness would require that she tap into the unifying features of racial diversity while depicting the struggle to understand and accommodate the position of the racial Other. But the hard line that differentiates between skin colors in the narrative suggests otherwise. Aibileen and Minny remain not only pitiable, granted dignified, characters but also conspicuously alien. Despite the author's disclaimer in the "Too Little, Too Late" afterword that the "point of the book" was "for women to realize, We are just two people. Not that much separates us. Not nearly as much as I'd thought," there is much that draws a firm color line in the novel (451). Stockett preserves her idealistic childhood spectacles, filtered by a contemporary politically correct approach to race relations in order to portray the help.[4] Aibileen, Constantine, and Minny are the sacrificial—almost beatific—maids who display extraordinary domestic and nursing skills, making them as endearing and asexual as fairy godmothers. In fact, the same unrealistic perspective applies to Stockett's depiction of the historical and social setting. She admits that her attempt to understand the black maids' life in the 1960s was not "something any white woman on the other end of a black woman's paycheck" could accomplish (451). Ultimately, that "black woman" to whom the writer refers constitutes a different species for the impromptu anthropological experiment that Skeeter undertakes. The author's linguistic choices are just as baffling. Black women speak in a thick, black Southern vernacular, but they easily switch to the unaccented (why?), grammatically correct language of their employers when they recall the latter's conversations.

Perhaps the most grating aspect of the novel is Skeeter's portrayal as the white savior who takes personal risks (while risking her subjects far worse) to make the downtrodden black life known to Northern white audiences. Assessing the ripple effects of the white savior theme in Hollywood, Julio Cammarota warns that in such "treatments of race, people of color appear to lack the agency necessary to enact positive changes in their own lives. The underlying assumption is that people of color, on their own, fail to enact resilience, resistance, and success" (245). Furthermore, that black servants would allow a white mistress into the inner sanctum of the black community—the literal and symbolic black kitchen—and would trust their personal stories to a white employer, particularly in a time and place when race relations were so tense, is a problematic premise. That would have gone against a long-standing and historically justified fear and distrust of whites even in what appeared as pro bono endeavors. Moreover, Skeeter is hardly a William Lloyd Garrison, Lydia Maria Child, or Samuel J. May, particularly as she leaves behind her "sources" to fend for themselves once she achieves her end goal to escape home to New York. With a plot set on the background—though somewhat remote—of the civil rights movement, it seems proprietary that the protagonist, the heroine, is Miss Skeeter and not the help, Aibileen or Minny. Equally irksome is Skeeter's transferring Aibileen's written narrative (albeit with Aibileen's permission in the novel, who, again, conveniently overcomes the black servant atavistic mistrust in the white mistress) into her project. Aibileen, following her teacher's advice to "read *and write* every day," is "writing [her] prayers instead of saying 'em," suggesting that those are her most intimate, most secret thoughts (22). For black audiences nowadays, this transfer triggers the long-standing concern with assumed white ownership/authorship of black culture. In fact, Ablene Cooper—the alleged inspiration for Aibileen—filed a lawsuit against Kathryn Stockett, citing the author's "unpermitted appropriation of her name and image," thus reenergizing this age-old racial discord (Robertson).

Sharing their traumatic history with a white audience was a risk of manipulation and a sacrifice of privacy that escaped slaves took upon themselves in order to help the abolitionist movement. Such testimonies came with high costs for the narrators. In bearing witness to his or her ordeal, the black narrator has traditionally negotiated with an unsympathetic—at best tolerant—listener, a process that further exacerbates his or her torment or trauma. The universal self-representational concern regarding balancing the private life with the public forum has a new meaning when the public likely already has a demeaning, sometimes hostile, viewpoint of the witness. Dori Laub emphasizes the crucial role of the listener to trauma as a "participant and a co-owner of the traumatic event" (57). Although "a separate human being [who] experience[s] hazards and struggles of his own, the listener has to feel the victim's victories, defeats and silences, know them from within, so that they can assume the form of testimony" (58). A victim of trauma thus needs an ally: a sympathetic audience to help his or her narrative come through. It is crucial that the teller finds solace and support in the listener's compassion. This subtle understanding of the process of bearing witness not only to oneself but also to a community raises suspicion in regard to the credibility of the exchange between Skeeter and her sources. *The Help*'s endeavor to bear witness to the suffering of black life is twofold: On the one hand, we have Skeeter, who directly fulfills the role of listener to the black women's traumatic narratives. Looking beyond Skeeter's goal to achieve her freedom by finding a journalistic position up North, at the risk of exposing her subjects, she *is* portrayed as an unlikely but sympathetic and involved listener. In the (farfetched) logic of the narrative, she acts as the auspicious channel for the narrators to tell on their aggressors (e.g., Hilly Holbrook in the novel). But outside the logic of the narrative, when we look at *The Help* itself as bearing witness to black history, the enterprise fails, as does Stockett as an ad-lib historian of black life in the early sixties. As Ida Jones of the Association of Black Women Writers sums it, "Despite efforts to market the book and the film as a progressive story of triumph over racial injustice, *The Help* distorts, ignores, and trivializes the experiences of black domestic workers. We are specifically concerned about the representations of black life and the lack of attention given to sexual harassment and civil rights activism." Stockett indeed only briefly mentions Skeeter's recording stories "of white men who've tried to touch [the help]" (258).

The mystique and popularity of black culture for white audiences are reflected in how whites emulate blackness—granted, a blackness that is filtered through white ideology. Noting the large number of black characters who inhabit white popular fiction today, Earni Young quotes Kimberly D. Blockett of Pennsylvania State University, who unsurprisingly assesses that these characters "are not as well developed as the writers think they are, and they are always **black** Americans as seen through the dominant culture's eyes" (26). In her editorial, Young draws from opinions of literary agents and black authors to conclude that while the white cross-racial portrayals of blacks are subpar, shallow, and often exploitative, they have the merit of bringing black characters to the mainstream. Young quotes one African American author, Bebe Moore Campbell, stating, "It is a step forward when they try" (28). Young's conciliatory stance toward unsatisfactory white cross-racial writing sadly relays the low expectations blacks have of whites in terms of effectively representing them and their culture and doing justice to black history. It is a resignation that in fact stems from acknowledging that although blacks have had a need to understand the white culture in order to survive, whites have demonstrated an insufficient interest in understanding the culture of the racial Other or have simply ignored it by taking refuge in a color-blind philosophy. Whereas blacks have been historically well versed in the practice of "double consciousness," that "sense of always looking at one's self through the eyes of the others," whites' privileged power position did not compel such a split (Du Bois 279).

The enterprise of assuming a black voice and of vicariously experiencing the toils of racial discrimination is nevertheless an achievement in its own right *if* the writer declares the ideological parameter within which he or she operates. In other words, the cross-racial representations of the racial Other ought to take into account the specific experiences racial groups have had in their common history. Noticeably, whites and blacks perceive and appropriate these common experiences differently, and in response, they devise dissimilar representations. That white cross-racial representations of history reflect the white ideology of race is not surprising in light of the racial contract and the trend of antiracialism.

The progression toward racial equality and a fairer assessment of US racial history are bound to demand a finer tuning in representing the Other. The long period of racial segregation demonstrated the harms of existing in separate quarters. The color divide, physical and ideological, only leads to alienation, suspicion, and misunderstanding. So the sincere desire to walk in the Other's shoes, if only by means of literary or cultural imagination, is crucial in the nation's pursuit of racial understanding. We are to expect an ever-wider interest in portraying the life and history of the Other, and undoubtedly, such undertakings will not be without controversy, readjustments, and doubts. Cross-racial representations are a necessary, creative part of a complicated process that grows and adjust to reflect America's social realities and needs. To a large extent, they are as satisfactory as the nation's racial status quo.

Keeping in mind the lesson learned from the *Confessions* controversy and the caveats that come with cross-racial representations of the Other, they hold a positive potential for interracial understanding and reconciliation. They are an effort, albeit often maladroit, to pay a debt to a painful and complicated history and assuage present racial tensions. The worth of Stockett's novel lies not in its attempt to restore history but in reflecting on race relations in the present: more specifically the move, although misguided and reductionist, toward racial reconciliation. Charles Joyner, referring to Styron's "boldest choice" to assume the persona of Nat Turner, suggested that, "preoccupied with the moral problems of white people and guilt-stricken at white brutality towards blacks, modern white writers had often been guided by impulses of contrition and expiation" (186). Ultimately, Stockett's novel cannot claim to show history "how it actually happened," to cite Leopold von Ranke's famous dictum; rather, it needs to be envisioned as making an intervention in the present. By imagining history as such, Stockett sheds light on the present through the prism of the past. In other words, this is how a white writer in the twenty-first century can handle the common racial history that she creates out of white imagination, nostalgia, and a good deal of defensive guilt. If *The Help* has any claim to bearing witness to history, it does so to the present, not to the past.

Notes

1. I purposely put the phrase in quotation marks in order to call attention to the misuse and abuse of politically correct discourses for the purpose of concealing, rather than eradicating, racism. The "political correctness" (PC) to which I refer throughout this chapter is drawn from John L. Jackson's assertion in his extensive study, *Racial Paranoia: The Unintended Consequences of Political Correctness* (2008), where he warns that "political correctness has proven tragically effective at hiding racism, not just healing" (91). As Jackson explains, due to Americans' lack of transparency, PC policies lose the capacity to encourage the honest dialogues. Instead, "blacks are stuck in the structural position (vis-à-vis white interlocutors) of their ancestors' white masters: they see smiles on white faces and hear kind words spilling from white mouths without the least bit of certainty about whether those gestures are representative of the speakers' hearts" (77–78).
2. David Theo Goldberg, George M. Fredrickson, Matthew Frye Jacobson, Nancy Leys Stepan, Eric Lott, Shannon Sullivan, Robyn Wiegman, Robert J. C. Young, and W. Fitzhugh Brundage are among the white scholars writing successfully about race, black life, and history.
3. Aibileen's musing while staring at the cockroach is one of Stockett's most infamous patronizing statements: "He big, inch, inch an a half. He black. Blacker than me" (189).
4. John L. Jackson ties "political correctness" to what he calls "*de cardio* racism"— that is, "a racism of euphemism and innuendo, not heel-dug-in pronouncements of innate black inferiority" (78). This reinvention of racism is "about what law can't touch, what won't be easily proved or disproved, what can't be simply criminalized and deemed unconstitutional. It is racism that is most terrifying because it is hidden, secret, papered over with public niceties and politically correct jargon" (87).

Works Cited

Brundage, Fitzhugh W. *The Southern Past: A Clash of Race and Memory*. Cambridge, MA: Belknap Press, 2005. Print.
Cammarota, Julio. "Blindsided by the Avatar: White Saviors and Allies Out of Hollywood and in Education." *Review of Education, Pedagogy, and Cultural Studies* 33.3: 242–259. Print.
Du Bois, W. E. B. *The Souls of Black Folk*. New York: Penguin, 1989. Print.
Goldberg, David Theo. *The Threat of Race: Reflections on Racial Neoliberalism*. Malden, MA: Blackwell, 2009. Print.
Jackson, John L. *Racial Paranoia: The Unintended Consequences of Political Correctness*. New York: Basic Civitas, 2008. Print.
Jones, Ida E. "An Open Statement to the Fans of *The Help*." *Association of Black Women Historians*. January 17, 2012. Web. http://www.abwh.com.

Joyner, Charles. "Styron's Choice: A Meditation on History, Literature, and Moral Impera-
    tives." *Nat Turner: A Slave Rebellion in History and Memory*. Ed. Kenneth S. Greenberg.
    New York: Oxford UP, 2003. 179–213. Print.
Laub, Dori. "Bearing Witness or the Vicissitudes of Listening." *Testimony: Crises of Wit-
    nessing in Literature, Psychoanalysis, and History*. Ed. Shoshana Felman and Dori Laub.
    New York: Routledge, 1992. 57–74. Print.
Mills, Charles M. *The Racial Contract*. Ithaca: Cornell UP, 1999. Print.
Morrison, Toni. *Playing in the Dark: Whiteness and the Literary Imagination*. New York:
    Vintage, 1993. Print.
Rewald, Alice. "William Styron." *Conversations with William Styron*. Ed. James L. W.
    West III. Jackson: UP of Mississippi, 1985. 80–82. Print.
Robertson, Campbell. "A Maid Sees Herself in a Novel, and Objects." *New York Times*,
    February 17, 2011. Web. http://www.nytimes.com/2011/02/18/books/18help.html?
    _r=4.
Stockett, Kathryn. *The Help*. New York: Amy Einhorn Books, 2009. Print.
Urban, W. J. "Black Subject, White Biographer." *Writing Educational Biography: Explora-
    tions in Qualitative Research*. Ed. Craig Alan Kridel. New York: Garland Press, 1998.
    103–13. Print.
Young, Earni. "Writing While: An Unprecedented Number of Black Characters Inhabit
    Today's Mainstream Fiction Best-Seller Lists, but Few of Them Are Created by Black
    Authors." *Black Issues Book Review* 6.4 (July/August 2004): 26–28. Print.

CHAPTER 2

"Must the Novelist Ask Permission?"

Authority and Authenticity of the Black Voice in the Works of Eudora Welty and Kathryn Stockett's *The Help*

Ebony Lumumba

I was scared, a lot of the time, that I was crossing a terrible line, writing in the voice of a black person. I was afraid I would fail to describe a relationship that was so intensely influential in my life, so loving, so grossly stereotyped in American history and literature.

—Kathryn Stockett, *The Help*

Kathryn Stockett ends her 2009 *New York Times* bestseller *The Help* with fear. In the opening quote, the first-time author expresses the apprehension she experienced in employing the voices of two middle-aged black domestic workers, Aibileen and Minny, as narrators within her text. Her fear of "crossing a terrible line" denotes a feeling of separation between the author and her black characters (Stockett 450). Such a statement spurs curiosity into why Stockett felt the voices of Aibileen and Minny were off limits to her authorship yet not the voices of Skeeter, Hilly, Elizabeth, or any of the novel's other white characters. Since its inception, Stockett's novel has garnered copious criticism for its portrayal of the lives of several white families and their hired black domestic laborers in Jackson, Mississippi, during the 1960s. In interviews, Stockett, a white female author, seems most concerned with having somehow overstepped a boundary by penning a work with two-thirds of its narration being spoken by black female characters. The overwhelming concern for media outlets, such as *Time* magazine and *CBS News*, has been the irony in Stockett confessing to have written a story so near to her personal history that lacks a clear connection to the author's professed identity. The afterword to this work, titled "Too Little, Too Late," contains memories of the author's childhood and Demetrie McLorn, the maid employed to assist in the care of generations of Stockett children. After 444 pages of narration detailing the intricate and complicated relationships among Aibileen, Minny, their employers, and a host of other Jacksonians, both black and white, in four additional pages, Stockett enlightens the reader as to her impetus for writing the bestseller. She asserts that *The Help* exists as a tribute to Demetrie and apologizes for perhaps having "told too little" while simultaneously dreading that she had "told too much" (Stockett 451). It is here, in these final four pages, where Stockett attempts to mitigate her lack of precision and literary acumen—undoing what she possesses the potential of achieving in the previous four-hundred-plus pages. The author diminishes her right to the stories she tells and separates herself from the community she attempts to voice.

With the publication of *The Help*, Stockett joins a long tradition of white Southern writers creating black characters and their voices within their works. Renowned twentieth-century Southern authors such as William Faulkner, Flannery O'Connor, Margaret Mitchell, and Eudora Welty have all peopled their texts with members of the African American community, whether as central figures or peripheral characters. Each of these writers incorporated the presence of African American characters and life in diverse ways. For the purposes of this study, I have selected the works of Eudora Welty in order to provide a solid canon of literary texts in which a white Southern female author meticulously writes the experiences and lives of those outside of her own community. It is useful to consider Welty's negotiation of the black community within her work in discussing Stockett, not only because of the parallelism of their race, gender, and geographical space, but also because Welty achieves what Stockett could not by thoughtfully considering distinct elements of the black community—namely, language—in telling her stories. As with Stockett's lone text, Welty explored the black community and its inhabitants in many of her fictional works. Perhaps the critics who have rendered their reproach on the provocative telling of the complex nature of interactions between black female domestic workers and their white employers enhance the anxiety Stockett admits to feeling in having written black voices in her text.

Ablene Cooper, a black middle-aged woman employed as a housekeeper and nanny by Stockett's brother, offers her disapproval of Stockett's work in the form of litigation. In a lawsuit filed in February 2011, Cooper accuses Stockett of using her name and likeness without her permission and contends that the character Aibileen Clark bears a striking resemblance to her own image. Both Cooper and the fictional Clark are middle-aged women, have a gold tooth, and provide care to white children who affectionately refer to them as "Aibee." They each also tragically lose their adult sons months before their employers' families welcome newborns. In 2010, one year after the book's release, Stockett provided Cooper with a copy of her text accompanied by a note in which she shared that despite the variation in the spelling of the name Aibileen, she felt the need to "reach out and tell" Cooper that the character had not been based on her in any way. The fear that Stockett speaks of in her afterword presents itself again in her message to Ablene Cooper. The intimate letter dispelling any relationship between the formation of the fictional character and Cooper assumes that a similitude exists between the two women, fictional and actual, that would be apparent to readers—namely, Cooper. Stockett undeniably dreads confrontation with others who also feel that she has crossed that "terrible line," not only in writing the voices of black women, but also in writing their lives (Stockett 450). A court of law has yet to accurately respond to the question of whether or not Stockett embezzled distinct traits from Cooper in the development of her fictional character. Cooper's case was dismissed by Hinds County judge Tomie Green due to the lapse in time between Cooper's receipt of the text and the filing of her claim. While this summary judgment leaves the interrogation of the authenticity of Stockett's writing up for critical grabs, what is clear is the question of permission in terms of the author's use of a black character and her voice. As her lawsuit contended, Cooper maintains that Stockett intruded into a space where she was not welcomed. After Judge Green issued her ruling, a discernibly distressed Cooper left the Jackson, Mississippi, courthouse shouting, "She's a liar! . . . tell her to tell the truth!"

When asked why she had decided to write *The Help* in a 2009 interview with *Time* magazine, Stockett states that the novel had its beginnings immediately following the September 11 tragedy, when the author resided in New York City, and that Aibileen found her basis in the memory the author possesses of her childhood caregiver, Demetrie. Stockett attaches the necessity of that particular memory to connect her with her home, stating, "Like a lot of writers do, I started to write in a voice that I missed. I was really homesick—I couldn't even call my family and tell them I was fine. So I started writing in the voice of Demetrie, the maid I had growing up. She later became the character of Aibileen [in *The Help*]" (Suddath 1).

Asserting that the voice of Demetrie and later the transformation of that voice into Aibileen was one that she missed indicates the author's familiarity with a voice that was not her own; however, Stockett's perception of the separation that exists between her, the voices she creates, and the communities from which these voices derive is problematic to the legitimacy of her work.

In a 2010 *CBS News* interview, anchor Katie Couric asked Stockett how she responded to criticism, supposedly from the African American community, for writing the black characters' dialogue in a nonstandard dialect and white characters' words in more standard English. Stockett replied, "My grandmother spoke so properly, my stepmother speaks so properly. Almost all of my friends' parents spoke this beautiful Southern eloquence and I honestly just wrote it like I remembered it . . . My mother's generation, oh gosh, the language was lovely, but I have to say I think the African American language is lovely as well" (Stockett 2010).

In these lines, the author speaks to having observed and assigned a variance in speech patterns between the African American community and white Southern speakers of English, designating the former of the two communities its own language altogether—coining the terribly problematic term "African American language"—and admitting an affinity to the latter group's verbal styling. Stockett's awareness of certain shifts and nuances in the voices she alleges to remember and record from her childhood is apparent; however, the author appears unaware of the context of the language she claims to channel from her past.

Style of language and dialect possess significance in literature of the South. The region's various communities and cultural groups each retain a practice of communication that is distinct to their separate needs and experiences. Of Southern African American author Margaret Walker Alexander, scholar Joyce Pettis writes that as "a black Southerner whose ear for the distinctive rhythm of spoken words developed precociously," Walker was aware of "the cadences of Southern speech, sermons, and Negro spirituals" (Inge 9). Like Stockett, Walker observed a distinguishing element present in African American dialect; however, disparate from *The Help*'s author, Walker is noted as having been aware of the variant rhythms and their cloaked meanings. This study considers the African American community, especially the factions of that community in the American South, as a high-context culture in terms of communication.

Anthropologist Edward T. Hall outlines the correlation between culture and the effect it has on communication with his discussion of cultures in the high and the low contextual frameworks. Within Hall's work, high-context cultures are those that place emphasis on inference and transfer information in more intimate and less direct and verbal fashions. High-context communication relies on messaging that is "either in the physical context or internalized in the person, while very little is coded [or] explicit" (Hall 91). According to this theoretical premise, America is considered to exist as a low-context culture, or one whose communication is widely reliant on information "vested in the explicit code"— that is, standard American English (Hall 91). As an ethnic countercommunity of American culture, the African American community possesses traits that deem it distinctive from the dominant culture. Language and modes of communication developed by this community serve as a marker for its uniqueness. The possession of this definitive trait of the transfer of information appears central to effectively voicing a character of the community from which it stems.

Stockett confesses that had she known her novel would be "so widely disseminated," she "probably wouldn't have written it in the type of language" that she did—speaking of the dialect of Aibileen, Minny, and other black characters in the world of the text (Suddath 1). In indicating that the vernacular of these central black characters could have been disposed of had the author anticipated the success of the novel, Stockett diminishes the value of an element vital to the genuine portrayal of the community she writes in so much of her text. In contrast, Welty's portrayal of the black community of Holden in "The Demonstrators" surfaces a signature trait adopted by the African American community as well as the folklore and modes of communication significant to that community: signifying. A dissimilarity existing between the communities to which Welty and Stockett belonged during the mid-twentieth century and the African American counterpart of those communities, literally just across the tracks,[1] is present in the variety of intricate methods of communication, including signifying. The African American communities that exist in their works should be considered high-context cultures, and the appearance of the folkloric element of signifying provides an example of the heightened communication context that exists within African American English.

Signifying in the black community is a derivative of double-talk or trickery taken from the character Esu-Elegbara and his monkey. Within Yoruba mythology, Esu-Elegbara is a character that served as a trickster messenger figure depicted with a monkey by his side (who possessed the same trickster ways). Esu is considered to be the Pan-African cousin of the Signifying Monkey of African American folklore. African American literary scholar Henry Louis Gates Jr. describes the character as: "the figure of a black rhetoric in the Afro-American speech community. He exists to embody the figures of speech characteristic to the black vernacular. He is the principle of self-consciousness in the black vernacular, the meta-figure itself. Given the play of doubles at work in the black appropriation of the English-language term that denotes relations of meaning, the Signifying Monkey and his language of Signifyin(g) are extraordinary conventions, with Signification standing as the term for black rhetoric, the obscuring of apparent meaning" (53).

Gates's scholarship provides a working definition for signifying, within the African American community specifically, and demonstrates the uses of this convention. The strong presence of signifying in the black community represents the real-life rhetoric of that cultural space. The concept of signifying deals specifically with language and its interpretation. Gates describes this concept as: "a meta-discourse, a discourse about itself. These admittedly complex matters are addressed, in black tradition, in the vernacular, far away from the eyes and ears of outsiders, those who do not speak the language of tradition" (Gates xxi). He explains that the use of the vernacular within the African American community in a signifying manner is a "protective tendency" that is "free of the white person's gaze" and that "black people created their own unique vernacular structures and relished in the double play that these forms bore to white forms" (Gates xxi, xxiv).

Literary critic Kenneth Bearden identifies similarities between the Signifying Monkey and the protagonist of Welty's "Powerhouse"—perhaps a character fashioned after sightings during her visits to Jackson's predominately black Farish Street district (Switzer 35). Gates states that "signifyin(g) in jazz performances is a mode of formal revision, it depends for its effects on troping" (53). Welty experienced the tendency that members of the African American community in Jackson had to communicate with double-speak firsthand. Much like the myths of Esu-Elegbara, where community outsiders retreat feeling cheated, angry, and confused, Dr. Strickland in Welty's "The Demonstrators" leaves the home of an African American patient with no straight answers to the questions he poses and having perhaps exceeded cultural restrictions in his communication to those present in the house. Although there exists a myriad of features specific to black American speech, signifying represents a tradition that extends deep into the cultural origin of the community—rendering the trope vital in the construction of authentic dialogue of black characters in a close-knit environment such as that of the women in *The Help*. Welty displays an understanding of the necessity of this component, whereas Stockett renders the dialect she writes as disposable to the narrative.

Having both lived as white women in a city and in a time period where privilege accompanied their racial status, Stockett and Welty's similarities also converge in their writing. Welty's published work and photography integrate varying themes of race and class. The formation of characters such as Phoenix Jackson, Ruby, Dove, Livvie, Solomon, and the other ethnic personas throughout Welty's fiction appear to be derivative of her first-person observation of similar communities in her hometown of Jackson and other areas of Mississippi. "Ida M'Toy" and "A Pageant of Birds" exist as nonfiction pieces penned by Welty that meaningfully remember and retell the lives and experiences of black women Welty encountered and photographed. While the author's work has at times been denigrated for what was regarded as an understated political position, especially considering the tumultuous climate of race relations during the time in which she was writing most, the author maintained that she was writing about life and all its realities—both the beautiful and the dreadful. As for writing politically or in order to champion a particular message of consciousness, Welty argued in her 1965 essay "Must the Novelist Crusade?" that, as a writer of fiction, she could not "set people to acting mechanically or carrying placards to make their sentiments plain" and that people were not "Right and Wrong, Good and Bad, Black and White personified; flesh and blood and the sense of comedy object" (105). In this piece, penned at the height of the civil rights movement in the American South, Welty also cautioned her contemporaries against "looking at people in the generality—that is to say, of seeing people as not at all like us" and notes that if "human beings are to be comprehended as real, then they have to be treated as real, with minds, hearts, memories, habits, hopes, with passions and capacities like ours," regardless of race or class (105). African American author Toni Morrison revered Welty's presentation of disparate communities and credited Welty as one of "certain fearless women who have lived in segregated societies" and "are able to write about black people in a way that few white men have ever been able to write . . . not patronizing, not romanticizing" (Flower 8).

When asked whether or not she had "known any black women . . . Really known them" by African American author Alice Walker in a 1973 interview, Welty responded, "I think I have. Better in Jackson than anywhere, though only, as you'd expect, within the framework of the home. That's the only way I'd have had a chance, in the Jackson up until now. Which doesn't take away from the reality of the knowledge, of its depth of affection—on the contrary" (Prenshaw 136).

Within her response, Welty fails to mention the friendship she professed to possess with Maude Thompson, the creator and organizer of the bird pageant that served as the source of Welty's 1942 "A Pageant of Birds," or that she had made regular visits to see Ida M'Toy before her death in the 1960s and considered her an old friend—both claims she made in a 1989 interview regarding her photography. These assertions present the possibility that Welty had known black women—really known them—and that she considered their existence as part of her world that exceeded the realm of domestic servitude. Stockett's response to her personal relationships with black women, like those who lead her novel's narration, shares similar traits with Welty's 1973 comments in that the woman she claimed to have been closer to "than the other kids," whose resounding voice had provided the framework of her novel, had occupied what Welty described as "the framework of the home" (Stockett 448; Prenshaw 136). However, a vast difference between the manners in which both women handle these figures in their work surfaces in each author's acknowledged conceptualization of their position in relation to those alternate communities. Welty contends that despite the complications that the political climate of Jackson, Mississippi, and the South placed on the potential to know—really know—any person of color during the middle of the twentieth century, the way in which she had grown to know black people and black women was valid and true. In her response to Walker's inquiry, Welty admits that, like Stockett, her only close interactions with blacks would have been with domestic workers. Yet the thoughtful and precise portrayal of Phoenix Jackson in "A Worn Path" seems to illustrate a deeper observance on the part of Welty. Jackson stands as the short story's only named character. She is the purpose of the tale, while the white characters possess a diminutive role that reinforces the elderly black character's dominance. She is essential.

In contrast to Stockett, Welty reifies the worth and legitimacy of her relationships with black women without sentimentalizing them. During her travels across Mississippi as a photographer for the Works Progress Administration and frequent visits to the black districts of Jackson, Welty realized her alternate position as an outsider to these communities but did not permit her placement to limit her observations of their customs, traditions, and varying modes of communication with one another. The majority of the subjects in *Eudora Welty Photographs* (1989) are African Americans in their homes, in their neighborhoods, at work—within their space—positioning Welty as a witness to the community through a literal and figurative lens. The author deliberately acted within her voyeuristic role in an effort to ensure that the communities and situations she observed remained authentic and untainted by her outsider presence. The black Farish Street Baptist Church parishioners hold a place within *Photographs* as well as Welty's 1942 nonfiction work named for their beautifully peculiar fundraising pageant. When questioned as to how she had been taken as a middle-class white woman venturing into disenfranchised minority communities to photograph the lives of the inhabitants, Welty admitted that there had been a "casual curiosity" on the part of her black subjects given her identity but that she had been "politely received" and that "there were connections" (xxvi). Allusions to these connections surface in her autobiography, *One Writer's Beginnings*, as Welty recalls the "ancient and familiar figure of the black lady" who tended to the patrons of a train station in Meridian, Mississippi (937). This character later finds her way into the pages of "The Demonstrators." Welty reveals an undeniable intellectual concern with a cultural space outside that of her own with the thoughtful and measured placement of African Americans or ethnically othered individuals in other works as well, such as *Delta Wedding*, "Powerhouse," "Livvie," and "Music From Spain."

The black voice has a vital role to play in detailing Southern life. The product of a region with an infamous history of racial tension, Southern writing often incorporates aspects of this thread of the region's social fabric. With plantation life existing as an integral facet of Southern living during the antebellum period, the early works of Southern writers are widely inclusive of the people and voices of those plantations: owners, masters, overseers, house and field slaves, and so on. The writings of early Southern authors such as Julia Mood Peterkin needed more than the white viewpoint and voice to possess accuracy. Peterkin received criticism from prominent critic H. L. Mencken for producing writing that was overwhelmingly "about white people, especially white people like herself" (Lewis 22). The monotony in the voice of Peterkin's work begged for the incorporation of a contrasting perspective and articulation. Mencken approved of the work produced by Peterkin that possessed a "more pointed emphasis on black culture," which eventually encouraged the writer to focus her writing less on the voice of "petty, self-absorbed white people" (Lewis 22).

Stockett borrows from this tradition by not relying solely on her seemingly autobiographical character, Skeeter, to convey the entire story. Stockett holds that the creation of the overtly attitudinal and cross Minny character was necessary because of the ability to voice thoughts with a brashness through her that was uncharacteristic of the "older, soft-spoken" Aibileen; however, both black characters served a distinct purpose that Skeeter could not (Suddath 1). The use of a personality closer in emotion and proximity to a particular community to tell of the intricacies of their experiences makes sense; however, the challenge of the truth of the voice surfaces when the writer or creator of such personalities is not a member of that community. I do not contend that only an African American can relay the struggle of that community with care and precision; I assert that thoughtful research and a humanizing perspective or sympathetic imagination is paramount in attempting to voice a character from another community. By "humanizing perspective," I mean that the characters created outside of one's own experience must be viewed as people, not as Others who can never be understood by an author who possesses an ostensible cultural difference. In an early letter to her agent, Diarmuid Russell, Welty describes this as the need to consider people (and thus characters) "one by one in the world" because "that is the way they are loved, believed, or understood, and when we are told to think in masses, we are lost for the one thing that is the essence and holy is gone" (Letter to Diarmuid Russell December 1941). She further criticizes other writers for lacking the sensibility to see people unlike themselves as equal and for writing with blinded prejudice that lacked purpose. She expressed her distaste of this handling of characters in another letter written in 1941 to Russell after reading a draft of Katherine Anne Porter's work, remarking, "She wishes to show the superiority of some races and the inferiority of others, and I can not think this is worthy of the work—the characters will have to contract and shrink in size in order to fit into a prejudice that should have nothing to do with them" (Letter to Diarmuid Russell November 1941).

In the afterword of her novel, Stockett confesses that she and her family felt as though Demetrie was "lucky to have . . . a secure job in a nice house, cleaning up after white Christian people" and that they felt as though they "were filling a void in her life" (Stockett 448). From her earliest memories, Stockett situated herself outside of the world of her black maid and the black community. Although the social climate of the mid-twentieth-century South would undoubtedly separate Stockett and her family from that of Demetrie or any other black citizen in her hometown, the author's negotiation of her lack of relation to that community complicates her storytelling. Other Southern women who have written across community lines, such as Eudora Welty, have done so with thoughtful contemplation and a "depth of affection" of which Stockett's work proves deficient (Prenshaw 136).

While Stockett laments that she felt "a little ashamed" that she had not considered the implications of the cultural difference that existed between her family and her childhood maid until well into adulthood, Welty admitted to considering this difference with vigor early on (Stockett 2010). Welty penned the majority of her works while Stockett was a young girl. Despite the obvious strictures perpetrated onto Welty's writing at that time, the author portrayed courage and a conscious intention within her work. Welty openly questioned whether it was the obligation of the writer to act as a crusader or an activist, as is evident in her essay "Must the Novelist Crusade?"; however, her writing during the sixties proved provocative, covertly political, and undeniably honest. Of Welty's 1963 short fictional piece "Where Is the Voice Coming From?"—a work written in response to the murder of civil rights activist Medgar Evers—author Suzan Harrison notes that "Welty does 'interrogate whiteness' and examine 'the effect of racist inflection on the subject'" (631).

In *One Writer's Beginnings*, Welty reflects fondly on an "old black sewing woman" hired by her mother during her childhood: "This was Fannie . . . [A]long with her speed and dexterity, [she] brought along a great provision of up-to-the-minute news . . . Fannie was the worldliest old woman to be imagined . . . [S]he could speak in a wonderfully derogatory way with any number of pins stuck in her mouth" (853).

The description of her childhood seamstress is particularly similar to Stockett's discussion of Demetrie. In the novel's afterword, Stockett states that Demetrie told her and her siblings "all kinds of stories about picking cotton as a girl. She'd laugh and shake her finger at us, warning us against it, as if a bunch of rich white kids might fall to the evils of cotton-picking, like cigarettes or hard liquor" (Stockett 447). While Welty describes an apparent admiration for Fannie, her skillful way with words, and the excitement of her stories, Stockett shares a condescending skepticism for Demetrie's tales and consents to her socially elevated position over Demetrie and her community. In identifying herself as a "rich white kid," Stockett steps farther outside of the reality of the stories Demetrie tells. This acknowledgment of a static separation between Demetrie as a black domestic worker and Stockett as a "rich white kid" detaches *The Help* from the literary tradition set forth by Welty (447). Just as Fannie decides for herself when she will begin and end her stories despite Welty's mother's discouraging chidings in *One Writer's Beginnings*, Demetrie's agency exists in her deliberate lack of response to any inquiries about her relationship with her husband, who Stockett describes as a "mean, abusive drinker named Clyde" (Stockett 447). The two authors reflect on these similarities in the character traits of the black domestic workers they had known as children in dissimilar ways. Welty acknowledges Fannie's power and choice of defiance, while Stockett notes that this was the only subject her maid would deny her to investigate. Welty witnessed a strong, confident figure; Stockett observed a child with an embarrassing secret.

Welty's response to critics such as Linda Orr who feel that Welty and other Southern (mostly female) writers "have participated in hiding that which is 'unspeakable' in Southern history" and the horror of racial discrimination in their works peopled by black characters differs from Stockett as well (Harrison 632). Orr describes Welty as an "ahistorical" writer whose work does little to incorporate the historical turmoil of the South (Harrison 632). She goes on to critique the author's work as "not concerned primarily with the larger cultural, racial, and political themes" of the time (Harrison 632). Although Welty never claims to intentionally focus on issues of race in her work or to write as an activist, she admits to "having a feeling of uneasiness over the things being written about the South at that time" and to writing "well-intentioned stories" with "generalities written from a distance to illustrate generalities" (Prenshaw 83). Of her regional home, the author observed that "wrenchingly painful and humiliating" events had colored and stained the history and that an "added . . . atmosphere of hate" during the sixties complicated the South's images indefinitely (107). Welty creates an environment that allows her reader to view her own surroundings as she had seen them and to witness those communities that were unlike her own the way she had. When asked by Alice Walker if the black people she met throughout her life ever "crept into" her fiction, Welty responded, "what I put into a short story in the form of characters might be called certain qualities of people in certain situations—no, pin it down more—some quality that makes them unique. I try to dramatize something like this in a way that can show it better than life shows it" (Prenshaw 137). In stating that she forms characters (specifically speaking of black characters) with "certain qualities of people . . . that makes them unique," Welty exercises what I have termed a *humanizing perspective* (Welty 137). She identifies the traits of people of color that she has observed as those of people, not the ways of the help.

Before "Where Is the Voice Coming From?" was published, an anonymous caller made the accusation that she (Welty) did not "understand anything about black people," to which she responded that she "had been writing about injustice" all her life (Harrison 633). Unauthorized Welty biographer Ann Waldron defended Welty and her concern with race relations in the South in much the same vein by asserting, "Eudora by no means ignored them (Blacks). She showed them to us without editorializing. You can't read *Delta Wedding* without seeing that the black servants and field hands are treated like children, deprived of basic rights, and living in poverty. Eudora, however, directs our gaze elsewhere. She . . . let others write political tracts" (Flower 4–5).

Stockett receives similar criticism from her readership; however, the author's response departs from Welty's self-assured tone. She admits to being hurt and disoriented by an African American woman who, during a book signing in Raleigh, North Carolina, exclaimed, "She didn't love you, you just think she did" when Stockett declared the affection she assumed Demetrie felt for her as a child (Stockett 2010). Stockett maintains a relentless avowal of intimacy with Demetrie throughout the course of interviews with media outlets and within the pages of her text that is complicated by the fact that she admits to not having been allowed to go to her home (due to its location on the black side of town), never having made inquiries into her emotional state, and only having seen her out of her white uniform "when she was in the casket" (Stockett 2010). Welty acknowledges very openly that although she had known black people, she could not have intimately known them outside of their predominately domestic capacities of the time period. She did not pretend or believe to possess a closeness that did not exist. Stockett's fictional characters, Minny and Constantine, exhibit similar traits to the real-life Fannie and Demetrie in their separation of personal and occupational duties. Minny is constantly perturbed with Skeeter—the young, white woman who clandestinely interviews black maids for her budding manuscript—for asking too many questions about her family, especially her abusive husband, Leroy, and "making this too personal" (183). Minny also shields the abuse she suffers at home from her employer, Celia Rae Foote, not wanting that to be a part of her story in the eyes of a white woman. Constantine, the beloved maid of Skeeter and the Phelan family, shields pieces of her world from the sight of her white employers as well, most notably her illegitimate daughter, Lulabelle, and the adoption she was forced to place her into because the baby was a "negro with white skin" (Stockett 358). Skeeter felt betrayed that despite feeling so close to Constantine, she had never known of Lulabelle. Although Stockett contends that she is most like the Marilyn Monroe doppelgänger Celia Rae Foote, the revelations that Skeeter makes about the true identities of the black women who have surrounded her throughout her life seem to correlate to the author's experience.

Welty's incorporation of black characters and distinct elements of black life exists as candid renderings of what she observed. Upon theoretically contemplating the question of whether or not the novelist must crusade on the side of right, the author observes that fiction writers must not consider themselves as disparate from any of the characters they produce and must certainly be equipped and able "to enter into the minds and hearts of our own people, all of them, to comprehend them (us) and then to make characters and plots in stories that in honesty and with honesty reveal them (ours-selves) to us, in whatever situation we live through in our own times" (108).

Here, Welty describes her intention to exercise creative equity in her penning of characters deemed socially and racially opposite. Stockett's representations of Demetrie, Aibileen, Minny, Yule Mae, Pascagoula, Constantine, Treelore, Leroy, and the host of other black characters in her past and her work differ as her observations illustrate a less attentive perspective of their community. Of her knowledge of the voices of the black women within her past who inform those in her work, Stockett claims to have "played it back like a tape recorder" (Stockett 2010). Perhaps lack of consideration for the depth and finesse imperative in relaying the feelings and struggle of that particular community exists as the author's deficiency. This absence of literary tact is also evident in a minor detail in Stockett's narrative where she speaks of the only black high school located in Jackson before integration. Within the text, Stockett writes of Minny speaking of her son Leroy Junior's school, Lanier High; however, the text reads "Lenier High" (219). This grammatical misstep could have likely occurred during editing by parties unfamiliar with Jackson's structural terrain; nevertheless, other edifices and figures native to the areas of Jackson with which Stockett would have been familiar, such as Power Elementary and Murrah High, are incorporated with accurate detail.

In a response to an inquiry into her purpose for fashioning works with overt political tones while refusing to associate them with a dogmatic goal or principle, Welty conceptualizes the reason for which she writes voices from any community, especially those of Jackson during the 1960s:

> All of it was a reflection of society at the time it happened. Every story in effect does that [. . .] They all reflect the way we were deeply troubled in that society and within ourselves at what was going on in the sixties. They reflect the effect of change sweeping all over the South—of course, over the rest of the country too, but I was writing about where I was living and the complexity of those changes. I think a lot of my work then suggested that it's not just a matter of cut and dried right and wrong—"We're right—You're wrong," "We're black, you're white." You know, I wanted to show the complexity of it all. (Prenshaw 259)

Stockett's critics question whether her novel exaggerates the level of intimacy in the relationships between white families and their black domestic workers during the 1960s; I assert that the possibility of a narrative that possesses relevance and authenticity although written outside of the community it depicts exists. Despite this evident interrogation of Stockett's work, the experiences of those who have witnessed the nuances of black life in America from the sidelines presented in a thoughtful manner offer a perspective that is germane and valuable. Margaret Walker Alexander describes the South's relationship with its literature as "a reflection of the life of the people" that is "too varied and too myriad an experience to deal boldly and comprehensively with" (Walker 135). Stockett's singular vantage point contrasts significantly from Welty's submersion and heightened sensibility to the subtleties of the black community in her home state. Although still on the periphery, Welty possessed a willingness to move beyond her microcosmic reality to observe and produce characters that were not only authentic but also human—and worthy of that attention to detail.

Note

1. During the early to mid-twentieth century, black citizens in Jackson, Mississippi, occupied housing predominately located on the west side of the city. The train tracks that run through the city, even unto current day, serve as a divider between downtown Jackson and communities with lower socioeconomic standing. Stockett says "she lived on the other side of the tracks" when responding to where her childhood maid, Demetrie, lived and whether or not she had ever been to her home (Stockett 2010).

Works Cited

Couric, Katie. "@KatieCouric: Kathryn Stockett." *CBSNews.com*. 2 March 2010. Web. 3 April 2011. http://www.cbsnews.com/video/watch/?id=625994n.

Flower, Dean. "Welty and Racism." *The Hudson Review* 60.2 (2007): 1–7. Print.

Gates, Henry Louis, Jr. *The Signifying Monkey: A Theory of African-American Literary Criticism*. New York: Oxford UP, 1989. Print.

Hall, Edward T. *Beyond Culture*. New York: Anchor Press/Doubleday, 1977. Print.

Harrison, Suzan. "'It's Still a Free Country': Constructing Race, Identity, and History in Eudora Welty's 'Where Is the Voice Coming From?'" *The Mississippi Quarterly* 50.4 (1997): 631–643. Print.

Inge, Tonette Bond, ed. *Southern Women Writers: The New Generation*. Tuscaloosa: Alabama UP, 1990. Print.

Lewis, Nghana Tamu. *Entitled to the Pedestal: Place, Race, and Progress in White Southern Women's Writing, 1920–1945*. Iowa City: Iowa UP, 2007. Print.

Prenshaw, Peggy Whitman. *Conversations with Eudora Welty*. Jackson: UP Mississippi, 1984. Print.

Stockett, Kathryn. *The Help*. New York: Amy Einhorn Books, 2009. Print.

Suddath, Claire. "Q&A: Kathryn Stockett, Author of *The Help*." *Time Magazine* November 11, 2009: 1–3. Web.

Switzer, Robert. "Signifying the Blues." *Alif: Journal of Comparative Poetics* 21 (2001): 25–76. Print.

Walker, Margaret. *How I Wrote Jubilee and Other Essays on Life and Literature*. New York: Feminist Press at CUNY, 1990. Print.

Welty, Eudora. *Eudora Welty Photographs*. Jackson: UP of Mississippi, 2001. Print.

———. Letter to Diarmuid Russell. November 24, 1941. MS. N.p. Print.

———. Letter to Diarmuid Russell. December 23, 1941. MS. N.p. Print.

———. "Must the Novelist Crusade?" *The Atlantic*, October 1965: 105–108. Print.

———. *One Writer's Beginnings*. Cambridge, MA: Harvard UP, 1984. Print.

CHAPTER 3

Blackness as Medium

Envisioning White Southern Womanhood in Eudora Welty's "A Worn Path" and *Delta Wedding* and Kathryn Stockett's *The Help*

Elizabeth J. West

White-authored texts asserting authoritative examination of black life and experience have prevailed in US discourse since before the nation's founding. As the editors of this volume have argued in the introduction, in literature as well as media, we continue to see the import of white-authored narrations on blackness. Generations of white authors have conditioned readers to accept their racially cast lens as authoritative and, yes, even "objective." Too often, however, challenges to this critical slant result in a reinscription of that very authority: as we focus on the pervasive misrepresentations of blackness in these texts, whiteness again evades scrutiny, and blackness remains the object under surveillance. Certainly, we must critique white characterizations of blackness for their historical and ongoing impact on racism. This need notwithstanding, however, we should commit as much attention to the disrobed and gutted effigy of whiteness that so often goes unacknowledged, though glaringly present. To my mind, nothing in recent times has highlighted this need more than reactions to Kathryn Stockett's novel, *The Help* (2009).

In conversations with colleagues, students, and recreational readers about this novel, I have again been reminded of how the focus on white-authored representations of blackness can stifle meaningful scrutiny of whiteness. I do not propose that my personal recollections stand as a scientific survey but rather that these anecdotal encounters reflect established lines of inquiry for white writings about race. In my conversations with black colleagues and black students, the overwhelming view was that *The Help* and its author seemed like just another in the long history of white writers capitalizing on black people's struggles and experiences. They seemed most offended by a white woman assuming the knowledge and understanding of black servants and the authority to represent them. Many told me they refused to read or to purchase such an enterprise. These fervent objections prompted me to include *The Help* among required readings in my 2010 undergraduate introductory course in literary studies. I thought this a fitting opportunity to challenge students with questions of authorial voice and authenticity, and selfishly, I wanted to educate myself further on reader response to the novel. Students ranged from sophomores to graduating seniors—representing the "traditional" college-age demographic. Of the total 17 students, 5 were African American and 12 were white. All but two white students praised Stockett's novel as an exemplary representation of black Southern experience. Two white female students and the five black female students argued that the novel was little more than the white author objectifying blackness as a means to reconcile white guilt. Black students unanimously expressed their dislike of the story, and they rejected suggestions that though written by a white author, the text might tell us something meaningful about black life.

Outside academia, I happened upon a few opportunities to discuss *The Help* with people in my personal world. I listened to white friends and acquaintances express their marvel at Stockett's achievement in telling the stories of black women in the era of Southern racism. Of the few blacks I know who decided to include *The Help* in their recreational readings, I did not hear the kind of staunch rejection voiced by my colleagues and students in the halls of academia. Perhaps the difference in reception—if my own observations reflect at all the larger social reception—may rest in the impulse of black nonacademics to interrogate whiteness rather than be driven by concerns with the white gaze. Perhaps, then, recreational black readers of *The Help* are not particularly disturbed by a white author writing black speech in dialect because they find the matter of a white writer interrogating whiteness through black cultural tropes a much more intriguing consideration. For example, when black readers envision the narrator's account of Hilly Holbrook, one of the leading white ladies of the community, unknowingly eating the feces of her black housekeeper, Minny, the laughter at this outrage originates from connections to familiar cultural contexts. In the halls of academia, some may be inclined to read this psychoanalytically as an example of the white fetish over the black body. However, through a black cultural lens, the depth of the insult rests in the association of this act with lower animal instincts, particularly that of the canine species. In African and African American folklore and casual discourse, the dog is commonly employed as symbol of lowliness and/or wickedness. While Americans see themselves as lovers of their canine friends, derogatory tropes alluding to dogs abound in our culture—today and certainly in the 1960s South. In our everyday experiences, most of us have had an occasion to witness a heated exchange in which one person extends to his rival the invitation to eat his waste, and in African American discourse, a frequent adage that signals the depth of an insult is when someone has been talked about like a dog. Dog owners know well that on excursions in the outdoors with canine companions, one must bury one's waste lest the dog gets whiff of it and consumes this delicacy. The message signified here is not lost on black readers who understand Minny's cultural lens: the human who is reduced to consuming the waste of another human holds a value far down the chain of being. Whether Stockett understands the depth of the insult is irrelevant to the black readers who do. Stockett's black recreational readers laugh and cry throughout their reading of *The Help*, but their reactions cannot be presumed to be the response to a white or universal read of race—black or white.

For the most part, I found that my white colleagues and students liked the book, praising Stockett for being a champion of blacks in the South. I found few whites who did not express a favorable impression of the novel. Of those few dissenting white readers that I encountered, two stand out in my recollection: one a colleague and the other a graduate student, both female and Southern, and both from households that had the luxury of hiring black nannies. In our discussion, my colleague expressed her ill ease with the novel's depiction of white Southern women. She recalled being particularly perturbed by her white middle-class Northern-transplanted friends who told her that after reading Stockett's novel, they now understood the truly horrid conditions under which blacks suffered. To be clear, these women were not speaking of the antebellum South and its legacy of labor exploitation that is tied to patriarchy. Their revelation came instead through Stockett's fictional white Southern women, in a postslavery world, exploiting and terrorizing black laborers in what can readily be seen as postemancipation, modern-world slavery. These women did not see Stockett's heroine, Skeeter, as the final symbol of the white Southern woman. They found the villainous and self-serving white women who ruled Stockett's fictional Southern elite community the definitive image of the text.

In the case of the graduate student whose reaction I recall here, I recommended Stockett's novel as an engaging read during the semester break. I thought her reaction might be interesting because frequently, in her visits to my office to discuss her work, she volunteered unsolicited recollections of her black nanny, who she declared had been the real mother figure in her life. Months later, in one of our office consultations, I asked whether she had gotten around to reading Stockett's novel. She did not indicate how long ago she had read it, but she shrugged her shoulders and told me that the book left her feeling very uncomfortable. She told me that she did not like the way Stockett represented the relationships between black maids and the white women who employed them and that she thought Stockett left no possibility for real human connectedness between black and white Southern women. She did not tease this analysis to its final implication—that is, that Stockett's representation of the black female gaze suggests a view of white womanhood that is hard to reconcile with dominant white paradigms of ideal white humanity.

These two disturbed readers of Stockett's novel reminded me that white authors represent blackness in ways that tell us much more about whites than blacks and oftentimes convey a base and unredemptive picture of whiteness. Rather than critically examining the import of these troubling depictions of whiteness, however, we continue to direct the focus to characterizations of blackness. This deflection is predicated on the Anglo-centric presumption that blacks have no capacity to gaze whiteness and that white dismissal of or silence regarding failed images of whiteness effectively renders those images nonexistent or unreal. Forefronting blackness as powerless, vilified, and/or denigrated, these works invisibilize unseemly images of whiteness: by virtue of our continued deliberations on these white-constructed images of blackness, blacks are maintained as lesser than and whites are reinscribed as symbolic and authoritative humanity.

In the long history of white writing black, white authors create a playing field in which they wrestle with questions of their humanity and with the disturbing blemish of slavery cast against the myth of white valor and decency. Not infrequently in these authorial quests, whiteness is rescued at the expense of those, specifically blacks, not invested in its preservation. We find the beginnings of this sacrificial practice in this nation's most sacred document—a "compromise" remembered recently by Emory University president James Wagner in the winter 2013 issue of the university's alumni publication, *Emory Magazine*. In a column emphasizing compromise as invaluable to the gridlock in our current national Congress, Wagner deemed the founding fathers' mathematical deduction of blacks to three-fifths human a model of compromise diplomacy. He summarized what he deemed the ingenuity of this hallmark concession: "As the price for achieving the ultimate aim of the Constitution—'to form a more perfect union'— the two sides compromised on this immediate issue of how to count slaves in the new nation." The end result, according to Wagner, was that the country was drawn "more closely together." In this battle to save the newly formed nation, blacks are not considered part of the citizen body, and they have no voice, yet their rights, freedom, and humanity will be further pilfered to secure the formation of the newly formed union. War often results in the destruction and victimization of innocent and uninterested populations, and the victors often explain that this fallout, or collateral damage, is unavoidable. In his assessment of the Wagner controversy, Kevin Kiley explains the chilling similarity between the shame of the founding fathers' compromise and the hushed, inconvenient shame of Emory's founding: "Emory has a complicated history of racial issues that predates Wagner's time on campus, extending all the way back to the institution's founding by slave owners" (2010). In both instances—the founding of the United States and the founding of Emory University—we are to believe that sacrificing black bodies and black humanity in the interest of white-sanctioned institutions is without question, acceptable, and in fact praiseworthy.

The compromise of black humanity in our nation's sterling document paves the way, then, for the relative ease with which blackness is cast as disposable and other in early white-authored texts—especially those contemplating national identity and legacy.[1] It is a literary template not lost on succeeding generations of white writers. The interpretive sleight of hand continues: readers and critics remain willing to debate how reinscribed white depictions of blacks impact blacks, but few are willing to examine how white depictions of blackness play into self-constructed myths of white humanity and achievement. Perhaps we might better understand the historical persistence of white domination if we examine the silenced or disregarded intimations about whiteness that are a by-product of white-constructed visions of blackness. Such a study might reveal that while the white gaze clearly has a destructive impact on dominant perceptions of blackness, this end result does not altogether salvage whiteness. In its more unacknowledged image, whiteness emerges as a gilded humanity: like a brilliant counterfeit gold coin, the inner material is only dull, valueless filler.

The literary and critical feats that feed the white-writes-black legacy depend on the narrator's noncritical yet assumed authoritative lens, the narrator's presumption that blacks lack the capacity to see or judge whiteness, and, of course, the readers' acceptance of these foundational premises. Deemed unempowered, uncritical, and uncurious, blacks are then reduced to entities acted on, measured, and assessed by a superior white power. With this black-white relational paradigm also articulated in public discourse, readers readily accept contrasting images of innate black frailty cast against white will—whether good or evil. Texts that originate out of this framework generally insinuate frequent and overused maxims that detract from the principal role of whites in a disturbing historical institution and its continued impact in our society. They lead the way to familiar innocuous recollections of the "tragedy" of Southern slavery, or the "unfortunate" and "unavoidable" historical blemish on this otherwise "great" nation. Stockett's novel is no less informed by this legacy, as the novel invites these kinds of readings. But this is the easy read. I propose we explore the less obvious in the novel and examine its resonance—both its accord and its discord—with the well-established tradition of white writing black. Through comparison of Stockett's *The Help* with two selected works by native Mississippian and author Eudora Welty, this chapter considers Stockett's link to a legacy of white female writing that has become most recognized in Welty's fiction. This comparison then informs analysis of the contrast in their works, which allows us to explore how blackness works in the white imagination to compromise the white authoritative lens.

While "the help" are ostensibly the narrative subjects of *The Help*, readers might arguably view Skeeter as the central (and, yes, white) voice and the novel's main character. In this regard, the novel seems yet another in a line of fiction by white women authors whose constructions of Southern, white female identity rest in affirmations of a subordinate and helpless black presence. Margaret Mitchell's *Gone with the Wind* (1936) stands as the foremost work of this tradition; however, before Mitchell's work, this fictional format was evident in Harriet Beecher Stowe's pre–Civil War novel, *Uncle Tom's Cabin*. Just as their male counterparts, white Southern women authors readily invoke a black subservient presence that then authenticates the privileged and superior place of whiteness—even when, as in the case of *Uncle Tom's Cabin*, the author aims to reveal the inhumane behavior of white slaveholders. Whether the presumed subjects of the text (as in Stowe's novel) or part of the narrative backdrop (as in Mitchell's novel), blacks are not represented as human equals to the whites whose Southern, female identity depends on their black presence.

In *The Help*, readers meet yet again a white protagonist in a Southern world still mired in its unsettling legacy of racism. In this world of white privilege and rule, the white protagonist, Skeeter, emerges into self-realization through her relationships with the black laboring underlings. As Skeeter searches for the source of her own anxieties and restlessness, she considers the lives of the black servants who have been central yet involuntary players in a legacy of white Southern privilege that clearly has informed her own history of wealth and ease. Stockett's novel breaks from tradition, however, with a narrative that employs black women's voices as markers of normative humanity. Although the leading narrative voice is Skeeter's, whiteness is othered and the black maids stand as the normative subjects. In the end, Stockett turns the lens, and we find ourselves gazing at whiteness, and the black maids provide the "authoritative lens" through which we see.

Skeeter evolves into an autonomous and authoritative self through her relationship with the presumed powerless and alienated black maids. With her independent spirit, Skeeter may stir memories of Mitchell's Scarlett O'Hara. Unlike Scarlett, however, Skeeter acknowledges the interior world and character of the blacks who are customarily marginalized in the minds of the whites they serve. In this regard, we might connect Skeeter to Little Eva, the sympathetic slave mistress of Stowe's nineteenth-century novel. In the fiction of twentieth-century white women writers, post–*Gone with the Wind*, we find the paternalistic white matrons of the Little Eva type, the self-consumed individualist Scarlett type, and variations between. Whatever the model employed, readers repeatedly meet a white female protagonist whose identity emerges through either an ancillary or focused gaze at the black servants who have been central to the legacy of white Southern wealth and privilege. In the fiction of white women authors whose works have more recently garnered critical attention in academia, this fictional prototype and staging abounds. Eudora Welty stands as one of the more studied authors of this demographic group; however, the case can be argued for the works of authors such as Carson McCullers, Ellen Glasgow, Flannery O'Connor, and Ellen Douglass.

The works of any or all the aforementioned authors would offer insightful comparative texts for analysis of *The Help*. To make the case for the novelty of Stockett's fictionalized racial perspective, however, I turn to the fiction of Eudora Welty, one of Stockett's celebrated literary predecessors. Though generations apart (and Welty deceased), Stockett and Welty share origins and source materials that invite critical scrutiny of their works. Both authors are Mississippi natives who found their home state and its inhabitants fitting subjects for their fiction, and both write from the vantage point of white, educated, privileged, Southern females. Though decades separate them and their works, Welty and Stockett paint similar pictures of Jim Crow Mississippi; however, they do not posit complementary narratives regarding white female complicity. To understand this difference between the two authors, a look back at the influence of one of the South's leading literary sons proves edifying.

For almost a century, critics have examined William Faulkner's fiction for its controversial representations of a dysfunctional South shaped by a racist past. Despite the myth of a glorious and golden Southern legacy that framed white Southern discourses of identity and history at the dawn of the twentieth century, whites in Faulkner's fictional world cannot free themselves from the harsh narrative of race relations that subsides just beneath the veneer of the prevailing narratives of an honorable and grand Southern past. Though women are not represented as central characters in Faulkner's fiction, they are nevertheless pervasive and vital to his image of a fallen postbellum American South. White Southern women in Faulkner's turn-of-the-century South signal the chaos and uncertainty of Southern society moving into the future. In the era of the antebellum South, though he did not represent the station of the white Southern male population at large, the image of the plantation lord, with his grand estate, massive land holding, countless slaves, and idle, dependent wife symbolized Southern order and affirmed white male rulership.

In the postwar world of the South, with the plantation system ruptured, the wealth and status of the old, white male guard was no longer certain. His financial and social uncertainty then informed the world of his once pampered plantation matron. In the fiction of Faulkner, this former icon of Southern gentility is transformed into the embodiment of mental dilapidation. The image of this helpless, neurotic plantation mistress is most memorable in Faulkner's fictional Compson matriarch of *The Sound and the Fury* (1929). This senior remnant from antebellum plantation grandeur stands as the icon of failed Southern womanhood in the postbellum American South. Mrs. Compson comes from a long line of Southern matriarchs who in the postbellum era find themselves in a world unlike that of the South's golden era. Their wealth and authority—and likewise their class status—have dwindled. The black family that serves the Compsons allows them some connection to their esteemed plantation past when their wealth, power, and relevance were marked by their lordship over their population of black underlings. In this grand world, white matriarchs had ongoing access to household help—primarily black female slaves—who came to be regarded as the behind-the-scenes masterminds of the plantation household operations. White women were little more than showpieces, dressed and displayed as exhibits of the master's/white male's massive material holdings. Idle, dependent, and mentally and physically frail, these plantation matrons were often the wards of their capable black female slaves. In the postslavery era, with these once prosperous plantations now barely economically sufficient, upper-class white male authority and power are now tenuous, and white female privilege is also destabilized. This is the condition of Faulkner's twentieth-century Compson household, and the senior Mrs. Compson symbolizes the turn-of-the-century white matron out of sorts and threatened by a South whose hierarchy no longer affirms her station as preeminent among its members. She is the image of white Southern female neurosis that manifests itself in a self-consumed hypochondriac who is unable to attend to her household or her children. Mrs. Compson is dependent on the black help to maintain her household. There is nothing flattering or redeemable in Mrs. Compson, and as a symbol of the white matron of the golden plantation era, she suggests that there is little substance or meaning in the lives of these women. Similarly, in Faulkner's "A Rose for Emily" (1930), Emily Grierson represents white Southern womanhood at the dawn of the twentieth century, still tied to the legacy of the antebellum South. Miss Emily is unable to make the transition to a new South: there is no chivalrous suitor fit to claim her and ensure her social station. She thus retreats into a world of macabre fantasy as the real world around her moves on.

The popularity of and reverence for Faulkner's fiction results in a more complex critique of white Southern male identity and experience, but the contrary has been the case for that of white Southern women. In general, Faulkner's fiction leaves a rather simplistic and unflattering image of white Southern womanhood: his fiction suggests a legacy of privilege that, in the aftermath of the plantation era, left white matrons unable to adapt to the changing South or to emerge into a functional level of self-reliance or independence. Their lack, in general, is exemplified in their continued dependence on their black help. Through Faulkner's fictional lens, white Southern women are ill equipped to transition into the emerging modernist world that will ultimately reshape Southern life and society. These women survive in this tumultuous era of a changing South by maintaining a domestic world that mirrors plantation society. In their world, they remain entitled to idleness and helplessness and, though no longer legally bound to them, blacks remain obligated to labor in the interest of these less-than-capable female remnants of a bygone era.

Eudora Welty was a Southerner herself and, like her contemporary, William Faulkner, a Mississippi native. Welty's works never garnered the acclaim of Faulkner's; however, her writings have emerged as serious texts of study in Southern literature, and her short story "A Worn Path" (1941) is among the most anthologized in American literature. This story has been heralded for its presumably sympathetic depiction of black experience in the American South. Readings asserting this interpretation are compiled in the 1998 Harcourt edition of the story. Among these is "Eudora Welty's Negroes: A Note on 'A Worn Path,'" in which Elmo Howell concludes that "Old Phoenix is a triumphant human being because even at her great age, she still reflects the primal joy of creation" (41). In "Life and Death in Eudora Welty's 'A Worn Path,'" Roland Bartel proclaims that Welty's fictional black heroine, Phoenix Jackson, is "one of the most memorable women in short fiction" (46). Elaine Orr credits Welty for the creation of a character whose identity and plight "challenge the reader both to unlearn and to relearn, that is, to enter the process of creation" (71). In the final essay included in the Harcourt edition, Joseph H. Gardner compares Welty's fictional Phoenix to Rannie, Alice Walker's fictional black mother (in the short story "Strong Horse Tea") who sets out on a journey to find needed treatment for her deathly ill child. Speculating that Walker's story may have been an answer to Welty's representation of black Southern female experience, Gardner concludes that Walker's desperate heroine contrasts sharply to Welty's more triumphant Phoenix. According to Gardner, "because Welty is outside the world of black women . . . she can envisage a Phoenix Jackson in all her mythic grandeur" (106). More recently, Welty scholar Pearl McHaney lauds Welty for her photographic recordings of the South: McHaney proclaims that in Welty's "haphazard, non-propagandist method of taking photographs of people who 'captured her imagination,' Welty demonstrates her subtle crusade for human rights."

While proclamations of Welty's racial altruism may capture the spirit of her art, and while her fictional heroine, Phoenix Jackson, may be interpreted as a sympathetic representation of black Southern experience, Phoenix Jackson is perhaps more critically representative of Toni Morrison's read of blackness in the white imagination. In her acclaimed and widely cited text *Playing in the Dark*, Morrison unveils the importance of blackness—in absence as well as presence—in American fiction by white writers. Morrison's interest in "the way black people ignite critical moments of discovery or change or emphasis in literature not written by them" (viii) is precisely that element in Welty's work pleading for inquiry. Examining Welty's fictionalized characterizations of blacks promises an answer to Morrison's call for "studies of the technical ways in which an Africanist character is used to limn out and enforce the invention and implications of whiteness" (53). Reading Phoenix Jackson, and even less prominent black characters by Welty, beyond suppositions of Welty's intent or authoritative gaze ultimately exemplifies how studies of racialized representations in white-authored texts can "reveal the process of establishing others in order to know them, to display knowledge of the other so as to ease and to order external and internal chaos" (Morrison 54). In short, by employing Morrison's critical prism, we can move beyond the presumed authoritative white gaze cast on the presumed diminutive blacks of Welty's narratives and instead explore the more intriguing exercise of turning that gaze back on itself and considering what it reveals about the narration of white female anxiety at work in Welty's fiction.

In the case of Phoenix Jackson, this aged black woman provides the mechanism for Welty to challenge unflattering stereotypes of white Southern women. As such, perhaps Phoenix Jackson tells us more about the South than Welty desires and, more specifically, Southern womanhood as she would have it. With the portrait of Phoenix Jackson as a simple, primitive (a nature or core that leaves her an outsider in Western [i.e., white] civilization), and dependent being, Welty maintains a recognizable and commonplace depiction of black Southerners. This is the standard discourse for narratives of the plantation South, most notably depicted in popular fiction by white authors from the turn-of-the-century nostalgic dialect tales of Thomas Nelson Page, Joel Chandler Harris, and Washington Cable to what has become the seminal text of the South's glorious antebellum past: Mitchell's *Gone with the Wind*. In their dialect tales, Page, Harris, and Cable employ black characters speaking in dialect to tell entertaining and sentimental tales of a bygone South made up of genteel white plantation lords and their simple-minded slave charges. And with their naturally helpless but sentimental dispositions, white Southern matrons further served to mark the superior station of the plantation lord, who both provided for and protected them and placed at their disposal black servants who were only too happy to care for them and their households. While Mitchell's saga introduces a Southern heroine who is central to the story and defies the conventional plantation narrative portrait of the weak, innocent white Southern matron, *Gone with the Wind* does not stray from the stereotype of simple-minded, dedicated, and happy slaves. In *The Help*, Stockett reminds us of this with Skeeter's reference to Mitchell's novel. As she attempts to convince the New York editor that her book will not be just another white work on the South, Skeeter explains that the black women in her story will break the mold: "Everyone knows how we white people feel, the glorified Mammy figure who dedicates her whole life to a white family. Margaret Mitchell covered that" (106).

Although we would not characterize Welty's fiction in the same light that Skeeter paints *Gone with the Wind*, "A Worn Path" still reminds us of the short-falls when white authors attempt to represent black Southern life. Published two years after Mitchell's 1936 novel had been transformed into its popular 1939 film version, "A Worn Path" stays away from idyllic plantation narrative images of white Southern female weakness and dependency, as well as any likeness of Mitchell's cunning white matron, Scarlett O'Hara. "A Worn Path" is ostensibly the story of a poor, aged black ex-slave journeying through the woods to the town where she can secure medicine for her grandson. The subordinate status of Welty's black protagonist, Phoenix Jackson, is established at the start and maintained throughout the story through the distinct contrast of her dialect and the regularized or generic speech of the white characters—although they are Southerners. This speech difference marks the boundaries of *primitive* and *civilized*, highlighting Phoenix Jackson's outsider status. In this respect, Welty is true to the legacy of nostalgic representations of the South that, while ignoring the distinct speech or dialect of white Southerners, maintain black Southerners as singular in their irregular and presumably deficient speech and, by extension, their prescribed inferior station.

Old and feeble, Phoenix Jackson is momentarily disoriented when she arrives at the doctor's office for her grandson's medicine. The attendant, who is unfamiliar with Phoenix, names her "Grandma," much like the white hunter in the wood who does not bother to ask her name but simply names her "granny." The nurse has encountered Phoenix on previous visits and recognizes her as "old Aunt Phoenix . . . [who] makes these trips just as regular as clockwork" (Welty, "A Worn Path" 21). Initially, Phoenix sits "silent, erect and motionless," until finally "there came a flicker and then a flame of comprehension across her face" (22). Her momentary memory loss after such a long, repeated journey suggests that the old woman suffers from feebleness of mind as well as body, but her state of dependency is cast in familiar racialized discourse. Reminiscent of plantation narratives and nostalgic white discourses of the South, the assumptions of familiarity in the names ascribed to Phoenix echo Southern codes of black-white relations. Well into the twentieth century, in intimate as well as casual encounters, white Southerners employed any array of names that suggested intimacy and subordination when they addressed adult and aged black women. In these exchanges, blacks were not awarded the authority to accept or reject the informal and subordinate terms whites used when addressing them: they had only to answer. In particular, the nurse's generic prefix to Phoenix's name signals Phoenix's subordinate station and her position as object of the white gaze. Unlike the hunter, the white woman who laces Phoenix's shoes, or the office attendant, the nurse knows Phoenix, and she knows her name. Nevertheless, she refers to Phoenix with the addition of "Aunt," a term suggestive of intimacy and familiarity—an intimacy and familiarity that Phoenix has no apparent authority to reject.

Representing Phoenix as needy, childlike, and in a dwindling cognitive state prior to the nurse's charitable gift (the medicine for Phoenix's grandson), Welty constructs a power dynamic that mirrors standard Southern race discourse. Phoenix is the embodiment of the mythical South's black archetype whose survival is ensured only by the benevolent oversight and intervention of white authority figures. In "A Worn Path," those white icons of authority are not just white men but also the white women who care for the poor, helpless Phoenix as she journeys to town, in need of their charity. Welty paints the portrait of white Southern benevolence toward blacks, and she positions white women not only as a power source of benevolence but as more genuine than their white male counterparts. This she suggests through the contrast of the hunter's dispassionate presence and the doctor's dispassionate absence. The hunter rescues Phoenix from a ditch that she has fallen into, but his humorous and condescending tone and his disingenuous nature undermine what might otherwise be read as an act of compassion. Phoenix provides him momentary amusement: he is shocked that a woman of Phoenix's age has set out on such a long and potentially dangerous journey. Rather than consider that a serious matter prompts her trip, he simply laughs at what he concludes is just another example of "old colored people" who would risk the dangers of the woods to get to see Santa Claus (19). With his suggestion that he would offer Phoenix some change (a dime) if he had some, the hunter further reveals his less-than-noble nature. As the nickel falls unknowingly from his pocket, his callousness is confirmed. In similar fashion, although it is the doctor who ultimately prescribes the medicine that is given to Phoenix, his absence suggests callousness as well. Phoenix has made this journey numerous times over several years seeking a remedy for a young child who has been suffering from a severe accident. The doctor does not consult directly with Phoenix, and we are not led to think that he has ever made a visit to see the young child. Phoenix and her young grandson are outcasts, worthy of little more than the depth of compassion required to toss a coin in a fountain.

In the end, Welty's Phoenix Jackson is little more than the silhouette of blacks that populate her 1946 novel, *Delta Wedding*. The interaction between the novel's heroine and matriarch, Ellen, and the local blacks illustrates Welty's alternative portrait to the likes of Faulkner's Mrs. Compson and Miss Emily. Throughout *The Sound and the Fury*, the Compsons' longtime servant, Dilsey, is the maternal figure for the Compson children and, along with her family, is the primary force in maintaining the Compson household. This is no more apparent than in Mrs. Compson's answer to her son Jason's admonishments for her inability to manage the servants. Her explanation serves as a confession of weakness and dependency: "I have to depend on them so completely. It's not as if I were strong. I wish I were. I wish I could do all the house work myself" (166). Similarly, in "A Rose for Emily," Faulkner's narrator explains early on that Miss Emily represents a legacy of female dependency interwoven in a bygone South: "Alive, Miss Emily had been a tradition, a duty, and a care; a sort of hereditary obligation upon the town" (15). Welty's Ellen, as well as the family of Fairchild women, defies Faulkner's faltering Southern matriarchs and the conventional frail Southern matriarchs of the mythical plantation South. The narrator explains that this legacy of strong Fairchild women can be traced back generations: "It was notoriously the women of the Fairchilds who since the Civil War, or—who knew?—since the Indian times, ran the household and had everything at their fingertips—not the men" (144–45). The women are the power brokers in the Fairchild household, and the example of the central matriarch's rule is her dominion over the unruly and dependent blacks that work on the Fairchild estate or reside nearby.

In *Delta Wedding*, blacks are strewn throughout the narrative, but not as part of the human elements. Instead, their presence works as a border on a canvas portrait: they accent the humanity of the Southern whites who reside within the borders. We get a sense of this at the novel's start through the reflections of nine-year-old Laura McRaven. As she anticipates her arrival to the home of her dead mother's kin, she remembers past visits and experiences. In her litany of recollections, pressed between a memory of her cousin's paper dolls and patterns in the stairway carpet, the narrator tells us that "she remembered the Negroes, Bitsy Roxie, Little Uncle, and Vi'let" (8). No details of this memory are offered— simply that she remembers them. They will be there when she arrives, much like the lifeless paper dolls and the patterns in the stairway carpet. The blacks in *Delta Wedding* live at the margins, but their presence adds meaning to and empowers whiteness. The silhouettes of blacks about the Fairchild estate and their virtual irrelevance suggest the higher relevance and authority of whiteness. Blacks work the fields and serve in the household, and just as the mythical blacks of the nostalgic slave era, the Fairchild blacks must be cared for by their wise, benevolent white lords. When blacks, even beyond the Fairchild estate, become rowdy and violent, it is Battle Fairchild who steps in "to protect them from the sheriff or prevail on a bad one to come out and surrender" (12). In a reversal of the relationship between Faulkner's Dilsey and Mrs. Compson, we find Ellen tending to her ailing, mindless nursemaid, Partheny. Ellen's benevolence is evinced in Partheny's assurance that she should leave her to return to the preparations for her daughter's wedding (78). Ellen is, as Laura has noted early in the narrative, "the mother of them all" (10). There is no greater testament of this than her selfless vigil at her servant's side.

A similar portrait of white female selflessness is suggested in the picture of the white female passerby who stops to lace Phoenix's shoes. Carrying an armful of Christmas presents and giving off an odor of perfume that catches Phoenix's attention, this lady is clearly of the class that hires the likes of Phoenix and other black women as servants. When Phoenix stops her along a busy street to ask that she tie her shoes, the lady instructs Phoenix to stand still. Addressing

Phoenix as "Grandma," she then "put her packages down on the sidewalk beside her and laced and tied both shoes tightly" (21). The scene calls to mind young children who, having not yet learned the simple skill of shoe lacing, must depend on their mothers. The white lady extends this benevolent act and moves along. There is no communication between Phoenix and this nameless lady; she extends no kind word, no smile, and no gesture suggesting an emotional human connection. The indifference shown by this anonymous white lady is replicated by the nurse. While she greets Phoenix and even offers her a seat upon entry, she quickly becomes impatient with her as she experiences a momentary cognitive lapse. When Phoenix fails to quickly answer the nurse, she does not consider that Phoenix has arrived after many miles of walking, which, as the hunter observed, seemed too many for a woman her age. Showing no patience, the nurse chides the old woman for taking up their time: she demands that Phoenix quickly tell them the condition of her grandson and "get it over" (22). The nurse frowns when Phoenix indicates that she had momentarily forgotten the reason for her journey, and the nurse speaks to Phoenix "in a loud, sure voice" (22). Again, the nurse's charity is symbolic of the mythical white benevolence extended to the childlike black population of the South: blacks are the "white man's burden,"[2] and in Welty's fictional world, they are the white woman's burden as well.

Phoenix Jackson is the burden of a Southern white world in which she is marginalized and dehumanized, and this black creation of Welty's imagination has no connection to black community or family either. Phoenix apparently lacks any knowledge of or access to the folk healing practices commonplace in black Southern society. The narrative suggests that this old—ancient in the narrator's eyes—holdover from slavery lives in isolation. With no obvious connection to a supportive black community, Phoenix Jackson must journey into the world of civilization and whites to secure the needed aid for her grandson. Perhaps more than Welty's sympathetic look at a black heroine, "A Worn Path" reveals Welty's inability to penetrate black life. Her black heroine suggests that just as many whites in the early to mid-twentieth century, Welty was only able to imagine black people and black life through the prism of her white Southern gaze. While she might have desired to create an endearing and humane black heroine, her attempt was compromised by the legacy of white racialized discourses from which her narratives fail to disconnect.

To connect Welty's work to a new South and to presumed postracial discourses of the South requires some intellectual gymnastics. The argument that Phoenix Jackson is an invention of a heroic artistic imagination—that is, Welty's—suggests that Welty has broken from tradition: that she offers a new vision or new possibilities. It is to suggest that Welty wants a South that will break free from its racialized origins. To make the case for or against this interpretation of Welty's intent contributes little to critical analysis of the text. Attempts to define creative works as the fruition of authorial intent too often lead to mere wishful thinking or, worse, imposing meaning that the text cannot substantiate. This gymnastic feat has been attempted throughout Southern history: from antebellum and postbellum myths of a genteel, bucolic South to the more recent celebration of the seventy-fifth anniversary of Mitchell's *Gone with the Wind*, there have been those committed to envisioning the South free of its tainted racial history. In its June 2011 documentary,[3] Georgia Public Television offered commentary from scholars touting Mitchell's philanthropic generosity to local black institutions. The implication is that by recognizing Mitchell's real-life benevolence, we can then ignore the damaging representations of blacks in her work as well as her highly sentimentalized depiction of the Confederate cause. It would be perhaps an intriguing study to explore the paradox of Mitchell's real-life generosity toward blacks and her artistic trivialization of black slave experience. However, speaking strictly of the text, *Gone with the Wind* minimizes the white South's exploitation of black labor and maintains the dismissive representation of slaves as simple-minded, childlike wards of white Southern benefactors. Blacks are part of the landscape that frames Southern life, and their presence helps define the centrality and the power of whiteness. Welty's objectification of blacks in *Delta Wedding* mirrors that of Mitchell's in *Gone with the Wind*. In both texts, we are asked to imagine Southern white womanhood differently—to replace the archetype of the frail, helpless plantation mistress with the image of a postslavery white matron seeking and wielding agency and power. As with the mythical plantation lord, a subservient and primitive black presence frames the narrative of this power-wielding white Southern matron.

While we cannot overlook the narrow lens through which white authors typically see authentic black identity and experience, we should not dismiss the possibility that occasionally we encounter white authors who find the depth of perception to see the South through the lens of its black inhabitants. That whiteness—that is, the white protagonist—ultimately surfaces as the central subject of the text should not hamper our analysis of the author's ability to represent the interior lives of blacks beyond Anglocentric convention. If we will suspend the supposition that the white writer's imposition of herself in the narrative necessarily impedes the subjectivity of the black protagonists, we can make the case that *The Help* offers a unique look at blackness in a white-authored text.

Stockett clearly wants readers to view Skeeter as exceptional, and that assessment rests in Skeeter's whiteness: we would not consider Skeeter's insight into the humanity of the black help extraordinary were she not white. Although Stockett frames Skeeter's heroism in her whiteness, the narrative does not paint whiteness as a universal heroic. With the exception of Skeeter—and arguably the ostracized, would-be socialite, Celia Foote—Stockett does not salvage the South or white Southerners. Janet Maslin points this out in her *New York Times* review of *The Help*. Maslin begins with a plot summary that echoes countless reviews of the novel: she describes the novel as a story about "black domestic servants working in white Southern households" and the white protagonist, Skeeter, as the heroine "slaving away on a book that will blow the lid off the suffering endured by black maids." Maslin moves momentarily away from this predictable interpretation to highlight the novel's problematic representation of whites. According to Maslin, "it's not the black maids who are done a disservice by this white writer; it's the white folk." Maslin recognizes the novel's lasting sting with its unfavorable depiction of whites. Stockett does not attempt to transform the ugliness and evil of her Southern white characters into a romanticized story of Southern loss and longing. The white female characters, in particular, are unlikeable, overly weak, overly manipulative, and easily corrupted. And while Skeeter arrives at this assessment of her peers, the black help lead her to this revelation. Moreover, even though Skeeter's presence seems to guide the narrative, her identity unfolds in large part through the experiences and narratives of the black maids rather than her own self-descriptive narrative. In chapter 5, the first chapter titled "Miss Skeeter," Skeeter's recollection of the family maid, Constantine, underscores the centralness of the maids' gaze in our understanding of Skeeter as well as the other white female characters. Here, in her recollection of Constantine, we learn more about Skeeter than through Skeeter's own self-reflective analysis. One of Skeeter's earliest memories of herself is the story of her brother who, having seen her shortly after her birth, proclaimed that she was not a baby; she was a "skeeter" (57). By her own estimation, she entered her teenage years overly tall and "not pretty," and her mother viewed her likewise (57, 65).

Only through Constantine does Skeeter imagine herself as more than the defective offspring that spawned her mother's disappointment. It is through Constantine's gaze that Skeeter comes to recognize her self-worth and the possibility that she is not ugly (65). With Constantine as her voice and guide, Skeeter learns to discover and believe her own feelings, even with regard to two matters that lay at the heart of Southern social codes: race and gender (65). If readers see Skeeter as courageous and maverick-like, it is spawned from the influence of Constantine. She has no white female model in this regard. Skeeter's mother is little more than the stock melodramatic, superficial, whining, and weakly matron of so many Southern novels. The young Skeeter learns to see the world differently from her parents and the whites of her circle because she has learned to see through Constantine's gaze. It is after Constantine reveals the truth of her biracial identity that Skeeter begins to see the black-white South differently. In the absence of Constantine, the adult Skeeter learns her harshest lessons on race through the lens of Constantine's friend, Aibileen.

Skeeter's first visit to Aibileen's house compels her to confront the reality that blacks see with their own gaze and that, in general, what they see does not corroborate white narratives of whiteness. Skeeter's visits to Aibileen's house reveal the more serious and critical lens through which blacks see whites. Now an adult, Skeeter enters the interior world of blacks who do not greet her with smiles and that sense of warm familiarity that she remembers from her childhood visits to Constantine's house. Skeeter now enters more deeply into the world of the black help as she compiles their narratives, and the result is that she begins to see her white female peers in a different and disturbing light. She relates this new vision as it comes to her during one of their scheduled social gatherings: "Hilly raises her voice about three octaves higher when she talks to colored people. Elizabeth smiles like she's talking to a child, although certainly not her own. I am starting to notice things" (157). The maids' narratives have caused the veil to be lifted; Skeeter sees whiteness as it appears to the maids, and she finds no counternarrative.

Through the lens of Aibileen and Minny, we view the presumed best of white Southern society, particularly its women, and the best leaves a disturbing picture. While the novel certainly maintains the dynamic of whites gazing and thus valuating black life, this is not the definitive gaze of the novel. The more sustained gaze is that of the maids, who, in general, see these white socialites as little more than beings with broken moral and ethical centers, with little work ethic, with little capacity to love or feel compassion for others, and who foremost lack courage. This is strikingly evinced in Aibileen's recollections of working in white households, particularly in the household of Elizabeth Leefolt, who has no capacity to love her own children. She blindly follows Hilly Holbrook, who is the self-serving power broker in this female world of white social elites.

It is through Minny's lens that we view the interior of Hilly Holbrook, only to find little there. Like the trickster figure in African American folklore, Minny triumphs in the end because she has the greater wit. Hilly certainly has the upper hand, but ultimately her shallowness and her vanity provide the safety for Minny and the other maids who have exposed the ugliness of Jackson's presumed finest ladies. The image of Hilly having consumed a pie consisting of the very waste she considered too foul to be deposited in her white-only toilet stands as an ironic but fitting statement of her own vileness. Minny sees Hilly at her destructive core, and the pie made of Minny's own defecation speaks to her valuation of Hilly's humanity. While Minny's contrasting valuation of Celia Foote might lead readers to argue the case for an ultimate redemptive vision of white women in the text, Celia's outcast status compromises this read. Celia and her husband, Johnny, live physically and socially outside the inner circle of Jackson's white elites. It is Celia's isolation—her exile—that leads her to notions of racial harmony. At the end of the novel, however, she and Johnny still live in isolation.

Readers may rightfully argue that with Skeeter as the central voice, *The Help* is yet another fictional journey of white self-realization had through objectifying blackness; however, the novel's end complicates this conclusion. In the closing chapters, we find white women in near hysteria over the possibility that the anonymously published novel about the help in fact recounts the intimate details of their not-so-flattering treatment of black maids. In contrast to the white female hysteria, the black maids, who have risked the most, proceed with calm and courage. In this contrast, readers again see the shallow and perverse world of those in the white inner circle. And in the final picture of Aibileen leaving Elizabeth Leefolt's house for the last time, Aibileen's perspective will provide our final look at Jackson's (i.e., the South's) treasured white womanhood: "I start down the driveway . . . feeling, in a way, that I'm free, like Minny. Freer than Miss Leefolt, who so locked up in her own head she don't even recognize herself when she read it. And freer than Miss Hilly. That woman gone spend the rest a her life trying to convince people she didn't eat that pie . . . Miss Hilly, she in her own jail, but with a lifelong term" (444).

Aibileen's departing gaze defies the nostalgic portrait of genteel white Southern womanhood and, in contrast, returns to Faulkner's image of the unstable, self-consumed, overly proud, and unlovable Mrs. Compson. Elizabeth and Miss Hilly are Mrs. Compson, and in *The Help*, they are white Southern womanhood seen through the eyes of black Southern women.

Notes

1. For further discussion of early white writers contemplating race and national identity, see West 126–31.
2. "The White Man's Burden: The United States and the Philippine Islands," is the title of Rudyard Kipling's 1899 poem that predicated American expansionism on presumptions of white paternalism and the "half devil and half child" nature of conquered native people.
3. Information on Georgia Public Broadcasting's 2011 documentary on the 75th anniversary of Margaret Mitchell's *Gone with the Wind* can be found at http://www.gpb .org/files/mmfiles/mmamericanrebelpresskit.pdf (or http://www.gpb.org/margaret -mitchell).

Works Cited

Bartel, Roland. "Life and Death in Eudora Welty's 'A Worn Path.'" *"A Worn Path."* Ed. Elizabeth Sarcone. New York: Harcourt Brace College Publishers, 1998. 45–48. Print.

Faulkner, William. "A Rose for Emily." 1930. Ed. Noel Polk. New York: Harcourt Brace College Publishers, 2000. Print.

———. *The Sound and the Fury*. 1929. Ed. David Minter. New York: W. W. Norton, 1987. Print.

Gardner, Joseph H. "Errands of Love: a Study in Black and White." *"A Worn Path."* Ed. Elizabeth Sarcone. New York: Harcourt Brace College Publishers, 1998. 97–106. Print.

Howell, Elmo. "Eudora Welty's Negroes: A Note on 'A Worn Path.'" *"A Worn Path."* Ed. Elizabeth Sarcone. New York: Harcourt Brace College Publishers, 1998. 37–41. Print.

Kiley, Kevin. "Amending the Record." *Inside Higher Ed*, February 28, 2013. Web. June 13, 2013. http://www.insidehighered.com/news/2013/02/28/emory-presidents -controversial-column-sparks-broader-discussion-leadership.

Maslin, Janet. "Racial Insults and Quiet Bravery in 1960s Mississippi." Books of the Times. *New York Times*, February 19, 2009. Web. June 13, 2013. http://www.nytimes .com/2009/02/19/books/19masl.html?_r=0&pagewanted=print.

McHaney, Pearl. "Race, Rights, and Resistance in Southern Literature in the Age of Obama." *American Studies Journal* (Center for American Studies, Harle-Wittenberg, Germany) 56. 2012. Web. http://asjournal.zusas.uni-halle.de:8001/workplace/235 .html.

Morrison, Toni. *Playing in the Dark: Whiteness and the Literary Imagination*. New York: Vintage, 1993. Print.

Orr, Elaine. "'Unsettling Every Definition of Otherness': Another Reading of Eudora Welty's 'A Worn Path.'" *"A Worn Path."* Ed. Elizabeth Sarcone. New York: Harcourt Brace College Publishers, 1998. 70–85. Print.

Stockett, Kathryn. *The Help*. New York: G. P. Putnam's Sons, 2009. Print.

Wagner, James. "As American as . . . Compromise" *Emory Magazine*, Winter 2013. Web. http://www.emory.edu/EMORY_MAGAZINE/issues/2013/winter/register/president .html.

Welty, Eudora. *Delta Wedding*. 1946. New York: Harcourt Brace Jovanovich Publishers, 1973. Print.

———. "A Worn Path." *"A Worn Path."* 1940. Ed. Elizabeth Sarcone. New York: Harcourt Brace College Publishers, 1998. 16–23. Print.

West, Elizabeth. "Blacks." *American History Through Literature 1820–1870*. Ed. Janet Gabler-Hover and Robert Sattlemeyer. New York: Twayne, 2005. Print.

CHAPTER 4

"Taking Care a White Babies, That's What I Do"

The Help and Americans' Obsession with the Mammy

Katrina Dyonne Thompson

In 2005, the coffee shop was my home. I personified the diligent doctoral student, armed with stacks of books and my laptop, venturing to the local Starbucks almost daily in an attempt to write my dissertation. One day while I was working, an older white gentleman approached me with a slight smile and asked, "Are you here to interview for a nanny job?" Shocked, I looked at my papers on the table, trying to restrain the sudden anger I felt. "No, I am not here to interview for a nanny position," I sarcastically responded. Then he smiled and asked, "Would you be interested in the position?" I felt the burden of hundreds of years of stereotypes in this one exchange. "No, I am not interested in taking care of your children," I stated flatly as I looked directly into his eyes. He stood there awkwardly, attempting to ignore my penetrating stare with a slight smile before politely leaving my table. I sat for a moment wondering why I had been approached, and then it struck me as I looked around the room. Out of all the young college-aged men and women in the coffee shop, I was the only African American. Having grown up in the South, I was fully aware of the history of black women as caretakers in white households and well understood that, due to a tradition of racism and sexism in the United States, women of color often had limited opportunities to enter other professions. However, I was in Long Island, New York, not the South, and this was no longer a Jim Crow society.

True enough, there are more than 200,000 women who serve as nannies or housekeepers in New York State, with majority of them being women of color (Venjara). The majority of these domestics are illegal immigrants from Latin

America or the Caribbean or of African descent, resulting in a common scene of black and brown women walking with strollers or by hand with young white children throughout the area. Therefore, the coffee shop stranger choosing me, the only woman of color in Starbucks, may seem to simply be a by-product of this trend. However, he not only expected me to be a nanny but also further assumed that I could easily transition into that vocation. Beyond the overt racial and class divisions present in America today, the assumption that black (and brown) women are innate caretakers has a much longer history than the current domestic employment practices. Many black feminist scholars have recognized that black women in postbellum America emerged in popular culture as either the "mammy" or the bad black woman. This socially constructed label is a part of the "controlling images" scholar Patricia Hill Collins discusses in her path-breaking work *Black Feminist Thought*. The first "controlling image"—that is, of the black woman as the "faithful, obedient domestic servant" or simply "mammy" (Collins 72)—has been an aspect of American culture for almost two centuries, with the main distributor being mass media. Recently, while reading the stories of two fictional black women, Minny Jackson and Aibileen Clark, in the acclaimed novel *The Help* by Kathryn Stockett, I was reminded of my experience in the coffee shop (Stockett). The novel, like the white gentleman who had approached me, represents a long history of assuming that black women are innately capable of taking care for white families and white America's unshakeable nostalgia of black women's controlling image of the mammy.

"You is smart, You is kind, You is important," were the daily affirmations Aibileen Clark chanted to the young white child she cared for (Stockett 521). Six days a week, Clark, a black domestic in 1960s Jackson, Mississippi, took the number six bus from the colored side of town to the white suburbs. For Aibileen, the best part of her job was the family's three-year-old little girl, Mae Mobley Leefolt. "Taking care a white babies, that what I do," she proudly boasts with a gleam from her gold tooth while reflecting on the 17 children she has raised (Stockett 1). Unlike other domestics in the region who prided themselves on their cooking, such as her good friend Minny Jackson, Aibileen knew babies: "I know how to get them babies to sleep, to stop crying, and go to the toilet bowl before they mamas even get out a bed in the morning" (Stockett 1). These women were known throughout Jackson: Aibileen as an excellent caregiver and Minny as an exceptional cook. Both women worked for numerous white families throughout the city. Entering white households daily to care for their children, clean their homes, and cook their dinners, Aibileen and Minny, although fictional characters, were constructed to represent many real-life black women who, for centuries, were "the help."

The Help is presented as a sympathetic story about three women—Aibileen Clark, Minny Jackson, and Eugenia "Skeeter" Phelan—who defied the rules of race in segregated Jackson, Mississippi, in the early1960s. After graduating from college, Skeeter, a young white woman, returns home to find her beloved black female caretaker, Constantine, mysteriously absent, which contributes to her new perspective on life. Centering on her desires to leave Mississippi for potential fame and freedom as a writer in New York City, Skeeter decides to interview black domestic workers regarding their experiences within white households. The main storyline focuses on Skeeter writing her novel, also called *The Help*. While Skeeter conducts secret interviews with black women throughout Jackson, she reveals the lives of Aibileen and Minny. Minny Jackson, married with five children, offers humorous liveliness to the story, despite her abusive marital relationship and continual existence on the periphery of poverty as a domestic. Her best friend, Aibileen, is a pious maid who has dedicated her life to nurturing white children during their primary years and has served more than 15 families throughout Jackson. The memories of Constantine, Aibileen's devotion to Mae Mobley, and Minny's superlative cooking skills invoke throughout the novel the fictional black caricature of the mammy that has plagued American literature for more than a century.

This chapter will offer a historical analysis that will compare Stockett's main characters to earlier mammies, often created by white female authors, to illustrate the consistent characteristics of the caricature and the manner of her appearance in popular culture that represent nostalgia for the old South within American society. Understanding that the mammy caricature's appearance in popular culture may be a social thermometer of the racial climate in the United States, juxtaposing past mammy characters will illustrate the larger issue of the regressive nature of race in an era continually referred to as postracial. This chapter will illustrate that Stockett's novel is part of an American tradition that continually perpetrates the mammy caricature in order to assert whiteness and justify past racial and gender injustices while denigrating the black female experience—all in an effort to revise history.

The mammy represents the most enduring black woman in American culture. Whether referred to as aunt, by her first name, or simply as mammy, this caricature often symbolizes an exaggerated idea of black women that we can trace from antebellum America to today. In folklore, the mammy is celebrated for her religious integrity, wide grin, hearty laughter, and loyal service (Morgan). For almost two centuries, she continues to love white families even more than her own family. White authors often construct the mammy caricature as a defense for the institution of slavery through plantation stories, literature, theater, advertisements, and other manifestations in mass media. Historically, the mammy traces her origin to the plantation households of the Southern states, where domestic female slaves performed the duties of maid, washerwoman, cook, caretaker, butler, and nurse (and even suckled white babies). These bondswomen often experienced some of the worst hardships of slavery, exposed to the violent whims of their mistresses and the sexual exploitation of their masters. Although elderly female slaves often were referred to as "aunt or auntie" on plantations by those within the enslaved community and by whites, the mammy as portrayed in American popular culture never existed (White; Gaspar and Hine; Parkhurst).

Historian Micki McElya, in *Clinging to Mammy*, traced the mammy's first fictional literary reference to the *Southern Literary Messenger* in 1836 (McElya). In a series titled "Diary of an Invalid," Mammy Marget was the "devoted and faithful" servant who nurtured the white family. First appearing in a proslavery fictional tale, mammy continues to emerge and reemerge in American popular culture in various derivatives, especially during transitional times in American society. In 1852, the first full-length narrative was written on the life of a mammy in Mary Henderson Eastman's proslavery novel *Aunt Phillis's Cabin*. A response to the abolitionist novel *Uncle Tom's Cabin*, this novel portrayed Aunt Phillis as a pious, faithful slave who, even when offered freedom by an abolitionist, emphatically states, "I'll never *take* my freedom . . . If my master would give it to me, and the rest of us, I should be thankful" (Eastman). The book ends with Aunt Phillis surrounded by the enslaved community and the white planter family upon her deathbed, a scene quite similar to Uncle Tom's death. Aunt Phillis, like other mammies that appeared in antebellum society, was strategically constructed to defend the slavery system during the rise of abolitionism and political and social debates on the expansion of slavery in the new western territories. During slavery, the mammy was used as a defense for the institution, while after the Civil War, she reemerged as a nostalgic icon of the old South to justify racial and sexual oppression and reassert dominant racial ideologies.

A few decades after the Civil War, a new ideology arose among white Americans known as the *lost cause*. The lost cause is a reinterpretation of America's antebellum and Civil War history; it offered a romanticized view of the South with happy slaves and paternal whites within a tranquil society while congruously allowing for a collective overlook of the horrors of slavery. By the late nineteenth century, the faithful "Old Negro" had become a staple of the Southern reminiscence of the lost cause. In literature, songs, orations, and media, white Southerners (and many throughout the United States) conducted daily rituals to the memory of their most beloved caricatures of black slave life—in particular, their doting mammies. This was influenced by whites throughout the South who expressed fear toward the "New Negro" that was "born in freedom and undisciplined by slavery," as astutely stated by historian Leon F. Litwack (198). As one Atlanta woman reported on the trepidation of Southern society in the 1890s to a Northern reporter, "You should have known the old darkeys of the plantation . . . Every year, it seems to me, they have been losing more and more of their carefree good humour . . . I'm free to say I'm scared of them!" (Baker 28). The lost cause ideology offered solace to many whites in a time of racial and social change; through popular culture, white Americans found comfort in reimagining their racial past. The media was and continues to be a conduit of America's long-held racial politics. According to media theorist Dan Laughley, in political economy theory, "the social consciousness is determined by . . . the ruling classes who own the means of production" (Laughey 122–25). Therefore mammy continues to thrive along with other black caricatures: although she is no longer a faithful slave, but instead a devoted servant, she continually emerges in times of white fears of change as a continual shrine to whiteness.

The emergence of Aunt Jemima—a robust black woman serving ready-made pancakes at the 1893 World's Fair—introduced a media frenzy that lasted more than a century (Manring; Kern-Foxworth). Like past mammies, Aunt Jemima comforted white fears of the time and placed black women in their proper place: in the kitchen and subservient. The mammy continued to materialize in popular culture mediums of the time, appearing at moments of heightened racial hostility. The fears whites had of the new generation of blacks that "possessed neither the temperament, demeanor, nor humility of former slaves" were never more apparent than in writer Thomas F. Dixon's 1905 fictional novel *The Clansmen* and its film adaptation, *Birth of Nation*, released in 1915 (Guerrero; Litwack 197–99; Dixon). By the early twentieth century, the mammy had become an American cultural exhibition and a consistent form of entertainment. Foreshadowing the fight for political and social rights of the civil rights movement, the popular mammy caricature entered America's homes through the new medium of television in the form of the popular series *Beulah* (Bogle, *Toms*; Bogle, *Primetime*). This show brought the comforting yet sassy black woman into every white home to serve their families, placate white fears, and reassert whites as dominant in American society. By the end of the twentieth century, mammy in her various representations had undergone slight physical changes, beginning as a large, dark-skinned woman with a checkered headscarf and sometimes becoming a slim woman in a maid's uniform in contemporary society. Despite the superficial changes to mammy, the defining characteristics of the caricature have not changed as she is continually reincarnated in American popular culture.

Kathryn Stockett's novel and its subsequent film adaptation follow in the tradition of the incessant appearance of the mammy in American mass media. Initially popular among female reading groups, *The Help* sold more than five million copies and remained on the *New York Times* bestseller list for more than one hundred weeks. Set in the segregated South at the time of the tragic murder of civil rights leader Medgar Evers and in the midst of the civil rights movement, *The Help* "spins a story of social awakening as seen from both sides of the American racial divide," praised the *Washington Post* (Steinberg). Many critics praised this book as a reflection of race in America more so than simply a fictional tale. Although issues of class, gender, and race repeat themselves in Stockett's work, her portrayal represents nostalgia more than it does a critical assessment of a time when hegemonic whiteness dominated and forced black subjugation was the norm. In fact, the propaganda surrounding *The Help* closely parallels another famous novel that purported to expose racial injustices by illustrating the pious nature of blacks: *Uncle Tom's Cabin* (Stowe).

American author Harriet Beecher Stowe published *Uncle Tom's Cabin* in 1852 and sold more than three thousand copies on its first day of release (see Tandy). Within the first year, more than three hundred thousand copies were in circulation. Written as an antislavery tract, Stowe wanted the book to appeal to Christian sympathies by emphasizing enslaved blacks as docile, innocent creatures forced into an unjust, immoral institution. Quite reminiscent of Stowe's objective, Stockett created her main character, Aibileen, to be "a true heroine" and "a devoted servant of the Lord" (Oldenburg). Though intended as an antislavery novel, Stowe's work portrays a romanticized view of enslaved blacks based on the stereotypes of the era. As the bestselling novel of the nineteenth century, the durability of *Uncle Tom's Cabin* has spurred its reincarnation in all forms of mass media. Stowe's antislavery text has been distorted, adapted, and performed thousands of times on the theatrical stage, and Uncle Tom is the most enduring character throughout these representations (Hirsch). Though *Uncle Tom's Cabin* was not the first exhibition of the mammy, Stowe's short discussion of Aunt Chloe greatly influenced the image of the mammy in popular culture, creating a template for this caricature (Stowe). More than 150 years later, Stockett's main characters represent a consequence of the incessant resurgence of the mammy and closely parallel the famous antebellum novel.

The manifestations of mammy in popular culture may vary in setting and political and social meaning; however, there have been similarities in racial and gender characteristics that continue to appear in American culture. Although more than a century separates Stowe's and Stockett's works, both women publicly create a text intended to assist in race relations, and they both propagate their books within a cause larger than merely profit or notoriety. Simultaneously, both white female authors claim to speak for and, more importantly, give agency to their black characters. Understanding the congruous aspects of the mammy in Stowe's, Stockett's, and various other mainly white female writers' work illustrates the powerful nature of the caricature. More important than the continual presence of mammy are the consistent characteristics over such a long and continually shifting timeline.

Almost every attribute assigned to the mammy contributes to her role in society and public memory as maternal and happily submissive. One of the most recognizable attributes of the caricature is her external appearance that only supports her role in fictional society. The physical characteristics of the mammy in popular culture have experienced changes throughout the years; however, Stowe's and Stockett's renditions are quite comparable. As Stowe described, Aunt Chloe has "a round, black, shining face . . . so glossy as to suggest the idea that she might have been washed over with white of eggs, like one of her own tea rusks. Her whole plump countenance beams, with satisfaction and contentment from under her well-starched checkered turban" (Stowe 66–67). Her weight and innate jolliness contribute to her role on the plantation as a nurturing, faithful slave to her white family. Analogously, Aibileen Clark credits her rapport with white children to her "fat" (Stockett 2). She emphatically proclaims that "babies like fat. Like to bury they face up in you armpit and go to sleep. They like big legs too" (Stockett 2). Her appearance sharply contrasts with that of the white mother and her employer, Elizabeth Leefolt, who is "lanky . . . her whole body be so full a sharp knobs and corners, it's no wonder she can't soothe that baby" (Stockett 191). Skeeter refers to Aibileen as having a "friendly softness" due to her physique, contributing to her role as an innate nurturer. Similarly, Minny's full figure signifies her status as an expert cook. Fitting well within the mammy mold, Stockett mentions Minny's weight of "hundred-and-sixty-five pound," on a "five-foot-zero" frame several times throughout the novel (Stockett 42). Referring to her as "fat and short and strong" brings to mind the most popular mammy of all, Aunt Jemima, whose physique suited her role as breakfast cook to American families, while her predecessor, Aunt Chloe, was "universally held and acknowledged" for her skills as a cook (Stowe 66–67). Minny's body type reminds Americans that black women, with their superb cooking talents, should be present in the kitchen. Assigning particular physical attributes to domestic abilities simply due to the external qualifiers, such as weight or beauty, contributes to placing black women into a monolithic group that lacks individual experiences.

Traditionally, literary works depict the mammy as unattractive to distract from the racial and sexual degradation of black women (Wallace-Sanders). Stowe and Stockett both use disparaging physical descriptions to illustrate their characters' lack of beauty. Aibileen's complexion is compared to a cockroach that is "black . . . Blacker than me" (Stockett 191). In fact, Stockett's reference to this insect illustrates the character's lack of appeal. Furthermore, Minny's skin is described as "blacker than Aibileen's by ten shades, and shiny and taut, like a pair of new patent shoes" (Stockett 191). Neither woman appears particularly attractive, with their complexions used as evidence of their stark difference from whites. The mammy's physical appearance supports her role as a natural domestic; however, it also provides an avenue by which to desexualize these black women, allowing them to inconspicuously enter white households.

Many white writers attempt to distract from or negate the centuries of sexual abuse by white men that actual black women experienced. Historian Deborah G. White pointedly recognizes that "white male exploitation of black women . . . is overlooked" (White 152). Stockett's physical constructions of Minny and Aibileen distract from any notion of attraction and therefore evade any opportunity for sexual harassment. However, the author ignores the continual threat of sexual harassment and violence within these homes, therefore neglecting the experiences of real-life black female domestics.[1] Interestingly, in *The Help*, Constantine, the former maid and caretaker for Skeeter, ambiguously introduces the topic of miscegenation; however, rape and sexual harassment are noticeably missing from the story. "My daddy was white," Constantine reveals to Skeeter with a smile on her face while she continues to state that "my daddy looooved me . . . Always said I was his favorite" during his weekly Saturday afternoon visits. In the novel, Skeeter is shocked at this revelation, as miscegenation was "against the law" in Jim Crow Mississippi; however, to downplay this complicated disclosure, Stockett chose to focus on how well Constantine's white father treated her. In the book, Constantine explains that her white father "used to come over . . . he give me a set a ten hair ribbons, ten different colors . . . Brought em over from Paris, made out a Japanese silk." Also, the clandestine weekly short visits of the white father are depicted as a festive occasion, almost a holiday resembling Christmas, where Constantine "sat in his lap" and received gifts "until he had to leave" (Stockett 77–78). The racial ancestry of Constantine is definitely not a common aspect of the mammy caricature in literature; however, Stockett's mixed-race domestic has been seen before.

The first full-length novel on the mammy, *Aunt Phillis Cabin*, "depicted a faithful 'mulatto'" (Eastman 102) mammy, an aspect of Eastman's storyline that is never fully explored. Stockett, similar to the antebellum writer Eastman, distracts from the potential rape and social ramifications of this state of affairs by emphasizing the mutual love between Constantine and her obscure father figure. The tragic mulatto caricature postdates the mammy and often illustrates these children as being the victims of a divided racial inheritance and oversexualized (Bogle, *Toms, Coons*). However, by placing mixed-raced women as mammies, Stockett can redefine or reconstruct past historical events to reassert in memory an improved image of white male identity. This revisionary history ignores the white males' sexual abuse of black women and replaces them with black men who are responsible for all violence against black women.

Stockett disguises her desire to defend whiteness while revising Southern history by identifying the most violent persons in the Jim Crow South as black men. Throughout the novel, the black men in Minny's life—from her alcoholic father to her husband, Leroy—are physically abusive (Stockett 60). To illustrate Minny's husband's violence, Stockett presents a scene in which, after being fired, Leroy returns home and "throws the kids in the yard and lock me [Minny] in the bathroom and say he gone light the house on fire with me locked inside!" (Stockett 514). He epitomizes the violent black brute and is the main black male character in Stockett's novel. Other black male figures in Aibileen's life are purposefully absent: Aibileen's son, Treelore, was killed prior to the beginning of the novel, and her husband, Clyde, abandoned Aibileen and his son "for that no-count hussy . . . Cocoa" (Stockett 26) years earlier. Therefore, Stockett's only depictions of black husbands, Clyde and Leroy, are violent and frenzied alcoholics or philanderers that either desert their families or abuse them. Stockett's novel suggests that white men should not be blamed for past abuses against black women and instead places black men as the only threat to black women.

Contrastingly, the white men Minny comes in contact with seem to be quite friendly and positive in her life. Throughout the novel, Celia Rae Foote is trying to conceal from her husband, "Mister Johnny," that she's hired Minny to work as a domestic. The trepidation of her husband discovering this secret causes the reader to think that he may get angry, even violent, if this is revealed. However, when Mister Johnny discovers Minny freely in his home, he simply smiles and compliments that she was "the best cook I've ever known . . . Hell, I haven't eaten like this since Cora Blue was around" (Stockett 162). Mister Johnny clearly associates Minny with romanticized memories of his own mammy as a child and therefore is happy that his wife intentionally concealed hiring a maid. Concerning his wife, he states, "I don't care if she can cook . . . I just want her here" (Stockett 162), emphasizing that white women did not need to fulfill the gendered expectation of womanhood because black women instinctively were able to portray that role. Also, Mister Johnny's cheerful acceptance of his wife's deception, when compared to the torture inflicted by Leroy, offers a sharp contrast between white men and black men to Minny and the reader. Stockett depicts her novel as an empowering story for women that centers on the lives of women. Men, black or white, overall are minor aspects of the storyline. In attempting to accomplish this task, *The Help* alters a tumultuous time of gender and racial inequality into an era in which white country club women have the most power in society. White men financially support their wives and sincerely care for their happiness, while black husbands abandon their wives or abuse them while also not providing financial support for their families; this is made evident by Leroy being terminated from his job within the novel. Interestingly, cooking secured Minny's job while it also offered her personal pleasure within her own turbulent life.

Stockett's emphasis on Minny's cooking skills was a central role in the novel and also was a consistent characteristic associated with mammies for centuries. Stowe's Aunt Chloe is a "cook . . . in the very bone and centre of her soul" (Stowe 67). Similarly, Minny is "such a good cook" that her culinary skill "sometimes . . . makes up for her smart mouth," according to Aibileen (Stockett 30). Both Aunt Chloe and Minny gain personal satisfaction from their skills in the kitchen. In Aunt Chloe's household, there was "not a chicken or turkey or duck in the barnyard" that was safe, and while "trussing, stuffing and roasting . . . she would shake her fat sides with honest pride and merriment, as she would narrate the fruitless efforts that one and another of her compeers had made to attain to her elevation." Aunt Chloe happily fed the planter's family and their guests, always excited to see a "pile of traveling trunks" indicating the "arrival of company at the house" (Stowe 67). She cherished cooking for her white family, broadcasting the culinary skills attributed to the mammy caricature. Stowe details Aunt Chloe's preparedness and excitement toward cooking in order to emphasize that mammies are meant to be in the kitchen and that they themselves recognize this inevitable talent. Similarly, Aunt Jemima was always excited when the "Colonel's guest[s]" arrived "prompt to breakfast" so that she could demonstrate her prowess in the kitchen (Manring 130). Mammies throughout history have excellent culinary skills. Continuing this tradition, Stockett also details Minny in the kitchen, emphasizing how she "lay the battered raw chicken on the rack . . . I watch the chicken sizzle, try to forget . . . Frying chicken always makes me feel a little better about life" (Stockett 263).

Aunt Chloe and Minny excel in the kitchen, while the white women they work for lack such natural domestic prowess. Ironically, both women attempt to teach the white women in the household how to cook. Aunt Chloe inspired Miss Sally to attempt to bake a cake, and Minny repeatedly gave Miss Celia lessons on preparing dinner; however, their attempts (at least initially) ended disastrously. Interestingly, Aunt Chloe openly admits that she turned "kinder sarcy" during the cooking tutorial with the plantation mistress. This retort and Minny's character being referred to as sassy parallel a popular derivative of the mammy archetype.[2] The most popular mammy character of the twentieth century was performed by African American actress Hattie McDaniel. In her roles as the mammy in film and television, she often appeared with rolling eyes, witty retorts, and playful impertinence while ever remaining the faithful servant. The sassy mammy offers comedic relief and periodically shines through in Aunt Chloe's and Minny's characters. During her moment of impudence, Aunt Chloe openly announces during the cooking lesson, "Now Missis, do jist look at dem beautiful white hands . . . and look at my great black stumpin hands. Now don't ye think dat de Lord must have meant me to make de pi-crust, and you to stay in de parlor?" (Stowe 72).

The stark contrast between, as Stowe describes, the "beautiful white" hands of the plantation mistress and the "black stumpin hands" of Aunt Chloe illustrates a dichotomy that Stockett incorporates throughout her novel. Blackness represents subjugation and intrinsic servant abilities, while whiteness illustrates cleanliness and an inability to perform particular household duties, such as cooking, child-care, and numerous other tasks. Stockett and Stowe wanted to assure their reading public that black women cooked for white families due to their skills, which white women were unable to acquire. As Miss Celia Foote states while hiring Minny, "I just can't seem to get the hang of the kitchen work" (Stockett 37). Aunt Chloe and Minny come from two different eras; however, their happiness comes from cooking for whites even though, paradoxically, they both have their own families.

Ironically, in Stockett's work, black women are innately good with domestic duties, while white women lack those abilities. This theme of white women as clueless domestics has been successfully used in other mediums. In the 1939 film adaptation of the book *Gone with the Wind*, also written by a white female author, Margaret Mitchell, the main character Scarlett O'Hara is childlike and is only able to become a somewhat autonomous figure under direct duress (Mitchell). Therefore, it is an interesting dynamic. White women hold a conflicting duality in society: they are both naïve domestics and fully capable supervisors. Simultaneously, this aspect of narratives supports the role of black women as innate domestics. The resurgence of this theme in Stockett's work is a lingering trait of the lost cause ideology and has been an aspect of popular books, films, and television shows. Also, the idea of white women as unsuitable for full domestic duty supports the need for the dutiful mammy and rewrites a history of forced labor and limited opportunities to a tranquil society that is rational, in which whiteness dominates and the cult of domesticity is protected.

Stowe and Stockett both create black women who neglect their own families to cater to white families. Aunt Chloe lives with her husband, Uncle Tom, in a cabin on the plantation along with several black children. In one scene, after feeding the planter's family, Aunt Chloe returns to her quarters to "get her ole man's supper"; however, Master George, the young white master from the big house, also enters the slave quarters for dinner. Upon his arrival, Aunt Chloe praises, "How easy white fols al'us does things!" in reference to Master George's ability to read and write, and she attends quickly to preparing his meal while conveniently ignoring her own family. "But, Aunt Chloe, I'm getting mighty hungry," the young planter complains with a jubilant smile. Aunt Chloe responds, "Mose done . . . Now, Mas'r George, you jest . . . set down now with my old man, and I'll take up de sausages, and have de first griddle full of cakes on your plate in less dan no time." Within her quarters, Aunt Chloe hurriedly prepares Master George's and Uncle Tom's plates while she neglects the "woolly heads and glistening eyes which were regarding their operations hungrily from the opposite corner" (Stowe 69–70). The presence of these children in Aunt Chloe's cabin was insignificant in Stowe's work. Aunt Chloe cares only that the planter's child eats first, even within the slave quarters, viewing the black children as merely nuisances. As a mammy, Aunt Chloe's personal life, experiences, and status as a mother are never fully explored. This seems to be a common aspect of the black female caricature.

This blatant neglect was quite apparent with the main black female characters in Stockett's work. Stockett does not fully explore Minny's children within her novel. In fact, the only solace Minny receives from her family is evident when she states that her "house is always full of five kids and neighbors and husband. Most days when I come in to Miss Celia's I am grateful for the peace" (Stockett 55). Although Stockett establishes firmly that Minny is in an extremely abusive marital relationship, the manner in which her children cope in this hostile household never enters into the storyline. Meanwhile, Aibileen's only son, Treelore, was killed in a work-related accident and never appears in the storyline outside of her memories. Therefore, as mothers to their own black children, Minny and Aibileen are never fully developed. Similarly, while Aibileen's relationship with her son is neglected, her adoration for the young white Mae Mobley appears as a constant theme. Aibileen does not interact with her best friend Minny's children, nor does Stockett explore any interpersonal relationships within her black community that may contribute to the intricacy of Aibileen's life. In the novel, Aibileen raised 17 children; however, the language does not specify if that number includes her own son. Aibileen's devotion to the young Mae Mobley extends beyond the threat of physical abuse or dismissal of employment. With the release of Skeeter's book, *The Help*, and its revelation of the private affairs of white women throughout Jackson, Aibileen loses her employment and tells the young Mae Mobley, "It's time for me to retire. You my last little girl, I say because this is the truth, it just ain't by my own choosing." At the time of Aibileen's dramatic termination from her job at the Leefolt residence, her only concern is not for her personal safety or livelihood but for her separation from Mae Mobley. During this denouement, Aibileen chants with Mae Mobley, "You is kind, you is smart, you is important," in a last effort to praise the potential of the young white child and show her adoration (Stockett 520–21). One of the most enduring qualities of the mammy caricature is her relentless adoration for white families, especially the white children in her care.

Central throughout the novel was Skeeter's love for and desire to find her family maid. After returning from college, Skeeter discovers that her friend and maternal figure Constantine mysteriously left the Phelan residence due to the unexpected return of a secret daughter. The story is eventually revealed by Aibileen that Constantine "had to send her away up north" to escape the scrutiny of having a "high yellow" child (Stockett 100). Upon discovering this secret, Skeeter fearfully says, "Oh . . . Aibileen . . . you don't think . . ." due to an "ugly thought," which is never fully divulged. However, Aibileen replies to Skeeter's fright: "No no, no ma'am. Not . . . that Constantine's man, Conner, he was colored" (Stockett 100). This response comforts Skeeter, who was "ashamed for having thought the worst." The question remains, what is Skeeter's "ugly thought?" Through the dialogue Stockett offers, it is evident that Skeeter is fearful that Constantine's daughter was fathered by a white man. Could Skeeter's fear derive from the thoughts that her father may have raped or had a sexual relationship with Constantine, which would explain her mother's privacy on revealing the details of the maid's disappearance? Or did Skeeter fear that a local white man raped Constantine, or maybe she had a secret, illicit relationship with a white man? Stockett evades these topics by solving the possible racial quandary of Constantine's daughter and by vanishing the female character and her voice from the narrative. In opening the possibility of rape or interracial relationships into the storyline, Stockett does not allow readers to draw their own conclusions; instead, she comforts some readers through her reaffirmation of whiteness and a sanitized version of the old South. Although Skeeter accepts Constantine's mixed heritage, the thought that Constantine had a relationship with a white man was too "ugly." By removing Constantine's daughter, while also not fully developing the black children overall, Stockett is able to focus her mammy caricatures within their main roles as caretakers to white families.

Constantine may be the most neglectful mother within the entire text; however, she is one of the most praised caregivers to the white family in which she was employed for over a decade, the Phelans. Throughout the novel, Skeeter praises Constantine as a nurturer who would bring her home to the black segregated side of town simply due to the love that she had for the white child in her care. To justify the situation, Skeeter states that "Constantine's love for me began with missing her child. Perhaps that's what made it so unique, so deep. It didn't matter that I was white" (Stockett 424). Skeeter's white skin does not affect her relationship with the family maid; however, Constantine's own daughter's complexion was a major hardship that resulted in her removal from the South. Black women are expected to love their white families unconditionally while, as Stockett illustrates, the same admiration is not necessarily allotted to their own families. Skeeter's assessment may be more of a reflection of Stockett's personal admiration of and disregard for her own experiences with black caretakers throughout her life.

The parallels between Kathryn Stockett and Harriet Beecher Stowe go beyond their similar descriptions of black women; they also venture into the utility of the caricature and the manner in which it is continually maintained in popular culture. Stowe created characters and a storyline that would appeal to the white populace for the antislavery case. The antebellum writer wanted to maintain whiteness and patriarchy while creating black (and white) characters that were sympathetic and nonthreatening and not overly confrontational to the potential white readers. Similarly, Stockett wrote a book that only minimally treaded the line of black agency and was historically reflective.

A native Mississippian, Stockett indirectly illustrates her personal nostalgia for the old South and black mammies in her novel. Stockett, in describing her real-life childhood domestic worker, remembers that her "cooking was outstanding . . . you felt loved when you tasted Demetrie's caramel cake." She always reminded Stockett and her siblings that "this is where you belong . . . Here with me." With such fond memories of "listening to . . . stories and watching her [Demetrie] mix up cakes and fry chicken," for the author, Demetrie was more than simply "the help" but the woman who faithfully nurtured and self-sacrificed for the Stockett family. Never fully understanding the tumultuous world of a black woman in Mississippi, Stockett constructed a false reality in which Demetrie satisfied all her infantile needs while ironically never having any needs herself. Similar to her fictional character Minny, Demetrie was also an "outstanding" cook and married to an "abusive drinker" (Stockett 525–30). However, instead of focusing on her own life, Demetrie spent her days catering to the Stockett family, according to the author's personal memories.

Kathryn Stockett and Harriet Beecher Stowe are two white female writers who never fully understood the complexities of Southern African American life; however, their literary flaws do not repudiate other white writers who accurately depict the black experience. As a Northern abolitionist, Stowe's novel was based on research from slave narratives and her own interpretation of black life and culture. Regardless of her antislavery stance, she still held expectations of black behavior imposed by the prevailing racial attitudes of the era; these tailored her characters in *Uncle Tom's Cabin*. Analogously, Stockett possesses a white, privileged perspective of her youthful encounters with the family maid, Demetrie, thus causing her to neglect the complexity of the African American female experience in the Deep South. Demetrie was "poor, colored, and female on a sharecropping farm," born on the eve of the Depression in Mississippi, and relayed some of her hardships to the white children in her care, according to Stockett. As one of those children, Stockett claims to have been "too young to realize that what she was telling us wasn't funny," and throughout her portrayal of black female domestics, it is evident that she never fully grasped the experiences of black women. Her fictional storyline of a white Southern female—Skeeter—attempting to write a book about the help in an effort to obtain professional success while also reconciling her own admiration and questions concerning her family maid, Constantine, who mysteriously and without warning (to Skeeter) leaves the Phelan family was in many ways a fictional autobiography of Stockett's own life. Although placed in a different time setting, the relationship between Skeeter and Constantine may reflect Stockett's own ideals of her relationship with Demetrie. Similar to the mammy, the women in her book are monolithic caregivers to white children. The violence, sexual abuse, and poverty of Stockett's youth and within her storyline are either rationalized or ignored, with the only major violence being marital abuse relegated to the black community. *The Help* allows for some whites to reconcile the changing social and racial terrain of twenty-first century American society: more specifically, the arrival of the first African American family in the White House and the use of the buzzword *postracial* on Saturday-morning news programs. Stockett is one in a long line of white authors who claim to focus on race and the black experience in order to recast whiteness in a more positive light and have continually used the mammy to rectify past wrongs at periods of uncertainty. Stockett's neglect, whether intentionally or naïvely, illustrates the continual struggle African Americans have in some white-authored fictions and racial struggles in the current era. However, why does the mammy continue to be reinvented and maintained in American popular culture?

In 1923, after several years of campaigning, the Daughters of the Confederacy submitted a proposal to Congress to erect a monument to the mammy in the nation's capital. The *New York Times*, in a May 15, 1910, editorial, glorified the mammy as having no "model or counterpart in all of history . . . How intense was her pride in her 'white folks.' How tender, how constant was her love for her white 'chillums' . . . A monument in honor of the black mammies would be unique among memorials, because the 'black mammy' was unique . . . especially of the people of the South" ("Deserves a Monument"). After a vociferous protest from black organizations and leaders, this monument eventually was rejected. Even though the stone monument to mammy was never built, she is continually memorialized in literature, advertisements, television, films, and ceramic and celluloid figurines. With the personal intention for women to realize, regardless of their racial and economic background, that "not that much separates us," as Stockett proclaims *The Help*, the novel and later film adaptation, serve as another honor to the mammy as she continually lives in American popular culture and memory (Stockett 530).

The popularity of *The Help* reflects the racial climate in present-day America, similar to the way Stowe's text represented its era. In 2008, the first African American president, Barack Obama, was elected, resulting in an outcry in the news media on two issues: that we now are living in a postracial society and that white men are losing power in society. The fear of whiteness or white power being lost in this new climate was a topic that was continually discussed during his first election and contributed to nostalgia for a simpler time. This changing racial climate parallels the rise of the mammy in the past; although Stockett does not re-create the lost cause due to her time period, she does offer a somewhat nostalgic look at a time of racial polarity and social violence. The random historical events mentioned in the book, such as the murder of Medgar Evers, assist in presenting *The Help* as historical fiction, more so than a romanticized view from a white perspective of female solidarity. Also, the writing style of the book, which illustrates the voice and experiences of two black female domestics and one white young woman, is deceitful. Although the main black female characters, Minny and Aibileen, are displayed as going against social norms, they actually stay within the racial lines and hierarchy of the period. There is a false sense that all three characters are explored equally; however, the book ignores the complexity and solidarity of the black community.

In retrospect, I realize that only a few years ago the presence of my books, computer, and stacks of paper within ten miles of a university could easily be ignored in that coffee shop. The details of my life may be dismissed due to the very American belief that as a young, black woman I was willing and able to properly care for a white family. Stockett's attempt to capture the help and her desire to pay homage to her own childhood maid contribute to the black female voice being silenced and the caricature of the mammy enduring. Scholar Trudier Harris stated in her path-breaking work *From Mammies to Militants* that black women are "Called Matriarch, Emasculator, and Hot Momma, Sometimes Sister, Pretty Baby, Auntie, Mammy and Girl . . . The Black American Woman has had to admit that while nobody knew the troubles she saw, everybody . . . felt qualified to explain her, even to herself" (Harris). *The Help* should be included in the long history of white female-authored works attempting to tell the black woman's story, though always protecting whiteness and all the while contributing to the continuation of stereotypes that have plagued the African American community for centuries.

Notes

1. The sexual violence black women experienced while working in white households has been a well-documented aspect of life for many domestics. For further reading on the topic, please refer to the works by Tucker; Hunter; and Clark-Lewis.
2. In the film adaptation, Octavia Spencer, who performed the role of Minny, was awarded the 2012 Academy Award for Best Supporting Actor. Similarly, Hattie McDaniel won the same award in 1940 for her performance of a sassy mammy in the acclaimed film *Gone with the Wind*.

Works Cited

Baker, Ray Stannard. *Following the Colour Line: An Account of Negro Citizenship in the American Democracy*. New York: Doubleday, Page and Company, 1908. Print.

Bogle, Donald. *Primetime Blues: African American on Network Television*. New York: Farrar, Straus and Giroux, 2001. Print.

———. *Toms, Coons, Mulattoes, Mammies, and Bucks: An Interpretive History of Blacks in American Films*. New York: Continuum, 2007. Print.

Clark-Lewis, Elizabeth. *Living In, Living Out: African American Domestics and the Great Migration*. Washington, DC: Smithsonian Institution Press, 1994. Print.

Collins, Patricia Hill. *Black Feminist Thought: Knowledge, Consciousness, and the Politics of Empowerment*. 2nd ed. New York: Routledge, 2000. Print.

"Deserves a Monument: Plan to Memorize the 'Black Mammy' Wins Southern Favor." *New York Times*, May 15, 1910. ProQuest Historical Newspapers X10. Web. February 20, 2012.

Dixon, Thomas. *The Clansman: An Historical Romance of the Ku Klux Klan*. New York: Grosset and Dunlap, 1905. Print.

Eastman, Mary Henderson. *Aunt Phillis's Cabin, or, Southern Life as It Is*. Philadelphia: Lippincott, Grambo and Co., 1852. Print.

Gaspar, David Barry, and Darlene Clark Hine. *More Than Chattel: Black Women and Slavery in the Americas*. Bloomington: Indiana UP, 1996. Print.

Guerrero, Ed. *Framing Blackness: The African American Image in Film*. Philadelphia: Temple UP, 1993. Print.

Harris, Trudier. *From Mammies to Militants: Domestics in Black American Literature*. Philadelphia: Temple UP, 1982. Print.

Hirsch, Stephen. "Uncle Tomitudes: The Popular Reaction to 'Uncle Tom's Cabin.'" *Studies in the American Renaissance* (1978): 303–330. Print.

Hunter, Tera W. *To Joy My Freedom: Southern Black Women's Lives and Labors after the Civil War*. Cambridge, MA: Harvard UP, 1997. Print.

Kern-Foxworth, Marilyn. *Aunt Jemima, Uncle Ben, and Rastus: Blacks in Advertising, Yesterday, Today and Tomorrow*. Westport, CT: Praeger, 1994. Print.

Laughey, Dan. *Key Themes in Media Theory*. New York: Open UP, 2007. Print.

Litwack, Leon. *Trouble in Mind: Black Southerners in the Age of Jim Crow*. New York: Vintage, 1998. Print.

Manring, Maurice M. *Slave in a Box: The Strange Career of Aunt Jemima*. Charlottesville: UP of Virginia, 1992. Print.

McElya, Micki. *Clinging to Mammy: The Faithful Slave in Twentieth-Century America*. Cambridge, MA: Harvard UP, 2007. Print.

Mitchell, Margaret. *Gone with the Wind*. New York: Macmillan, 1936. Print.

Morgan, Jo-Ann. "Mammy the Huckster: Selling the Old South for the New Century." *American Art* 9.1 (1995): 86–109. Print.

Oldenburg, Ann. "'Help' Author Kathryn Stockett Responds to Lawsuit." *USA Today* February 23, 2011. Web. February 20, 2012.

Parkhurst, Jessie W. "The Role of the Black Mammy in the Plantation Household." *Journal of Negro History* 23.3 (July 1938): 349–369. Print.

Steinberg, Sybil. "Book Review: 'The Help' by Kathryn Stockett." *Washington Post* April 1, 2009. Web. 20 February 2012.

Stockett, Kathryn. *The Help*. New York: Berkeley Books, 2009. Print.

Stowe, Harriet Beecher. *Uncle Tom's Cabin*. Cutchogue, NY: Buccaneer Books, 1982. Print.

Tandy, Jeanette Reid. "Pro-Slavery Propaganda in American Fiction of the Fifties." *The South Atlantic Quarterly* 21 (January 1922): 41–50. Print.

Tucker, Susan. *Telling Memories among Southern Women: Domestic Workers and Their Employers in the Segregated South*. Baton Rouge: Louisiana State UP, 1988. Print.

Venjara, Sana. "Stroller Surveillance: Race, Class and New York City Nannies." *Next City Newsletter* April 2, 2012. Web. July 8, 2013.

Wallace-Sanders, Kimberly. *Mammy: A Century of Race, Gender, and Southern Memory*. Ann Arbor: U of Michigan P, 2008. Print.

White, Deborah Gray. *Ar'n't I a Woman? Female Slaves in the Plantation South*. New York: W. W. Norton, 1985. Print.

CHAPTER 5

"When Folks Is Real Friends, There Ain't No Such Thing as Place"

Feminist Sisterhood and the Politics of Social Hierarchy in *The Help*

Shana Russell

During the early 1960s, my great grandmother, Josephine, was employed as a domestic worker by Miss Horowitz, a wealthy Jewish woman in Kansas City, Missouri. At age 13, my mother, the eldest girl of seven children, worked with her some weekends as Josephine polished silver, ironed, dusted, and set up for bridge parties. Miss Horowitz lived in an exclusive high rise known as Twin Oaks. Josephine and my great grandfather, Reverend Alfred Weldon, lived in a basement apartment in the building. My mother lived across town in government-subsidized housing, a home she shared with five of her siblings and her mother.

My mother describes domestic labor as transformative. It allowed her to cross the boundaries of poverty once a week into "a new world . . . another side of the city where they had beautiful things." Josephine and Miss Horowitz, she reflected, "made the world bigger." While my mother is always very open with me about her life, I never knew about her stint as a teenaged domestic laborer. It wasn't until her book club read Kathryn Stockett's *New York Times* bestselling novel, *The Help*, that she and several other women of color between the ages of forty and seventy began delving into their own histories as household laborers or the children of domestic workers as they pored over the details of the novel. Reading the book in the solitude of my New Jersey apartment left me uncomfortable with its representations of black women as complacent, apolitical, and doting caretakers of white children. Yet the novel allowed my mother to reflect on her experience in a new way. Despite my visceral reaction to the novel and its 2011 film adaptation, I cannot deny the impact of this narrative of black life, written by a Southern white woman, on my mother. I wonder how many other children sat at the kitchen tables of their childhood homes, talked with their mothers and grandmothers about *The Help*, and heard stories of what it was like to work in white women's kitchens. I must confess, my mother's critical and introspective engagement with the film was far more compelling than any scholarly analysis.

Yet it is Stockett's perceived inability to account for the experiences of black domestic workers in the South that incited the wrath of scholars who publicly critiqued the film in print, on television, and on the web. This criticism is best summarized by a statement composed by the Association of Black Women Historians shortly before the film's release. They state, "The Association of Black Women Historians finds it unacceptable for either this book or this film to strip black women's lives of historical accuracy for the sake of entertainment." The association directs their statement to fans of the film, rather than Stockett or Tate Taylor, the film's director, who is also white. Perhaps they were not anticipating its popularity among women like my mother.

The statement includes a suggested reading list of alternative fictional narratives about domestic workers. One in particular, Alice Childress's *Like One of the Family*, stands out as that which *The Help* so ambitiously attempts to be. Published as a collection in 1956, *Like One of the Family* is a series of monologues delivered by the singular narrator, Mildred, to her best friend and fellow domestic worker, Marge. In many ways, Mildred is a foil for Aibileen Clark, the central black female character of *The Help*. Like Aibileen, Mildred is a day laborer and a keen observer of the racial and gendered dynamics of domestic work. Despite the success of the novel's initial release, it quickly disappeared and was out of print for two decades until it was resurrected in 1986 by literary scholar Trudier Harris. It's almost as if Mildred foresaw the fictitious sisterhood between black women and their employers perpetuated by films like *The Help*. She states prophetically in one monologue, "I know that maids don't be carryin' on like that over the people they work for, at least none of 'em that I've ever met" (Childress 125).

At the same time, *The Help* and its supporters suggest that the bonds of womanhood and motherhood mitigate the racial hierarchies that characterize the relationships between white housewives and black women workers. To ease her own anxiety about writing, Stockett offers this statement in her afterword, one that she considers the prized passage from her debut novel: "Wasn't that the point of the book? For women to realize, *We are just two people. Not that much separates us. Not nearly as much as I'd thought*" (*The Help* 520). To understand how *The Help* is shaping contemporary discourses on the possibility of narrating women's history through this perceived sisterhood among liberal white women and their female employees of color, this essay places *The Help* in conversation with other cinematic representations of domestic labor that demonstrate the significance of the domestic worker not only to American historical mythology but also to configurations of feminism, labor, and cultural consumption.

The title of Stockett's novel misleadingly suggests that it is solely "the help" who narrate the story of domestic workers in Jackson, Mississippi. Two-thirds of the novel's chapters are written in the vernacular voices of friends and fellow domestics Aibileen Clark and Minny Jackson. Eugenia "Skeeter" Phelan, a recent Ole Miss graduate and aspiring writer, narrates the remainder of the story. She secretly interviews Aibileen, Minny, and several other black women working in the homes of her middle-class friends. These interviews, coupled with memories of her relationship with her former caretaker, Constantine, make up the bulk of the novel.

Skeeter is the standout protagonist. Her coming-of-age story, from an awkward twentysomething to a budding writer headed for New York City, propels the narrative. The film adaptation of the novel magnifies the centrality of Skeeter's character. Although Aibileen, played by Viola Davis, serves as the only voice-over, the film emphasizes Skeeter's transformation. Her position as a marginal figure in the community of women—due to her awkwardness, her education, and her inability (or refusal) to marry—transforms into a willingness to challenge, even in secret, the racial dynamics of Jackson.

Critics of the novel, including political scientist and MSNBC commentator Melissa Harris-Perry and historian Valerie Boyd, assert that it would be impossible to think of the narrative as anything other than a product of Stockett's racial imagination. Both scholars conclude that the novel is not at all what its title suggests. In a candid interview with Oprah Winfrey, Viola Davis, who received a significant amount of praise and even more criticism for her role as Aibileen, exhibited a sense of uneasiness about her character. As an actor, she wanted to show more of Aibileen's interior life and less of her outward docility. She, too, was skeptical about the narrative voice. "It was about 'the help,'" she exclaimed. "That's what it's about" ("African-American Women in Hollywood"). My mother and those who made *The Help* a bestselling novel and summer blockbuster feel differently. The voices of Minny and Aibileen, I heard women argue repeatedly, are authentic, or at the very least empathetic, representations of black women of the era, making Stockett's role as author (and perhaps her race) irrelevant to her ability to present the "truth" about black women's lives.

As I talked with women, family members, and colleagues about the novel and film, I noticed a clear tension in their responses along lines of class and education. In the spring of 2012, I was tasked with organizing a panel discussion titled "What's Up with *The Help*: Domestic Labor, Black Feminism, and the Politics of Representation." My copanelists, both women—a white historian and a black sociologist—severely critiqued the film's disregard for the horrors of domestic labor and racial oppression and rallied in defense of the real domestic workers who had been wronged by such a historically inaccurate portrayal. When asked by a local high school student in the audience whether or not there was anything productive or good to take away from the film, we, "the experts," were at a loss. It was then that my mother, a woman who never had the educational opportunities that she was able to provide for me, raised her hand. She shared the story of her own experience working with her grandmother and somehow changed the tide of the conversation. Other audience members began sharing the stories of their families and the love that the women in their lives had for the film's representation of their labor. It rendered my copanelists and I completely speechless.

Six months after Harris-Perry shared her critique of the film on MSNBC's *The Last Word*, she was given her own show on the network and used the platform to return to her critique of the film, this time with a panel that included comedian and political commentator Elon James White; Micki McElya, author of *Clinging to Mammy: The Faithful Slave in Twentieth-Century America*; and Barbara Young, a household worker with 17 years of experience and representative of the National Domestic Workers Alliance. The twenty-minute segment began with Harris-Perry's impassioned commentary about the film's numerous missteps. White and McElya echoed her sentiments and lambasted the film for its inaccurate portrayal of the realities of racial oppression. Young, on the other hand, found the film endearing. In her eyes, it exposed what she called "America's best kept secret," the women who work for white American families. "I am the real domestic here!" she stated, a powerful exclamation that seemed completely lost on Harris-Perry and the show's remaining guests ("*The Help* Doesn't Help").

Thus, as a scholar, I was faced with a problem: how do I negotiate the novel's mythological history with my own, as the product of four generations of domestic workers? Perhaps the answer to that question lies within the white woman who proclaims to tell their story—or, should I say, the women: the narrator, whom Aibileen and Minny refer to as "Miss Skeeter," and Stockett, the novel's author. The voices of the novel's black narrators are mitigated and interpreted by Skeeter. This mirrors Stockett's own experience as a white woman who penned the story as a means of materializing her memory of Demetrie, the black woman who worked for her family when she was a child. Like, Stockett, Skeeter is bound by the limits of her own imagination. *The Help* is a product of Skeeter's guilelessness and the unreliability of Stockett's memory.

Skeeter's antagonistic relationship to her peers, the elite white women of Jackson, reveals a great deal about her role as an interpreter of black life and history. Skeeter, a single working woman with aspirations beyond the confines of Southern white gentility, exists on the precipice of second-wave feminism. Although her insistence on female independence is generally self-serving, it also makes her a perfect fit for challenging Jackson's sociopolitical reality. Placing black women at the bottom of the Southern racial caste system is necessary to bolster the superiority of the community's white women. Skeeter returns from Ole Miss on the outskirts of her own social circle, naturalizing the intimate bond she develops with Aibileen and Minny, one that obfuscates the dynamics of privilege between them as though her antiracism is a natural extension of her feminist awakening. This, like the novel's fabricated sisterhood, is fiction. In 1963, when the novel is set, mainstream feminism had not yet made room for women of color. And Skeeter certainly didn't discover either at Ole Miss. In spite of this, the novel gestures toward a racially optimistic future. Released just one month after Barack Obama urged Americans to "choose our better history" in his 2009 inaugural address, *The Help* confirmed, for some, that we were already living the postracial ideal. "Choosing our better history," for Stockett, meant privileging the sister-hood between black and white women and the affective relationship between black women and the white children for which they care. In the author's own words, "I took liberties that made me feel like I was telling the story in the way it should be told" (Stockett interview).

The novel begins as Aibileen narrates, "Taking care a white babies, that's what I do, along with all the cooking and cleaning . . . I know how to get them babies to sleep, stop crying, and go in the toilet bowl before they mamas even get out a bed in the morning" (*The Help* 1). It is not until after Aibileen confesses her undying love for Mae Mobley, the two-year-old daughter of her employer, Eliza-beth Leefolt, that the reader learns about Aibileen's biological son, Treelore, who died in a horrific accident.

Admittedly, I found the triangular relationship between Aibileen, Mae Mob-ley, and Treelore unsettling. The juxtaposition of Aibileen's affection for Mae Mobley and the gruesome death of her son suggests that she is able to mourn Treelore's death by caring for her employer's child. Once Aibileen's narration begins, we learn that hearing Mae Mobley exclaim, "I love you, Aibee," as she plays outside reminds her of her own son doing the same (*The Help* 107). My visceral reaction is perhaps best described by the "real" Aibileen, Ablene Cooper, the former employee of Stockett's brother. In an interview with *Essence* magazine, Cooper explains, "I began working for the Stocketts . . . in October 1998, three months after my youngest son died from leukemia . . . I've read Ms. Stockett's book . . . Losing a child is hard enough without having to relive that moment as part of someone else's story. I feel as if she invaded my privacy and exposed one of the most awful times in my life to the world" (Viera 73).[1] The affirmation of Aibileen's relationship with Mae Mobley, alongside the deemphasis of her grief was, for me, another instance where the narrative voice is no longer that of "the help." Barbara Young, the "real domestic worker" and organizer, disagrees. She expressed a fondness for the relationship between Aibileen and Mae Mobley. To her, it was the most humanizing aspect of the film ("*The Help* Doesn't Help"). Young is not alone. A number of domestic workers expressed a fondness for the film's portrayal of their labor. I have never worked in a white woman's kitchen or cared for her children. Thus I cannot dismiss praise for the film's humanistic portrayal of domestic laborers (for which credit has to go to the actors). So I must return to Skeeter, the translator of the text and the center of its feminist sister-hood: a trope that seems almost formulaic when one considers representations of black domestic workers on screen dating back to the thirties.

The intimate bond between recently widowed Bea Pullman (the protagonist of the original film adaptation of the Fannie Hurst novel, *Imitation of Life*) and her maid, Delilah Johnson, embodies a feminist logic that, in 1934, was decades away from becoming a part of popular discourse. Hurst was an early advocate for women's rights and became exposed to racial disparity through her interac-tions with the writers of the Harlem Renaissance, particularly Zora Neale Hur-ston. Hurst had a close relationship to Hurston, a "sisterhood" characterized by race and class hierarchies. She observed black life through the protected lens of privilege and then adapted her observations to works of fiction (Caputi 702). Like Stockett, Hurst became the author of black life, which allowed her to choose her own history.

In many ways, Bea and Delilah are parallel characters differentiated only by color. They are single mothers, working class, and struggling to support small families on their own despite the obstacles presented by gender. Delilah finds herself at Bea's doorstep as a part of a desperate search for live-in domestic work and an employer that is willing to take in her daughter, Peola. Bea takes over her late husband's door-to-door maple syrup company to support her daughter, Jessie, but finds it nearly impossible to convince potential clients to take her seriously as a widow. Shortly after Delilah's arrival, Bea discovers her exceptional pancake recipe. The women go into business together and eventually develop a million-dollar pancake franchise that bears Delilah's name and likeness.

Delilah is incredibly complacent and even enthusiastic about domestic work. This blurs the race and class boundaries that characterize the relationship between the two women. While negotiating the ownership of the "Aunt Delilah" pancake franchise, Bea shares with Delilah that with her portion of the earnings she can finally own her own home. Delilah replies, "How am I gonna take care of you and Miss Jessie if I ain't here . . . I's your cook and I wanna stay your cook." The loyalty of black women to their employers, or to their liberal white female allies in the case of *The Help*, is a repeated trope in filmic representations of household laborers. Harris-Perry explains, "The fidelity of black women domestics is more important than the realities of the lives and the pain, the anguish, the rape, the lynching that they experienced" (Harris-Perry interview). Yet Delilah's response to Bea is necessary to the illusion that domestic labor is a choice, as opposed to a form of labor to which black women have historically been restricted. Evidently, Hurst and the film's director chose a history that absolves liberal white viewers of guilt.

Delilah's illiteracy magnifies her dependence on Bea and is illustrated by her minstrel-like affect and vernacular speech. Her gestures and facial expressions provide the audience with moments of humor in an otherwise emotionally charged narrative. When Bea observes Peola's superior ability to recite world capitals, for instance, she tells Delilah that Peola is much smarter than Jessie. In one of the film's many moments of comic relief, Delilah replies, "We all starts out that way. We don't get dumb until later." The dialogue is not clear as to which "we" Delilah is referring. On the one hand, this could be a straightforward gesture toward black people's innate illiteracy, a dehumanizing caricature created for entertainment, which is part of the representational history that the Association of Black Women Historians assigns to *The Help*. Or it could be another universalizing gesture underscoring the innate sisterhood that has been obscured by the ignorance produced by the social forces that draw artificial distinctions between women of different races. Regardless of whom the "we" refers to, insofar as this is wrapped up in a narrative about what is a very intimate relationship between a white woman and her black employee, it becomes necessary to naturalize Delilah's lack of intelligence and her desire to care for white families in order to make this relationship sympathetic.

The 1959 remake of *Imitation of Life* is a familiar yet seemingly more progressive narrative. Businesswoman Bea Pullman becomes aspiring actress Lora Meredith, played by Lana Turner. The burgeoning civil rights movement warranted a radical change in the domestic worker figure. Delilah becomes Annie, played by Juanita Moore, a prideful and well-spoken single mother who, like Delilah, is unable to find work. In some ways, this revamped adaptation of Hurst's novel prefigures the postracial politics of *The Help*.

The black female protagonists of *The Help* are certainly not superficial caricatures. But there are remnants of Delilah in Minny, played by Octavia Spencer in the film. While teaching her employer, Celia Foote, the basics of cooking, Minny conjures Aunt Jemima and sings praises to Crisco and fried chicken. What is unsettling about Minny's humorous outbursts is the way the figure of the domestic worker, who is supposedly the subject of the narrative, becomes the target of ridicule.

The 1959 adaptation of *Imitation of Life* resurrects Delilah with subtlety. Annie's daughter, Sarah Jane, satirically performs the doting black servant when her mother requests her assistance in catering to Lora's dinner party guests. Sarah Jane enters the living room carrying a silver tray high above her head as she exclaims, "Fetched y'all a mess a crawdads Miss Lora for you and your friends . . . No trick to totin' Miss Lora. I learned it from my mammy and she learned it from old massuh before she belonged to you." The scene emerges in a way that suggests that Sarah Jane's performance is a political commentary on representations of domestic workers in the American racial imagination, an image that she is removed from because of her ability to pass for white. It is also a bitter renunciation of her mother's profession. Sarah Jane's shuck-and-jive routine is a declaration of alienation, a critique of slavery's "belonging," and also a sign of her unbelonging to Annie's world.

Imitation of Life is not the only film to use passing and racial performance as locusts for political commentary. The 1949 film *Pinky* opens as the title character returns to the South after spending several years up North, passing for white and training to become a nurse. Her grandmother, Dicey, relies on domestic labor to support Pinky's education. Like Delilah, Dicey is overwhelmingly childlike and painfully loyal to her employer, Miss Em, who considers Dicey her faithful servant and friend. Dicey dismisses her servitude by stating, "When folks is real friends, there ain't no such thing as place."

Eventually, the local doctor commissions Pinky to nurse Miss Em, who has recently fallen ill. Miss Em treats Pinky like a maid, a constant reminder of the racial hierarchy at play. Pinky questions the expectation of racial performativity by saying, "What should I do? Dye my face? Grovel and shuffle? Say yes'm and no'm . . . so I won't upset you?" At the conclusion of the film, Pinky must submit to domestic labor as a means of financially supporting herself, but she does it without the proclamation of cross-racial sisterhood.

The trope of the passing daughter who exposes the fiction of sisterhood returns in *The Help* in the form of Constantine's daughter, Lulabelle. Constantine sent her four-year-old daughter to an orphanage in Chicago due to an inability to care for her while working for the Phelan family. As an adult, Lulabelle returns to Jackson to reunite with her mother. Her ability to pass for white (like Sarah Jane and Pinky) affords her the privileges of class and education but alienates her from Constantine's world.

Lulabelle enters the Phelan home by passing as a white woman during a meeting of the Daughters of the American Revolution. She is quickly discovered by Charlotte Phelan, who demands that she leave immediately. Before exiting, Lulabelle responds, "What, you don't allow colored Negroes in your living room if we're not cleaning up?" With that, she spits in Charlotte's face and storms out (*The Help* 427–28). She is followed by Constantine, who, without a second thought, leaves her position working for the Phelan's to be with her daughter. Although Lulabelle is significantly more defiant than Pinky and Sarah Jane, her disruption of the illusion of her mother's unwavering fidelity to the Phelans complicates the notions of family that permeate the discourse surrounding domestic work.[2]

The mystery of Constantine's firing is one that looms over the entire narrative. Skeeter returns home from Ole Miss to find that her beloved maid is nowhere to be found. Whenever Skeeter needs reassurance, she remembers Constantine's words. In the film, elaborate flashbacks stand in for Skeeter's vivid memories. Eventually, she aggressively demands that her mother tell her the real story. The dramatic scene represents Skeeter's rejection of her mother's worldview and that of Jackson's elite. This, coupled with her identification with Aibileen and Minny as surrogate mothers/mammies, offers a post–civil rights and postfeminist response to Sarah Jane, Pinky, sisterhood, and motherhood redeemed through a postracial affiliation as "sisters" that ameliorates the trauma of both mother/daughter and interracial relationships.

Conclusion

The maid's daughters are not the only ones passing. In *The Help*, and other whiteauthored narratives of black life, racial performativity passes as nostalgia. American mythology passes as history. Wage labor passes as sisterhood. Second-wave feminism passes as radical antiracism. And the voices of naïve white women, who are merely observers and interpreters, pass as the thoughts and feelings of the black women whose experiences they appropriate to create narratives of racial progress.

Unlike Peola, Sarah Jane, Pinky, and Lulabelle, my mother was never ashamed of the fact that her grandmother, who we all called Nanny, worked in a white woman's house. When I asked her about this, she responded simply, "Why would you be ashamed of someone for working?" In Mildred's words, "There's many a doctor, many a lawyer, many a teacher, many a minister that got where they are 'cause somebody worked in the kitchen to put 'em there" (Childress 37). What Stockett remembered and then used her protagonist to interpret mattered very little to my mother. In fact, I doubt that she even noticed Skeeter at all. My mother and other black women like her were not looking to Kathryn Stockett to reveal an uncertain truth about a history they did not get to choose. The problem of white authorship, then, is not an inability to tell our story on screen. It's a refusal to follow these fictional narratives into the mundane spaces, like my mother's kitchen, where they are given life.

Notes

1. In 2011, Cooper filed a complaint against Stockett citing emotional distress. This case was ultimately dismissed by the Hinds County Court in Alabama.
2. This scene in the novel is significantly altered in the film adaptation. Lulabelle is renamed Rachel for the film. She is brown skinned and no longer passes for white. Instead, she simply storms into the Phelan home and, after a long, heated argument with Charlotte, storms out with Constantine following her.

Works Cited

"African-American Women in Hollywood." *Oprah's Next Chapter*. The Oprah Winfrey Network. June 23, 2013. Television.

Association of Black Women Historians. "An Open Statement to Fans of *The Help*." 7 August 2011. Web. 29 Feb. 2012. http://www.abwh.org/index.php?option=com_content&view=article&id=2%3Aopen-statement-the-help.

Boyd, Valerie. "Review: 'The Help': A Feel-Good Chick Flick Set in Civil Rights Era." *ArtsATL.com*. 11 August 2011. Web. 29 February 2012.

Caputi, Jane. "'Specifying' Fannie Hurst: Langston Hughes's 'Limitations of Life,' Zora Neale Hurston's *Their Eyes Were Watching God*, and Toni Morrison's *The Bluest Eye* as 'Answers' to Hurst's *Imitation of Life*." *Black American Literature Forum* 24.4 (1990): 697–716. Print.

Childress, Alice. *Like One of the Family: Conversations from a Domestic's Life*. Boston: Beacon Press, 1986. Print.

Harris-Perry, Melissa. Interview by Lawrence O'Donnell. *The Last Word*. MSNBC, August 10, 2011. Television.

The Help. Dir. Tate Taylor. Perf. Emma Stone, Viola Davis, Bryce Dallas Howard, and Octavia Spencer. DreamWorks, 2011. Film.

"*The Help* Doesn't Help." *Melissa Harris-Perry*. MSNBC, February 25, 2012. Television.

Imitation of Life. Dir. Douglas Sirk. Universal International Pictures, 1959. Film.

Imitation of Life. Dir. John M. Stahl. Universal Pictures, 1934. Film.

Pinky. Dir. Elia Kazan. 20th Century Fox, 1949. Film.

Stockett, Kathryn. *The Help*. New York: Berkeley Books, 2009. Print.

———. Interview by Michelle Norris. *All Things Considered*. National Public Radio. WNYC, New York. December 23, 2009. Radio.

Viera, Bene. "In Her Own Words: The Real Aibileen?" *Essence*, August 2011: 73. Print.

CHAPTER 6

Black Girlhood and *The Help*

Constructing Black Girlhood in a "Post"-Racial, -Gender, and -Welfare State

Julia S. Jordan-Zachery

Introduction

"If you white you alright / If you black step back": the lyrics of this 1967 folk song capture the storyline of black and white girlhood in Kathryn Stockett's *The Help*. *The Help* is primarily a story of two women: a young college-educated woman nicknamed Skeeter and an older black domestic, Aibileen, who has raised a number of white children. After completing college, Skeeter returns to Jackson, Mississippi, to a way of life that she finds stifling. As such, she seeks to find an alternative via a career as an author. She fosters a relationship with Aibileen, to the extent that one is possible in 1962 in the Deep South, as a means of writing the great novel that would allow her to escape the trappings of a middle- and upper-class life of a white Southern belle. With reluctance, Aibileen and other maids agree to help Skeeter in her clandestine project that tells the stories of the black maids. *The Help* is set as a story of multicultural and multiclass female relationships—which can be touted as an ideal of postfeminism and postracism. Postracialism and postfeminism are ideologies that function to suggest that racial differences and gender discrimination are no longer salient (see McRobbie). While *The Help* attempts to situate itself in the ideologies of postracialism and postfeminism, the discursive practices deployed actually work to reinscribe racialized and gender tropes.

In this chapter, I argue that the construction of black girlhood in *The Help* relies on historical stereotypes of black womanhood and as such reinforces white understandings of black life in a manner that normalizes the contemporary inequitable position of black women and their offspring. The story of the black girl, although a minor character, characterizes the continuation of a particular regime of race-gender-class hegemony. *The Help* deploys historical narratives of the contented, silent, and "dignified" black woman. This fictional portrayal tapped into a cultural and political moment of nostalgia—a desire for the "beauty" and "simplicity" of the past—at the same time the United States elected its first multiracial president, Barack Obama. This yearning for nostalgia requires black girls and the women they eventually become to play the role of the mammy—the content and docile enslaved woman who cared for and protected white interests. This is the type of woman who does not advocate for equality and who knows her "place" in society. Thus, by analyzing and contrasting the construction of girlhood, we are able to see how such tropes are reinscribed and as such unveil the incongruence between the notion of "equality" often celebrated in relation to *The Help* and the inequality it advocates between black and white women.

I admit that girls, and particularly black girls, are not the primary characters of the novel *The Help*. However, the fleeting discussion and characterization of black girlhood warrants analysis. Kindra, the daughter of domestic Minny Jackson and the central black girl of this analysis, can be read as an intergenerational cultural text. Although she is a young child (girlhood is thought of as girls from birth to age ten), she provides us with a means of investigating the underlying societal assumptions about girls and the women they become. The construction of girlhood is not monolithic and is indeed shaped by various social processes and ideologies (see Jiwani, Steenbergen, and Mitchell). However, black girlhood tends to be overlaid with the stereotypical construction of black womanhood. From girlhood, the black body is marked along racialized gender boundaries for a particular function in society. The dominant discursive practices tend to represent black girls in a rather monolithic manner and portray them as failing to conform to the ideals of virtue, piety, and hard work. This representation can be read as part of the cultural backlash to the modern civil rights movement (see Springer). Consequently, the construction of black girlhood produces and reproduces a narrative that is familiar in terms of our understandings of race, class, and gender.

These fleeting glimpses of black girls in *The Help* introduce a possible starting point for an analysis of the politics of how we construct black girls in this "post"-race, -gender, and -welfare era. The depiction of black girlhood in the novel begs the question, "How do we think of black girls in our society?" As argued by Bobo, "fictionalized creations of black women," and I add black girls, "are not innocent; they do not lack the effect of ideological force in the lives of those represented in that black women are rendered as objects and useful commodities in a very serious power struggle" (36). This essay attempts to examine the identity construction of black girls in the novel, *The Help*. Informed by black feminist theory, I explore Anglocentric perspectives and representations of black girlhood. Such an analysis is important, as it focuses not only on the short-term treatment of this population but also on how they are treated in the long term as they grow into womanhood. Black feminists have a tradition of asking who speaks on the behalf of black women and what is being said about them (see Cole and Guy-Sheftall; Collins; Lorde). In an attempt to (re)claim black womanhood from its often negative construction by those in the majority, black feminists have engaged in critiques of social, economic, cultural, and political structures, institutions, and processes. Using the theories developed from such critiques, I attempt to situate black girls not only within *The Help* but also within the larger contemporary society. Specifically, I look at how the tropes of race, class, and gender are used to frame black girlhood and the political and social work done via these frames. The tropes of race, class, and gender allow us to see how this "fictional character" set in a historical time period of the 1960s transcends time and can be viewed as "futuristic" in terms of Anglocentric understandings of the roles of black girls in our more contemporary society.

Seeing and Constructing Black Girlhood

Black girlhood is not a typical subject of social science research. Ruth Nicole Brown asserts, "So in conversations about girls, what about Black girls? . . . In girls' studies, the demonstrated narrative discrepancy calls attention to girlhood, yet ignores the ways girlhood is produced differently given the intersection of diverse categories of identity" (36). In our conversations on race, black girlhood also seems to disappear. According to Rozie-Battle, many studies of black youth focus on males because their problems manifest in more overt ways, such as over-representation in the juvenile justice system. When, and if, black girls or teens are the center of social science research, they are typically constructed as *pathological*, as research tends to concentrate on issues of teen pregnancy, poverty, welfare use, juvenile delinquency, and (poor) school performance, for example, to negativize black girls' behavior.

As I discuss next, *The Help* constructs black girls as uncontrollable and womanish, poverty-stricken, living in violent and unstable homes, and unredeemable. In essence, the black girl is a failure in the making—a long-term potential societal problem. Construction of black girlhood hints at anxieties in this new so-called social and economic order. This manner of "seeing" black girls is then used to justify their surveillance, both by the state and by private individuals. There are a number of storylines running throughout *The Help*; some see the storyline of friendship. However, if one were to unpack the novel, there is a storyline of innocence (but only directed at white girlhood), one of violence as normal (in the black community), and one of redemption. I start with the storyline of innocence.

Who Can Be an Innocent?

The tropes of gender, race, and class suggest that it is impossible for black women to be perceived as innocent and therefore as warranting protection from destructive and harmful forces (Crenshaw). Hegemonic constructions are used to suggest that black women are "improper" and "immoral" and as such cannot be innocent (see Davis; D. White). Instead, these women, and girls, are constructed as overly aggressive, "strong," violent, and dangerous. Sapphire, the embodiment of this stereotype, has in the "post" era morphed into the image of the "angry Black woman" (see Childs; Collins; Davis; West). The angry black woman not only is unjustifiably upset but also tends to also be disproportionately upset. She is emotional; however, in the case of black women, she is also easily provoked to hostility—in words and deeds. The angry black woman is sometimes portrayed and depicted in reality TV shows—such was the case of Omarosa Manigault-Stallworth of the NBC series *The Apprentice*. Bill O'Reilly, on his show *The O'Reilly Factor*, suggested that First Lady Michelle Obama embodied the angry black woman stereotype (O'Reilly, Tabacoff, and Sohnen). By asserting that Mrs. Obama "looked like an angry Black woman," O'Reilly told the audience that she was driven, outspoken, achievement-oriented, self-centered, mistakenly angry, troubled, and not to be trusted.

Even at the tender age of five, Kindra is constructed as embodying the qualities of Sapphire, the angry black woman stereotype. To understand the construction of Kindra, it is important to juxtapose her character with that of Mae Mobley Leefolt (Aibileen's white charge). As the story unfolds, we see both Kindra and Mae Mobley Leefolt at the same age of five. Kindra is five at the start of the book, and Mae Mobley is five at the end of the book. This is the only similarity these girls share, except for their gender. At the tender age of five, there is no innocence surrounding Kindra. In contrast, Mae Mobley is constructed as pure and innocent. Consider Minny's description of her daughter, Kindra:

> "Mammy, fix me something to eat. I'm hungry." That's what my youngest girl, Kindra who's five said to me last night. With her **hand on her hip and her foot stuck out**.
>
> I have five kids and I take pride that I taught them *yes ma'am* and *please* before they could even say *cookie*.
>
> All except one.
>
> "You ain't having nothing till supper," I tell her.
>
> "Why you so mean to me? I *hate* you," she yelled and run out the door.
>
> I set my eyes on the ceiling because that's a shock I will never get used to even with four before her. The day your child says she hates you, and every child will go through the phase, it kicks like a foot in the stomach.
>
> But Kindra, Lord. It's not just a phase I'm seeing. That girl is turning out just like me. (Stockett, 51; words in bold are my emphasis)

In another interaction, Kindra's perceived innate anger and defiance is also portrayed. Again, through the eyes of her mother, we are told,

> At home that night, I get the butter beans simmering, the ham in the skillet.
>
> "Kindra, get everybody in here," I say to my six year old. "We ready to eat."
>
> "*Suuuuppperrrrr*," Kindra yells, not moving an inch from where she's standing.
>
> "You go get your daddy the proper way," I yell. "What I tell you about yelling in my house?"

Kindra rolls her eyes at me like she's just been asked to do the stupidest thing in the world. She stamps her feet down the hall. "*Suuupperrr!*"
"*Kindra!*" (Stockett 218)

Minny, in detailing her interactions with Kindra, employs the characteristics of the angry black woman, thereby suggesting that there is no such thing as girlhood for young black female children. Here we see that Kindra appears to be easily moved to hostile words and anger. She is emotional and behaves in what might be called a "womanish manner." More important, her mother seems to hold little to no hope that Kindra might be "cured" of her disposition when she foreshadows that she will turn out to be just like her. Similar to the generational arguments made about the culture of poverty (see Jordan-Zachery; Murray; Neubeck and Cazenave), Stockett suggests that there is a generational transmission of anger between black women and girls. Minny is the sassy grown-up version of Kindra. She is the maid who is constantly in trouble because of her often emotional, "unprovoked," over-the-top responses to her employers. Kindra, the fictitious character, is one iteration of real-life black women, including the likes of Mrs. Obama, who are often portrayed as angry and defiant toward societal beliefs that black women are content with their position in society. In this sense, Kindra is used to project a type of futurism that is mapped onto the bodies of young black girls and women as she is used to suggest that this behavior is normal unless the girl is properly trained and controlled.

In addition to being defiant, Kindra is consistently portrayed as possessing an insatiable appetite—this could also be read as an inability to be satisfied and to control one's feelings/emotions. Once more through the eyes of Minny, we learn that

Leroy looks at me through one eye because he knows something's up. He knew it last night at supper and smelled it when he walked in at five o'clock this morning.
"What's eating you? Ain't got no trouble at work, do you?" he asks for the third time.
"Nothing eating me except five kids and a husband. Y'all driving me up a wall."
The last thing I need him to know is that I've told off another white lady and lost another job . . .
"Mama, where you going?" yells Kindra. "I'm hungry."
"I'm going to Aibileen's. Mama need to be with somebody not pulling on her for five minutes. I pass Sugar on the front steps. 'Sugar, go get Kindra some breakfast.'"
"She already ate. Just a half hour ago."
"Well, she hungry again." (Stockett 226; words in bold are my emphasis)

The depiction of Kindra's questioning of racial hierarchies also characterizes her as angry.

Kindra props her arm on her hip. "Nuh-uh. Ain't nobody putting my mama in jail. I beat those white people with a stick till they bleed."
Leroy points his finger at every one of them. "I don't want to hear a word about it outside this house. It's too dangerous. You hear me, Benny? Felicia?" Then he points his finger at Kindra. "You hear me?"

> But Little Miss Something slaps her fork down on the table, climbs out of her chair. "I hate white people! And I'm on tell everybody if I want to!" (Stockett 220)

Again, this characterization is indeed futuristic, as it maps the perceived behavior of a real-life adult woman onto the body of this "imagined historical" child, thereby predicting the woman that she is likely to become. For example, this construction is very reminiscent of the characterization of Michelle Obama. As part of a 2008 campaign speech for her husband, Mrs. Obama proclaimed "for the first time in my adult life I am proud of my country because it feels like hope is finally making a comeback." Both assertions—that of Kindra and that of Mrs. Obama—upset notions and norms of the proper place of black girls or women. They are questioning their black girlhood or womanhood as racialized gendered subjects in a society that views itself as democratic and equitable. As such, both are viewed as a threat and a danger. These assertions invoke questions of patriotism and racial loyalty, leaving some to wonder whether Kindra or Mrs. Obama is suitable for serving white interests. Consider Tennessee Republican Beverly Watson's view of Mrs. Obama: "I don't much care for her and it has nothing to do with her color or race or anything, she just seems to have a big attitude, like she's just above everyone else" (qtd. in Romano). Unfortunately, neither the girl nor the woman (real or imagined) can be thought of as serving the interests of white Americans, because they are perceived as self-absorbed and narcissistic (see Healy; Malkin).

In comparison, Mae Mobley is characterized as innocent. Given Mae Mobley's construction as innocent, she is deemed worthy of comfort, self-worth, protection, and love. Consider how Aibileen (the black help and the other mother) comforts Mae Mobley:

> I rush to get her but Miss Leefolt get there first. Her lips is curled back from her teeth in a scary smile. Miss Leefolt slap Baby Girl on the back a her bare legs so hard I jump from the sting. Then Miss Leefolt grab Mae Mobley by the arm, jerk it hard with every word . . . [I] pick up Mae Mobley, try to hug her to me, but she bawling and her face is red and she fighting me. "Come on, Baby Girl, it's all right, everything—" Mae Mobley make an ugly face at me and then she rear back and bowp! She wack me right on the ear . . . I'm so mad at Miss Leefolt, I'm biting my tongue. If the fool would just pay her child some attention, this wouldn't happen! . . . "You okay Baby Girl?" I whisper . . . I look down and see read fingermarks on the back a her legs. "I'm here, baby, Aibee's here," I rock and soothe, rock and soothe. But Baby Girl, she just cry and cry. (Stockett 19)

A few pages later Stockett writes,

> I can hear the grip she [Minny] got on the phone, sound like she trying to crush it in her hand. I hear Kindra holler an I wonder why Minny already home. She usually don't leave work till four.
> "I ain't done nothing but feed that old woman good food and look after her!"
> "Minny, I know you honest. God know you honest."

Her voice dip down like bees on a comb. "When I walk into Miss Walters', Miss Hilly be there and she try to give me twenty dollars. She say, 'Take it. I know you need it', and I bout spit in her face. But I didn't. No sir," She start making this panting noise, she say, "I did worse."

"What you did?"

"I ain't telling . . ."

Kindra gets to crying in the background. Minny hang up the phone without saying goodbye. I don't know what she talking about a pie. But Law knowing Minny, it could not have been good. (Stockett 21)

Not once during this conversation did Aibileen stop to inquire as to why Kindra was in distress. Neither did she speak directly to Kindra to offer her a word of comfort or encouragement. Given Kindra's construction as sassy and grown, she is often denied the protection of the self-proclaimed "other mother" Aibileen. Instead, Kindra is ignored, treated with suspicion, and/or chastised. Consequently, Kindra is denied of innocence primarily because she is seen as "grown" and womanish. Furthermore, Kindra cannot be perceived as innocent because she defies her "place" in white society. A good black girl or woman would celebrate her place, as in the case of Aibileen. Because of her behavior, there is no protection, from the state or individuals, of her decisions as a nonadult; any punishment or suffering she receives is warranted.

Violence as Normalized

In *The Help*, the story of Kindra Jackson and her siblings is also one constructed around the trope of violence and its intersection with race and class. This particular narrative of violence and black girlhood is configured through the language of the family. Kindra's family life is used to suggest that she is "lost" and therefore not worth protecting and nourishing. Instead of protecting Kindra and Minny's other four children, Aibileen hurries away from their violent home while claiming,

As usual, Minny's house be like a chicken coop on fire. Minny be hollering, things be flinging around, all the kids squawking. I see the first hint a Minny's belly under her dress and I'm grateful she finally showing. Leroy, he don't hit Minny when she pregnant . . . "Kindra! Get your butt off that floor!" Minny holler. "Them beans better be hot when your daddy wakes up!"

Kindra—she seven now—she sass-walk her way to the stove with her bottom sticking out and her nose up in the air . . . "Why I got to do dinner? It's Sugar's turn!"

"'Cause Sugar at Miss Celia's and you want a live to see third grade." . . .

"Kindra, I don't want a see so much as a bean setting in that sink when I get back, Clean up good now." Minny give her a hug. "Benny, go tell Daddy he better get his fool self out a that bed." "Awww, Mama why I-"

"Go on, be brave. Just don't stand too close when he come to."

We make it out the door and down to the street fore we hear Leroy hollering at Benny for waking him up. I walk faster so she don't go back and give Leroy what he good for.

"Glad we going to church tonight," Minny sigh. (Stockett 396–97)

However, in discussing finding Mae Mobley in distress, Aibileen states, "but the help always know" (Stockett 5). With her depth of knowledge about comforting (white) children, she then goes on to comfort Mae Mobley. Mae Mobley's mother is characterized as neglectful toward her children. However, she has Aibileen, who serves as a surrogate mother, to protect and nourish the innocence of white girlhood. Because Aibileen serves as a nurturing and protective figure and because the family is not constructed as being consumed by daily violence, Mae Mobley's girlhood is protected. The duality of the construction between white and black girlhood is told via Aibileen:

> "Mae Mobley, you know you're not supposed to climb out of your crib!"
> Baby Girl, she looking at the door her daddy slammed, she looking at her mama frowning down on her. **My baby**, she swallowing it back, like she trying real hard not to cry.
> I rush past Miss Leefolt, pick Baby Girl up . . .
> I lay Baby Girl on the changing able, try to keep my mad inside. Baby Girl stare up at me while I take off her diaper. Then she reach out her little hand. The touch my mouth real soft.
> "Mae Mo been bad," she say.
> "No, baby, you ain't been bad," I sway smoothing her hair back. "You been good. Real good." (Stockett 15; words in bold are my emphasis)

This child, in the eyes of Aibileen, is an extension of her—indeed, she sees Mae Mobley as her baby. She extends to Mae Mobley kindness, love, and tenderness. Aibileen offers her positive affirmations as a means of countering the abuse and neglect this young girl experiences. However, she fails to do so with Kindra. This is because Aibileen plays the stereotypical role of mammy, while Kindra is locked into the role of the angry black girl in whose life violence is the acceptable norm. Kindra is not only violent (or at least has the potential to be violent) but also accustomed to living in violent situations. Thus violence becomes normalized in this girl's life. These two characters, the mammy and the angry black girl, cannot coexist. Consequently, the mammy's role is to eradicate the angry black girl or at least lessen the damage she can inflict on the "innocents" of society.

Race, gender, and class hierarchies and privileges are often communicated via an ideology of difference in terms of cultural norms, practices, and behaviors. As Razack posits, violence is constructed as resulting from cultural norms and practices while often ignoring how structural inequalities promote, encourage, and sustain violence. In representing violence, the white community seems immune; there are no representations of interpartner violence, and the children are shielded from mistreatment by the ever present, all-knowing mammy. This stems from the belief that not only is the black man inherently violent, but black women, in an attempt to protect the black man and family, will endure such violence with little to no challenge. The black family as dysfunctional is then mapped onto not only adults but their children (thus giving way to the culture of poverty argument used to frame our social welfare debates). The futurism of *The Help* suggest that blackness is doomed and ill fated regardless of race, gender, or age.

Surveillance and Muting

Given the discursive constraction of Kindra—who is only seven by the end of the novel and is still clearly a girl, if only in terms of age—one is left to wonder if there is any hope for this child. I argue that, even with Aibileen's surveillance, there seems to be little hope of redeeming Kindra. I turn to Nannie Helen Burrough's National Training School, a model of racial uplift, and the ideology of black female respectability to help me make the argument that Kindra is not redeemable and as such must be constantly surveyed and eventually muted.

The motto of the National Training School was "Bible, Bath and Broom." Stockett (knowingly or unknowingly) employs this model in the construction of Aibileen, who I argue plays the mammy figure. Aibileen was able to play this mammy figure because she is constructed as churchgoing, sexually modest (indeed, she is asexual, as she was abandoned by her husband and has no romantic interest), she is always clean and properly presentable to the white community, and she exhibits strong house-cleaning and child-rearing skills. While Stockett appropriated the motto of the school, she failed to incorporate the activism component (for a detailed analysis of the National Training School, see Wolcott). Although the story takes place during the modern civil rights era, the story omits activism, as Aibileen is given no agency. She is given agency in terms of individual interactions, such as encouraging and teaching Mae Mobley about the civil rights movement. However, she lacks agency in terms of offering a critique of systemic and institutionalized racism and in terms of sensitizing and advising Kindra about her civil rights.

While Stockett fails to give Aibileen such a sensibility, she affords her agency to police other blacks. She employs a rather static and limited understanding of racial uplift in the sense that it is only directed inward to the black community. As such, Aibileen polices other blacks. Aibileen engenders a form of racialized-gendered accommodation. In contrast, even at the age of five, Kindra does not embody such a racialized-gendered accommodation. She is not a dutiful daughter in terms of her biological family and her racial family. This break in attitudes about black obedience to whites suggests a type of panic about black life in this *post*racial, -gender, and -welfare state. If blacks are allowed to question the hierarchies of race, class, and gender, there is a fear that they might rebel and demand equality. Thus Kindra, and real-life black girls, becomes a threat to be eliminated via social policies.

Black women engage in policing and muting other black women in response to white middle-class patriarchal ideals (see Gaines; E. White). This is often thought of as the politics of respectability (Higginbotham). By failing to hear the cries of Kindra, by failing to offer her positive affirmations, and in essence, by seeing her only as pathological, Aibileen sees her as unable to or incapable of engaging in the project of racial uplift. This begs the question, what type of girl is deemed worthwhile to participate in such a project, to engage in such political work? According to Stockett, it is Mae Mobley. There is an expectation that Mae Mobley will be empowered to speak on behalf of those who are subjected to injustices and inequalities. Aibileen teaches Mae Mobley about the civil rights movement; at such a young age, Mae Mobley knows how to protect Aibileen when she is caught teaching her younger brother about civil rights. Mae Mobley is being empowered to enter the public sphere, while Kindra is being groomed to be a domestic worker—and particularly a quiet domestic worker who does not challenge inequalities. In the *post*race, -feminism and -welfare state, a black child like Kindra is being controlled to be silent about and unquestioning of social inequalities and injustices: "As some kind of twisted neoliberal citizenship formation would have it, rather than encouraging Black girls' way with words, they are often not only punished for what they say but also how they say it" (Brown 49).

Conclusion

Black girlhood is often overlooked, categorizing black pubescence in terms of womanhood compared to white girls; black girlhood thus becomes inconsequential and arguably negativized and sexualized perhaps before pubescence. Consequently, "young Black girls also face the fact that not only are they even less visible than White girls in popular culture, [but] those images and representations that do appear tend to be grounded in the controlling images of Black womanhood" (Emerson 88). When *The Help* speaks of black girls, they are constructed as "troubled" and as "failing." Furthermore, the often-negative images imposed on black women's bodies are mapped onto the bodies of black girls. Thus there are really no "black girls"; there are only "black women."

Given the construction of black girlhood in such modern-day depictions in this so-called *post*race, -gender, and -welfare state, there seems to be no future for the bodies of black girls. We are given a hint as to the future of Kindra via her older sister, Sugar Jackson. Sugar also works as a maid—her mother is a maid and her grandmother was a maid. The value of these girls/teens is seen only in their ability to work as "the help": more specifically as "the help" to promoting white interests. These children escape a valuation process that centers on protecting children and encouraging them to soar and do better than the generations before.

If we juxtapose *The Help* and the 1996 and post-1996 welfare reform efforts, in effect, it seems that there is *no* black girlhood. In both instances, black girls (and teens) are never constructed as embodying the characteristics associated with youth—innocence, nonsexuality, and the need for protection and guidance by adults. Instead, in being constructed as infinite adult women, black girls are conniving, inherently sexual beings without sexual maturation; mannish and defying gender norms; and seen as not needing protection; they are combative and hostile to critique even by progenitors.

Thus it should not be surprising that, similar to the policies of the welfare state, *The Help* also suggests the use of surveillance (see Harris for a discussion of the surveillance of girls). Kindra, while being a girl, is characterized as the urban teen mother—a caricature of black teen girls that was used in the 1996 welfare reform discourse. Jordan-Zachery characterizes the urban teen mother image as communicating "the intergenerational transmission of welfare dependency . . .

The *Urban Teen Mother* is the image of selfish desire and bodily urges run amok, coupled with an unquestionable attitude of entitlement associated with the *Welfare Queen*" (45). Kindra, through the eyes of black women, is constructed in a similar manner. In both instances, *The Help* and welfare reform policies suggest that these girls/teens must be controlled. They must be controlled through work (via non–livable wage jobs), marriage, and/or denial of services and protection. These actions are necessary to protect the good members of society—read white interest (see Jordan-Zachery). So in this *post*feminism, -race and -welfare state, black girls are expected to, or required to via public policies, step back and allow others to prosper. When Kindra is placed in the context of the historical and ongoing construction of black women in the United States, it is possible to view her as part of an ongoing and evolving tension. She captures a race-gender tension of the "rightful" place of black women in the United States—culturally, politically, and economically. It is in this manner that black girlhood in *The Help* can be read as a response to a race-gender crisis that, while grounded in slavery, is ever present in contemporary society regardless of the public accomplishments of black women.

Works Cited

Bobo, Jacqueline. *Black Women as Cultural Readers*. New York: Columbia UP, 1995. Print.

Brown, Ruth Nicole. *Black Girlhood Celebration: Toward a Hip Hop Feminist Pedagogy*. New York: Peter Lang, 2009. Print.

Childs, Erica. "Looking behind the Stereotypes of the 'Angry Black Woman': An Exploration of Black Women's Response to Interracial Relationships." *Gender and Society* 19.4 (2005): 544–561. Print.

Cole, Johnnetta Betsch, and Beverly Guy-Sheftall. *Gender Talk: The Struggle for Women's Equality in African American Communities*. New York: One World, Ballantine Books, 2003. Print.

Collins, Patricia Hill. *Black Feminist Thought: Knowledge, Consciousness, and the Politics of Empowerment*. New York: Routledge, 1991. Print.

Crenshaw, Kimberlé. "Mapping the Margins: Intersectionality, Identity Politics, and Violence against Women of Color." *Stanford Law Review* 43.6 (1991): 1241–1299. Print.

Davis, Angela. *Women, Race and Class*. New York: Random House, 1981. Print.

Emerson, Rana. "African-American Teenage Girls and the Construction of Black Womanhood in Mass Media and Popular Culture." *African American Research Perspectives* 8.1 (2002): 85–102. Print.

Gaines, Kevin. "Uplifting the Race: Black Leadership, Politics, and Culture in the Twentieth Century." *Journal of Southern History* 63.2 (1997): 443–444. Print.

Harris, Anita. *Future Girl: Young Women in the Twenty-First Century*. New York: Routledge, 2006. Print.

Healy, Patrick. *New to Campaigning but No Longer a Novice*. October 28, 2008. Web. January 10, 2011.

Higginbotham, Evelyn B. "African-American Women's History and the Metalanguage of Race." *Signs* 17.2 (1992): 251–274. Print.

Jiwani, Yasmin, Candis Steenbergen, and Claudia Mitchell. *Girlhood: Redefining Limits*. Montreal: Black Rose Books, 2006. Print.

Jordan-Zachery, Julia. *Black Women, Cultural Images and Social Policy*. New York: Routledge, 2009. Print.

Lorde, Audre. *Sister Outsider: Essays and Speeches*. New York: Crossing Press, 1984. Print.

Malkin, Michelle. *2 Michelles, 2 Americas*. February 20, 2008. Web. January 10, 2011.

McRobbie, Angela. "Post-Feminism and Popular Culture." *Feminist Media Studies* 4.3 (2004): 255–264. Print.

Murray, Charles. *Losing Ground: American Social Policy, 1950–1980*. New York: Basic Books, 1984. Print.

Neubeck, Kenneth, and Noel Cazenave. *Welfare Racism: Playing the Race Card against America's Poor*. New York: Routledge, 2001. Print.

O'Reilly, Bill, Dave Tabacoff, and Amy Sohnen, prod. "Does Michelle Obama Dislike America?" *FOX News*, February 20, 2008. Web. January 10, 2012.

Razack, Sherene. *Looking White People in the Eye: Gender, Race, and Culture in Courtrooms and Classrooms*. Toronto: U of Toronto P, 1998. Print.

Romano, Lois. *Michelle's Image: From Off-Putting to Spot-On*. 2009. Web. January, 10 2011.

Rozie-Battle, Judith. "African American Girls and the Challenges Ahead." *Journal of Health and Social Policy* 15.2 (2002): 59–67. Print.

Springer, Kimberly. "Divas, Evil Black Women, and Bitter Black Women: African American Women in Postfeminist and Post-Civil Rights Popular Culture." *Interrogating Post Feminism*. Ed. Y. Tasker and D. Negra. Durham, NC: Duke UP, 2007. 248–276. Print.

Stockett, Kathryn. *The Help*. New York: Amy Einhorn Books, 2009. Print.

West, Carolyn. "Mammy, Sapphire, and Jezebel: Historical Images of Black Women and Their Implications for Psychotherapy." *Psychotherapy* 32 (1995): 458–466. Print.

White, Deborah Gray. *Ar'n't I a Woman? Female Slaves in the Planation South*. New York: W. W. Norton, 1985. Print.

White, E. Frances. *Dark Continent of Our Bodies: Black Feminism and the Politics of Respectability*. Philadelphia: Temple UP, 2001. Print.

Wolcott, Victoria. "'Bible, Bath and Broom' Nannie Helen Burroughs's National Training School and African-American Racial Uplift." *Journal of Women's History* 9.1 (1997): 88–110. Print.

CHAPTER 7

Second (and Third, and Fourth . . .) Helpings

Black Women, Size, and Spectacle in *The Help*

Mecca Jamilah Sullivan

Until more recently than I'd like to admit, I constructed my identity in direct opposition to the image of the mammy. As a big black girl who loved to smile, I insisted on playing the father, the neighbor, the gardener—anything but the mother—in games of house. When bandanas were fly in high school, I made sure to rock mine in outlandish neon greens, underscored by purple extensions and lipstick the color of blood. Every chance I got, I made sure the second signal the world got from me—after the unmissable sign of my size—was the clear message: I will not take care of you. To this day, I sometimes suck in my bulges and harden my eyes when white toddlers gurgle at me on the bus, their mothers often looking on with ambiguously pleading smiles.

These were the memories, distant and not so distant, that arose in me while watching *The Help*, Hollywood's adaptation of Kathryn Stockett's novel of the same name, which filled many a black woman with frustration in 2009. Directed by Tate Taylor, the film follows young white college grad Eugenia Phelan (Emma Stone), whose nickname, "Skeeter," signals her status as a misfit: the sweaty, prickly girl in a community of flatironed perfects. (I need not mention that the superskinny Skeeter never really sweats, has pristinely Pantined ringlets, bats her lashes with the best of them, and is damn near *perfect* herself.) Skeeter is a rabble-rouser and decides to make a name for herself as a writer by profiling the domestic servants of her hometown, Jackson, Mississippi. *And oh yeah*, she thinks, *my*

An earlier version of this piece appeared on the *Feminist Wire*. See Sullivan.

writing might help them too. This afterthought of civil rights soon takes center stage as key historical events (particularly the murder of Medgar Evers) converge with her postpubescent awakening about the hard life of her own beloved maid, Constantine (Cicely Tyson), and a pretty white savior is born.

It's a classic American feel-good plot—a narrative of white-faced altruism and silenced black salvation so familiar that American audiences have come to crave it. *Feeling good* on the backs of caricatured black bodies is one of America's greatest compulsions, and *The Help* is poised to deliver contemporary audiences their fix.

Among the domestic workers Skeeter sets out to "help," the most prominent is Aibileen Clark (Viola Davis). Aibileen is the employee of one of Skeeter's frenemies, who ends up gathering subjects for Skeeter and hosting her in her own home while she writes. Viola Davis is startlingly good, as always. I was intrigued by Taylor's choice to give Aibileen a sometimey narrative authority, offering her spots of voice-over throughout the film. But this potentially subversive structure ends up serving more to distance American viewers from civil rights–era racist ideologies than to expose them to poor black women's inner lives. We learn little from Aibileen about her life, less about her pain, and nothing about her anger. But when Skeeter begins reading up on Mississippi's segregation law to research her book project, it is in Aibileen's voice—not Skeeter's—that we hear the elaborate, careful, logic of Jim Crow spelled out.[1] Because to hear phrases like "books shall not be interchangeable between the white and colored schools, but shall continue to be used by the race first using them" from a young white girl's mouth might not feel so good . . . and this is a feel-good movie, after all (*The Help*; "Remembering Jim Crow").

The Help offers several selfless, self-silencing black figures to sate America's addiction to racialized caricature. But as a big black woman, my eyes were fixed on Minny Jackson (Octavia Spencer), Aibileen's loud-mouthed, wide-hipped, and comparatively thick-fleshed best friend. Minny does a lot of work in the movie: she is at once selfless mammy and angry black woman, moral center and comic relief. She helps everyone and everything on the levels of both action and narrative, helping herself only to another glistening piece of fried chicken, as needed.[2] She is the insubordinate Negro who propels the story's plot to its climax; she is also the balm that cuts the tension for viewers by staging her insurrection through a breathtaking blend of comfort food and potty humor. And of course, she brings the comic relief like only big black women can, offering poetic odes to Crisco, cutting people down to size with exaggerated dagger glares, and swallowing slim white women into her hugs, even though she's not really that big. In one scene—the film's lowlight—we see her leaning forward, eyes expanding to light-bulb size as she exclaims, "I sho' do love me some fried chicken!" and then takes an aggressive bite of a glistening drumstick (*The Help*).

Minny is, of course, not the film's only pernicious image package deal. The movie offers a greatest hits of America's black woman iconography: worn brown hands on babies' milkpool skin;[3] a black woman bloodied by an abusive husband named Leroy; the requisite cure-all church scenes; and many, many a bulging eye.

But Minny seems to offer all this in a single package, and more. There is something about the image of the capacious flesh and generous smile of big black women that America cannot get enough of. This is one of our country's many compulsions: a relentless belief in the availability of the big black other to define and pacify the "regular" white self. And no one serves up pacifying comfort like mammy. Her largess and her unthinkability beyond the bounds of the kitchen create white litheness, mobility, and cross-class access. Her indefatigable mirth and tirelessly open arms usher in white emotional complexity, offering a haven for white vulnerability, a receptacle for white anger, and an antidote to white pain. And like any addicted body in search of easy salve, America keeps going back for more and more and more of the bountiful, boundless *all* that mammy has to offer.

To attempt a catalog of the black woman figures that do this work would be exhausting and impossible—and unnecessary. We all know mammy and her iconic progeny. We feel them peeking at us from pancake boxes and cereal ads and cleaning supply commercials and tear-washed talk show sofas.[4] We see so much of them that some of us begin to see them even when they are not there: in black woman media moguls, in the thick-cheeked teenager on the bus, and in ourselves.

I would be remiss if I did not say Octavia Spencer, in the role of Minny Jackson, reminded me of my mother: not in the character's oozy, oafish moments, but when we see her anger, her pain. Truth fully told, in this respect, she reminds me of many black women I know who can deftly communicate disdain in the wrinkle of an eye or the slow downward turn of a frown. This is all a credit to Spencer and what she does with the script. But for Minny Jackson, these subtle executions of power are limited to communications with other black people—with Aibileen, for example, when she first introduces the idea of sharing her stories with little white Skeeter, or with her own daughter, Sugar, whose few seconds onscreen compose the film's only sustained depiction of black familial intimacy. Under white gazes, Minny's moments of self-expression and sophisticated punition are quickly obfuscated by comedy—a sharp turn of the hip and an exaggerated sigh of "Hnh!" or its dialogic equivalent.

This is a stand-in for black female voicing, the gesture toward triumphal expressivity and unsilenced speech that is supposed to give the movie its "feel-good" sheen. And for many people, it does just that. Following the release of the film and the eruption of brilliant black feminist criticism of both the film and novel versions of *The Help*, I've had several conversations with smart black women, many of whom I love and respect, who were glad to "see our stories" and "hear our voices" in Stockett's pseudohistorical-fictive text.

Davis and Spencer themselves joined this chorus of supporters in their February 2012 interview on the PBS television show *Tavis Smiley*, which aired two weeks before the announcement of the 2012 Academy Awards (for which both Davis and Spencer were nominated, with Spencer winning for Best Supporting Actress). In that interview, Davis and Spencer defended themselves, Stockett, and black actors in general against the critiques of figures like Smiley, for whom, as he put it, "there's something that sticks in [his] craw" about celebrating black women actors for roles as domestics several decades after Hattie McDaniel's 1939 Oscar win for her role as mammy in *Gone with the Wind*. "Here we are all these years later," Smiley said to *The Help* actors, "and I want you to win, but I'm ambivalent about what you're winning for" ("Actresses Viola Davis and Octavia Spencer").

The conversation this "ambivalence" sparked among Spencer, Davis, and Smiley illustrates the difficulty America has in looking critically at its cultural iconography and at the image of mammy in particular. Their dialog points to the traps that the rhetoric of representation sets for productive talk about blackness and demonstrates the perils of representation gone wrong. Davis responds immediately to Smiley's critique with the stirring claim that "that very mindset . . . is absolutely destroying the black artist." She continues: "The black artist cannot live in a revisionist place. The black artist can only tell the truth about humanity, and humanity is messy." Thus, for Davis, "If the [black] woman next door killed her baby and was 100 lbs overweight and ate a piece of fried chicken and then went next door and killed someone else, that's what we have to do as black artists." Affirming this obligation, Spencer praises Minny and Aibileen as icons because they offer spaces for big brown women's bodies outside of narratives of pathology. For her, what matters is that they push past the limited roles available for "African-American women, and women of a certain size, women of a certain age" ("and Hue," Davis adds) and that "there's nothing ignoble about what they do." Spencer's list of representational priorities provides a rapprochement of sorts when Smiley echoes her logic, explaining his longing to see "upstanding, outstanding, celebratory African-American figures" onscreen ("Actresses Viola Davis and Octavia Spencer").

Spencer's references to race, gender, size, and age highlight the intersectional dimensions of America's erasures, silencings, and willful misunderstandings of black women and underscore how those intersections are written onto big black female bodies. Yet her crucial critique—which screams from Stockett's screen—is lost to a discussion of "upstanding" black iconography and its presumably damaging, disturbed alternatives. By and large, this conversation presents black pathology as one side of "truth" and black nobility as its distant, partly imaginary foil. The possibilities of greater complexity, emotional range, and subjective nuance within blackness come up only in the subjunctive (i.e., contrary-to-fact) tense, as Davis reflects: "If you were to come to me and say you felt the writing was not balanced . . . that you didn't feel there were a lot of colors to the character[s], that you just saw a blank, flat, unrealistic stereotype, then I would go with you" ("Actresses Viola Davis and Octavia Spencer"). This possibility is quickly buried under debate about the culpability of black producers, rappers, and basketball players for the dearth of positive black representation. Yet Davis's hypothetical critique is precisely what needs to be said about a film like *The Help*. By pitting the longing for "positive" representation against famished celebrations of *any* representation, the conversation misses the major point that is as gleaming and silent as mammy's pie-slice eyes: representation itself is the problem.

Those of us who are "happy" to see these figures can only be happy in relation to what seems like the more common alternative—complete erasure from the American cultural imaginary. But when black women are reduced to vessels of others' "good" feelings, this same erasure claims new reach, evacuating black women of the range of complex emotionality that constitutes the human and presenting them only as foils, conduits, receptacles, and salves for more pressing (i.e., white) emotions, both onscreen and off. So we have mammy, big and strong and smiling steadily over centuries, convincing black women that she represents them and inviting generations of white folks to make of her what they will. And who, in the end, feels good about that?

These images are the opposite of new—they are the dirt from which America's ideas about black women grow. Yet they are here now, as we speak, in wide-eyed, open-armed, wobbly bosomed splendor. And there's much more to come: of the previews shown before the screening I saw, the last was for the crime comedy *Tower Heist* (2011), in which a slimmed-down Gabourey Sidibe (from *Precious: Based on the Novel Push by Sapphire*) plays another two-for-one black female stereotype—the loving, angry, sidekick-of-a-sidekick domestic worker who is also hilariously desirous of sex—opposite Eddie Murphy and Ben Stiller ("*Tower Heist* Movie: Trailer").

America clearly craves these images and doesn't have the *something*—the insight? the willpower? the courage? all of the above?—to do the work, deal with its issues, and get off the stuff. Instead, it contents itself with the mantra "I'm getting better—really, I am" and numbly shoves another big black woman caricature down consumers' throats.

And does this really help anyone? One of the film's recurring motifs is the affirmation Aibileen offers her boss's child, a chubby blond toddler whose face that warns that, as Aibileen puts it, she won't likely "be no beauty queen." To this child, Aibileen delivers the affirmation "You is kind, you is smart, you is important" several times throughout the film. Dialect stereotypes aside, it's a welcome feminist critique in a "civil rights" film ironically lacking in real interrogations of oppression. For that reason, I could not help but hold a sip of breath for some halfway analogous message to reach a black child on screen. The analog? When Minny indoctrinates Sugar with the "rules" of domestic work, number one on the list is "*no sass-talkin'!*" Minny repeats this rule to herself throughout the film as well—"*no sass-talkin'!; no sass-talkin'!*"—as if willing herself to stay on the mammy end of the two-pronged black woman pendulum, even as the red-hot lure of the angry black woman calls (*The Help*).[5] And that's to say nothing of Minny's scatological pie.

And we, the audience, are meant to be content with that. This is supposed to suffice for complexity: a character that embodies two whole stereotypes in one and is funny to boot. For many of us, it is this self-policing face of Minny with which we most identify—the one that says "hold it together; speak carefully and purposefully; don't push me cause I'm close to the . . ." It's the face that's in constant dialogue with the meat it covers, ever reminding the self inside to measure, monitor, and translate its anger. For others—like me—it's the struggle *not to contain my joy*, to insist on experiencing my mirth and generosity on my own terms, that defines my dealings with mammy and her matrix of black female iconography. Either way, black women's lives are rerouted around America's centuries-old expectations, while our elations, despondencies, and rages are beaten beyond recognition—even self-recognition.

This has never been clearer to me than it was during the film's closing credits. The young black woman next to me, who had laughed and cried and murmured convivial "mmhms" at all the chicken jokes, smiled at me as the lights came up, hoping to chat and bond. I thought about sharing my reactions with her. But I knew it would exhaust me (in an already depleted state) and might burst an important bubble for her and mar a dim highlight in a heavy day. So I gave her a deep, genuine smile and turned away, deciding to write down my thoughts instead. And I wondered if that would help anything at all.

Notes

1. For a small sampling of Jim Crow laws arranged by topic, see "Remembering Jim Crow."
2. See "The Mammy Caricature."
3. In the twenty-first century, the United Colors of Benetton's print advertisements have been among the most recognizable of such images. See, for example, "United Colors of Benetton and Its Shocking Adverts."
4. For a humorous critique of the evolution of these images in contemporary commercial culture, see Gay.
5. See "Sapphire Caricature."

Works Cited

"Actresses Viola Davis and Octavia Spencer." *Tavis Smiley*. PBS Thirteen, New York, NY. February 10, 2011. Television.

Gay, Roxane. "A Brief Retrospective of the Pine-Sol Lady." *Thought Catalog*, n.p. April 29, 2011. Web. August 12, 2011.

The Help. Dir. Tate Taylor. Perf. Emma Stone, Viola Davis, Bryce Dallas Howard, and Octavia Spencer. DreamWorks, 2011. Film.

"The Mammy Caricature." *Jim Crow Museum of Racist Memorabilia*. Ferris State University. n.d. Web. August 11, 2011.

"Remembering Jim Crow: Presented by American Radio Works." *American Radio Works*. Publicradio.org. n.d. Web. August 12, 2011.

"Sapphire Caricature: Jim Crow Museum at Ferris State University." *Jim Crow Museum of Racist Memorabilia*. Ferris State University. n.d. Web. August 11, 2011.

Stockett, Kathryn. *The Help*. New York: Penguin, 2008. Print.

Sullivan, Mecca Jamilah. "Second (and Third, and Fourth . . .) Helpings: A Big Black Woman's Thoughts on The Help." *Feminist Wire*. n.d. Web. August 19, 2011.

"*Tower Heist* Movie: Trailer." *Official Site for the Tower Heist Film*. Universal Pictures, n.d. Web. August 12, 2011.

"United Colors of Benetton and Its Shocking Adverts." *Controversial Advertising in the 21st Century*. n.p. January 8, 2008. Web. August 11, 2011.

CHAPTER 8

Mae Mallory and "The Southern Belle Fantasy Trope" at the Cuyahoga County Jail, 21st and Payne/"Pain"

Paula Marie Seniors

Introduction

In Monroe, North Carolina, in 1958, after the attempted rape and brutal beatings of two African American women by white men and the loss of the court cases that sought justice for these crimes, African American women compelled the president of the National Association for the Advancement of Colored People (NAACP), Robert F. Williams, to found the Negroes with Guns Movement. Williams proposed protecting women and children with arms, meeting "violence with violence," and "repel[ing] on the spot attacks by white persons."[1]

In 1961, African American working-class self-defense and radical activist Mae Mallory, a devotee of Williams's Negroes with Guns Movement, traveled to Monroe to support him and the visiting Freedom Riders sent down by the Congress of Racial Equality (CORE) and others to show the effectiveness of passive resistance over self-defense.[2] On Sunday, August 27, 1961, five thousand armed Ku Klux Klan members, including the police, viciously attacked the demonstrators and invaded the heavily armed and trained black community. A Ku Klux Klan couple—the Stegalls—pushed their way into Williams's home, where he sheltered them from angry blacks. They left unharmed.[3] Mallory recalled that Chief Mauney "threatened to have us all hanging by our heels within thirty minutes."[4] Williams and his family abandoned Mae Mallory and made their way to Cuba, Julian Mayfield[5] traveled to Ghana, and Mallory escaped first to New York and then to Cleveland, Ohio.[6] Accused of kidnapping the Stegalls, she was incarcerated in Cleveland at the Cuyahoga County Jail at 21st and Payne/"Pain," where she faced extradition to Monroe.

Mae Mallory spent 13 months in jail, and her writing offered her an important strategy for surviving incarceration. Her writing challenged state repression aimed at those who resist hegemony.[7] Mae Mallory's diary entries "The Gun Moll," "Miss Deep South," and "The Alcoholic Relic"; "Of Dogs and Men" from the *Workers World*; and the pamphlet *Letters from Prison by Mae Mallory: The Story of a Frameup* provide us a window through which to view her inner life and personal experience as one of the many children and women incarcerated at 21st and Payne/"Pain." Using these texts, as well as Kathryn Stockett's *The Help* and Tony Kushner's *Caroline or Change*, I explore how Mallory used her writing to fight white female supremacy in prison and to survive incarceration. I also look at how white women and, in the case of Kushner, white men used the Southern belle fantasy trope and the mammy trope to maintain white privilege to keep African American women in a subjugated position in US society. By exploring *The Help*, *Caroline or Change*, and Mallory's "The Gun Moll," "Miss Deep South," "The Alcoholic Relic," and "Of Dogs and Men," I investigate the historical trajectory of the maintenance of these tropes by white authors such as Joel Chandler Harris in 1800s to the present. By looking at Mallory's writing, as well as the writing of Alice Childress, Louise Thompson, and others, I explore African American resistance to these representations. Finally, this essay excavates a history erased and offers students an alternate narrative of the civil rights movement centered on the self-defense movement to which Mallory belonged, moving away from the palatable and popular civil rights discourse of the passive resistance of Martin Luther King, Rosa Parks, and others.

I will begin with Mae Mallory's discussion of the arrival of "The Gun Moll," "Miss Deep South," and "The Alcoholic Relic" at 21st and Payne/"Pain": "September 1st 1962 I've been here in Cuyahoga County Jail [for] 6 months. [F]or the most part the 6 months were uneventful, except for the delaying of my mail, holding of perishables until they were rotten" the overflowing of cell block 7A, the "quarantine for a case [of] infectious hepatitis," the denial of visitors, and the fact that "[m]ost of us were edgy and a quarrel was very easy to start. At this time I have been in jail here longer than any of the others."[8]

Audrey Proctor and Ruthie Stone of the Monroe Defense Committee found it necessary to lodge a complaint personally with the sheriff over Mae Mallory's ill treatment at 21st and Payne/"Pain": "Miss Proctor pointed out that the committee was received in a very undemocratic way. She said that an appointment was confirmed by her several days ago for five persons, but when a delegation of five showed up only two were permitted to see the Sheriff." They won assurances of a resolution, but the mistreatment continued.[9]

Mae Mallory writes that the arrival of "The Gun Moll," "Miss Deep South," and "The Alcoholic Relic" at 21st and Payne/"Pain" marked a cacophony of chaos instigated by these women through an onslaught of racialized conflict and clashes. According to Mallory, before they came to the jail, little if any racial ruptures occurred. With their ingress, they brought racialized pandemonium and dissension, which compounded tensions that already existed due to overcrowding, *not race*. Mallory indicates that the white supremacist triumvirate "cohorts from the deep south" boasted "of their achievement of getting the colored girls moved out of their rooms and across the hall."[10] They successfully encouraged prison authorities to use racist practices of transferring African American inmates over whites to relieve the overburdened prison.[11]

I would like to suggest that underlying their actions remained the claim of the privileges of white womanhood. Tera W. Hunter, Cynthia Skove Nevels, and Crystal Nicole Feimster all contend that white women participated in the oppression of African American women to claim whiteness, womanhood rights, and power and to raise their status in white society. Skove Nevels adds another layer to the demand for white womanhood rights by arguing that they participated in lynching and racialized violence to assert their white womanhood.[12]

The Use of Tropes of True Womanhood

Like the middle-aged white woman whom the Irish American communist and political prisoner Helen Gurley Flynn met during her stint at Alderson Prison, West Virginia, in the 1950s, "The Gun Moll," "Miss Deep South," and "The Alcoholic Relic" used white womanhood tropes to oppress African American women prisoners. Gurley Flynn recalls that this middle-aged white woman employed true womanhood tropes by "weep[ing] hysterically and protest[ing]" her lot of living with African American prisoners. Her actions gained her the promise from a white officer of a single room in an effort "to calm her" and protect her from the contagion of the black prisoners.[13]

Comparably, by demanding that the state remove the "colored girls" from their presence, "The Gun Moll," "Miss Deep South," and "The Alcoholic Relic" argued that the very sight of the black women impinged on their womanhood and their whiteness. By demanding that the state answer their whims and commands, they successfully negotiated their position from criminal to the Southern belle fantasy trope, fully inhabiting the trope through white female supremacist racism and violence, for the Southern belle could not exist without the two.[14] By controlling their living situation within the prison through white privilege bestowed on them by the state, they claimed an elevated position, masked and obscured their criminality, and asserted white supremacy by positioning themselves above the African American female inmates. Again, the Southern belle could not exist without her oppression of the black subject.

For example, in 1890s Bryan, Texas, Italian American Fannie Palazzo claimed white womanhood privileges by accusing African American Jim Reddick of rape. Due to her Italian heritage, the white authorities did not take her case seriously until she "fainted": a true marker of whiteness and womanhood. Upon the faint, the Anglo community conferred upon her white womanhood status through the suppression of the black using lynching.[15] Similarly, in Kathryn Stockett's über-popular 2010 novel *The Help* (and the movie directed by Tate Taylor), the white female protagonist, Skeeter, like Stockett, aspires for literary success and uses her white womanhood status to achieve this goal. Like Joel Chandler Harris, who appropriated African American folktales for his own gain and to claim a

Southern planter stock heritage (which he did not inhabit, and to erase the stain of his Irishness, given his low caste position as the illegitimate and deserted son of Mary Harris and an Irish laborer), Skeeter/Stockett also exploited the lives of African American women maids by resurrecting the mammy trope for the twentieth and twenty-first century.[16] Skeeter/Stockett offers the fictional Minny Jackson: "short," "big," strong (given she "could probably lift [a] bus over her head"), and manly, because she sits "with her legs splayed" and with her "thick arms crossed."[17] Skeeter/Stockett also appropriated the life of Aibileen Clark, modeled after Aibileen's real-life double, Abilene Cooper, Stockett's brother's maid. For this infraction, Cooper sued Stockett.[18] In *The Help*, Stockett also introduces us to Hilly Holbrook, Celia Foote, and the low-caste white trash Elizabeth Leefolt, who all claim white womanhood status through their ability to hire African American maids.[19] In Jewish playwright Tony Kushner's 2003 Broadway musical *Caroline or Change*, set in 1963 St. Charles, Louisiana, Rose, the Jewish stepmother from Brooklyn of eight-year-old Noah, ascends as a Southern belle given her African American maid, Caroline. Caroline is a 39-year-old divorced mother of four who works all day in the laundry room "sixteen feet below the sea." Noah adores her; he sings that Caroline is king and queen but, most importantly, "stronger than my dad."[20] Thus Harris, Stockett, and Kushner maintain both the mammy trope and the Southern belle fantasy trope. Through their writing and its popularity among readers, they also claim an expertise on blackness, so much so that while Stockett appropriated the life history of Abilene Cooper for monetary gain, Cooper lost her court case; thus the state maintained the white power and privilege of Stockett over the blackness of Cooper's life story.

The Spanish Heritage Fantasy and the Southern Belle Fantasy Trope

The incarcerated white supremacist triumvirate, Fannie Palazzo, the white women in *The Help,* and the Jewish stepmother Rose all positioned themselves at the center of the Southern belle fantasy trope. Similarly, Harris placed himself at the center of Southern planter stock. Like David Gutierrez's and Carey McWilliams's Spanish heritage fantasy, in which the Mexican elite profess to a direct link to Spain to distance themselves from working-class Mexicans and the stigma of being Mexican, the Southern belle fantasy trope contends that *all* Southern white women are in direct line and descendants of the Southern planter class and grew up with the requisite happy, black, corpulent, dialect-spewing, manless, manly, nameless mammy, who took care of their every whim and waited on them hand and foot.[21] The Southern belle fantasy trope fits with the cult of true womanhood trope of the beautiful, innocent, pure, and virginal white woman in need of protection: the antithesis of black womanhood.[22] These tropes conveniently ignore the brutality of the Southern belle; her role in maintaining white power; her subjugation and humiliation of African American women in her service; her active participation in the beating and lynching of black women, men, and children; and her white supremacist savagery.[23] This trope ignores the reality that not all white Southern women *or men* descended from the mythic planter class.

Some—like the white supremacist triumvirate, *The Help*'s Celia Foote, and Joel Chandler Harris—came from the indentured servitude stock or the poor white degraded class and lived and worked side by side with African Americans, with neither the wealth nor the ability to hire a requisite happy, fat, black, compliant maid.[24] Comparable to the Spanish heritage fantasy, some, such as the white supremacist triumvirate and many a Southern belle, positioned themselves at the center of the fantasy to distance themselves from their inherited class position and claim their superiority as the antithesis of African American women.

The Transfer Scheme at 21st and Payne/"Pain"

In 1962, at 21st and Payne/"Pain," the new transfer scheme concocted by "Miss Deep South," "The Gun Moll," and "The Alcoholic Relic" with the aid of the state marked a definitive way in which white supremacist women prisoners claimed whiteness and womanhood. Mallory writes that the new transfer practice broke with the previous custom of moving new inmates over old regardless of color. African American women protested on the grounds that the new transfer scheme remained racist. They tried to induce Chief Narducci to return to the old method. He refused. Mallory recalled that, because of their demands, the police inflicted pain and violence on the African American incarcerated women by dragging two of them "hand and feet" across the floor. Mallory tried to prevent the state-sanctioned savagery against one of the women, and for her actions, Mallory recalled that the new matron "put her feet on my pelvis bone and pushed with all her might" in an effort to crush Mallory physically and emotionally.[25] Mae Mallory's diary indicates that she fully blamed the white supremacist triumvirate for the new transfer practice, the violence, the actions of those in the melee, and vigorous efforts to cause racial strife. But what really incensed Mallory was their bragging about compelling the state to remove the "colored girls" and their uninhibited swanking about: "This was too much. I made a break to chase [The Alcoholic Relic] into her room. Instead of running into her room, she ran for The Gun Moll's room and fell. The matrons on duty were the Tom Stooge and this new white matron [who] had previously kicked me in my pelvis were called. They called the chief and claimed that I had beaten this alcoholic old relic. This charge was substantiated by Miss Deep South and the roommate of the Gun Moll's."[26]

Mae Mallory and Self-Defense

Whether Mae Mallory actually fought with "The Alcoholic Relic" or not, the truth remains that the prison melee in Cleveland illuminated several key strategies used by Mae Mallory, including her physical, psychic, and intellectual resistance to hegemony and state repression. As an advocate for self-defense, it remains unsurprising that Mallory would fight back. A little over a year before she entered prison, she used her body to fight state tyranny at a June 13, 1961, rally at the United Nations protesting the murder of the Republic of the Congo's first prime minister, Patrice Lumumba, and physically defended herself against two white police officers.[27] African American civil rights lawyer Conrad Lynn writes in *There Is a Fountain* that, at the UN rally, "when the police waded in swinging clubs," Mallory "took two policemen and cracked their heads together and knocked them unconscious."[28] By chronicling the prison melee and by physically fighting back at the UN and 21st and Payne/"Pain," Mae Mallory took a stand against white female supremacy, domination, and state authority. She asserted *her rights and her black womanhood*; endured imprisonment; and challenged state, class, and race oppression. The prison clash also elucidated the white supremacist triumvirate's efforts to elevate their class status within the jail by claiming whiteness and womanhood even in the face of *their own* criminality. This leads to the question of how they ended up at 21st and Payne/"Pain."

"The Gun Moll," "The Alcoholic Relic," and "Miss Deep South"

The agitation for all this started when a white woman who reportedly helped to beat and rob an old man (there take was 29 cents) with her boyfriend so they could get money to divorce and exchange spouse[s]. This woman came very pregnant and very boastful of the fact that she was captured with two guns on her. Immediately she started to irritate most of the inmates and expected to ride rough shod over everyone using her pregnancy as protection.[29]

Although a criminal, "The Gun Moll" claimed the cult of motherhood status reserved for white Anglo women, ultimately reconfiguring her class and criminal position. At 21st and Payne/"Pain," she positioned herself within the "Republican motherhood" framework and discarded her low caste status through her pregnancy. She firmly situated herself within this framework to, according to Allison Berg and Marilyn S. Blackwell, provide the nation with citizen sons and daughters as wives for these citizens, thus contributing to the prevention of racial suicide. Berg and Blackwell contend that the "Republican mother" endeavored to keep "her body pure for racial reproduction" and protect the nation from the black and the Southern and Eastern European mothers who overproduced.[30] For "The Gun Moll," this also meant discarding her criminality. The "Republican mother" was charged with, according to Blackwell, "ensuring the virtue of future generations" and, as eugenicist Albert Edward Wiggam wrote in *The Fruit of the Family Tree*, becoming a vessel for the creation of a great race, the ultimate "guardian of the blood."[31] Ultimately, "The Gun Moll" positioned herself as the definitive mother at 21st and Payne/"Pain" in full need of protection and special treatment, because she protected the nation and the jail from African American women.

Mae Mallory presents the second member of the white supremacist triumvirate: "Another old cohort was The Alcoholic Relic [who] was brought in on a drunk charge. This old relic would agitate and annoy [everyone]."[32] Mallory muses, "This ancient one would wear hard bottom shoes at breakfast time and clomp around making as much noise as possible," deliberately disturbing the inmates.[33]

Finally, Mae Mallory introduces us to the third member of the triumvirate: "Miss Deep South." Mallory writes that she "thought [the African American inmates] delighted in her talk about the nice old colored lady that used to work for her mother. This nice old colored lady died on the day of this inmate's graduation from high school."[34] With this story, "Miss Deep South" lets the African American women prisoners know that she and society relegates them to the low-caste worker stock in charge of taking care of white folks. Her remembrances were not unusual, given the attempt to maintain white power. Irish American Helen Gurley Flynn detailed her encounters with white Southern women at Alderson Prison who attempted to maintain white supremacy through the mammy trope: "White women from the South were particularly obnoxious, expecting Negro women to wait on them, work for them," and even service them sexually. She writes that they treated African American women "rudely and contemptuously."[35]

Stockett's final chapter of *The Help*, "Too Little Too Late," resembles "Miss Deep South's" and Gurley Flynn's story and offers us a way to view the maintenance of the Southern belle fantasy trope and the black mammy trope. Stockett, a self-described rich white girl who grew up in Mississippi *in the 1970s*, takes great pleasure in telling the readers that she wrote the novel about black mammies in Mississippi in the 1960s to honor her *very own colored maid*, Demetrie, a "stout," "dark skinned" mammy who, like her novelistic doppelgänger and "Miss Deep South's" black maid, conveniently died when Stockett was in her teens. This is convenient because neither "Miss Deep South's" nor Stockett's maid lived to tell *her story*, and thus white women can claim an expertise on African American womanhood and build the perfect black mammy grateful for their silence due to death.

By introducing the readers to the white supremacist triumvirate, Mae Mallory resists the mammy trope and continues this resistance through her essay "Of Dogs and Men."

"Of Dogs and Men"

While incarcerated at 21st and Payne/"Pain," Mae Mallory wrote "Of Dogs and Men" in 1962 as a riff on *Of Mice and Men*, a groove on Robert Burns's "To a Mouse": "The best laid schemes of mice and men often go awry."

> Just recently, I read of the case of a dog fighting for his life in the courts. This dog is accused of killing six sheep. For this the courts have ordered him to be put to death. The case is now before the Supreme Court. Chances are that this dog will be allowed to remain in its home pending the outcome of litigation.
>
> I, too, have a case before the United States Supreme Court. But look where I have to stay pending the outcome of litigation. For many months, I have been locked up in the Cuyahoga County Jail, denied the companionship of my family and friends. This dog is actually accused of killing six sheep. I killed no one. I am guilty of no crime. But the charge against me is kidnapping a white couple. This couple was protected and given safe conduct out of an enraged community.

> Nevertheless, this constituted kidnapping in the eyes of the racists. This dog will probably get more consideration from the courts than I will.[36]

In "Of Dogs and Men," Mallory wrote of the effort by a white supremacist woman to maintain the status quo during World War II in New York City: "An [upper middle class] white woman I used to babysit for when I was but a teenager once said that having me around was like having a pet."[37] Mallory's employer regarded her in the same way that white elites viewed Chinese houseboys of nineteenth-century San Francisco and black women of Mallory's historical milieu of New York's Bronx Slave Market (1930s–1940s). Chinese houseboys/domestics symbolized upper-class position and wealth for white folks who prized these "men" as status symbols. One man, Younghill Kang, experienced dehumanizing treatment because the whites he worked for treated him as one would treat a house pet. African American women day laborers found themselves treated similarly.[38] According to Dayo Gore and Erik McDuffie, due to the economic downturn of the 1930s and the loss of jobs within World War II industry in the 1940s, African American women found themselves relegated to selling their labor daily (day work) on the street corners of New York City to predatory white women, who undermined their dignity and humanity to maintain white womanhood rights, a la the Southern belle fantasy trope, New York style.[39] Analogous to African American women slaves who, through their exploited labor, made it possible for white woman to fit snugly within the Southern belle fantasy trope, African American leftists Marvel Cook and Louise Thompson Patterson contended in "The Bronx Slave Market"(1935) and "Toward a Brighter Dawn" (1936), respectively, that black women domestics in New York also enabled white middle- and upper-class women to sustain their positions in society, with those of a lesser social ilk elevating their status through African American women's labor. Ultimately, by hiring black maids *all white women* undergirded their identity, white supremacist ideologies, and "class privilege."[40] Like African American women in the Bronx Slave Market, whom white women treated as commodities and undressed with their eyes to, according to Cook, "measure their strength to judge how much work they [could] stand" and whom they bought at an undercut price as one would "a cow or horse in the public market," Mae Mallory's presence in the white woman's household symbolized these black women and that of the ornamental Chinese houseboy.[41] By defining Mallory as a pet, the white supremacist woman ensured Mallory's position in the white household as the personification of the ultimate trophy domestic, stripped of her humanity. Her pet status in the household ultimately allowed the white woman to uphold hegemonic power.

In "Of Dogs and Men," Mae Mallory considers her transfiguring from human to pet as well as the other identities that black domestics hold in the mind's eye of white women: "I wondered about that statement [that having me around was like having a pet]. For it was different. The usual statement of this nature concerning a Black servant goes something like 'She's just like one of the family.'"[42] Consequently, Mallory reflects on the dual identity of the black servant as dog and honorary family member, which is very much in line with the honorary white status that some nonwhites held in South Africa during apartheid.

Working-class African American leftist, activist, actress, and intellectual writer Alice Childress's African American domestic, Mildred, in *Just Like One of the Family*, set in 1956 New York City, helps us understand Mallory's metamorphosis from human to pet. Childress modeled Mildred after her militant Aunt Lorraine and drew on her own experience as a domestic.[43] According to Trudier Harris, Childress's exit from domestic service remained quite dramatic, for she "surprised her employer by throwing keys at her head," her insurgent approach to resigning. Notwithstanding or perchance because of this transgression of decorum, the white woman wanted her to return to work![44] Accordingly, Mildred's rebellious spirit emerges from Childress and Aunt Lorraine's work life. Similar to Mallory, Mildred found herself confronted with the dual identities of dog and honorary family member. In the story, Mildred could not help but hear Mrs. C., the white woman she worked for, brag loudly and purposely to her friend and for Mildred's benefit that "we *just* love her! She's *like* one of the family."[45] Mildred, like Mallory, felt that something more lay within this statement, that Mrs. C. transformed Mildred into an anthropomorphic pet rather than a family member. Mildred, with an insurrectionary nature reminiscent of the Louisiana slave uprising of 1811, Sojourner Truth, Harriet Tubman, Frederick Douglass, and Nat Turner and with a sharp tongue, upbraided Mrs. C.: "You are a pretty nice person to work for, but I wish you would please stop talkin' about me like I was a *cocker spaniel* or a *poll parrot* or *kitten*." Thus Mildred fully rejects Mrs. C. situating her as a prized pet.[46] The teenaged Mae Mallory also questioned the designation of pet: "This time it was like having a pet around the house. The usual American household pet is a dog. Could this woman have intended to imply that having me around the house was like having a dog around? No doubt she did!"[47] Like the African American women at the Bronx Slave Market whom white women treated as merchandise, undressed with their eyes, and bought as one would buy livestock, Mallory discovered that she *too* symbolized a treasured and prized animal—no less, no more.[48]

Both Mildred and Mallory discovered a way to push back against the efforts to dehumanize them. Mildred informed Mrs. C. that she *was* "not *just* like one of the family at all," for she remained confined to eating in the kitchen while the white family ate in the dining room. Unlike the fantasy rendering of *The Help*, where Celia Foote and her husband inconceivably break with white Southern custom and sit Minny down to a meal *and serve her*, Mildred could not entertain guests in the parlor as Mrs. C.'s son did, she could not borrow the lace like Mrs. C.'s mother did, she could not nap in the living room like little Carol did, *and unlike the dog* she could not sleep on the satin spread. She told Mrs. C. that she cleaned, cooked, and kept the house, and that "if I dropped dead or had a stroke you would get somebody to replace me," so no, Mildred argued she was not like one of the family but rather a servant due a raise![49] Like Alice Childress, who rendered her resignation by assaulting her white female employer with keys only to find that for this transgression in decorum she received an invitation to return to work, Mildred's employer promised to ask her husband about a raise for Mildred. Mildred personified black women domestics whom Louise Thompson contended advocated for "freedom and dignity" and whom African American leftist Esther Cooper Jackson characterized as both oppressed and revolutionary. Jackson and Thompson founded the Domestic Workers Union to buffer black women workers. Thompson argued that these black women remained at the center of "transformative change," "challenged prevailing cultural representations of black women domestics as servile and unworthy of protection," and *fought back*.[50] Mae Mallory epitomized Mildred and other domestics as she rallied against white female supremacy through "Of Dogs and Men." Through writing, Mallory, Childress, Thompson, and Jackson resisted white writers' discourse about the black maid. Another way in which white female supremacists attempt to suppress and control the black maid is through the concept of love between the black maid and her white charge.

Love, Wage, and the Colored Maid

In "Too Little Too Late," Kathryn Stockett earnestly expresses the belief that Demetrie, *her very own colored maid*, remained "lucky to have us [the white family to work for]. A secure job in a nice house cleaning up after white Christian people."[51] Demetrie, she contends, remained lucky because she "had no babies of her own, and we felt like we were filling a void in her life," and "if anyone asked her how many children she had, she would hold up her fingers and say three. She meant us: my sister, Susan, my brother, Rob, and me."[52] How magnanimous of Stockett, how noble, how astute, and how sickeningly altruistic. Stockett, in maintaining the mammy trope, remains convinced that Demetrie loved the little white children in the family, but especially little homely Kathryn. Stockett, and legions of others who maintain the mammy trope, never give a thought to the reality of the relationship. Alice Childress resists this concept. Childress's Mildred contextualizes the relationship—Mrs. C. bragged loudly to her friend that Mildred "*just adores* our little Carol!" Mildred felt compelled to inform her "I do not *just* adore your little Carol. I think she is likeable, but she is also fresh and sassy."

> *Luckily* my mother taught me some inhibitions or else I would smack little Carol once in a while when she's talkin' to you like you're a dog, but as it is I just laugh it off the way you do because she is *your* child and I am *not* one of the family. Kushner offers a similar stance of resistance. Caroline in *Caroline or Change* does not hold warm sentimental feelings for Noah who remains constantly under foot in the basement where she tells him "Now muse yourself, I got no use for you. This basement too darn hot for two."[53]

When Noah leaves his holiday money of twenty dollars in his pants pocket and he demands that Caroline return it, her initial inclination is to return it—notwithstanding the fact that his stepmother humiliatingly gave Caroline permission to keep any money left in the laundry in order to teach Noah not to carelessly leave money in his pockets. Because of the mounting viciousness in

Noah's tone, she refuses to return the twenty dollars as she sings, "Now I can take my boy to the dentist!, Now I can buy real presents for Christmas."[54] Noah responds,

> There's a bomb!
> President Johnson has built a bomb
> Special made to kill all Negroes!
> I hate you!
> I hate you
> Kill all Negroes!
> Really! For True!
> I hope he drops his bomb on you!
> Caroline.[55]

Without a word to the family, Caroline does not return to work, but she soon must return for financial needs. When Noah tries to make amends in the basement and asks, "Will we be friends then?" Caroline answers, "Weren't never friends."[56] To further understand the relationship between the black maid and white child, Mae Mallory's experience offers an abject lesson. In "Of Dogs and Men," the white children remain nonentities, nonexistent, faceless, and nameless; they do not register or play *any* role in Mallory's story. Therefore Mallory fully contests the contention that love exists between the black mammy and the child. How can anything exist when the child does not exist in the narrative?

As Alice Childress's *Just Like One of the Family*, Tony Kushner's *Caroline or Change*, and "Of Dogs and Men" illustrate, and according to Evelyn Nakano Glenn, "caring has been mythologized as love, rather than labor, as a private matter, and as an activity natural to women" ultimately unworthy of proper pay because the maid in this business arrangement is defined as "part of the family." Mildred so aptly asserts, "I do not feel like no weekend guest. I feel like a servant" in need of a raise. Or, as in many cases, she is an invisible member, with no name and no social life.[57] Comparably, *In Raising Brooklyn*, Mose Brown discusses the concept of maid work in the twenty-first century as caring work. She writes of how white families in Brooklyn exploit West Indian maids who work for them by "asking providers to work later than usual by making them feel as if all 'family' members had to chip in."[58] Nakano Glenn aptly notes that "caring work" in the United States was and is ultimately performed under "conditions of un-freedom and dependency," beginning with African enslavement and the tracking of African Americans, Mexicans in the West, and Japanese in Hawaii into domestic labor as children. This is similar to the African American nurse who reported in 1912 that she began working at the age of ten or the case of Hawaiian plantation owners who coerced Japanese workers to give them a wife or daughter to care for their white children. The consignment to "caring work" ultimately shut these women out high school, college, and other forms of labor and education.[59]

But back to Kathryn Stockett, who laments that alas—alas—she never asked Demetrie "what it felt like to be black in Mississippi, working for our white family," nor about her dreams or her aspirations.[60] Stockett centers the question on the white family, not on a singularly African American life unencumbered by whites. It never occurs to her that perchance Demetrie wished for a life free from this white family, that she held fast to the idea of family and a life for herself. That Caroline in *Caroline or Change* might want to stay home and *raise her own children* rather than find herself confined to a below-sea-level laundry room. That Mildred in *Just Like One of the Family* does not like her little charge or that, in the teenaged Mallory's case, these children do not exist or register in her universe.

Tony Kushner's *Caroline or Change* remains in conversation with Gurley Flynn's, "Miss Deep South's," and Stockett's accounts. The Jewish playwright regales the playgoers with the story of eight-year-old Jewish Noah and African American Caroline in 1963 St. Charles, Louisiana.[61] The play is a reminiscence of sorts of Kushner's childhood growing up with *his own* requisite black maid. In the play, Caroline remains confined to the basement laundry room "sixteen feet below the sea," with singing appliances, washing machines, dryers, and African American women and male performers who magically metamorphose into super mammies and super Uncle Toms.[62] Think about it! Kushner gives Broadway audiences and white supremacists their idealized dream of black womanhood as singing working machines, the definitive representation of the mammy reminiscent of the stereotype of the happy singing slave, the ultimate stage Negro that materialized after slavery to make the argument that African Americans "liked" being slaves, that it was good for them.[63] Caroline makes thirty dollars a week, like her real-life doppelgängers described by Mose Brown; Nakano Glenn; 1912's "More Slavery in the South"; Marvel Cook's "The Bronx Slave Market"; Claudia Jones's 1949 "An End to the Neglect of the Problems of the Negro Woman"; and the *New York Times* articles by Kirk Semple, Monique P. Yazigi, and Constance Hays. They all contend that black maids make below the minimum wage and experience exploitation given that they work more than fifty hours during the week.[64] Or, as Mae Mallory wrote in "Of Dogs and Men," "for both the lady and her dog to be dressed in mink and 'go strolling down Fifth Avenue' was considered smart. But if I were paid a decent salary by her, it would be considered stupid; if I would have demanded more money, it would have been considered impudent. The dog really led the best life."[65]

Mae Mallory's experience challenges us to consider the government's role in ensuring unfair labor practices aimed at keeping nonwhite domestics in a marginal position in US society by defining domestic work and "babysitting" as not real work. The government denied these workers Social Security through the 1935 Social Security Act, which excluded domestics and farmworkers from coverage, the majority of whom were black, Asian, and Mexican. The ultimate refusal by Congress in 1974 to define households as workplaces and domestics as workers rather than as family members excluded them from protection under the 1938 Fair Labor Standards Act and sealed the fate of nonwhite domestics as exploitable, low-wage laborers.[66] This, according to Nakano Glenn, ensured "the ideology of caring work" as not work "and therefore not deserving of protection and entitlements formalized by U.S. legal and regulatory structures." These laws and acts ultimately maintained African American, Mexican, and Japanese domestics as a working poor class, very much like Caroline in *Caroline or Change*, Mildred of *Just Like One of the Family*, and the Bronx Slave Market domestics.[67]

Politics, the Black Maid, and the Reality/Her Life

Caroline in *Caroline or Change* remains uninterested in the civil rights struggles going on around her, while her daughter admires Martin Luther King Jr. and Noah's Brooklynite grandfather envisions African Americans leading the revolution, a stance very much in line with the Trotskyist Workers World Party.[68] Similarly, *The Help* trivializes the civil rights struggle, conflating it to a struggle by black domestics to use white folks' toilets. Unable to conduct their own battle, they rely on white Southern belle Skeeter to lead the charge. Stockett puts white women at the center of the civil rights movement, when in reality the white women of Jackson, Mississippi, remained active participants in maintaining white supremacy through Jackson's Citizens' Council; they were the Ku Klux Klan in dresses and suits. They held positions of power like Marion Simpson, an officer, and Mrs. Sara McCorkle, the director of women's activities.[69]

Some, like "A Southern Lady," wrote for *The Citizen Council* of the African American threat and of maintaining segregation: "Do not belong to or make contributions to any group which advocates either present or future 'integration' or 'de-segregation . . .' Do belong to and do contribute to your community Citizens Council. Do your part to help multiply the strength that lies only in responsible organization by taking a public stand with those dedicated thousands of men and women who say '**It shall not happen here**'" (author's emphasis).[70]

Unlike Stockett's or Kushner's representations, African American women remained leaders in civil rights activism, worked for revolutionary change, and paid the price. Mamie Till Bradley sought justice for the 1955 murder of her son Emmett Till in Money, Mississippi. Fannie Lou Hamer, who worked as a child sharecropper in Mississippi, experienced sterilization, acted as the vice chairperson for the Mississippi Freedom Democratic Party in 1964, and faced brutal beatings by white supremacist police officers for her efforts.[71] In 1957, Mae Mallory sued to desegregate the New York City schools on her children's behalf. For her efforts, Mallory believed and the records confirm that the state targeted and incarcerated her for accepting $1,040 in welfare checks between July 1952 and March 1953 while working for six weeks (ironic, for the tax form is a 1040). Her FBI files verify this claim that the state actively worked to suppress her activism over a twenty-year period (or longer).[72] Mallory also rallied for communism in her union job and supported Fidel Castro, Patrice Lumumba, and third-world revolutions. She joined and then rejected the Communist Party and the Black Nationalists movement, became a devotee of the Negroes with Guns Movement, and founded the Crusader Family in Harlem to support them.[73] African American women in Louisiana also remained active in the civil rights movement. They held prominent positions in the NAACP, advocated for equitable pay for black teachers and equitable segregated schools, participated in voter registration drives, and paid the poll tax to vote. For their advocacy, the Citizens' Council successfully disenfranchised them and threatened them with the loss of their jobs for encouraging integration in high school or colleges, one of the key objectives of the NAACP. The Citizens' Council shut down the Louisiana NAACP for ten years.[74] The fictional renderings in *Caroline or Change* and *The Help* of impotent African American women does not resemble the real-life activism of these women or the price that many of them paid, like Mae Mallory, who in 1962 found herself confined to 21st and Payne/"Pain" in Cleveland, Ohio, subjected to the provocation of the white supremacist triumvirate and forced to listen to stories of "colored maids" who serviced "Miss Deep South." So how did African Americans fight back against the Southern belle fantasy trope and the mammy stereotype?

Pushing Back against the Southern Belle, the Black Mammy, and the White Supremacist Triumvirate

At 21st and Payne/"Pain," Mae Mallory discovered a way to resist white supremacy and the cacophony of chaos that was "Miss Deep South" and the white supremacist triumvirate. After "Miss Deep South" told the story of her "colored maid," Mallory wryly and with an ironic tone took great pleasure in relaying the story of *her white manservant*: "I informed [Miss Deep South] of the drunk old white man that worked for my mother and washed our windows because we lived on the twelfth floor, this immediately caused her to dislike me."[75]

By introducing the ever-loyal and loving white manservant, Mae Mallory played havoc with and vanquished "Miss Deep South's" hyperstereotypical rendering of black womanhood reflected through the requisite colored maid. By transforming the mammy into a white manservant, Mae despoiled the Southern belle fantasy trope by emasculating white men through black women's work, the ultimate humiliation for white supremacists. Mallory's white manservant worked to avenge African American women and the Chinese houseboy by reinvigorating black women with the tropes of true womanhood and infusing the Chinese houseboy with virile masculinity. No doubt the revelation of a white manservant catering to the whims of Mallory's African American family caused "Miss Deep South" to not only dislike Mae Mallory but despise her because Mallory rendered "Miss Deep South's" colored maid immaterial and irrelevant, which annihilated the Southern belle. Lest we forget, the Southern belle cannot exist without the antithetical, the antidoppelgänger mammy. Mallory ultimately disempowered "Miss Deep South" and the white supremacist triumvirate by rendering them incorporeal. She destroyed all notions of the hegemonic work hierarchy of color by flipping the script with the ever-loyal white manservant who proved his love of the black family in a fantastic feat of dexterity, prowess, and drunken splendor by washing the family's twelfth-floor windows on the outside of the building, acting as a human crane. Mallory's white manservant puts to rest any notion that people of color belonged at the bottom rung of society, forever in love with and in service to white folk.

"Of Dogs and Men" (November 1962) also acted as a form of resistance to white female supremacy and the white woman in New York who equated the teenaged Mallory to that of a household pet to sustain white women's status.[76] "Of Dogs and Men" taught us all that "pets" do bite and fight back. Mallory recalled that the white woman she worked for lived in a "No Dogs or Negroes Allowed" upper-middle-class apartment building. Mallory heard they considered allowing dogs, but "never had I heard a conversation about allowing Negroes." She also noted that some New York apartments allowed dogs to enter through the front entrance with or without their owners. Mallory elucidates that this indulgence did not apply to African Americans. Thus begins her sardonic push back against white supremacist rules and regulations: "When I was without my little charges I was instructed to use the 'Service Entrance.' Since I did not come to service the building, I paid no heed to such instructions and went brazenly through the front door. And no one raised a fuss! After all, a war was going on— and Afro-Americans were in it 'Fighting for Democracy.' Come to think of it, so were some dogs."[77]

Mallory knowingly and humorously comes to the following conclusion about the binary identities assigned her: "For after thinking about it and making a comparison of my life with that of the pooch's I found out that I could not only compare very well my life with this animal but I could also contrast it, with great similarity, the lives of Afro-Americans in general with those of America's most favorite household pets."[78]

And with this statement, Mae Mallory begins her critique of 1961 US systems of inequality affecting African Americans. She determines that "interestingly enough, from the comparison, I found out that it is the dog that leads the best life. Yes, perhaps the lady was right!"[79] Mallory's assertion proves true, for as a teenaged babysitter Mallory wore a threadbare coat while she observed white women on Fifth Avenue and their dogs attired in matching mink coats. Let us not forget that in *Just Like One of the Family*, the dog sleeps on a "satin spread."[80] Mallory contests her situation as a working-class girl confined to wearing a coat unsuitable to the New York weather and the utter absurdity, inhumanity, and waste of a dog and master in mink. It is at this point that "Of Dogs and Men" develops as a protest of ignominy, dehumanization, and the African American condition due to entrenched white supremacy and structural and institutional racism. Linking African Americans and dogs, Mallory writes, "Most negroes do not choose to lead a dog's life—whether it is as a lap dog, hunting dog, or one from the kennel. They do not want scraps from the master's table, neither crumbs, neither do we choose to be masters—only master of our fate. The thinking the Black man in America realizes [is] that he needs liberation. We live in shacks that no self-respecting dog would appreciate."[81]

Mallory cleverly connects African Americans to the varying breeds of dogs while simultaneously arguing that, unlike the dog, they don't want scraps in the form of substandard housing, low wages, and poverty; they don't choose supreme power over all but instead want agency and human rights. As Nina Simone sang, "You don't have to live next to me, just give me my equality."[82] Paradoxically,

Mallory suggests that while the dog readily takes leftovers from the table, the dog would not appreciate the housing of the African American poor.

Mae Mallory defines the different types of dogs by offering that Charlie Wilson, the head of General Motors, preferred hunting dogs ("dogs that feed their masters") rather than kennel dogs (dogs that "expected to be fed"). Consequently, Mallory points out that at GM, Wilson only hired African Americans as menials, thus his hiring practices reflected his belief that African Americans personify "hunting dogs" and should remain part of the low caste in US society.[83] Mallory's understanding of Wilson's stance and her support of African Americans labor issues at GM remained longstanding, as well as the union's support of Mallory. In 1963 in Detroit at the Northern Negro Grass Roots Leadership Conference, they made a resolution to support Mallory in her fight against extradition to Monroe. At the conference, Cleveland's CORE and Freedom Fighters also proposed a nationwide boycott of GM's Cadillac division such as the one already in effect in Cleveland. They suggested protesting unfair hiring practices that prevented African Americans from working as salesman, mechanics, and office staff.[84] One thing that Wilson did not anticipate in defining dog types or temperament was that when abused all dogs bite back and wound, as Mallory's critique of Wilson in "Of Dogs and Men," the 1963 GM boycott in Cleveland, and the organizing around labor issues by CORE, the Freedom Fighters, and the Northern Negro Grass Roots Leadership Conference indicate.

The Show Dog

> The average Afro-American does not want the People's Republic of China kept out of the United Nations, he does not support the blockade of Cuba, nor does he feel the need of an Atomic War to protect imperialistic interests. It is only the show dog and those that aspire to be show dogs who support these causes.[85]

Mae Mallory continues her groove on the relationship between dogs and African Americans by introducing the show dog. She writes that the state uses the show dog African American diplomats in Africa, Asia, and Latin America to vote against third-world independence, and with this she reveals the complicity with hegemony that some middle-class blacks use to gain power on the backs of the black working class and poor.

The relationship between African American diplomats and the State Department remained a complex one given that African Americans who wanted to serve found themselves fighting on two fronts—white racism and entrée into the diplomatic core given that the Eisenhower administration, the Kennedy administration, and the Johnson administration remained reticent to assign ambassadorships to African Americans because of the thought that blacks could not pass security clearance without the taint of communism sullying their record. By 1962, only two African Americans held diplomatic posts: Mercer Cook in Niger and Clifton Wharton in Norway. Given the difficulty of obtaining these posts, it remains questionable whether they held the type of power that Mallory suggests.[86] Perhaps Mallory referenced the cultural ambassadors like African American trumpeter Louis Armstrong, sent overseas in the hopes of arguing that African Americans did not experience oppression. This eventually backfired when, upon the murder of four black girls in Birmingham, Louis Armstrong refused to act as an ambassador.[87]

Mallory also exposes the eruptions of third-world revolutions and the explosion of revolutionary thought occurring in Africa, Asia, Latin America, and the Middle East. Mae Mallory uncovers the fear this most certainly instilled in the United States and Europe and the labor put forth both overtly and covertly to extinguish these revolutions as occurred in the Belgian Congo.[88] "Of Dogs and Men" acts as a continuation of Mallory's preincarceration writing and advocacy conjoining third-world revolutions with African American civil rights.[89] It also works as a form of resistance to white female supremacy and violence that she experienced at 21st and Payne/"Pain" at the hands of the white supremacist triumvirate and the administrators. Finally, "Of Dogs and Men" continues Mallory's critique of some middle- and upper-class African Americans who gain materially without concern for the black working class or poor. Mae Mallory offers that the show dog sold out African Americans to the world by promoting "foolish propaganda on how well the Black man is treated in America" and the "progress we are making." At a time when African Americans experienced violence from white supremacists and dire social economic conditions, Mallory contends that when confronted by the "Black Masses" about his complicity in upholding hegemony, the show dog runs to "his master for support," and the master either offers reassurance, throws him out, or throws him a bigger bone. Mallory concludes that "dogs are never made to stoop so low."[90]

In connecting the dog's life to that of African Americans, Mae Mallory reveals the African American condition: as a babysitter, she made low wages, and African Americans made poverty wages, experienced high unemployment "many months of the year," suffered infant mortality rates significantly higher than those of whites, and "[could not] afford proper medical care." Mae Mallory, in effect, reveals persisting issues in the African American community, presaging the state of African Americans in the late twentieth and twenty-first century. She elucidates the links of inequality over time.[91] She also evoked the refusal by Cuyahoga County in 1962 to offer her proper medical care at 21st and Payne/"Pain" as reported in the June 22 *Workers World* newspaper. This led Ruthie Stone and Audrey Proctor of the Monroe Defense Committee to file a complaint with the sheriff, who assured them that "the committee will be allowed to provide a private physician to examine Mrs. Mallory for treatment."[92] Mallory continues her discussion of the African American situation in "Of Dogs and Men": "We still fill the jails and hang on trees until we are dead. Our bodies are still found in bags weighted with concrete at the bottom of rivers. Our arms, heads, and legs are still being severed from our bodies. And we are still being found in rivers—no water in our lungs—dead. These deaths are always 'accidental' heart attacks, or of 'natural causes. No investigations needed.'"[93]

Mae Mallory reminds us of her own incarceration and alludes to the 1962 shooting of voter registration workers in Mississippi; the wounding of more than one hundred people and the death of two by US soldiers on the University of Mississippi campus because of James Meredith's acceptance to the school; and the suspicious 1962 death by "drowning" in South Carolina of twenty-year-old Raymond Johnson, son of the Mrs. E. A. Johnson, editor of the Negroes with Guns *Crusader* newspaper.[94] Mallory's observations act as a portent of the concerted effort to keep African Americans in a marginal position in society in the twentieth and twenty-first centuries, the building and funding of prisons rather than schools, the creation of schools as conduits to prison for African American and Hispanic or Latino/a students, and high incarceration rates that point to the fact that more blacks remain in prison today than during slavery.[95] By detailing the lynching of African Americans during her historic time period, the complicity of the state in these murders, and the lack of investigations or punishment for these crimes, Mallory's discloses these very same issues in the twenty-first century: the 1997 murder by dragging of James Byrd of Jasper, Texas; the 2006 murder of Sean Bell of Queens, New York; the 2007 kidnapping, rape, torture, and ripping out of hair of Megan Williams of Charleston, West Virginia; the 2012 murder of Trayvon Martin of Sanford, Florida; the 2012 cross-burning at African American women's homes in Swansea, South Carolina; and the 2012 attempted assault by car of black women joggers by a white woman in Salt Lake City, Utah.[96] Mae Mallory sums up the African American condition and concludes, "These things shouldn't happen to a dog. But they do happen to Negroes in America."[97]

Conclusion

"The Gun Moll," "Miss Deep South," and "The Alcoholic Relic"; "Of Dogs and Men"; *The Help*; and *Caroline or Change* all delve into the maintenance of the mammy trope, the Southern belle fantasy trope, and beyond while revealing these very same issues in the twenty-first century. We must question the resurrection of the mammy in the twenty-first century in literature and film, especially given that the very sophisticated, urbane, über-educated African American First Lady Michelle Obama resides and works in the White House. It appears that the response to an African American First Lady by white supremacists writers, filmmakers, and others manifests in the reemergence of the mammy, because they believe that African American women stepped out of place: that the only place for a black woman in the White House is the kitchen. Thus they resurrect the mammy to put African American women back in the kitchen.

While Kathryn Stockett, Tony Kushner, "Miss Deep South," Joel Chandler Harris, and legions of others re-create and reinvent the mammy stereotype, the *actual* lives of African American women domestic workers remain more intriguing because of their agency, their resistance to hegemony and white supremacy, and their efforts to make social and political change in their lives and the lives of those who surround them. John D'Emilio writes that African American civil rights activist Bayard Rustin's great grandmother Elizabeth Davis, the woman who raised him, spent her life working as a domestic in West Chester, Pennsylvania. She made it possible for her daughter Julia to attend the Friends School, graduate from high school, and receive nursing training. A teenaged Mae Mallory as a babysitter pushed back against white supremacy, and as an incarcerated woman, Mallory pushed back against the white supremacist triumvirate.[98] Mae Mallory and Bayard Rustin's great grandmother all remind us that the fight for humanity and civil rights was not fought for the trivialities offered in *The Help* or even in *Caroline or Change* but rather for real black women's experiences with oppression. They raged against white female supremacy in the guise of the Southern belle, fought state repression and the black mammy trope, and found meaning for their lives even in the face of the oppressive nature of incarceration, racism, and *real-life* experiences working as domestics.

Notes

1. Williams, *Negroes with Guns* 63; Williams, "Robert Williams President"; Mallory, "Memo from a Monroe Jail"; "Monroe NAACP."
2. Williams, *Negroes with Guns* 78; Lumumba, Mae Mallory Interview; Nelson. After the Freedom Riders' brutal defeat in 1961 in challenging the Jim Crow transit laws and segregationist policies in public facilities, which excluded African Americans from traveling desegregated on the Greyhound and Trail-ways bus lines and from using public facilities, they traveled to Monroe. See Nelson; Williams, *Negroes With Guns*; Tyson.
3. Williams, *The Crusader* 2; Mallory, "Memo from a Monroe Jail"; Lumumba, Mae Mallory Interview; Seniors, "Free Mae Mallory!"; Williams, *The Crusader* 7, 27; Johnson; Webb; Lumumba, Mae Mallory Interview. According to Williams, the police arrested, shot, and savagely beat a 17-year-old boy (Williams, *The Crusader*).
4. Mallory, "Memo from a Monroe Jail"; Lumumba, Mae Mallory Interview.
5. Julian Mayfield (1928–84) was an African American journalist, actor, and playwright. He was also a Professor in Residence at New York University in 1968. He wrote for newspapers such as *The Evening News*, Accra, Ghana, and wrote several books, including *The Grand Parade* (1961). Letter to Len Holt from Robert F. Williams, Robert F. Williams Papers, Reel 3, Robert F. Williams Papers, Bentley Historical Library, University of Michigan; "Dixie," Reel 11, Robert F. Williams Papers, Bentley Historical Library, University of Michigan; Julian Mayfield, "Save Mae Mallory: Frame-Up in Monroe," *The Evening News*, Accra, Ghana, March 29, 1962 (J. B. Matthews Papers, Duke University Archives); Julian Mayfield, "Why They Want to Kill Mae Mallory," *The Evening News*, Accra, Ghana, March 31, 1962 (J. B. Matthews Papers, Duke University Archives).
6. Mallory, "Memo from a Monroe Jail"; Lumumba, Mae Mallory Interview; Seniors "From Lynch Threat to Frame-up." An April 2, 1962, letter to the director of the FBI and May 1, 1962, letter to Mr. Belmont from A. Rosen both detail the Monroe Race Riot and Williams's flight to Cuba (Letter to Director of the FBI).
7. Davies 102–3; Harlow xiii, xvi–xvii, 2.
8. Mallory "County."
9. "It's a Struggle."
10. Mallory writes that Chief Narducci and the authorities transferred four African American women whose time exceeded the new white inmates (Mallory "County").
11. Mallory "County."

12. Nevels 35, 71, 72, 73, 76, 89–90; Hunter 2, 115–16; Feimster 125, 126, 135, 141, 142.

13. Flynn 179. Helen Gurley Flynn says that after talking to the woman, she was able to call on the woman's husband's experience as a union worker working with black men to convince her that the black women in the prison remained decent to change the woman's mind (179–80).

14. Nevels 35, 36, 64, 71, 72, 73, 74, 76, 89–90, 92, 71, 73; Feimster 125, 126, 135, 137, 138, 139–40, 141, 142, 166–67, 161, 169–70, 171, 172; White 29.

15. Nevels 35, 71, 72, 73, 89–90.

16. Bickley 15; Cousins 3; Harris, "A Rainy Day with Uncle Remus (Evening)" 608–16; Harris, "A Rainy Day with Uncle Remus" 241–48; *Scribner's Monthly* 443–53; Harris *Nights with Uncle Remus*; Stockett 13.

    Joel Chandler Harris was born on December 9, 1848, to a mother from "respected family in Newton Country, Georgia." He spent four years (1862–66) apprenticing with Joseph Addison Turner owner of the Turnwold Plantation, who ran the weekly *Countryman*. Bickley indicates that Chandler Harris drew inspiration for his stories from the plantation and the slaves that worked there, given his visits with the slaves "Uncle George Terrell, Old Harbert, and Aunt Crissy, the Turner slaves who were the prototypes for Uncle Remus, Aunt Tempy and other figures" (Bickley 15, 18–19; Cousins 3, 15).

17. Stockett 13.

18. Ibid.; Robertson; Chaney; Associated Press.

19. Kushner 17–18; *The Help*; Stockett.

20. Kushner 17–18, 36–37. The very talented Tonya Pinkins made a name for herself as "The Countess" in *All's Well That Ends Well* and *Measure for Measure* in New York's Shakespeare in the Park, Livia Frye the lawyer on the soap opera *All My Children*, and on Broadway as glamorous, beautiful African American women in *Thoroughly Modern Millie, Radio Golf, Jelly's Last Jam, The Wild Party, Play On*, and *Chronicle of a Death Foretold*, only to be consigned to the angry character of Caroline.

21. Gutierrez 32–33; McWilliams 43.

22. White 29; Welter 152.

23. White 29; Welter 152; Nevels 35, 36, 64, 71,72, 73, 74, 76, 89–90, 92; Feimster 125, 126, 135, 137, 138, 139–40, 141, 142, 166–67, 161, 169–70, 171, 172.

24. Du Bois 3–31; "Landscape of Slavery"; Morris; Schafer. The Kingsley Plantation clearly shows that the African Americans and whites lived side by side. For example, Anna, the concubine of Kingsley, lived in the kitchen underneath the house, while other enslaved people lived in dwellings in close proximity to the plantation. I visited the plantation in summer 2003. Comparably, at Jefferson's Monticello, the white workers lived side by side with the slaves on Mulberry Row. I visited this plantation in spring 2011.

25. Mallory "County" 1–6.

26. Ibid., 13–14.

27. Lynn 163; Joseph 2.

28. Lynn 163.

29. Mallory, "County" 12.

30. Berg 1–2, 79; Blackwell.

31. Wiggam 280; Berg 1–2, 79; Blackwell; Aanerud 27; Berg 79.

32. Mallory, "County" 13.

33. Ibid.

34. Ibid., 12–13.

35. Flynn 178. The government criminalized communism through the Smith Act of 1940 and the McCarran–Walter Act (Immigration and Nationality Act of 1952). The government used these laws to imprison Helen Gurley Flynn, Claudia Jones, and others. The government repealed these acts in 1990.
36. Mallory, *Letters from Prison* 27.
37. Mallory, "Of Dogs and Men," *Workers World*; Mallory, "Of Dogs and Men," *Letters from Prison* 25–26.
38. Le Espiritu 34–35.
39. Gore 19, 104, 106–7, 108; McDuffie 112.
40. Gore 110; McDuffie 113.
41. Gore 110.
42. Mallory, "Of Dogs and Men," *Workers World* 4; Mallory, "Of Dogs and Men," *Letters from Prison* 25–26.
43. Harris, "Introduction" xiii; Childress; Gore 1–2, 44, 66, 74–75, 85, 95, 108–9. Alice Childress was a leftist who supported Paul Robeson during his battle with the House Un-American Activity Committee. She founded the leftist Committee for the Negro in the Arts, "which challenged Hollywood's dual black list for radial black artists" (Gore 66); worked on the case against Rosa Lee Ingram, who killed a white man during an altercation in Georgia, and published in *Masses and Mainstreams* and "Conversations from Life" about black domestic Madge in Paul Robeson's *Freedom*, and in *Baltimore Afro-American which* would become *Just Like One of the Family* (Gore 74–75, 44, 66, 85, 95, 108–9; Martin 251–53).
44. Harris, "Introduction" xiii; Childress 1–2.
45. Childress 1–2.
46. Childress 2; see also Rasumussen.
47. Mallory, "Of Dogs and Men," *Workers World* 4; Mallory, "Of Dogs and Men," *Letters from Prison* 25–26.
48. Gore 110.
49. Childress 1–2.
50. McDuffie 114, 116.
51. Stockett 448.
52. Ibid.
53. Kushner 104.
54. Ibid., 38, 104.
55. Ibid., 104.
56. Ibid., 123.
57. Glenn 48; Childress 3.
58. Glenn 48; Brown 17
59. Glenn 53–54; Negro Nurse.
60. Stockett 250; Taylor.
61. Kushner 17–18.
62. Ibid., 17–18, 36–37. The very talented Tonya Pinkins made a name for herself as "The Countess" in *All's Well That Ends Well* and *Measure for Measure* in New York's Shakespeare in the Park, Livia Frye the lawyer on the soap opera *All My Children*, and on Broadway as glamorous beautiful African American women in *Thoroughly Modern Millie*, *Radio Golf*, *Jelly's Last Jam*, *The Wild Party*, *Play On*, and *Chronicle of a Death Foretold*, only to be consigned to the angry character of Caroline.
63. Seniors 79; Carby 34; Tanner 8; Huggins 250–51, 255; Malone 51–52; Smith 11; Toll 36, 54, 67; Hatch and Hill 104.
64. Brown 23–25, 39, 45–46, 49–51; Negro Nurse 196–97; Glenn 46; Gore 104, 107, 110; McDuffie 167; Davies 45; Semple 1; Yazigi 1–2; Hays 4–5; Glenn.

In 1912, an African American nurse reported that she worked from sun up to sun down "fourteen to sixteen hours a day. I am compelled by my contract, which is oral only, to sleep in the house" (Negro Nurse 196). She writes that she doesn't "know what it is to go to church; I don't know what it is to go to a lecture or entertainment or anything of the kind; I live a treadmill life" (ibid.). Her salary as a maid was ten dollars a month. She wrote about her inability to pay her bills and support her children on such a small salary (Negro Nurse 196–97; Glenn 46).

In *The Help*, Abilene makes $172 a month in Jackson, Mississippi, in 1963 (Stockett 16). In 1994, Rhonda Allayn from Barbados made $200 in New York City as a maid. Allayn says, "That was no money. You had to clean the whole house, and the house was humongous . . . [t]he day I was ready to leave was the day they fired me. I was going home. There was no way I was going to be a slave" (Hays 5). In 1994, a Guyanese nanny's salary was initially $310 a week until she began cleaning, and then it rose to $425 a week (Hays 4). In the 2000s, West Indian maid Arlene found herself working for $340 a week (Brown 49–50).

65. Mallory, "Of Dogs and Men," *Letters from Prison* 25–26.
66. Lipsitz 5; Williams; Glenn 53–55; McDuffie 113, 126–27, 132.
67. Lipsitz 5; Williams; Glenn 53–55; McDuffie 113, 126–27, 132.
68. A. Seniors, "FBI files"; C. Seniors, "FBI files"; *Workers World* 1959–1966; Logo- "Colored and White Unite," "Black and White Unite."
69. *The Citizen's Council*, October 1955, 2; *The Citizen's Council*, December 1955, 2; *The Citizen's Council*, January 1956, 2; "Mrs. Sara McCorkle Takes Council Post."
70. "Women of the South Take Your Stand Now!"
71. Bennett, *Before the Mayflower: A History* 377, 368–369, 590, 604–6, 607, 610; Lee 85, 21–22; Hine 533–36, 544; Feldstein 89–94.
72. Mallory, "Constant Desperation" 1–4; Lumumba, Mae Mallory Interview 523; Mallory, "FBI files" 1957, 2; Tyson 190; Mallory, "FBI files" 1958, 1–4. The FBI kept meticulous records on Mallory, beginning in 1957 and ending in 1978 under what they termed subversion control.
73. Mallory, "Constant Desperation" 1–4; Lumumba, Mae Mallory Interview 2, 10–11; Mallory, FBI files, 1957, 2; Tyson 190. The FBI kept meticulous records on Mae Mallory, beginning in 1957 and ending in 1978 under what they termed subversion control.
74. Lee; Federal Bureau of Investigation; Sartain 51, 58, 99, 82–83, 85, 101–2; "History of the New Orleans Branch"; Fairclough 194, 199–202, 209, 225, 228; Bartley 194–98, 209, 215, 225, 228, 209, 215, 225, 228. According to the April 10, 1946, FBI report, the NAACP women on the board of directors in 1946 included Mrs. A. T. Bently, Mrs. Mildred C. Byrd, Miss Mada Porter, Mrs. Molli Cunningham, Mrs. G. G. Dorney, Mrs. E. R. Ladix, Miss, Edna Dandridge, Mrs. Estelle Adams, and Mrs. Hilda Daresbourg (Federal Bureau of Investigation). The March 30, 1948, FBI report noted that officers of the NAACP, according to the *Louisiana Weekly*, included the following women who held positions on the board of directors: Mrs. Mildred C. Byrd, Mrs. Katie Wickham Chapman, Mrs. G. G. Downey, Mrs. Hilda Darensbourg, Mrs. Zerita Davis, Mrs. Ethel Humphrey, Mrs. Irma Landix, Miss Mada Porter, and Mrs. Alma Valley. It also lists A. P. (Alexander Pierre) Tureaud and John E. Rousseau as board members (ibid.).
75. Mallory, "County" 12–13.
76. Mallory, "Of Dogs and Men," *Workers World* 4; Mallory, "Of Dogs and Men," *Letters from Prison* 25–26.
77. Mallory, "Of Dogs and Men," *Workers World* 4; Mallory, "Of Dogs and Men," *Letters from Prison* 25–26.

78. Mallory, "Of Dogs and Men," *Workers World* 4.
79. Ibid.
80. Ibid., 25–26; Mallory, "Of Dogs and Men," *Letters from Prison* 25–26.
81. Mallory, "Of Dogs and Men," *Workers World* 4.
82. Simone.
83. Mallory, "Of Dogs and Men," *Workers World* 4; Mallory, "Of Dogs and Men," *Letters from Prison* 25–26.
84. "Freedom Fighters."
85. Mallory, *Letters from Prison* 27.
86. Krenn 94–95, 97, 115–16, 120–21, 126–28. African American academics and politicos made a concerted effort to gain diplomatic posts other than Liberia, "the black post" for African Americans, given especially the independence movements in Africa and Asia that people like African American Congressman Charles African American and African American journalist Ethel L. Payne saw as intertwined with the African American condition (Krenn 115–16).

    By 1959, Eisenhower appointed John H. Morrow (D) as US ambassador to Guinea with a white Elbert G. Matthews taking over "the black post" as ambassador to Liberia. By 1965, President Johnson named African American Patricia Roberts Harris as ambassador to Luxemburg. With the African independence movements, many African countries saw African Americans as second-class citizens and scoffed at them being assigned to their countries, but despite this, Franklin H. Williams gained the ambassadorship to Ghana in 1965 (Krenn 109–10, 125, 127, 124, 151–52, 157–58).
87. Painter 251.
88. Ghana gained independence on March 6, 1957; Congo gained independence on June 30, 1960; Patrice Lumumba was murdered in 1961 and the CIA's hand in his murder remains evident. Somalia gained independence on July 1, 1960; on August 1, 1960, Dahomey, Niger, Upper Volta, Ivory Coast, Chad, Congo Brazzaville, Gabon, and Senegal all proclaimed independence. Mali claimed independence on September 22, 1960. Sierra Leone claimed independence April 27, 1961; Tanzania claimed independence on December 9, 1961, Jamaica gained independence on August 6, 1962, Trinidad and Tobago gained independence in 1962; and Uganda gained independence in October 1962 (Bennett, *Before the Mayflower: The History* 593, 598, 600–601, 602–3, 604–5).
89. Mallory, *Letters from Prison* 26–27. Mallory pamphlet collection included "Angola A Theatre of Atrocities, A Portuguese War of Genocide against African freedom Fighters," "For the Immediate Independence of Uganda" (issued by Uganda National Congress), and "Caribbean Revolutionaries Speak Out! What are the relationships between Latin American Revolutionary Movements and the struggle for Afro-American Liberation?," which dealt with Revolutionary movements in Puerto Rico, Guyana, and the Dominican Republic. Her pamphlet collection indicates her vast knowledge of the eruptions of revolutionary movements and successful independence struggles emerging around the world, which must have made the United States and Europe take a great pause, and then work to figure out how to end these movements. As the founder of *The Crusader* family, she wrote of Castro's 1960 visit to New York, linking his visit with the United States with the murder and overthrow of Lumumba (Latin American Pamphlet; Mallory, "Fidel Castro in New York 1960"; Africa Handbills; Mallory, "Tshombe as Tool").

    As the executive secretary of the African American Committee in Defense of the Congo, Mallory and the committee questioned Lumumba's murder and asserted in a flyer that "Tshombe was the tool the American and Belgian imperialists used to murder Lumumba. We are deeply suspicious that the bloody hand has struck again . . . These are the same bigots that are murdering innocent black people and our supporters here in the U.S.A—Harlem, Chicago, Mississippi and Alabama. These were the same criminals that actively supported the wanton slaughter at the Bay of Pigs" (Mallory, "Tshombe as Tool").

90. Mallory, *Letters from Prison* 26–27.
91. In 2012, the US Department of Labor, the *Washington Informer*, and CNN Money reported on the high unemployment rates of African Americans. The Department of Labor and CNN Money listed the unemployment for African Americans in 2011 at 15.8 percent "compared to whites at 7.8 percent." Black women's salaries remain lower than those of black men, African American women's unemployment rates declined significantly, and ultimately African American women make less than black men and white women. See Department of Labor; Maestras and Ellison; Censky.

> In addition, once unemployed, Blacks are less likely to find jobs and tend to stay unemployed for longer periods of time. Blacks remained unemployed longer than Whites or Hispanics in 2011, with a median duration of unemployment of 27.0 weeks (compared to 19.7 for Whites and 18.5 for Hispanics). Nearly half (49.5 percent) of all unemployed Blacks were unemployed 27 weeks or longer in 2011, compared to 41.7 percent of unemployed Whites and 39.9 percent of unemployed Hispanics. Once a worker is unemployed for a prolonged period, it becomes harder to find a new job. Job search becomes harder for such an individual because the worker may not have the networks of employed friends and family to refer them to jobs and because they may become disconnected and depressed the longer they remain unemployed. (Department of Labor)

> The Office of Minority Health and Timothy Williams reported in 2011 that African American babies are 2.4 times more likely to die before the age of one than white babies. African American babies' infant mortality rates remained worse than those in China, Mexico, and Sri Lanka, and major cuts of "federal and state programs aimed at reducing infant deaths have hampered progress." The Office of Minority Health also reported that African American children are "four times as likely to die as infants due to complications related to low birth-weight as compared to non-Hispanic white infants" and that "African Americans had 1.9 times the sudden infant death syndrome mortality rate as non-Hispanic whites, in 2007" (Williams, "Tackling Infant Mortality Rates among Blacks").

92. "It's a Struggle."
93. Mallory, "Of Dogs and Men," *Workers World* 4.
94. Letter from Mae to Conrad Lynn and Williams; Letter from Mallory to Mabel Williams; Burlage 115; Bennett, *Before the Mayflower: The History* 604, 605; Painter 269.
95. According to the *New York Times*, one in every four African American male school dropouts faced incarceration in 2009; Chicago Youth Justice Data Project reported in April 2012 that in 2011 83 percent of black youths, 14 percent of Latino/Hispanic youths, and 3 percent of white youths were incarcerated in Illinois. They report that students are criminalized through suspensions, expulsions, and dropping out. That they are targeted and placed in the justice system for school absences, curfews, running away, and possessing cigarettes, thus pointing to the criminalization of youth and the school-to-prison phenomenon. See Dillon; Chicago Youth Justice Data Project; "Misplaced Priorities."

96. In 1997, three white supremacists would beat, chain, and drag African American James Byrd to death in Jasper, Texas; in 2007, six white men and women (including two mothers) kidnapped, tortured, sexually assaulted, and tore out the hair of twenty-year-old Megan Williams in Charleston, West Virginia; Sean Bell was murdered by New York police officers during a hail of fifty bullets after his bachelor party in 2006; in 2012, a cross was burned at the home of two black women in Swansea, South Carolina; in Topeka, Kansas, the Ku Klux Klan left calling cards at black-owned businesses in February 2012; a white woman in Salt Lake City attempted to run down three black joggers in March 2012; and the murder of 17-year-old Trayvon Martin while walking in his gated community in Florida by white supremacist George Zimmerman in 2012. See "West Virginia Protesters Demand Hate Crime Charges"; "Final Call Exclusive"; "Race Torture in West Virginia"; McFadden; Baker; Wilson; Chen and Baker; "Third Defendant Convicted in Dragging Death in Texas"; Herbert; Southern Poverty Law Center, "Cross Burning"; "Ku Klux Klan Calling Cards"; Southern Poverty Law Center, "White Woman Calls Racial Epithets and Attempts Assault with Vehicle"; Liston, "Trayvon's Killer"; Liston, "Family of Florida"; Liston, "Outrage Builds"; "Trayvon Martin's Killer to Ask for New Release from Jail."
97. Mallory, "Of Dogs and Men," *Workers World* 4.
98. D'Emilio.

Works Cited

Aanerud, Rebecca. "The Legacy of White Supremacy and the Challenge of White Anti-racist Mothering." *Hypatia* 22.2 (Spring 2007): 27. Print.

Africa Handbills, Pamphlets 2, Folder 2–1, Mae Mallory Papers, Reuther Labor Library, Wayne State University. Print.

Associated Press, *New York Daily News* Staff Writer. "'The Help' Author Kathryn Stockett Sued by Brother's Maid for Basing Best-Selling Book on Her." *New York Daily News*, August 11, 2011. Web. http://articles.nydailynews.com/2011–08–11/entertainment/29890725_1_lawsuit-court-filings-character.

Baker, Al. "3 Detectives Are Indicted in 50-Shot Killing in Queens." *New York Times*, March 17, 2006. Print.

Bartley, Numan V. *The Rise of Massive Resistance: Race and Politics in the South During the 1950s*. Baton Rouge: Louisiana State UP, 1969. Print.

Bennett, Lerone. *Before the Mayflower: The History of Black America*. 7th ed. Chicago: Johnson Publishing, 2000. Print.

———. *Before the Mayflower: A History of Black America*. New Millennium ed. Chicago: Johnson Publishing, 2003. Print.

Berg, Allison. *Mothering the Race: Women's Narratives of Reproduction, 1890–1930*. Urbana: U of Illinois P, 2001. Print.

Bickley, R. Bruce, Jr. *Joel Chandler Harris*. Boston: Twayne, 1978. Print.

Blackwell, Mary S. "The Republican Vision of Mary Palmer Tyler." *Mothers and Motherhood Reading American History*. Ed. Rima D. Apple and Janet Golden. Columbus: Ohio State UP, 1997. 31. Print.

Brown, Tamara Mose. *Raising Brooklyn: Nannies, Childcare, and Caribbean's Creating Community*. New York: New York UP, 2011. Print.

Burlage, Dorothy Dawson. "Truths of the Heart." *Deep in Our Hearts*. Athens: U of Georgia P, 2000. 85–130. Print.

Carby, Hazel V. *Reconstructing Womanhood: The Emergence of the Afro-American Woman Novelist*. Oxford: Oxford UP, 1987. Print.

Censky, Annalyn. "Unemployment Falls but Not for Blacks." *CNN Money*, June 6, 2012. Web. http://money.cnn.com/2012/01/06/news/economy/black_unemployment_rate/index.htm.

Chaney, Jen. "'The Help' Lawsuit against Stockett Is Dismissed." *Washington Post*, August 16 2011. Web. http://www.washingtonpost.com/blogs/celebritology/post/the-help-lawsuit-against-kathryn-stockett-dismissed/2011/08/16/gIQAiCWqJJ_blog.html.

Chen, David W., and Al Baker. "New York to Pay 47 Million for Sean Bell." *New York Times*, July 28, 2010. Web. http://topics.nytimes.com/top/reference/timestopics/people/b/sean_bell/index.html.

Chicago Youth Justice Data Project. n.d. Web. 2013. http://www.chicagoyouthjustice.com.

Childress, Alice. *Like One of the Family: Conversations from a Domestic's Life*. Boston: Beacon Press, 1986. Print.

The Citizen's Council. 1.1 (October 1955). Louisiana State University Archives. Print.

The Citizen's Council. 1.3 (December 1955). Louisiana State University Archives. Print.

The Citizen's Council. 1.4 (January 1956). Louisiana State University Archives. Print.

Cousins, Paul M. *Joel Chandler Harris*. Baton Rouge: Louisiana State UP, 1968. Print.

"Cross Burning." *Southern Poverty Law Center*, March 16, 2012. Web. http://www.splcenter.org/get-informed/hate-incidents?page=2.

Davies, Carole Boyce. *Left of Karl Marx: The Political Life of a Black Communist Claudia Jones*. Durham: Duke UP, 2007. Print.

D'Emilio, John. *The Lost Prophet: The Life and Times of Bayard Rustin*. New York: Free Press, 2003. Print.

Department of Labor Report. "The African American Labor Force in the Recovery." February 29, 2012. Print.

Dillon, Sam. "Study Finds High Rates Imprisonment among Dropouts." *New York Times*, October 8, 2009. Web. http://www.nytimes.com/2009/10/09/education/09dropout.html.

Du Bois, W. E. B. *Black Reconstruction in America*. New York: Atheneum, 1992. Print.

Fairclough, Adam. *Race and Democracy: The Civil Rights Struggle in Louisiana, 1915–1972*. Athens: U of Georgia P, 1995. Print.

Federal Bureau of Investigation. "Communist Infiltration of the National Association for the Advancement of Colored People in New Orleans Division. 3/30/48. Internal Security." REEL 2, 9 m, New Orleans Public Library. Print.

Feimster, Crystal N. *Southern Horrors: Women and the Politics of Rape and Lynching*. Cambridge, MA: Harvard UP, 2009. Print.

Feldstein, Ruth. *Motherhood in Black and White: Race and Sex in American Liberalism, 1930–1965*. Cornell: Cornell UP, 2000. Print.

"Final Call Exclusive: One-on-One Interview with West Virginia Race Torture Victim Megan Williams." *Final Call*, October 7, 2007. Web. http://www.finalcall.com/artman/publish/article_3997.shtml.

Flynn, Elizabeth Gurley. *The Alderson Story: My Life as a Political Prisoner*. New York: International Publishers, 1963. Print.

"Freedom Fighters." Resolution Passed at the Northern Negro Grass Roots Leadership Conference, Detroit, Michigan, November 9–10, 1963, No. Negro Grass Roots

Leadership Conference, 1963, Box 2, Folder 2–19, 1. Mae Mallory Papers, Reuther Labor Library, Wayne State University. Print.

Glenn, Evelyn Nakano. "Caring and Inequality." *Women's Labor in the Global Economy: Speaking in Multiple Voices*. Ed. Sharon Harley. New Brunswick: Rutgers UP, 2007. 46–61. Print.

Gore, Dayo. *Radicalism at the Crossroads: African American Women Activists in the Cold War*. New York: New York UP, 2011. Print.

Gutierrez, David. *Walls and Mirrors: Mexican Americans, Mexican Immigrants and the Politics of Ethnicity*. Berkeley: U of California P, 1995. Print.

Harris, Joel Chandler. *Nights with Uncle Remus*. Boston: Houghton, Mifflin and Company, 1911. Virginia Tech Special Collections. Print.

———. "A Rainy Day with Uncle Remus." *Scribner's Monthly Illustrated Magazine* 22.2 (June 1881): 241–248. Virginia Tech Special Collections. Print.

———. "A Rainy Day with Uncle Remus." *Scribner's Monthly Illustrated Magazine* 23.3 (July 1881): 443–453. Print.

———. "A Rainy Day with Uncle Remus (Evening)." *Scribners Monthly Illustrated Magazine, Midsummer Holiday* 22.4 (August 1881): 608–616. Virginia Tech Special Collections. Print.

Harris, Trudier. "Introduction." *Just Like One of the Family: Conversations from a Domestic's Life* by Alice Childress. Boston: Beacon Press, 1986. xi–xxxiii. Print.

Harlow, Barbara. *Resistance Literature*. New York: Methuen, 1987. Print.

Hunter, Tera W. *To Joy My Freedom: Southern Black Women's Lives and Labors after the Civil War*. Cambridge, MA: Harvard UP, 1997. Print.

Hatch, James, and Erroll, G. Hill. *A History of African American Theatre*. Cambridge: Cambridge UP, 2003. Print.

Hays, Constance, L. "The Nanny's Life." *New York Times Online*, August 28, 1994: 4. Web.

The Help. Dir. Tate Taylor. Perf. Emma Stone, Viola Davis, Bryce Dallas Howard, and Octavia Spencer. DreamWorks, 2011. Film.

Herbert, Bob. "In American Starring at Hatred." *New York Times*, February 28, 1999. Web. http://www.nytimes.com/1999/02/28/opinion/in-america-staring-at-hatred.html?ref=jamesjrbyrd#.

Hine, Darlene Clark. *African American Odyssey*. 2nd ed. Upper Saddle River: Prentice Hall, 2002. Print.

"History of the New Orleans Branch 1915–1990: 75 Years of Perseverance and Courage." no date probably 1990, The Amistad Research Center, Tulane University, New Orleans, Louisiana. Print.

Huggins, Nathan Irvin. *Harlem Renaissance*. Oxford: Oxford UP, 1971. Print.

"Infant Mortality Rates and African Americans." U.S. Department of Health and Human Services, The Office of Minority Health, 2012. Web. http://minorityhealth.hhs.gov/templates/content.aspx?ID=3021.

"It's a Struggle Just to Get Fresh Fruit in Jail! Mae Wins Round with Ohio Sheriff." *Workers World*, June 22, 1962: 1. Library of Congress. Print.

Johnson, Mrs. E. A., ed. *The Crusader*, February 1964, UNC Charlotte Manuscript, Harry Golden Papers Part 2, Box 62, Folder 26. Print.

Joseph, Peniel E. *The Chronicle Review*, July 21, 2006: 2. Print.

Krenn, Martin L. *Black Diplomacy: African American and the State Department 1945–1969*. Armonk: M. E. Sharpe, 1999. Print.

"Ku Klux Klan Calling Cards." *Southern Poverty Law Center*, February 23, 2012. Web. http://www.splcenter.org/get-informed/hate-incidents?page=6.

Kushner, Tony. *Caroline or Change*. New York: Theatre Communications Group, 2004. Print.

"Landscape of Slavery: Meet the People." *Monticello*. n.d. Web. 2013. http://www.slaveryatmonticello.org/mulberry-row/people.

Latin American Pamphlet 1961, 2–15, N.Y.C Pamphlets 1961–1965, Box 2, Folder 2–18, Mae Mallory Papers, Reuther Labor Library, Wayne State University. Print.

Lee, Chana Kai. *For Freedom's Sake: The Life of Fannie Lou Hamer*. Urbana: U of Illinois P, 1999. Print.

Le Espiritu, Yen. *Asian American Women and Men: Labor, Laws, and Love*. Lanham: Rowman and Littlefield, 1997. Print.

Letter to Director of the FBI from SAC Charlotte, April 2, 1962, United States Government Memorandum To Mr. Belmont from A. Rosen, May 1, 1962, Robert F. Williams FBI File, File 100-HQ-387728, Section 4, UNC Charlotte Manuscript 329 Robert Franklin Williams Collection, Box 1, UNC Charlotte. Print.

Lipsitz, George. *The Possessive Investment in Whiteness: How Whites Profit from Identity Politics*. Boulder: Westview, 1998. Print.

Liston, Barbara. "Family of Florida Boy Killed by Neighborhood Watch Seeks Arrest." *Reuters*, March 7, 2012. Web. http://www.reuters.com/article/2012/03/08/us-crime-florida-neighborhoodwatch-idUSBRE82709M20120308.

———. "Outrage Builds over Florida Vigilante-Style Killing." *Reuters*, March 19, 2012. Web. http://www.reuters.com/article/2012/03/19/us-usa-florida-shooting-idUSBRE82I17520120319.

———. "Trayvon's Killer Said to Make Self-Incriminating Statements." *Reuters*, May 24, 2012. Web. http://www.reuters.com/article/2012/05/25/us-usa-florida-shooting-idUSBRE84O00020120525.

Lumumba, Malaika. Mae Mallory Interview. Ralph J. Bunch Oral History Collection 523, February 27, 1970, 19, Moorland Spingarn Research Center, Howard University. Print.

Lynn, Conrad. *There Is a Fountain: The Autobiography of a Civil Rights Lawyer*. Westport: Lawrence Hill and Company, 1979. Print.

Maestras, Adriana, and Charles D. Ellison. "In Jobless Numbers, Obama Gets Black and Brown Bruises." *The Washington Informer*, June 4, 2012. Web. http://washingtoninformer.com/index.php/us/item/11078-in-jobless-numbers-obama-gets-black-and-brown-bruises.

Mallory, Mae. "Constant Desperation." Mae Mallory Writings, 1962–1963, Mae Mallory Papers, Box 1, Folder 1–6, Reuther Labour Library, Wayne State University, 1–4. Print.

———. "County." September 1, 1962, Mae Mallory Collection, Box 1, Mae Mallory Writings 1, [Diary of some sort], 13–14, Walter P. Reuther Library, Wayne State University. Print.

———. FBI files June 21, 1957, Freedom of Information Act, 2. Print.

———. FBI files, May 28, 1958, Freedom of Information Act, 1–4. Print.

———. "Fidel Castro in New York 1960." Crusaders for Freedom NYC 1960–1961, Folder 2–10, Mae Mallory Papers, Reuther Labor Library, Wayne State University. Print.

———. Letter from Mae Mallory to Conrad Lynn and Williams, 28 August 1962, reel 1 Robert F. Williams Papers, University of Michigan, Ann Arbor, Bentley Historical Library. Print.

———. Letter from Mae Mallory to Mabel Williams, October 11, 1962, Clippings Folder Robert F. Williams Papers, Bentley Historical Library, University of Michigan. Print.

———. "Memo from a Monroe Jail." *Freedomways: A Quarterly Review of the Negro Freedom Movement* 4.2 (Spring 1964): 203–214. Print.

———. "Of Dogs and Men." *Letters from Prison by Mae Mallory: The Story of a Frameup.* N.d., probably 1962 or 1963, Cleveland, Ohio, 25–26. The Monroe Defense Committee, The Schomburg Center for Research in Black Culture. Print.

———. "Of Dogs and Men." *Workers World*, November 23, 1962: 4. Library of Congress. Print.

———. "Tshombe as Tool of U.S. and Belgium." Probably 1964, Mae Mallory Papers, Reuther Labor Library, Wayne State University, Box 2, Folder 2–2. Print.

Malone, Jacqui. *Steppin' on the Blues.* Urbana: U of Illinois P, 1996. Print.

Martin, Charles, H. "Race, Gender, and Southern Justice: The Rosa Lee Ingram Case." *American Journal of Legal History* 29.3 (July 1985): 251–253. Print.

McDuffie, Erik. *Sojourning for Freedom: Black Women, American Communism, and the Making of Black Left Feminism.* Durham: Duke UP, 2011. Print.

McFadden, Robert D. "Police Kill Man after a Queens Bachelor Party." *New York Times*, November 26, 2006. Print.

McWilliams, Carey. *North from Mexico: The Spanish-Speaking People of the United States.* New York: Greenwood, 1968. Print.

"Misplaced Priorities: Over Incarcerate Under Educate." *NAACP*, April 2011. Web. http://naacp.3cdn.net/01d6f368edbe135234_bq0m68x5h.pdf.

"Monroe NAACP Defies National Office Decision on Williams." 1210, no date probably 1959, 1, Robert F. Williams Collection, MALP Box 16, The Schomburg Center for Research in Black Culture. Print.

Morris, Giles. "Life on Mulberry Row: New Exhibit Will Shed Light on Slavery at Monticello." *Cville Weekly* 23:13–19. Web. December 2011. http://www.c-ville.com/Article/News_Extra/New_exhibit_will_shed_light_on_slavery_at_Monticellospan_classApple_tab_span_stylewhite_space_pre_span/?z_Issue_ID=11801212114025590.

"Mrs. Sara McCorkle Takes Council Post." *The Citizen's Council* 3.4 (January 1958): 2. Print.

A Negro Nurse. "More Slavery at the South." *Independent* 72, no. 3295 (January 25, 1912): 196–197. Print.

Nelson, Stanley. *Freedom Riders.* Firelight Media, PBS, 2010. Film.

Nevels, Cynthia Skove. *Lynching to Belong: Claiming Whiteness through Racial Violence.* College Station: Texas A&M UP, 2007. Print.

Painter, Nell. *Creating Black Americans.* New York: Oxford UP, 2006. Print.

"Race Torture in West Virginia." *The Final Call*, October 14, 2007. Web. http://www.finalcall.com/artman/publish/article_3996.shtml.

Rasumussen, Daniel. *American Uprising: The Untold Story of America's Largest Slave Revolt.* New York: HarperCollins, 2011. Print.

Robertson, Campbell. "Family Maid Files Suit against Author of 'The Help.'" February 17, 2011, 2:14 PM. Web. http://artsbeat.blogs.nytimes.com/2011/02/17/family-maid-files-suit-against-author-of-the-help/#more-180261.

Sartain, Lee. *Invisible Acts: Women of the Louisiana NAACP and the Struggle for Civil Rights, 1915–1945*. Baton Rouge: Louisiana State UP, 2007. Print.

Schafer, Daniel L. *Anna Madigine Jai Kingsley: African Princess, Florida Slave, Plantation Owner*. Gainesville: U of Florida P, 2003. Print.

Semple, Kirk. "A Boon for Nannies, If Only They Knew." *New York Times Online*, April 14, 2011: 1. Web.

Seniors, Audrey Proctor. FBI files, Freedom of Information Act.

Seniors, Clarence. FBI files, Freedom of Information Act.

———. "Free Mae Mallory!" Reprinted from *Africa, Latin America, Asia Revolution* (Paris, France, November 1963), Harry Golden Papers Part 2, Box 16, Folder 49, Archives, University of North Carolina, Charlotte, North Carolina. Print.

———, Chairman. "From Lynch Threat to Frame-Up." September 16, 1964, Ephemera on the Monroe Defendants, The North Carolina Collection, University of North Carolina, Chapel Hill. Print.

Seniors, Paula Marie. *Beyond Lift Every Voice and Sing: The Culture of Uplift, Identity, and Politics in Black Musical Theater*. Columbus: Ohio State UP, 79. Print.

Simone, Nina. "Mississippi Goddamn." *Nina Simone Anthology*. New York: HMG, 2003 Print.

Smith, Eric Ledell. *Bert Williams: A Biography of the Pioneer Black Comedian*. Jefferson, NC,: McFarland and Company, 1992. Print.

Stockett, Kathryn. *The Help*. New York: Berkeley Books, 2009. Print.

Tanner, Jo A. *Dusky Maidens: The Odyssey of the Early Black Dramatic Actress*. Westport: CT: Greenwood, 1992. Print.

"Third Defendant Convicted in Dragging Death in Texas." *New York Times*, November 19, 1999. Web. http://www.nytimes.com/1999/11/19/us/third-defendant-is-convicted-in-dragging-death-in-texas.html?ref=jamesjrbyrd.

Toll, Robert C. *Blacking Up: The Minstrel Show in Nineteenth-Century America*. New York: Oxford UP, 1974. Print.

"Trayvon Martin's Killer to Ask for New Release from Jail." *Reuters*, June 4, 2012. Web. http://www.reuters.com/article/2012/06/04/us-usa-florida-shooting-idUSBRE85207Q20120604.

Tyson, Timothy. *Radio Free Dixie: Robert F. Williams and the Roots of Black Power*. Chapel Hill: U of North Carolina P, 2001. Print.

Webb, Constance. "Behind the Iron Curtain the Community Speaks." 1211, Robert F. Williams Collection, MALP Box 16, The Schomburg Center for Research in Black Culture. Print.

Welter, Barbara. "The Cult of True Womanhood: 1820–1860." *American Quarterly* 18.2 (Summer 1966): 152. Print.

"West Virginia Protesters Demand Hate Crime Charges." *The Roanoke Times*, November 4, 2007. Print.

White, Deborah Gray. *Ar'n't I a Woman? Female Slaves in the Plantation South*. New York: W. W. Norton, 1985. Print.

"White Woman Calls Racial Epithets and Attempts Assault with Vehicle." *Southern Poverty Law Center*, March 31, 2012. Web. http://www.splcenter.org/get-informed/hate-incidents.

Wiggam, Albert Edward. *The Fruit of the Family Tree*. Indianapolis: Bobbs Merrill, 1924. Print.

Williams, Rhonda L. *The Politics of Public Housing*. New York: Oxford UP, 2005. Print.

Williams, Robert F. *The Crusader* (August 1963), 7, UNC Charlotte Manuscript, Harry Golden Papers, Part 2, Box 62, Folder 26. Print.

———. *Negroes with Guns*. New York: Marzani and Munsell, 1963. Print.

———. "Robert Williams President of the Union County, N.C. NAACP." Document 1, 1, Robert F. Williams Collection, no date, probably 1959, The Schomburg Center for Research in Black Culture, MALP Box 16. Print.

Williams, Robert F., and Albert Edward. *The Crusader* 4.4 (October/November 1962). UNC Charlotte Manuscript, Harry Golden Papers. Print.

Williams, Timothy. "Tackling Infant Mortality Rates among Blacks." *New York Times*, October 14, 2011. Web. http://www.nytimes.com/2011/10/15/us/efforts-to-combat -high-infant-mortality-rate-among-blacks.html?pagewanted=all.

Wilson, Michael. "Judge Acquits Detectives in 50-Shot Killing of Bell." *New York Times*, April 26, 2006. Print.

"Women of the South Take Your Stand Now!" *The Citizens Council* 2.5 (February 1957): 4. Louisiana State University Archives. Print.

Workers World Logo (1959–1966). "Colored and White Unite." "Black and White Unite." Library of Congress. Print.

Yazigi, Monique P. "So Hard to Find Good Employers These Days." Style. *New York Times Online*, August 15, 1999: 1–2. Web.

CHAPTER 9

Bleeping Mark Twain?

Censorship, *Huckleberry Finn*, and the Functions of Literature

Robert T. Tally Jr.

*A*dventures of Huckleberry Finn is perhaps the most famous, most beloved, and most controversial novel featuring a prominent black character and written by a white author. Extremely popular in its own day and in the decades that followed, Mark Twain's novel became one of the most holy of the canonical texts of American literature once mid-twentieth-century critics discovered in it the key to the American experience and an uplifting illustration of the American spirit. The influential critic Lionel Trilling, in *The Liberal Imagination*, asserted that Huck Finn and Jim formed a "community of saints," and Trilling effectively established the novel as national monument (104, 106). However, the euepric effect of *Adventures of Huckleberry Finn* on the body politic is not as indisputable as many of its apologists would have it, and during the last thirty years, controversies have arisen over use of the novel in the classroom, particularly given the frequent appearance in the book of a well-known and offensive racial epithet. The story is presented as a meandering and quixotic tale of a poor, white boy and his boon companion, a runaway slave, as they make their way down river, deeper and deeper into the slaveholding South, until they reach a problematic but seemingly happy ending, in which the adventures come to an abrupt end with Tom Sawyer and Huck Finn playing a dangerous game with Jim. It is then discovered that, unbeknownst to both Huck and his companion, Jim had already been set free, so he was not a runaway slave after all, at which point Jim almost disappears from the text entirely. Twain's Mississippi River odyssey, with its local color and vaudeville-styled humor, is narrated by Huck himself, who manages to refer to Jim and to all African Americans by one of the most offensive terms in the modern English language more than two hundred times. For many readers, *Adventures of Huckleberry Finn* is therefore a work that causes embarrassment, pain, and resentment. As a hypercanonized text, one frequently included as required reading not only in college classrooms but also in high school and even earlier, Twain's 1885 novel continues to be a controversial touchstone for discussion of race in the United States today.

The controversy over the recently published NewSouth Edition of *Adventures of Huckleberry Finn* raises once more the question of censorship and of the functions of literature more generally (see Gribben; unless otherwise noted, all references to *Huckleberry Finn* and to Gribben's "Editor's Introduction" cited parenthetically in the text will be to this edition). Edited by Alan Gribben, an established Mark Twain scholar who teaches at Auburn University at Montgomery, Alabama, the NewSouth Edition notoriously substitutes what Gribben considers to be less offensive "synonyms" for Twain's original racial epithets, of which the "N-word" is both the most pervasive term in the novel and the least acceptable in civil discourse today. (A caveat to the reader: I will use the offensive word in the body of the text below, but only in direct quotations, some of which come from books routinely given to schoolchildren as required reading.) Predictably, following the publication of the NewSouth Edition in 2011, a public outcry arose against it, as Mark Twain's would-be defenders lashed out against the "censorship" as they rushed to the apparent rescue of a literary masterpiece that was thought to be imperiled by yet another "politically correct" assault. Ironically, Gribben's own justification of the project of this NewSouth Edition is, in part, that it might help *save* the great American novel by making it more suitable for classroom use in high schools or colleges. Gribben feared that, without a less-offensive alternative, the near-omnipresence of such an inflammatory and controversial word might otherwise keep *Huckleberry Finn* off the syllabus. In the cases of both Gribben's expurgations and the defense of Twain's original language, an implicit question is, what is the function of a work of literature in the classroom . . . and in the world?

Before examining the controversy over the NewSouth Edition of *Huckleberry Finn* further, I would like to begin with a brief autobiographical anecdote, and I promise to keep it well under 500,000 words (i.e., the length of Twain's own recently published, unabridged autobiography). It occurs to me that I did not read *Adventures of Huckleberry Finn* in high school; rather, I read it on my own during those years, but it was never an assigned text. I entered ninth grade in 1982, the same year that John Wallace, an African American teacher at the Mark Twain Intermediate School in Fairfax, Virginia, famously or infamously condemned *Huckleberry Finn* as "racist trash" (see M. Moore 1); Wallace went on to publish his own edition of the novel, which removed all instances of both the N-word and, for reasons presumably unrelated to racism, the word "Hell." I do not know if my high school or its teachers made any deliberate decision to avoid *Huckleberry Finn*, but I can imagine that the controversial repetition of the N-word might have made both teachers and students uncomfortable. This would have been in what was then thought of as a fairly progressive region of the "New

South" (yes!), North Carolina, and more particularly a somewhat urban, indus-trial, or technological locale in the Piedmont region of that state—Winston-Salem, specifically. Although the area was, and remains, quite conservative politically, most of its citizens, regardless of ethnicity, would pride themselves on their enlightened attitudes toward race and race relations, and no one at my high school would have embraced the rhetoric of racial bigotry openly. Thus I can imagine that it is at least possible that the presence of the N-word might have discouraged use of Twain's novel in the classroom.

One book that was in the ninth-grade classroom, both for me and for nearly everyone I know, was William Golding's haunting little novel from 1954, *The Lord of the Flies*. In the unforgettable, climactic moment of that book, the young heroes Piggy and Ralph approach the camp of the "wild boys," and Piggy, entreating them to embrace the mores of civilized society once more, makes this heartfelt plea: "Which is better—to be a pack of painted Indians like you are, or to be sensible like Ralph is?" (Golding 180). At least, that is how the line reads in the copy we were given. In the terrific 1963 film adaptation, Piggy's line is slightly different: "Which is better—to be a pack of painted savages like you are, or to be sensible like Ralph is?" However, in the 1954 original, the same line reads as follows: "Which is better—to be a pack of painted niggers like you are, or to be sensible like Ralph is?" Somehow, my edition was expurgated, with the term "Indian" replacing the incendiary N-word. In other words, someone had Bowdlerized this passage, substituting "Indians" for a more offensive term, but one that was also apparently intended to refer to a similar though distinct sort of "savage." (Let us leave aside for the moment the proposition that the phrase "painted Indians" might be *as* offensive.) One other note about my *Lord of the Flies* experience in high school: nowhere in my volume does it say that anything in the novel has been altered. The copyright date is still listed as 1954, and there is no evidence that the author himself, an editor, or the publisher might have emended any part of the text. I am not sure just who, but *someone* had protected me and my fellow (American) pupils from an offensive word, without comment and apparently without any controversy at all. (I believe that only the American editions were changed in this manner. As far as I can tell, in the United King-dom and in Commonwealth nations, the phrase "painted niggers" remained. For example, in the *Encyclopedia of Censorship*, Jonathan Green notes that, according to the Canadian Library Association, in 1988 "parents and members of the black community objected to a reference to 'niggers' and said it denigrates blacks" [see Green 331].)

Admittedly, one single use of the N-word is easier to replace, to "bleep" out, or to alter than some 213 uses, and a logic of comparative "savagery" or of com-parative terminological offensiveness would not really rescue *Huckleberry Finn* from the discomfort of schoolchildren, their teachers, or parents. The NewSouth Edition edited by Gribben substitutes the word "slave" for the nearly ubiquitous *N-word*. It also substitutes "Indian" for the more offensive *Injun* and "half-blood" for *half-breed*, a choice for which Gribben credits J. K. Rowling's *Harry Potter and the Half-Blood Prince* for giving "a degree of panache" (14). This editorial decision is obviously fraught with other problems, as I will discuss in a moment, but the intent behind the choice is clearly to make the novel more amenable to schoolteachers and more likely to be read by schoolchildren, both in middle schools and in high schools and perhaps also at the collegiate level. To put it another way, Gribben's aim is to make a text with "adult" language available to minors who would not, and perhaps should not, be exposed to that sort of diction at that particular time in their lives.

Leslie Fiedler famously suggested that the classics of American literature had come to be seen as children's literature, more particularly "boys' books" (Fiedler 28). (Fiedler's essay "Come Back to the Raft Ag'in, Huck Honey!" was originally published in the *Partisan Review* in 1948, and it may be worth noting that the phrase used as the title appears nowhere in *Huckleberry Finn* itself.) Fiedler was thinking of the intrigue and warfare of James Fenimore Cooper's *The Last of the Mohicans*, the sea voyages of Richard Henry Dana's *Two Years before the Mast* and Herman Melville's *Moby-Dick*, and above all Twain's *Adventures of Huckleberry Finn*, in which the youthful hero narrates his odyssey through a lawless wilderness. Of course, few or none of these writers intended that their audience be limited to, or even include, children, and Fiedler acknowledges this irony when he writes that modern American life seems typified by "its implacable nostalgia for the infantile, at once wrong-headed and somehow admirable" (Fiedler 27). Just as so many Americans long to be youthful, in looks or energy levels or some perceived innocence, perhaps we want to turn our mature literature back into child's play. But, as we sometimes rediscover on closer inspection, not everything in our library is suitable for all audiences.

This most recent controversy over the use of *that word* in *Adventures of Huckleberry Finn* highlights the interactions among writing, editing, teaching, and reading, and this serves as a point of entry into a discussion of the function of literature itself. What is literature? How ought it to be used? For many, works like *Huckleberry Finn* are themselves primary and fundamental texts for both enjoying and studying literature, inasmuch as the delights as well as the lessons of the novel spark an interest in further reading. Since its publication in 2011, Gribben's NewSouth Edition has been roundly criticized by scholars and laypersons alike, primarily because of its substitution of the word *slave* for the almost ubiquitous N-word. And the word substitutions do seem like a misguided attempt to clean up Huck's—and Twain's—language. However, as Gribben explains, the intent of this "censorship," as it is most often called, is to expand the readership and extend the influence of the novel. In fact, far from being an "attack" on an American classic, this edition is intended to save *Huckleberry Finn* from the oblivion to which it is destined as more and more teachers refuse to include the novel on their reading lists. In his introduction, Gribben emphatically endorses the use of other, nonexpurgated versions, and he specifically urges scholars to use other editions, but he insists that this NewSouth Edition is intended to bring new and younger readers to Twain's masterpiece. Most scholars and teachers of American literature would consider this a worthy goal. The question, then, is whether this form of "censorship" is an appropriate way to achieve such a goal.

Gribben's introduction straightforwardly explains the alterations in the text, as well as the rationale behind them, and Gribben explicitly directs "academic" readers to the "magisterial edition" produced by "the Mark Twain Project at Berkeley" (16). This honest acknowledgment and helpful guidance for more mature readers is welcome, I should think. This strikes me as far, far less of a sin against literature than the Orwellian erasure of history that occurs when Piggy warns against behaving like "painted Indians" in *The Lord of the Flies*, with no footnote or explanation concerning what had been altered.

Hence the intent behind the NewSouth Edition, if not the execution, is commendable. Despite the understandable outcry of voices condemning New-South's and Gribben's literary crimes against Mark Twain, we all know that it is not uncommon to "bleep" parts of even great works of art when the audience includes minors. For example, if *The Godfather*—one of the greatest films in American cinema—can have its dialogue altered and its brief nudity excised in order to make it suitable for television, then there is no inherent reason why *Huckleberry Finn* couldn't have its PG-rated version available in grade school, so long as the original can still be enjoyed elsewhere. Surely the "classic" works of American filmmaking deserve their own respect, and the films ought to have aesthetic integrity preserved, yet most of us will understand that certain words and images may be unsuitable for this or that audience, and we can make allowances accordingly. This brouhaha over the expurgated version of *Huckleberry Finn* again raises the question of how appropriate certain "classic" works of American literature may be for teenaged students. The publisher's rationale, in part, is that this edition will be more suitable for high school and college students embarrassed (or worse) by the repeated use of the offensive term. This is why Lorrie Moore, who is no fan of the NewSouth Edition, wants *Huckleberry Finn* to go to, and remain in, college (see L. Moore).

In this as in other controversies over the novel, some of Twain's would-be defenders have rolled out the old arguments about the sanctity of literature, the "realistic" language of the time, and the book's generally salutary depiction of a poor white boy and an African American man as bosom companions. In this effort, they sometimes overlook the textual and historical evidence that makes these positions much more problematic than they appear. Further, as Jonathan Arac pointed out in his *Huckleberry Finn as Idol and Target*, such arguments frequently pit (mostly white) persons of ostensible goodwill against (mostly black) students, teachers, and parents, who are told that they are ignorant or that they are plain wrong for not wholeheartedly endorsing the required reading of the hypercanonized novel—a book, it must be noted, that could not possibly be read aloud, word-for-word, on primetime network television. Defending Twain's use of the N-word, rather ironically, has sometimes meant forcing it on the very people most hurt by its use.

As someone who teaches a lot of early American literature (but only at the college or university level), I regularly encounter the N-word in print. But students reading these texts are seldom encouraged to sympathize or to identify with the utterer of the word, as they are likely to be when Huck uses it. The N-word appears a few times in *The Adventures of Tom Sawyer*, but that book is narrated by an omniscient and sometimes ironic third-person narrator, not by the actual hero of the story. A handful of Edgar Allan Poe's narrators use the term—surprisingly few, in fact—but readers never confuse any Poe narrator with a representative figure of a distinctively American national culture. In Frederick Douglass, it appears as a dirty word, used only by those whom the intended reader is invited to revile. Quite unlike many other such characters, Huck, while narrating his own story and using this word more than two hundred times, is rarely seen as an odd-ball rube who doesn't know any better, which, after all, may have been closer to Twain's original intent, but as the heroic and iconic American whom all students should applaud. This can cause discomfort for many students, African American or not, who are suddenly told that the offensive term is not only acceptable in this context but implicitly authorized by their teacher, by their school, and by the institution of American literature itself.

As James S. Leonard and Thomas Asa Tenney note in *Satire or Evasion?: Black Perspectives on "Huckleberry Finn,"* "it goes without saying that the word was at the time of Twain's writing, and remains today, a slap in the face for black Americans. It is inevitable that black children in a classroom with whites should feel uncomfortable with a word and a book in which it appears so often, and that black parents should wish to protect their children from what the word represents" (Leonard, Tenney, and Davis 5). And as Arac notes with some dismay, the institution of American literary criticism, particularly in its public face in newspapers and magazines, is at least as much to blame as the original text. Reviews appearing in such mainstream organs as the *New York Times* and the *Washington Post* have perpetuated a false impression of both the novel and the N-word, often to the detriment of concerned teachers, students, and parents, "who find themselves pained, offended, or frightened by the permission *Huckleberry Finn* gives to the circulation of an abusive term in the classroom and schoolyard" (Arac 30). Arac is referring in part to the long-standing critical usage of the name "Nigger Jim" to refer to the principal African American character in the novel. Astonishingly, given their apparently antiracist positions and generally liberal political leanings, critics and writers such as Lionel Trilling, Leslie Fiedler, C. Vann Woodward, Perry Miller, Harold Beaver, and Norman Mailer, among scores of others, have had no compunction about employing this moniker *even though* the phrase never appears in *Adventures of Huckleberry Finn* at all. Let me repeat that: the phrase "Nigger Jim," used by critics and scholars and writers for more than seventy years and presumably on the putative authority of Mark Twain himself, *never* appears in the novel. Not once.

The NewSouth Edition's attempt to ameliorate such problems in the text of *Huckleberry Finn*, while not wholly laudable, is therefore at least understandable and reasonable. Furthermore, it is certainly not the first attempt. The publishing house of Harper and Brothers released a 1931 edition, according to Robert B. Brown, "specially prepared to let 'Huck [. . .] step down from his place on the library shelf and enter the classroom'" (Brown 84). And ironically, the central complaint in a 1957 controversy in New York was that an edition of *Huckleberry*

Finn did not capitalize the word "Negro," a word that does not actually appear in Twain's original text (see Arac 63–66). Apparently, as with my own experience with *The Lord of the Flies* in the 1980s, the New York students were already getting an expurgated version, unbeknownst to them.

Still, although I think that its goals are praiseworthy in the main, I will not endorse the NewSouth Edition, since its means for achieving these aims are hamfisted and sometimes outright stupid. Gribben has chosen to replace the N-word with the word "slave," which (astoundingly!) he claims is a "synonym," as if he cannot imagine an African American living in the antebellum era could be a free man, a surmise rather obviously overturned by the merest glance at the historical record. Indeed, Gribben seems to have temporarily forgotten that the most prominent African American character in *Huckleberry Finn* is himself a free man! Hence we must grit our teeth through the nonsense of this famous (now-revised) line from the novel's denouement: "So, sure enough, Tom Sawyer had gone and took all that trouble and bother to set a free slave free!" (517). Slavery and racism in the United States are related, but quite distinct, matters, and the N-word certainly did not go away after abolition, as Gribben knows all too well. While Twain notoriously cautioned the illustrator of *Huckleberry Finn*, E. W. Kimble, not to make Huck look "too Irishy," Jim's looks had nothing whatsoever to do with his bondage or his freedom.

In fact, one could argue that Gribben's decision to conflate the historical condition of antebellum slavery with the seemingly perpetual problem of racism does *more* damage than the original, bigoted language of the novel was doing. Gribben cites a well-known moment in the text where Huck, disguised as Tom, lies to Sally Phelps, telling her that the steamboat "blowed out a cylinder-head," which leads to the following exchange:

> "Good gracious! anybody hurt?"
> "No'm. Killed a slave."
> "Well, it's lucky; because sometimes people do get hurt." (453)

(Needless to say, in Twain's original text, Huck says, "No'm. Killed a nigger.") Referring to this scene, Gribben explains that "the synonym 'slave' expresses the cultural racism that Twain sought to convey" (13). However, common sense alone suggests that Gribben is incorrect here. Were a "slave" to have been killed, then someone's valuable property would have been lost, and the tragedy of the accident, at least in the mind of Sally Phelps, presumably would be enhanced. By switching the terms, Gribben has lessened the power of any potential critique of racism that Twain (dubiously, in my view) may have had in mind. For example, Sacvan Bercovitch, pointing to the exact same spot in *Huckleberry Finn*, notes that Huck's use of the N-word is "profoundly racist" here. Observing the "full-stop" between Huck's "No'm" and "Killed a . . . ," Bercovitch writes, "We can't argue (as too many critics have) that it's just slang—a poor, ignorant boy's way of saying African American. What Huck *means* is far worse than what a bigot means by 'wop' or 'wasp.' Huck is saying that a 'nigger' is a *no one*, a nonhuman."

Huck's use of the term here is also entirely gratuitous; "Huck could have just as well stopped at 'No'm.'" The term was a "vicious slur," in the 1880s as today—for Huck, for Twain, for contemporary readers, and for other readers up to the civil rights movement (see Bercovitch 106–8). No, the word "slave" is not *in any way* a synonym for the far more offensive and still incendiary word uttered more than two hundred times in Twain's novel.

As is well known among even high school students, by the 1880s the question of abolition in the United States was settled, and slavery no longer had serious proponents or apologists, so Huck Finn's "decision" to "go to Hell" by electing not to return Jim to bondage was unlikely to be considered a controversial or even difficult choice by the contemporary reader. However, the bigoted view of a person referred to by the N-word as inferior to whites or even as not wholly human has persisted long after abolition, and this is the world in which *Adventures of Huckleberry Finn* circulates. Owing to the NewSouth Edition's flat-out foolishness in confusing race and slavery, I would not use this edition in a college-level class, and I would advise against its use in grade schools as well. But, in sum, it is not the NewSouth Edition's so-called censorship that makes the project objectionable but the specific means chosen.

Twain's heirs in comedic and incisive satire have found ways to use the mechanisms of censorship to their advantage. I think that television satires—for instance, *The Daily Show* or *The Colbert Report*—are very much in the tradition of modern American humor that Twain helped establish, and these shows routinely use those seven words that George Carlin taught us cannot be uttered on television (see, e.g., Tally). They "get away with it," as we know, by "bleeping" the words. The use of the bleep does not really erase the word entirely—that is, we all know what word is being bleeped—but the offensiveness is somehow mitigated. It would become very frustrating to have to hear that bleeping sound two-hundred-plus times over the course of *Huckleberry Finn*, I readily concede, but it might still be preferable to the hundreds of instances of a word that even the fiercest defenders of the novel would hesitate to use in polite company, if at all.

The very existence of the silly term I have been using, the N-word, demonstrates the degree to which this is true. As Arac points out, the term N-word gained popular currency during the O. J. Simpson trial, when Deputy District Attorney Christopher Darden argued that admitting into evidence Detective Mark Fuhrman's use of "the filthiest, dirtiest, nastiest word in the English language" would "blind the jury" (see Noble A10). As Arac observes and then pointedly asks, "many broadcast media bleeped out Fuhrman's use of the term, and *USA Today* would not print the term even in their front-page story revealing the contents of the Fuhrman tapes. So I ask before going on: should people of goodwill unhesitatingly maintain that a word banned from CNN and *USA Today* must be required in the eighth-grade schoolroom?" (Arac 24).

Of course, I'm not really suggesting that a textual equivalent of the "bleep" should be inserted in place of the N-word in *Adventures of Huckleberry Finn*, only that the sort of "censorship" we see in the NewSouth Edition is actually done all the time, with no real damage done to the original, to the reader, or to the institution of literature itself. Undoubtedly, many bright youngsters can profitably read the unexpurgated *Huckleberry Finn*, as well as *Moby-Dick*, *The Scarlet Letter*, and other great and complex books, just as they could watch great films like *Chinatown* or *Raging Bull*, but whether they should do so is another question, and whether all schoolchildren should be required to do so is a different matter entirely. Perhaps *Huckleberry Finn* does belong in college, as Lorrie Moore suggests, but if a PG or PG-13 version can be used in the high schools, so much the better. This is less a question of censorship than a question of how we wish for literature to function in culture and society more broadly. Are these texts to be worshipped as idols, which *Huckleberry Finn* has most certainly become for some, or can they become active participants in a vibrant, changing social milieu? My own terminology and phrasing give me away, of course, as I find the value of Twain's novel to lie not in our scrupulous attention to a boy's repetition of a naughty word but in the narrative's ability to help us imagine new and more interesting ways of seeing ourselves (white, black, and other) and the world we live in. Just because Huck himself wished to avoid being "sivilized" doesn't mean we or our students need to do so.

Works Cited

Arac, Jonathan. *Huckleberry Finn as Idol and Target: The Functions of Criticism in Our Time*. Madison: U of Wisconsin P, 1997. Print.

Bercovitch, Sacvan. "Deadpan Huck, or, What's Funny about Interpretation." *The Kenyon Review*, New Series, 24.3/4 (Summer–Autumn 2002): 90–134. Print.

Brown, Robert B. "One Hundred Years of Huck Finn." *American Heritage* (June–July 1985): 81–85. Print.

Fiedler, Leslie. "Come Back to the Raft Ag'in, Huck Honey!" *Leslie Fiedler and American Culture*. Ed. Steven G. Kellman and Irving Malin. Cranbury, NJ: Associated UPs, 1999. 26–34. Print.

Golding, William. *The Lord of the Flies*. 1954. New York: Perigree, 1959. Print.

Green, Jonathan. *Encyclopedia of Censorship*. New rev. ed. Ed. Nicholas J. Karolides. New York: Facts-on-File, 2005. Print.

Gribben, Alan, ed. *Mark Twain's Adventures of Tom Sawyer and Huckleberry Finn*. Montgomery, AL: NewSouth Books, 2011. Print.

Leonard, James S., Thomas A. Tenney, and Thadious M. Davis. *Satire or Evasion? Black Perspectives on "Huckleberry Finn."* Durham, NC: Duke UP, 1992. Print.

Moore, Lorrie. "Send Huck to College." *New York Times*, January 16, 2011: WK12. Print.

Moore, Molly. "Behind the Attack on 'Huck Finn': One Angry Educator." *Washington Post*, Metro Section, April 21, 1982: 1. Print.

Noble, Kenneth B. "Simpson Judge Permits Evidence on Racial Bias of Detective." *New York Times*, January 21, 1995: A10. Print.

Tally, Robert T., Jr. "I Am the Mainstream Media (and So Can You!)" *The Stewart/Colbert Effect: Essays on the Real Impact of Fake News*. Ed. Amarnath Amarasingam. Jefferson, NC: McFarland, 2011. 149–63. Print.

Trilling, Lionel. *The Liberal Imagination: Essays on Literature and Society*. New York: Doubleday, 1950. Print.

CHAPTER 10

White Lies and Black Consequences

Margaret Jones and the Complex Dynamics of the Publishing Industry

Josephine Metcalf

Numerous autobiographies have been released over the past two decades documenting contemporary African American and Mexican American urban life, including themes of violent gangbanging, drug hustling, and the inner-city search for economic stability and social recognition. This cycle of contemporary street gang memoirs commenced in 1993 with Sanyika Shakur's *Monster* and Luis Rodriguez's *Always Running* and often took as its setting Los Angeles (LA), the city that has been dubbed "the gang capital of America" (Serjeant). A relatively recent contribution to this literary trend is Margaret Jones's *Love and Consequences*, published 2008; its subtitle is *A Memoir of Hope and Survival*.

Some reviewers of *Love and Consequences* labeled the narrative "survival" or "misery" literature, while most, like the *New York Times*'s respected Michiko Kakutani, deemed it a contemporary street gang memoir (e.g., Kakutani; Reed; Alexander). Though Jones is half-white and half–Native American, her tales about growing up in an African American foster family in South Central LA and becoming a drug dealer for notorious black neighborhood gangs meant that the text was more often classified by reviewers as such. Kakutani praised Jones for her "humane and deeply affecting memoir," and the author even received critical acclaim from Oprah's *O Magazine* (Kakutani; Hinckley). (Critical studies of Oprah Winfrey remind us how influential her seal of approval can be for authors [see Konchar Farr; Konchar Farr with Jaime Harker].) *Love and Consequences* sold swiftly—that is, until the *New York Times* ran a writer's profile on Jones, which prompted her sister to call the newspaper and expose her as a white university graduate named Peggy Seltzer who had grown up in an affluent and stable suburban family. Jones confessed, and within a day of Seltzer's disclosure, the *Times* noted that attention turned to the publishing house responsible: Riverhead Books, a subdivision of Penguin (Rich "Tracking"). Scrutiny was piled on Riverhead in terms of their irresponsibility for letting this scam occur at all, but furthermore in terms of how low a publisher will stoop to profit.

In many ways, the Seltzer story is, according to Sherry Cohen of the *Connecticut Press Club*, "just another embarrassing gaffe in the publishing industry" (Shameer Cohen). The act of fabricating memoirs has a history, possibly as long as the American autobiographical genre itself.[1] Though if we consider the contemporary publishing climate into which Seltzer released her text, the literary world was still reeling from the scandal encompassing James Frey's 2003 memoir, *A Million Little Pieces*. Frey was a former alcoholic who appeared on *Oprah* to discuss the traumatic experiences detailed in his narrative about addiction. He sold several million copies before Winfrey frog-marched him back on to the show to apologize for inventing some of the events in his life story. It is important to note that much of the press coverage in the Seltzer case drew comparisons with Frey. But I would like to assert that the Seltzer scandal differs from the earlier literary exposé, because it sparked a particularly heated attack on the publishing industry and what many view as its exploitative racial politics. The intense criticism of Riverhead was arguably inflamed by the expectations that surround the subgenre of the gang memoir and the dangerous waters into which their client waded when she chose to construct and appropriate blackness without the authorial "authority" to do so.

Life-writing critic Paul John Eakin contends that while all people have the right to tell their stories, "we do so under constraints; we are governed by rules, and we can expect to be held accountable to others for breaking them" ("Breaking Rules" 113).[2] The revelation of Jones's true identity shattered the unspoken contract between readers of memoir and the writers themselves, sparking extensive criticism of Riverhead. A first-person narrator can certainly be unreliable (a classic example being Huckleberry Finn), but this is not so readily permissible within autobiography, a genre that purports to tell the truth and promises to be faithful and factual when used as a cataloging device in bookstores. Publishers hold a brokerage role that binds them into this moral contract, suggesting they too must respect Eakin's directives.

Yet life-writing scholar Timothy Dow Adams suggests that, regardless of any contract, all autobiographers are unreliable narrators simply because all humans are naturally liars (ix). Meanwhile, David Shields reminds us that "anything processed by memory is fiction" (57). From this viewpoint, lying in autobiography is rendered impossible because the audience begins with the assumption that the complete or unvarnished truth is not feasible (14). Nonetheless, the general literary public *do* still expect a "basically" truthful account when they purchase a memoir; editing tricks may repackage the life depicted, but what happened is fundamentally "real" at its core. Moreover, the quality of verisimilitude is actively encouraged by publishers who are working within a US tradition of autobiography that sells. Even though many readers may be aware of the calculated structuring of memoirs (including the condensing of time, the selection of material, and possible mediation of facts), they are willing to disregard such minor revisions for the "thrill" of perceiving the bulk of the material as legitimate.

The *Love and Consequences* scandal offers a fascinating case study of these broader issues concerning the discussion of "truth"; it is intriguing to consider how this memoir, with its topical themes and heated controversy, was interpreted by commentators. I examined 25 press pieces about the book itself and its author. While this was far from an exhaustive and formal reception study, it provided sufficient evidence to probe the dynamics at stake in the publication of such urban memoirs and to consider whether it is simply a case of black criminal stereotypes being deployed to fill the pockets of what one book reviewer labeled "the very white, insular publishing community" (Thompson).[3] Indeed, I allude to Riverhead as a "white" corporate publisher, bearing in mind—as the introduction to this collection contends—that while there have been numerous powerful nonwhite-authored narratives, "the stories that educational institutions authorize and that infiltrate our consciousness through popular culture arise from hegemonic power that remains unto this day primarily white." I sampled copy varying from the respected *New York Times* and *LA Times* through to the *New York Daily News* tabloid, as well as popular blogs such as *Undercover Black Man* (by the late television writer David Mills) and the *Suite101* website (for freelance writers). That reviewers and journalists censured the publishers more so than Seltzer herself suggests that, to some degree, they were alleviating the author of full responsibility for issues of representation and instead shifting public focus to the institutional politics of race and literature. In so doing, they opened up a number of beguiling consequences and lines of enquiry concerning a publishing industry in the supposedly "postracial" twenty-first century.

The production cycle of contemporary street gang memoirs arguably formed one key component of a wider body of gangsta culture that commenced with rap in the late 1980s. Gangsta rap has been praised by cultural scholars for engaging positively with the destructive social forces that impinged deeply on the ghetto as material for the music (e.g., see Kelley 183). Artists such as Ice Cube regularly rapped about the struggle to survive for African Americans in postindustrial urban California—for example, reflecting on the Reagan legacy of waning employment and welfare that was precariously situated alongside a burgeoning penal state. Ice Cube himself astutely referred to rappers as "underground street reporters" (Kelley 190). Cultural studies scholar Eithne Quinn argues that such music satisfied the "vast appetite for 'black ghetto realness' in the popular culture marketplace" by "mobiliz[ing] the authenticity discourse" (32). Though gangsta rap certainly had black fans, such "street-realist reportage" could offer white suburban audiences an immediate insight into black ghetto culture, feeding their curiosity and allowing them to figuratively traverse engrained racial and class lines within American society (10).

Contemporary street gang memoirs merit scholarly attention like their popular musical counterparts because they can be read as social transcripts.

Such narratives provide a window into the urban environment of LA, offering "exclusive" reports on disadvantaged and deprived young people and how they shape and organize their lives through aggressive street gangs. Publishers were prompted to turn to the 'hood in 1993 when news media responses to the LA riots of the previous year indicated a public fascination with life in areas like South Central. As one literary agent explained the allure of Shakur's *Monster*, "We see so much of the violence of the American inner-city; now here's a voice that comes from inside that can explain it to us" (Horowitz 28–37). Thus publishing houses swiftly responded to the commercial success of gangsta rap, channeling ghetto authenticity through another medium for popular consumption. Indeed, the lure of gangsta "realness" can be plainly traced into literary realms, with the first-person and experienced narrators of the autobiographical genre in particular feeding such cultural demands. As Shakur explains in the preface to his memoir, "I am a gang expert—period. There are no other gang experts except participants" (xiii).[4]

In *Monster*, Shakur is authoritarian and forceful from the outset, telling the reader what to think. Stanley Williams's *Blue Rage, Black Redemption* (2004) likewise offers a pedagogical narrative voice posing as a specialist on the topic of gangs. Like other contemporary street gang memoirs, *Love and Consequences* engages with "real" issues of youth unemployment, substandard education, rising poverty levels, and racial conflict in South Central LA. The streetwise and confident narrator assumes the reader is an outsider to the ghetto who has little understanding of its troubles. Likewise, the afterword to *Love and Consequences* states, "Part of what we offer is the perspective of having been inside the gang ourselves" (293). Thus, while appealing to the same principle of authority, Seltzer unashamedly complies with the first (and most familiar) of three primary transgressions identified by Eakin for which autobiographers have been reprimanded: the "misrepresentation of biographical and historical truth" ("Breaking Rules," 113–14). She constructs a version of the black experience, acting as a professional emissary on topics varying from the California prison system, homicide statistics, drug usage, and even wheel rims for cars (268, 273, 275, 277, 282). The unmitigated danger was that Seltzer's act of deception was cynically reinforcing and perpetuating white stereotypes and tropes about blackness: put simply, typecasting African Americans as prisoners, as violent, and as drug dealers driving flashy cars.

Performance studies scholar E. Patrick Johnson asserts that an even more complicated dynamic (and potential hazard) occurs when whites appropriate blackness. As Johnson notes, "History demonstrates that cultural usurpation has been a common practice of white Americans and their relation to art forms not their own" (4). The likes of Eminem and Vanilla Ice have hijacked contemporary black rap styles, though white cultural annexing of blackness can be traced back to the minstrel shows that gained popularity in the mid-nineteenth century. Seltzer was clearly acutely aware of the (first-person) ghetto authenticity that underpins gangsta culture. In the opening pages of the text, she includes an "Author's Note on Language, Dialect and Kontent" because the Bloods gang, of which she professes to be a member, despises their rivals—the Crips—to the extent that she is not permitted to make use of the capital letter "C." Hence she implores the reader, "Please do not confuse the use of slang and my replacing C's with K's as ignorance or stupidity. I choose to write as we chose to speak in the world of my childhood" (2). Such linguistic styling remains in force throughout the memoir. But as Johnson explains, when white subjects perform "black" signifiers, "the effect is already entangled in the discourse of otherness; the historical weight of white skin privilege necessarily engenders a tense relationship with its others" (4).

The moment Seltzer was exposed, Riverhead had no choice—as the *New York Daily News* noted—but to quickly recall 19,000 copies of the book and cancel her upcoming book tour (Hinckley). This extreme reaction was arguably dictated by a (thwarted) appetite for realness embedded in gangsta culture (most evidently rap, but also film, memoir, and fashion), as well as the fact that Seltzer volunteered herself as a sociological expert. Riverhead's rejoinder speaks volumes about the complexity of the representational politics at stake with a gang memoir. In the aftermath of the scandal, several reviewers, such as Sherry Cohen, asked questions along the lines of, "If the writing is so good, why not just sell it as a novel?" (Cohen). Lisa Rufle, writing for *Suite101*, stated, "What makes these situations even more baffling is that these books could have been just as compelling had they been marketed as fiction novels" (Rufle). But such responses failed to note that the credibility and commercial success of such texts is predicated on the audience's belief in this experiential discourse of ghetto authenticity or hyperrealism. Former gang member Luis Rodriguez's decision to novelize his life story attests to the power of such a discourse; he received rejections from 22 publishing houses. *Always Running* only gained attention from publishers once he rewrote the book as memoir rather than fiction.[5] Perhaps Riverhead similarly deduced that there was no alternative to the autobiographical form.

Riverhead's decision to recall *Love and Consequences* further reminds us that such discourses are racialized in nature; there is a "special" burden of authenticity placed on African American autobiographers. By contrast, following Frey's exposé, his memoir suffered an initial lull in sales before returning to the *New York Times* bestseller list. *A Million Little Pieces* was never recalled, though readers were offered a refund by the publisher (fewer than two thousand were ever claimed). Human curiosity was too much for some who subsequently purchased Frey's book for an entirely different reading experience. That the narrative was not wholly fabricated perhaps partially dictated its continued ability to sell. That Seltzer's was utterly fictitious meant it needed to be erased from collective consciousness; no trace of the text nor its author can today be found on Riverhead's website. Frey's sustained popularity is arguably rooted in his sensational and melodramatic materials, including the mafia boss whom he meets in rehabilitation. Maybe such exaggerated theatricality encourages a fictional reading. By comparison, Riverhead's downfall was their preference for supporting an author who was forging links with a "real" subject: a memoirist who was purporting to present an unmediated and bona fide vision of the streets of LA. Of course, the crucial difference is race: Frey is not black nor posing as such in any way. Elements of race and racism ensure that the claims for authenticity made by African

American and nonwhite memoirs are more loaded and significant, as indeed Johnson reminds us.

It is unsurprising that the *LA Times* launched a particularly irate series of pieces aimed at Riverhead, sarcastically noting that South Central "is worlds away from the New-York based publishing industry" (Timberg and Getlin). The newspaper reported that Seltzer's readers felt betrayed and angry that they had been inspired by her courage but, more important, were disgusted on behalf of "the residents of South LA, whose real stories, and real pain, were appropriated and repackaged for the purpose of selling books" ("Opinion"; see also Kellogg). Aside from the betrayal of gangsta authenticity more generally, the specific treatment of the local LA community represents the point at which things began to get especially awkward for the publisher and espouses Eakin's second contravention: the "infringement of the right to privacy" ("Breaking Rules" 114). This statute of self-narration proposes that the autobiographer should not display the personal and privileged lives of others. Seltzer was professing to speak for all those embroiled in the gang wars; her dedication at the front of the text references "all the Bloods and Crips who lost their lives in the struggle—as well as those who are lost trying to find life within the struggle . . . everything I do, I do in your memory" (3).

African American life writing has a long tradition of standing for a deep-rooted sense of community (e.g., see Marcus 289; Mostern 12, 32, 51). In such historical memoirs, the narrators carry responsibility for representing both individual and collective experiences, often stemming from encounters with racism. The narrator of *Love and Consequences* contends, "White people always think I'm Mexican," so she can partake in the common experience of (and victimization by) dominant white racism, identifying herself as "other" (141). Her early life in several abusive foster homes is worn as a badge of "street realism" to provide her with access into the impoverished inner cities of LA. When John Howard Griffin released the diaries of his 1966 contentious journey into the Jim Crow South, passing as a black man as a means of understanding the plight of African Americans, he maintained, "I do not represent myself as a spokesperson for black people" (Bonazzi 199). By contrast, Seltzer methodically aligned herself with the communities of South Central, criticizing the mainstream media following the 1992 riots for taking "every opportunity to call *us* savages" (265, my emphasis). When the narrator discovers the name of her social worker, she states "Anna . . . seemed like about as suburban, white a name as you could get. With a name like that I couldn't even get mad that she didn't understand half of what I told her" (165).

Pretending you are a different person is potentially problematic enough in itself. But the stakes are raised further when a bogus memoirist alleges to be speaking on behalf of an entire (racial) community. As a result, Seltzer's deception distances her further from Frey's exaggerations; what Daniel Mendelsohn has labeled "the plagiarism of trauma" takes on a heightened significance when applied to the black urban community (Mendelsohn). Mendelsohn titles his *New York Times* article "Stolen Suffering" and reprimands Seltzer far more than Frey, because she was appropriating the anguish and distress of an oppressed group ("the impoverished African Americans of Los Angeles today"). On a palpable level,

Frey makes no generalizations on behalf of others who have undergone alcohol treatment. His was a solitary journey, and Frey himself created his own circle of blame when he accepted Oprah's initial invitation. Much of the immediate press criticism surrounding this scandal was targeted at the author himself (though his literary agent would appear on Oprah to suffer a similar grilling). Again, the key point here when relating Frey and Seltzer is that "authenticity"—or the case in point of the false memoir—is further charged in black life writing.

Seltzer was faithful to the conventions of the contemporary street gang memoir. Before being revealed as a sham, the text was praised (in stylistic terms) for being a strong example of the genre. For instance, like *Monster* and *Blue Rage* among others, *Love and Consequences* offered a conversion trajectory, journeying from immature and raw gangbanging adolescent, through to educated enlightenment—often through punishment—and renunciation of violence. Such a significant transformation holds importance not only for the narrator himself or herself, but for all those embroiled in the gangsta lifestyle and moreover all marginalized groups in such inner-city areas. Lisa Rufle was initially seduced by Seltzer's collective conversion: "One genuinely wants to believe, despite all of these atrocities, that if Jones is able to succeed there is hope for anyone who struggled through similar ordeals" (Rufle). Kakutani was also greatly enthused by this story that explored not just "a young girl coming of age in this world" but a focus on the "bonds of love and loyalty that can bind relatives and gang members together, and the craving after safety and escape that haunts so many lives in the 'hood" (Kakutani). Hence it was hardly surprising that the *New York Times* would lash out at the publisher, perhaps fueled in part by Kakutani's embarrassment and sense of having been emotionally manipulated.

Making the situation even more thorny for the publisher (or "real" for the reader), Seltzer concocted a charitable foundation, whose website was listed inside the back sleeve of the book, that aimed "to reduce gang violence and mentor urban teens." Not only did the publisher fail to properly vet this "www.brothersisterhood.com" foundation, but the website was set up in the name of Seltzer's literary agent at Riverhead, Faye Bender. Bender had obligingly provided Seltzer the capital to establish the website. The journalists and reviewers who discussed the website scam again implied that the publishers were particularly unethical because they were letting down a whole community by using the website as a "book promotion vehicle" (Kellogg; see also Rich "Foundation"). The publishers seemingly had no option other than to shame-facedly recall the book and lay themselves open to an onslaught of criticism. "Fuck me," shouted David Mills (the *Undercover Black Man*), "this shit makes me sick" (Mills).

In the days following her confession, Seltzer made a statement in which she suggested that, despite the book's fabricated narrative, it had been written—quite earnestly—on behalf of the LA community: "I thought it was my opportunity to put a voice to people who people don't listen to. I was in a position where at one point people said you should speak for us because nobody else is going to let us in to talk" (Access Hollywood). Seltzer's intention can be read as seemingly noble (though incredibly naïve). There has been a long history of white silencing of African Americans, from slavery onward, including white authoring of history as a means of representing the black community. Furthermore, there are certainly other white cultural figures who have told stories of black struggles with less hostile reactions from those portrayed (consider Harriet Beecher Stowe, though most of the glowing reviews for *Uncle Tom's Cabin* in 1852 came from white abolitionists). Nonetheless, in making the bogus claim that it was *her* struggle too, Seltzer was precariously toying with the politics of race representation that have sparked heated contemporary debates—from Stuart Hall and other cultural studies scholars—over depiction and delegation (e.g., see Hall "New Ethnicities," "What Is This 'Black,'" *Representation*). Gangsta culture in many ways provides excellent materials to apply to Hall's criticism of the media's reproduction of popular (typecast) images of black people.

Following Seltzer's revelatory statement, sympathy for the publisher waned significantly. For instance, Amy Alexander in the *Nation* denied any pity for Riverhead, contending they were not "innocent victims" in failing to notice their author was a "sociopath" (Alexander). *Nation* referenced a medical definition of "sociopath" and observed that Seltzer fit all the criteria on the checklist. The *LA Times* appeared almost amused when Riverhead revealed Seltzer had provided them evidence to support her story, including photographs and letters (Timberg and Getlin). At this point, the memoirist adhered to Eakin's final misdemeanor: the "failure to display normative modes of personhood" ("Breaking Rules" 114). Quite simply, Eakin is referencing narrators who flout customary human behavior (oftentimes involving "clinical" contexts). Seltzer was no longer possibly naïve; instead, she was morally corrupt. There was now no redemption for the publishers. Even if Seltzer herself was branded psychotic, that failed to exonerate Riverhead; the exploitative damage had already been done to the community. Mills declared that recalling *Love and Consequences* was not sufficient. Instead, he asserted that "Seltzer's ignorant, tone-deaf editor—Sarah McGrath—owes an apology to the black community of South Los Angeles. McGrath's bosses at the Penguin Group should make some gesture of contrition [to the community for] peddling black pain and death to white readers" (Mills).

As detailed in the *LA Times*, the publisher's official statement on events proclaimed: "Riverhead relies on authors to tell us the truth . . . an author promises us the truth in their publishing agreement" (Timberg and Getlin). Professing innocence, the publisher attempted to align themselves with the deceived reader, suggesting they had been conned to the very same extent. McGrath and Bender had worked with Seltzer on the book for three years, and as a result, *Entertainment Weekly* flagged McGrath's announcement: "There is a huge personal betrayal here as well as a professional one . . . It's very upsetting to us because we spent so much time with this person" ("Memoir"). Furthermore, McGrath attempted to empathize with the black community, with the *New York Times* highlighting her comment that "we thought we were doing something good by bringing her story to light" (Rich "Gang Memoir"). These statements formed the focus of much disparagement from journalists. Despite the publishers trying to atone for their fundamental oversight, commentators believed that Riverhead was just as guilty—debatably more so—than Seltzer herself for exploiting white fascination with blackness.

White intrigue with black cultural representation was firmly entrenched prior to the cycle of gang memoirs released in the early 1990s. In the mid- to late 1980s, rap demonstrated how secretive street gang subcultures, inaccessible to the majority of the public, could provide captivating material for popular texts that appealed across racial and class lines. This interest was partially fueled by a long-standing white enthrallment with black masculinity that Norman Mailer branded "coolness envy" in his notorious 1957 essay "The White Negro" (Mailer). Contemporary historian Kevin Starr attempts to understand the culture of modern-day California by exploring the white exoticization of black gang culture—what he deems "gang chic." Starr contends that this style was, by the 1990s, "pervading music, clothing, and the jargon of more teenagers than there were gangbangers. Gangsta rap, after all, was bringing the most murderous sentiments of the gangland ghetto into the homes of the mostly white teenagers who bought such CDs" (Starr 87). Longings for black ("hip") culture certainly spurred the commercial success of rap and in many ways also stimulated a demand for gang memoirs.

Indeed, white fetishization of blackness was *already* a component of gangsta culture (and gang memoirs); Seltzer did not invent such ways of thinking but instead made an existing premise more starkly and uniquely visible. Writing in the *Washington Post*, Stacey Patton believed such coolness envy had fed Seltzer's actions. Patton was dumbfounded that Seltzer would take such a risk and livid at Seltzer's appropriation of black stories. Patton was troubled "that white America appeared ready to lap it up as an 'authentic' account of a world it knows so little about" (Patton). As a former foster child herself, Patton could only comprehend the narrative's deception by contending that Seltzer "seemed to be revealing her own secret admiration of and desire for blackness while catering to prurient and voyeuristic consumer appetites" (Patton). Seltzer was arguably conforming to cultural studies scholar Baz Dreisinger's notion of "cultural passing," a mode of white-to-black passing prompted by admiration for black culture (6). While a young child, the narrator of *Love and Consequences* asks her foster mother, "What if I don't wanna be white?" (46). While appropriation of blackness offers, as detailed by Johnson, "a fetishistic 'escape' into the Other to transcend the rigidity of their own whiteness," of perhaps greater significance in this case study was the ability of Seltzer's story to commodify blackness as a means of feeding the hunger of white mercantile publishers (5). Again, Seltzer's actions do not make her exceptional (it would be too easy to dismiss her actions as anomalous), but rather they shed light on a wider and ongoing trend: the institutional prejudice of the publishing industry.

When the Seltzer story broke, Sara Nelson—former editor of *Publishers Weekly* and now chief of Oprah's *O Magazine*—loosely attempted to defend the industry by noting "there are a lot of potential liars looking for book deals" (Nelson). Shakur's *Monster* serves as evidence of the economic propensity of contemporary street gang memoirs (though there is no evidence at all the text is falsified). In 1992, Shakur had quietly instigated a publishing bidding war for his manuscript, resulting in a lucrative contract (a $150,000 advance and the promise of additional payments of at least $100,000). When he was rearrested a couple of years after the release of his memoir, the police found him signing autographs on his front porch (Faludi, *Stiffed* 482). Several commentators dryly noted that Seltzer herself was given a $100,000 advance (e.g., Dawes). While Riverhead can complain that they were also duped, such a sum certainly insinuates that the publisher saw money-spinning potential in this text. Consequently, the incensed David Mills contends that as compensation for having already "counted the money they expected to make," Riverhead should offer not only offer a "gesture of contrition" to South Central (as already detailed) but a gesture of "goodwill also" (Mills).

There are some interesting dynamics worthy of note here. There has been an ongoing literary debate in recent decades concerning what black writer Leonce Gaiter called a "white media establishment incapable of concealing its innate racism" following the publication of *Monster* (Horowitz 28–37).[6] When contemporary street gang memoirs first began to appear in 1993, Susan Faludi, writing in the *LA Weekly*, criticized publishers for being selfishly "eager for a piece of the marketable LA riots drama in the black ghetto" (Faludi "Ghetto Star"). I wonder to what degree the rage in the black community over the Seltzer scandal emanates from a preexisting anger at publishers exploiting this material? Such a strange and unique case simply brought such matters to the surface. Perhaps Riverhead felt they were avoiding such criticism of representational exploitation by engaging with an atypical subject. In using a half-white, half–Native American narrator, were they alleviating some of the dangerous subjectivity that publishers must surely have been aware of when it comes to white fascination with blackness? Bio Laina Dawes, writing for the *BlogHer* publishing network, was conscious of this: "Cultural appropriation is a sticky subject. Dare us colored folk complain? Yes, sometimes our stories—stories that need to be told and thrown into the world, are indeed told . . . just by someone else that is deemed more socially palatable" (Dawes).

I have already suggested that publishers feel the worth of gangsta stories lies in their first-person authenticity and verisimilitude. Yet there is some proof that this is a weak contention on the part of publishers; there is some evidence that publishers *do* have options outside of autobiography, and in turn, black writers do have choices other than white-owned corporate publishing houses. In the second half of the twentieth century, there was a large-scale restructuring of the US publishing industry, producing a field dominated by only a handful of transnational media conglomerates (Nishikawa). One of these is Longman, Pearson, based in London, which controls Penguin, which in turn owns Riverhead. But the establishment of a number of independent black book publishing houses in the 1990s implies the reductiveness of assuming that black criminal stereotypes are being deployed solely to fill the pockets of so-called white corporate publishers. There are several such case studies of publishers—including Atlanta's Black Pearl Books or Brooklyn's Black Print Publishing—but of noteworthy significance is Columbus, Ohio's Triple Crown Publications. Not only were black publishers benefitting from documenting African American street life, but more important, over the past decade, such accounts were frequently released as fiction.

Triple Crown in particular has been responsible for a number of these novels. The publishing house was established by Vickie Stringer, whose first work of fiction was written while serving a seven-year prison sentence for drug dealing (Annesley 13–26). On her release in 2001, Stringer established the business, determined to publish both her own narratives and others, as well as creating legal employment in the process. Stringer's accomplishments highlight the notion that "blackness" as a commodity needs to be examined in more multifaceted terms; it is inadequate to assume that it is beneficial only to white capitalists.[7] Triple Crown continues to release often two or three texts a month, proving the 'hoods are still a relevant and interesting subject for literature. Though popular fiction and not necessarily worthy of the literary merit that secured *Love and Consequences* praise from Oprah and Kakutani, conceivably it does still serve to suggest that Riverhead did have choices and that the Seltzer controversy does not represent some essential or monolithic attitude on the part of the publishing industry. While Riverhead was convinced of Seltzer's legitimacy, perhaps they should have been more flexible in their choice of genre; paradoxically, autobiography in this instance put them in a financially compromised position.

Furthermore, the current struggles over race and literature are not unique to our contemporary age but rather speak to broader continuums, traditions, and struggles. Stringer's fiction is entwined with a need to become financially viable—a tradition that reaches back to the first African American novelist, Harriet Wilson. Wilson wrote *Our Nig* in 1859 in order to gain legitimate funds to support her and her young son. In fact, Seltzer's story also draws parallels with the long history of black narratives in a number of ways. On a palpable level, her memoir (like other contemporary street gang life stories) follows the tripartite structure of slave narratives: confinement, escape, and freedom, often accompanied by religious conversion too. The construal of Riverhead as an exploiter of sensitive (black) materials holds some resemblance to the controversy over fake slave narratives in the nineteenth century written by whites; many black authors of the authentic slave narratives were dismissed as mere "fronts." Since the 1980s, when many female-authored slave narratives were rediscovered by Henry Louis Gates Jr. and others, their legitimacy was, again controversially, challenged.

The notion of black literature perceived as needing a stamp of white credibility was an issue for slave narratives, which had to be "sanctioned" by a white abolitionist to be taken seriously (a more nuanced form of white authorial authority). Even Frederick Douglass's text was only initially viewed as legitimate because of William Lloyd Garrison's introduction. Late nineteenth-century writers such as Paul Laurence Dunbar were "sponsored" and instructed by white critics such as William Dean Howells. Something congruous occurred during the Harlem Renaissance of the early twentieth century with white benefactors such as Carl Van Vechten. Thus Seltzer's error of judgment is further imprudent when considered in light of the long and sensitive history of African Americans in the literary tradition. Even in the twenty-first century, America seemingly still has far to go in the quest for (literary) racial equality and justice.

Eakin asserts that "when life writers fail to tell the truth, then, they do more than violate a literary convention governing nonfiction as a genre; they disobey a moral imperative" (*Ethics* 2–3). Holding Seltzer accountable was not sufficient when there were moral constituency interests at stake, such as ghetto realness, the LA community, and white exploitation. Put simply, there was a lot of blame to go around for the memoir's lack of narrative mandate. That Seltzer broke not just one of Eakin's "rules" but all three arguably dictated that all those involved—not just the author—had to be held accountable. This is underscored when considering the subgenre of a contemporary street gang memoir, with gangsta culture offering a heightened sense of authenticity. Hence it is predictable that it was Riverhead who bore the brunt of the criticism; they were the powers energizing the project (what Kenneth Mostern deems "the construction of autobiographical truth in phenomenological terms"; 39).[8] Maybe the degree to which McGrath, Bender, and all those involved were held up to scrutiny was adequate punishment. Indeed, there was some (embarrassing) irony that among her numerous acknowledgments, Seltzer draws attention to "my winning literary team: my agent, Faye Bender, who just gets me when no one else does; my editor, Sarah McGrath, who had the courage to believe a no-name author like me . . ." (295).

Notes

1. Though there has seemingly been little scholarship on falsified American memoirs throughout history, see Browder. See also Rich, "A Family Tree of Literary Fakers," in which Rich notes that false American memoirs date back to at least 1863.
2. Note that Eakin approaches autobiography "not as a literary genre but instead as an integral part of a lifelong process of identity formation. Written autobiographies represent only a small if revealing part of a much larger phenomenon, the self-narration we practice day in day out" (114).
3. For further information on a "white" dominated publishing industry, see Young.
4. Though a little beyond the scope of this chapter, it is worth noting that this emphasis on reportage and pedagogy is a long-standing feature of popular black autobiographical writing, most notably in the bestselling text of all times along these lines, *The Autobiography of Malcolm X* (Malcolm X and Hayley). This is despite the fact that it was cowritten by Alex Haley, who had a different agenda to that of Malcolm X.
5. Information obtained from an author interview with Rodriguez in January 2008.
6. See also Staples; Barras; and French.
7. We are inevitably reminded of Stuart Hall's famed essay, "What Is This 'Black' in Black Popular Culture?," where he makes the same point (Hall "What Is This 'Black'").
8. Indeed, if there had been further room for analysis in this chapter, Mostern's text would be a valuable source. He deliberates an "institutional" definition of black autobiography—the extent to which (white-owned) publishers can legitimize the act of self-representation, and how the "real" person (or our sense of it) is a literary construct which forms the basis of the "contract" between reader and publishing house.

Works Cited

Access Hollywood. "Oprah Duped by Another Fabricated Memoir." *MSN Today*, March 5, 2008. Web. http://today.msnbc.msn.com/id/23486842/ns/today-entertainment.

Alexander, Amy. "Truth and Consequences." *The Nation*, March 24, 2008. Print.

Annesley, James. *Fictions of Globalization: Consumption, the Market and the Contemporary American Novel*. London: Continuum, 2006. Print.

Barras, Jonetta Rose. "Literary Lock-Up: The Self-Imposed Bondage of Black Writers." *Washington DC City Paper*, October 28–November 3, 1994. Print.

Bonazzi, Robert. "Afterword." *Black Like Me* by John Howard Griffin. New York: Signet, 1998. 194–211. Print.

Browder, Laura. "Fake Autobiographies: A Great American Tradition." *History News Service*, February 12, 2005. Web. http://historynewsservice.org/2005/02/fake-autobiographies-a-great-american-tradition.

Dawes, Bio Laina. "Another Memoir Bites the Dust—Love and Consequence Writer Ain't No 'Blood.'" *BlogHer Publishing Network*. March 6, 2008. Web. http://www.blogher.com/another-memoir-bites-dust-love-and-consequence-writer-aint-no-blood.

Dow Adams, Timothy. *Telling Lies in Modern American Autobiography*. Chapel Hill: U of North Carolina P, 1990. Print.

Dreisinger, Baz. *Near Black: White-to-Black Passing in American Culture*. Amherst: U of Massachusetts P, 2008. Print.

Eakin, Paul John. "Breaking Rules: The Consequences of Self-Narration." *Biography* 24.1 (2001): 113–127. Print.

———, ed. *The Ethics of Life Writing*. Ithaca: Cornell UP, 2004. Print.

Faludi, Susan. "Ghetto Star." *Los Angeles Weekly*, October 6, 1999. Print.

———. *Stiffed: The Betrayal of the American Man*. London: Chatto and Windus, 1999. Print.

French, Mary Ann. "For Black Authors, the Same Old Story? A Round-Table Look at Literary Roadblocks Facing African Americans." *Washington Post*, June 13, 1994. Print.

Frey, James. *A Million Little Pieces*. New York: Random House, 2003. Print.

Hall, Stuart. "New Ethnicities." Ed. Linda Alcoff and Eduardo Mendieta. *Identities: Race, Class, Gender and Nationalities*. Oxford: Wiley-Blackwell Press, 2002. 90–95. Print.

———. *Representation: Cultural Representations and Signifying Practices*. 5th ed. Milton Keynes: Open UP, 2001. Print.

———. "What Is This 'Black' in Black Popular Culture?" *Black Popular Culture*. Ed. Gina Dent. Seattle: Bay Press, 1992. 21–33. Print.

Hinckley, David. "Oprah's Mag Gushed over Memoir of Fake Gangbanger." *New York Daily News*, March 5, 2008. Print.

Horowitz, Mark. "In Search of Monster." *Atlantic* 272 (December 1993): 28–37. Print.

Johnson, E. Patrick. *Appropriating Blackness: Performance and the Politics of Authenticity*. Durham, NC: Duke UP, 2003. Print.

Jones, Margaret B. *Love and Consequences: A Memoir of Hope and Survival*. New York: Riverhead Books, 2008. Print.

Kakutani, Michiko. "However Mean the Streets, Have an Exit Strategy." *New York Times*, February 26, 2008. Print.

Kelley, Robin D. G. *Race Rebels: Culture, Politics and the Black Working Class*. New York: Free Press, 1994. Print.

Kellogg, Caroyln. "Hey, Margaret Seltzer, about That Nonprofit." *Los Angeles Times*, March 5, 2008. Print.

Konchar Farr, Cecilia. *Reading Oprah: How Oprah's Book Club Changed the Way America Reads*. Albany: SUNY Press, 2004. Print.

Konchar Farr, Cecilia, and Jaime Harker, eds. *The Oprah Affect: Critical Essays on Oprah's Book Club*. Albany: SUNY Press, 2008. Print.

Mailer, Norman. "The White Negro." *Dissent: A Quarterly of Politics and Culture*, Fall 1957. Web. http://www.dissentmagazine.org /online_articles/the-white-negro-fall-1957.

Malcolm X with Alex Haley. *The Autobiography of Malcolm X*. New York: Grove Press, 1965. Print.

Marcus, Laura. *Auto/biographical Discourses: Theory, Criticism, Practice*. Manchester: Manchester UP, 1994. Print.

"Memoir 'Love and Consequences' Revealed as Fiction." *Entertainment Weekly*, March 4, 2008. Print.

Mendelsohn, Daniel. "Stolen Suffering." *New York Times*, March 9, 2008. Print.

Mills, David. "Fucking Liar." *Undercover Black Man* (blog), March 4, 2008. Web. http://undercoverblackman.blogspot.com/2008/03/fucking-liar.html.

Mostern, Kenneth. *Autobiography and Black Identity Politics: Racialization in Twentieth Century America*. Cambridge: Cambridge UP, 1999. Print.

Nelson, Sara. "Reality Check." *Publishers Weekly* 255.1 (March 10, 2008). Print.

Nishikawa, Kinohi. "Black Book Production and the Culture of Conglomeratized Print." Conference paper at the American Studies Association conference, November 3–6, 2005, Washington, DC (paper requested from author). Print.

"Opinion: Margaret Seltzer's Fake Memoir." *Los Angeles Times*, March 6, 2008. Print.

Patton, Stacey. "The Rap on Whites Who Try to Act Black." *Washington Post*, March 16, 2008. Print.

Quinn, Eithne. *Nuthin' but a "G" Thang: The Culture and Commerce of Gangsta Rap*. New York: Columbia UP, 2005. Print.

Reed, Mimi. "A Refugee from Gangland." *New York Times*, February 28, 2008. Print.

Rich, Motoko. "A Family Tree of Literary Fakers." *New York Times*, March 8, 2008. Print.

———. "Foundation Is Questioned after Memoir Is Exposed." *New York Times*, March 6, 2008. Print.

———. "Gang Memoir, Turning Page, Is Pure Fiction." *New York Times*, March 4, 2008. Print.

———. "Tracking the Fallout of (Another) Literary Fraud." *New York Times*, March 5, 2008. Print.

Rodriguez, Luis J. *Always Running—La Vida Loca: Gang Days in LA*. New York: Curbstone, 1993. Print.

Rufle, Lisa. "Love and Consequences." *Suite101*, March 4, 2008. Web. http://www.suite101.com/content/a-memoir-of-lies-a46627.

Serjeant, Jill. "Little Glamour in LA, Gang Capital of America." *Reuters*, February 8, 2007. Print.

Shakur, Sanyika. *Monster: The Autobiography of an LA Gang Member*. New York: Atlantic, 1993. Print.

Shameer Cohen, Sherry. "Truth or Consequences." *Connecticut Press Club* (a subchapter of the National Federation of Press Women). n.d. Web. http://www.ctpressclub.com/blog.htm.

Shields, David. *Reality Hunger: A Manifesto*. New York: Penguin, 2011. Print.

Staples, Brent. "When Only Monsters Are Real." *New York Times*, November 21, 1993. Print.

Starr, Kevin. *Coast of Dreams: A History of Contemporary California*. London: Allen Lane, 2005. Print.

Thompson, Carla Ray. "Author Margaret B. Jones, 'Love and Consequences,' Be a Big Fat Liar." *The Ride: Popping Off about Popular Culture* (memoirist/journalist's blog), March 9, 2008. Web. http://www.cwrite.wordpress.com.

Timberg, Scott, and Josh Getlin. "Behind Book Scandal." *Los Angeles Times*, March 5, 2008. Print.

Williams, Stanley "Tookie." *Blue Rage, Black Redemption: A Memoir*. Pleasant Hill, CA: Damamli, 2004. Print.

Young, John K. *Black Writers, White Publishers: Marketplace Politics in Twentieth Century African American Literature*. Jackson: UP of Mississippi, 2006. Print.

CHAPTER 11

"A Secondhand Kind of Terror"

Grace Halsell, Kathryn Stockett, and the Ironies of Empathy

Alisha Gaines

Though it be a thrilling and marvelous thing to be merely young and gifted in such times, it is doubly so, doubly dynamic—to be young, gifted *and black* . . . Write about *our people*: tell their story. You have something glorious to draw on begging for attention . . . This nation needs your gifts.

—Lorraine Hansberry,
To Be Young, Gifted and Black: Lorraine Hansberry in Her Own Words

As Lorraine Hansberry had observed, it's a special time to be young, gifted, and black.
—Grace Halsell, September 16, 1969, journal entry

When Grace Halsell cited Lorraine Hansberry's affirmation of a talented generation of black youth, she had only recently "become" a black woman. Armed with the curiosity and mobility of a freelance journalist, the economic security of a former White House staff writer for the Lyndon B. Johnson administration, and the reckless courage of the daughter of an infamous cowboy and westward expansionist, Halsell attempted to abandon the presumed comforts of Southern white womanhood by undergoing a course of medication to darken her skin. For Halsell, experimental blackness had little to do with challenging structural racial inequalities or solving W. E. B. Du Bois's stubbornly and dangerously persistent "problem of the color line."[1] Instead, she chose blackness "to open my mind, my eyes, my pores, to the dilemma of race in America, and to share those experiences."[2] Privately citing Hansberry's motto, the title of both a posthumously produced play and a literary mosaic of unfinished works, interviews, and journal entries, Halsell appropriated the powerful rhetoric of a burgeoning Black Power movement by imagining herself among the intended audience of the playwright's loving and urgent charge to a new generation of black writers. With the hubris of privilege, Halsell timed the "specialness" of her new "young" and "gifted" blackness just as black separatists began to question and reject the place of white liberals in a movement starting to address issues such as white supremacy, capitalism, and the US imperialism evidenced by the Vietnam War. Her six-month experiment in both Harlem and Mississippi concluded with the publication of the 1969 bestselling memoir of "our people," *Soul Sister*. This chapter attends to the cultural investment in this seemingly radical version of empathy—to walk in someone else's skin rather than his or her shoes. Halsell's eagerness to "open" herself and "share" her new blackness is premised on a convenient and disavowing erasure of narratives by black women and reveals the imbalanced power dynamics implicit in the empathetic gesture. It is an erasure that enables and creepily anticipates Kathryn Stockett's nostalgic reimagining of the 1960s lives of black domestic workers in her 2009 *New York Times* bestseller, *The Help*. By detailing Halsell's experimental reracialization and its resonances with *The Help*, as well as the relationship between Halsell and her masquerade mentor, John Howard Griffin, this chapter reveals pervasively perverse assumptions about the meanings of black identity and the utility of cross-racial empathy by insisting that such complicated and fetishized assumptions can be a matter of life and death.

"I Could Be Black"

Although a self-described "descendent of slave-holders and Civil War veterans,"[3] Grace Halsell was no "belle." Born May 7, 1923, in Lubbock, Texas, to her then 63-year-old father and 30-year-old mother, Ruth Shanks, Halsell was encouraged to "exert free will"[4] by a father whose 1957 *New York Times* obituary headlined, "Harry H. Halsell, 96, Indian Fighter, Texas Rancher who Once Outfoxed Geronimo Dies." Despite growing up near native communities, Halsell puzzlingly insists "color was not a conscious fact in my early years" (11). She did not become "*personally* interested" (9, emphasis in original) in either the ethical or legislative gains made by the civil rights and Black Power movements or even the lives of people of color until a book recommendation at a State Department reception early in 1968 made race both immediately interesting and personal. Halsell gushes, "I bought *Black Like Me* and plunged into it . . . 'I could do that . . . I could be black'" (9). Written by another Fort Worth native, 1961's *Black Like Me*[5] chronicled John Howard Griffin's now iconic sojourn into what he calls "oblivion,"[6] a six-week trek through the Jim Crow South as a black man—one maintained through a combination of sun lamps, the vitiligo treatment medication Oxsoralen, and a topical skin stain. The resulting spectacle of Griffin's physical transformation and harrowing tales of a Jim Crow South ensured not only the wild success of his narrative but also its long-standing place in high school curricula as the primer of cross-racial empathy. Along with count-less generations of adolescent readers, Halsell found in the pages of *Black Like Me* the cure for acute racial myopia: radical empathy. Moved by Griffin's example, Halsell began an intimate correspondence with him in March 1968 that would last until Griffin's death in 1980. "I want to know you" (15), she writes. She receives her chance on April 3, 1968, with Griffin delivering a lecture at the University of Baltimore. Although many like-minded readers of *Black Like Me* sought Griffin's encouragement and advice for their own racial experiments, this initial meeting and ensuing friendship convinced Griffin that Halsell could and should attempt blackness. In a May 23, 1968, recommendation letter to Robert Gutwillig, editor of the New American Library, Griffin writes, "Let me just say that many people have approached me about such a [race-switching] project and I have consistently discouraged it, because it is dangerous and it takes very special gifts of perception . . . When Grace Halsell suggested this to me, I jumped at the idea enthusiastically, because she combines the experience and the perception and the 'feeling' more than any person I know:—I urged her to do what I have always discouraged everyone else from doing."[7] With the support and mentorship of the man she would call "Soul Brother Number One,"[8] Halsell prepared herself for an experiment in empathy that implicitly reveals the limits of the scopic regimes of racialization. Deeply invested in the idea that by temporarily "looking black" one can assume the authority of both experience and representativeness, Halsell con-structs a medicalized blackness developed and maintained by the same team of renowned dermatologists Griffin used almost ten years prior: Robert Stolar, John A. Kenney of the Howard University School of Medicine, and Aaron B. Lerner of the Yale University School of Medicine. Under their guidance, Halsell took a vitiligo corrective regimen of Tsiroralen and the topical ointment Zetar. She then supplemented the effect of the medications with weeks basking in the tropical suns of St. Thomas and Puerto Rico, hair dye, and black contacts. Along with the physical transformations of her body, Halsell learned to perform blackness by enrolling in what could only be considered John Howard Griffin's correspon-dence course, "Racial Empathy 101." Responding to her anxious queries on how to create the "identity . . . in mind,"[9] Griffin gives her this advice:

> I think the best thing is to keep the story as near the truth as possible . . . (We must avoid giving the racists the material to discredit you later—they will love to put on that you went there [Mississippi] under false pretenses.) Certainly with Negroes, I would tell the exact truth, that you are doing a kind of "lady" *Black Like Me*; you are from Fort Worth. Once you are in the Negro community it is just assumed that you are Negro, so you will not need to make any explanations because none will be asked . . . If Negroes ask questions you can give honest answers; if whites (especially strangers) ask questions just assume that cold-staring "sullen" attitude and mumble the minimum replies . . . this is what most Negroes do now, when the questions are unwarranted.[10]

Here, Griffin trains Halsell in a performance of blackness where instructive black women are not only conveniently absent but also rendered unnecessary. Instead, blackness is excavated from the white imaginary in all the complexity of its "sullen" and "mumbl[ing]" suspicion. With exclusive and assumptive authority, Griffin explicates the presumed schism between the public and interior lives of African Americans by suggesting that blackness must be staged for the appeasing benefit of white audiences. In his (il)logics of racialization, it is only in these moments of loaded interracial contact that blackness even becomes legible. Here, Griffin fails to acknowledge the performativity of racial difference and obscures anxieties about black authenticity and belonging often played out at the intersections of class and sexuality.

"A Kind of 'Lady' *Black Like Me*"

While readying Halsell for her curtain call, both she and Griffin were largely motivated by the gendered nuances Halsell could bring to a white readership's understanding of black America. "After all," Halsell writes, *Black Like Me* was written by a man . . . I wondered if it were possible for a white woman to expose herself to that mind-deadening malady of second-class citizenship and report its effects" (11–12). In the same pitch letter to editor Robert Gutwillig, Griffin anticipates the insights to be gained via Halsell: "I have also felt that this [project] should be done by a woman, and felt my own work deficient because I believe there are insights that only a woman can get."[11] Selling Halsell with invocations to a gynocentric ideal of female intuition, Griffin recognizes his blindness regarding the experiences of black women in his own exposé but still positions himself as the guiding authority on how to perform black womanhood. "Always act suspicious," Griffin warns, "especially of men asking questions, and especially of the police, suspicious, uneasy and ready-to-run; because certainly the fear of rape is widespread."[12] Prompted by either his masculine "impulse" to protect Southern white womanhood or the lingering fear of sexual violence stemming from his own racial (mis)adventures, Griffin's cautionary advice is still notably ambiguous (of whom is she to fear exactly?). However, in the logics of *Soul Sister*, Halsell interprets his warnings through her long-conditioned fear of black male sexuality: "The white man says the black man is a beast and marauder, he will rape you, rob you, he is mean as the devil (you know the devil has got to be black)" (50). Halsell reveals that proper Southern white womanhood is predicated on the paranoid expectations of a pathological black male sexuality animated by the not-exclusively-Southern fiction of the ubiquitous black male rapist. "Yes," she admits, "I've packed all of my old fears, right in with the nylons and hairbrush. I'm not *supposed* to go [to Harlem]" (50, emphasis in original). Halsell continues, "No telling what's going to happen to a good white woman like me" (51). Her fear spectacularly reinforces her white womanhood while supposedly ensuring that whiteness is protected from a willful and polluting miscegenation. Despite the medical and topical interventions darkening her body, it is as if the rapaciousness of black sexuality would undoubtedly hunt down and uncover the "real truth" of her whiteness. In other words, she may attempt black womanhood but would always be a white potential rape victim.

These regionally sanctioned mythologies directly impact how she chooses to embody her "synthetic blackness."[13] In a September 2, 1968, letter to dermatologist Robert Stolar, Halsell exclaims, "I'm beginning to see several benefits in being a man! I could wear long-sleeved shirts and trousers and just have a dark face and dark hands."[14] During a month of nearly nude sunbathing and almost overdosing on vitiligo corrective medication in the desperate attempt to get an even coloring on her entire body, Halsell fantasizes herself both black and in drag, longing for the masculine privileges of Griffin's seemingly easier black embodiment. Never anticipating displaying his entire body to the gaze of anyone aside from his own reflection, Griffin prepared his blackened body to pass only in public. Contrastingly, Halsell suggests that to successfully perform black womanhood, her *naked* body must be able to withstand the scrutinizing gaze of racializing surveillance. By readying her privates for the private sphere, Halsell gestures toward the vulnerability of black women, eerily foreshadowing the uncomfortably ironic end of her memoir.

Once Halsell's body reached a "beautiful color (good enough to eat I suppose—if you like caramel),"[15] she moves to Harlem to begin her (mis)adventures in blackness. "I have been on the outside looking in. I have smelled the colored people's collard greens and their living-up-close-together smells. I am now going to knock on their doors and say, black people let me in there with you!" (13). After months of being "let in" and working as a secretary at Harlem Hospital, Halsell felt frustrated in the urban "black enclave" (51). Disappointed by the other secretaries she pejoratively dismisses as "[holding] up whitey's standards" (116), she quits her job in pursuit of more "authentic" black folk. She eventually leaves Harlem after being unable to connect with the women with whom she shared a neighborhood guest house. Rather than taking these failures in cross-racial empathy as instructive moments to reconsider the superficial assumptions both she and Griffin made about black identity, she instead displaces her anxiety on a more acceptably familiar repository for it—black queerness. After realizing "that the Guest House has women who make love only with other women" (78), Halsell dismisses her queer housemates with the same ease she dismisses her bourgeois-aspiring Harlem Hospital colleagues.

"Mississippi Goddam"

After abandoning Harlem, Halsell continues to shape her black womanhood in Griffin's image by tracing his footsteps down to the deepest South—Mississippi. "I want to experience firsthand why so many believe it's the most backward state in the Union" (127), she writes. As the setting of the 1955 lynching of 14-year-old Emmett Till, the 1963 assassination of Medgar Evers, the voting registration drives of the 1964 Freedom Summer, and the subsequent lynchings of Mississippi Freedom Project workers James Chaney, Andrew Goodman, and Michael Schwerner, Mississippi had become the paradigmatic symbol for the South's need for, and resistance to, the demands of the civil rights movement. It was Mississippi's reputation as the seat of racial terror solidified by the Evers assassination that inspired Nina Simone to angrily croon "Mississippi Goddam" in 1963. If the South remains the "national other"[16] and repository for the sins of the rest of the country's racial past, Mississippi is the other's other.

When Halsell alights from the bus in Jackson, she does so conscious of the legacies of both the state's and region's blood-soaked history. Halsell writes, "Because I am a creature, so to speak, of 'the Confederacy,' this trip represents an excursion into the past, a reliving of a part of my life, with glimpses into old secrets long buried, yet still vivid and intimidating" (127). Recognizing the difficulty in assimilating into Jackson's black community knowing "all strangers in the South are suspect" (131), Halsell seeks protection and guidance from members of the local chapter of the National Association for the Advancement of Colored People (NAACP). The recipient of their gracious hospitality and over a plate of ribs, Halsell hears "several of the most gripping accounts of Klan bombings and lynchings . . . these acts of terror, all in Mississippi, I listen like any interested yet *detached* observer" (153, emphasis in original). For the first time in her narrative, Halsell sits as witness as the resilient black Mississippians articulate the threats to their own survivability. In the face of this frank truth telling, Halsell chooses this moment to disclose her whiteness, announcing the detachment she previously only felt. Postdisclosure, she is quickly made to realize the danger her presence puts them in: "'If the Klan find out where you're staying, they'll kill us and you,' Winson [director of Jackson's NAACP] cautions. 'If there's anything them peckerwoods hate worse than a *nigger* who talks back to them it's a white woman living with the *niggers*'" (155, emphasis in original). Rather than place this already vulnerable community in further peril, she decides she must continue her racial pilgrimage elsewhere.

Upon reaching the "Delta, an area of rich land and poor people, in the northwest corner of Mississippi" with "towns [that] seem self-contained, barricaded against strangers, fretful, and lonely" (166), Halsell suffers the consequences of violating the de facto segregation still lingering after the legal defeat of Jim Crow. Rather than serving as a camouflaged witness to the realities of living black in the Deep South, Halsell provokes the status quo. For example, the police are called on her after she asks to use a telephone in the white waiting room at the Greyhound bus station as well as for attempting to integrate a white, Southern Baptist congregation in the middle of Sunday morning service. Halsell undertakes these nonviolent, civil rights movement-inspired strategies without any contextual understanding and/or awareness of the needs and wants of this community. As Halsell becomes the agitator some Southern whites feared only came from the North, she experiences the conflicting duality of her new blackness. She writes, "I feel disembodied, a cipher floating in a void . . . I do not feel a Negro; yet . . . I cannot be my old self either" (192). It is a "secondhand kind of terror" (157). Stranded on the virgule between two racial realities, it is finally Halsell's employment as a domestic day laborer that sutures black authenticity to her embodied racial feeling.

In pursuit of both the folk and work, Halsell begins working with the Wheeler family after a recommendation by the Mississippi State Employment Office. On her very first day, she receives passing instructions from a hurried Mrs. Wheeler to "clean the commode, clean the tub, clean the floors, run the sweeper, do the washing, [and] do the ironing" (194) for her $3 daily wage. Halsell is then left alone in the Wheeler two-story colonial only to be surprised when Mr. Wheeler unexpectedly returns. She writes, "I do not look at him directly but keep my eyes to the laundry, yet I sense he is staring at me, and in that moment of silence, I feel he is somehow magnetized" (195–196). After asking the usual questions such as her name and where she's from, Mr. Wheeler retires to the upstairs master bedroom.

> Soon from [the] suite comes a thunderous clap . . . and simultaneously he shouts, "Come quick!"
>
> Hurrying upstairs, I walk swiftly into the bedroom. Instantly the door slams behind me and as I turn around I find myself encircled in Wheeler's arms. I am momentarily overwhelmed. He presses his mouth roughly against mine and forces his body against me, muttering hoarsely about his desperate need for "black pussy" . . .
>
> "Only take five minutes, only take *five minutes*," he mumbles, partly pleading, partly threatening. "Now quieten down! Just gotta get me some black pussy!" . . .
>
> I loose one arm enough to reach up and, with the last of my strength and will-power, I push the large framed [family] picture from its moorings and send it careening down. It grazes the back of Wheeler's head. His flushed face dissolves from lust into hatred. "You black bitch!" he cries, shaking with anger. More menacingly he adds, his voice lowered to a whisper: "I ought to kill you, you black bitch!"
>
> I suppose I should feel terror-stricken all over again; the lord and master is in a state of mind where nothing might faze him, and where the urge to satisfy himself as a punitive act may be strong. But curiously my feeling is one of utter relief. Then, feeling more contempt than fear: "Go ahead, you coward!" I dare him. "You wouldn't have the nerve!" (197; emphasis in original)

Halsell's blackness triggers Wheeler's fantasy of the lascivious and available Jezebel. In the presence of her black woman body, Wheeler performs an eager lecherousness that reveals his part in the well-rehearsed script dictating the interactions between white men and black women in the precarious space of the domestic. Halsell writes, "I have heard many Negro maids say that their greatest fear is being in the house alone when the white man comes in. As one bitterly commented, 'They pay you fifteen dollars a week, and then expect to get you too'" (198).

As readers are omnisciently aware that Wheeler craves five minutes with a not-so-black pussy, this scene spectacularly reveals the vulnerability of black womanhood while uncomfortably mired in the ironies of authenticity, empathy, race, and power. These ironies are not completely lost on Halsell herself: "Now I reflect how I had gone with trembling heart to the ghetto, Harlem, fearful that a big black bogeyman might tear down the paper-thin door separating my 'white' body from his lustful desires. And now it had been a white, not a black, devil whose passions had overwhelmed him" (202). As Halsell acknowledges her racist assumptions about black masculinity, she articulates a black womanhood constructed in the wake of white masculine rapaciousness and foreshadowed by her decision to affect a blackness that could pass naked. "I begin to see the role of the black woman in Wheeler's home objectively," she writes, "she is me" (201). While the medical interventions made to her body immediately cast Halsell's blackness in the visual logics of racialization, the spectacle of Halsell's near-rape is the generative act of her black womanhood. What makes this scene so incredibly perverse then is that Halsell needs this spectacle of racialized sexual violence for a proper racial belonging. After nearly six months experimenting in black woman-hood, it is this moment that finally allows her to empathize with real, Southern black women. With this discomforting paradox, *Soul Sister*'s gesture toward the vulnerability of black womanhood is simultaneously an affront to black women.

Bolstered by the credibility of her whiteness, Halsell's resistance to Wheeler is imbued with the legitimacy black women survivors of sexual violence lack. Rather than reveal the "truth" of her body, Halsell escapes back into whiteness comfort-ably knowing she does not need her $3 daily wage. She releases herself from the grip of her attacker and taunts her perpetrator with a defiance she assumes most black women can and/or will not demonstrate. Halsell writes, "Suppose the black woman in [Wheeler's] frenzied embrace had been a mother of hungry children, waiting for her to bring them food. Could she have resisted his advances? Run from home without collecting *any* money for her day's labor?" (202, emphasis in original). Halsell's necessary queries underscore the connections between eco-nomics, labor, and the maintenance of white supremacy. However, the disavowal of long histories of black women's narratives of resistance enables both Halsell's "exceptional heroism" as well as the historically inaccurate claim that a 2009 novel about black domestic workers is "breaking new ground . . . [with] a brand new perspective."[17]

How to Play the Help

Born in 1969 in Jackson, Mississippi, Kathryn Stockett gained literary celebrity due to the overwhelming success of her debut novel, *The Help*. Propelled into both the popularity and scrutiny of fame, the story of how *The Help* came to be is nearly the stuff of legend: a decade of writing; countless rejections; a promise to a struggling film director; and finally, a place on the *New York Times* bestseller list, an Academy Award–nominated film adaptation, upward of forty translations, and millions of novels sold. Stockett admittedly wrote *The Help* to understand the complicated relationship between her childhood self and her family's black domestic worker, Demetrie. She writes, "Although Jackson's population was half white and half black, I didn't have a single black friend or a black neighbor or even a black person in my school . . . Yet one of the closest people to me was Demetrie."[18] While it is unclear if Stockett ever made any black friends, she did regret never asking Demetrie "what it felt like to be black in Mississippi work-ing for our white family."[19] *The Help* is the balm to Stockett's white guilt. It is a nostalgic, mournful, and regretful lament—the imagined and hopeful answer to that nagging question.

As Stockett attempted to remedy her childhood ignorance, she did so through the corrective voices of Jackson's black domestic workers, whom she portrays as both unable to tell their own stories but still remarkably instructive, resilient, undereducated, loving, and full of stories. Although some of the narrative is told through the perspectives of sassy Minny and long-suffering Aibileen, the clear protagonist is the semiautobiographical, aspiring-writer protagonist, Eugenia "Skeeter" Phelan. Like Stockett, Skeeter establishes her literary career by crafting and coaxing a fantasized voice from Jackson's black domestics while precariously shuttling between cross-racial empathy and feigned indifference. However laudable on the surface, Skeeter's secret nighttime trysts with black women are mired in the complicated histories of Southern labor, race, and power, particularly since Skeeter wants to be the author, not the stenographer, of black life. Skeeter admits, "At first, I'm disappointed that Aibileen is doing most of the writing, with me just editing. But if Missus Stein [the New York editor] likes it, I'll be writing the other maid's stories" (175). Consequently, readers of *The Help* face a narrative trap. Since Skeeter's love life, disintegrating friendships, and career aspirations are the main concerns of the novel, we are coaxed into hoping Skeeter remains cocooned in white privilege and suffers nothing from her seemingly courageous decision to talk to the help.

Although temporally separated, Halsell and Stockett serendipitously meet on the common ground of a reimagined 1960s Jackson, Mississippi. In a tangible way, Halsell's brief experience as a "black" domestic worker firmly sutures the concerns of *Soul Sister* to those of *The Help*, but more important, both authors stage their redemption as "creatures . . . of the Confederacy" in the restaging of Mississippi-brand racism and the appropriation of the narrative voices of black women. In *Soul Sister*, Halsell writes a Jackson rightly unable to accommodate her new black body because of its storied racial violence. Halsell's dangerously ironic black womanhood spectacularly indexes Stockett's refusal to name the sexual violence endemic to the experience of Southern black domestic work. Although Skeeter briefly acknowledges that "angry stories come out, of white men who've tried to touch them" (304), Stockett cannot bring herself to write any scenes detailing the overwhelming and historical threat of sexual violence. For example, while portraying the precarious circumstances Minny endures working for the socially snubbed Celia Foote behind her husband's back, Stockett never fully acknowledges what might happen to Minny upon her discovery. "I'll tell you what he's gone do [if he finds me]," Minny worries. "He's gone get that pistol and shoot Minny dead right here on this no-wax floor."[20] Able to imagine Minny's dead but not "rapeable" body, Stockett obscures the very same realities of Southern sexual violence that Halsell exploits. For Stockett, this allows her to create a reimagined Mississippi much more palatable to, and subsequently celebrated by, a twenty-first-century liberal readership.

Both Halsell and Stockett develop grotesque fantasies of black womanhood that then underscore their own privileged positionalities. With self-absorbed good intentions, Halsell and Stockett sought to appropriate blackness as a representative mouthpiece for African American women. Although Halsell admits that she "never regarded Negroes as a part of my society. They were simply part of the landscape" (11), she also paradoxically insists she "was in a good position to notice all the fetters binding my darker sisters" (12). While it is "thrilling" to be a young, gifted, and *black* writer as Hansberry reminds, Halsell's and Stockett's strategic ignorance compels a racial ventriloquism premised on spectacularizing black suffering as sought-after and profitable secondhand terror. Halsell's temporary blackness cannot undo her family's "expansionist" hand in the genocide of native peoples, just as Stockett's portrayal of the relationships between wise maids and their microaggressive employers cannot undo the white supremacist violence structuring the lives of black domestic workers. As both Southern writers negotiate "home," ultimately both are projects of assuaging personal guilt. What *Soul Sister* and *The Help* do, rather extraordinarily, is expose the inequities of power in the empathetic gesture and the erasures and disavowals necessary to enact its logics.

It remains to be seen if *The Help* will gain the long-standing cultural currency of cross-racial empathetic texts such as Harper Lee's *To Kill a Mockingbird* or Griffin's *Black Like Me*. Its unprecedented book and box office sales predict it will be. However, while *Soul Sister* should have solidified Halsell's place alongside her more memorable mentor, Griffin's memoir was better suited to the tastes of a white reading public eventually uncomfortable with the salaciousness of her exposé. Case in point, when John Howard Griffin died in 1980 of diabetes complications, rumors abounded that his death resulted from skin cancer stemming from his racial masquerade. Ironically, it was Halsell who died in 2000 from a tragically long battle with the skin cancer multiple myeloma, a direct result of her six-month martyrdom to the "ineffable despair" (14) of blackness.

Warning: blackness can be fatal.

Notes

1. Du Bois vii.
2. Halsell, *In Their Shoes* 2.
3. Halsell, *Soul Sister*, 11. All subsequent citations of this text will be indicated by in-text citation.
4. Halsell, *In Their Shoes* 32.
5. Griffin, *Black Like Me*.
6. Ibid. 37.
7. Griffin, Letter to Robert Gutwillig.
8. Halsell, Letter to John Howard Griffin, 20 March 1978.
9. Halsell, Letter to John Howard Griffin, 19 April 1968.
10. Griffin, Letter to Grace Halsell.
11. Griffin, Letter to Robert Gutwillig.
12. Griffin, Letter to Grace Halsell.
13. Halsell, *Black/White Sex* 22.
14. Halsell, Letter to Robert Stolar.
15. Halsell, Letter to Aaron Lerner.
16. For more on this idea, see Baker and Nelson.

17. Ibid, 120. This claim is undone by many texts including Alice Childress's 1956 novel *Like One of the Family*, which chronicles through a series of monologues, the life of the outspoken black domestic Mildred
18. Stockett, "This Life" 1.
19. Stockett, *The Help* 530.
20. Ibid. 43.

Works Cited

Baker, Houston, and Dana Nelson, eds. "Violence, The Body, and 'The South.'" *American Literature* 73 (2001). Print.

Du Bois, W. E. B. *The Souls of Black Folk: Essays and Sketches*. Chicago: A. C. McClurg, 1907. Print.

Griffin, John Howard. *Black Like Me*. New York: Signet Books, 1961. Print.

———. Letter to Grace Halsell. 20 April 1968. Grace Halsell Collection. Special Collections Library. Fort Worth, TX: Texas Christian University. Print.

———. Letter to Robert Gutwillig. 23 May 1968. Grace Halsell Collection. Special Collections Library. Fort Worth, TX: Texas Christian University. Print.

Halsell, Grace. *Black/White Sex*. New York: William Morrow, 1972. Print.

———. *In Their Shoes*. Fort Worth, TX: Texas Christian University Press, 1996. Print.

———. Journal Entry. 16 September 1969. Grace Halsell Collection. Special Collections Library. Fort Worth, TX: Texas Christian University. Print.

———. Letter to Aaron Lerner. 13 November 1968. Grace Halsell Collection, Special Collections Library. Fort Worth, TX: Texas Christian University. Print.

———. Letter to John Howard Griffin. 19 April 1968. Grace Halsell Collection. Special Collections Library. Fort Worth, TX: Texas Christian University. Print.

———. Letter to John Howard Griffin. 20 March 1978. Grace Halsell Collection. Special Collections Library. Fort Worth, TX: Texas Christian University. Print.

———. Letter to Robert Stolar. 2 September 1968. Grace Halsell Collection. Special Collections Library. Fort Worth, TX: Texas Christian University. Print.

———. *Soul Sister*. Washington, DC: Crossroads, 1999. Print.

Nemiroff, Robert. *To Be Young, Gifted and Black: Lorraine Hansberry in Her Own Words*. Englewood Cliffs, NJ: Prentice-Hall, 1969. Print.

Stockett, Kathryn. *The Help*. New York: Berkeley Books, 2009. Print.

———. "This Life: Kathryn Stockett on Her Childhood in the Deep South." *Daily Mail*. 18 July 2009; 1. Print.

CHAPTER 12

"Savior," Good Mother, Jezebel, Tom, Trickster

The Blind Side Myth

Pearlie Strother-Adams

Introduction

Singer Madonna and actress Angelina Jolie, two of Hollywood's "bad girls" known in the past for their shockingly kinky sexual exploits, are now, ironically, hailed as America's "good mothers," modern-day Mother Theresas, and real-life symbols of Hollywood's new mammy: the protector and the savior of children, especially black children. Sandra Bullock won an Oscar for best actress for her performance in *The Blind Side* (2009), cast as Leigh Anne Tuohy, a real-life rich white woman who, with her husband, Sean Tuohy, takes in a homeless black teenage boy, Michael Oher, who goes on to become one of the National Football League's most prominent stars.

This chapter explores the representation of African Americans in the film *The Blind Side*. The film, directed by John Lee Hancock, appears simplistic on the surface; however, to the contrary, character representation and positioning are ideologically complex and methodical, seemingly by design. In order to study Hollywood's representation of African Americans in *The Blind Side* in roles that deliberately play to white mainstream audiences, it is necessary to give attention to the representation of the principal white protagonist, Tuohy (Bullock), because what emerges in her character represents Hollywood's true objective more specifically: the ideological meaning they seek to achieve and "fix" in the minds of viewers as reality, or the "norm" (Hall, *Representation: Cultural* 249). The purpose of this chapter is twofold. First, it argues that African Americans continue to be overwhelmingly framed as the "Other," defined as "dark, primitive, different" (hooks, *Black Looks* 21), a tradition that is maintained in *The Blind Side*; thus we will explore how Hollywood uses various techniques to maintain and manipulate age-old stereotypes of the African American male as the *victim, tom, savage,* and *trickster*. Second, the chapter looks at the major ideological shift in the roles of the white and black female: the white female's progression from "needy and incapable"—requiring constant "help" with caring for herself, her family, and especially her children—to "savior" (particularly for black children), a mythological *good mother*, a Christian saint, and an archetypal *mammy*, a role traditionally and historically devised to suit black women. To the contrary, the black female in *The Blind Side* is "cast out" as *mammy* to become the archetypal, stereotypical *sapphire/jezebel*. These mythological archetypes will be discussed in greater detail later in the chapter.

Hopefully, this chapter contributes to the literature in this area and seeks to answer the following research questions: (1) Is Hollywood's objective to establish the white female as a superwoman, the perfect wife and mother, and a savior of black children, while representing the black female as unfit as a mate and particularly as a mother and therefore detrimental to the survival of the black family and community? (2) Does Hollywood represent the black male in *The Blind Side* as alien, other, and criminal when he exists outside of and is therefore uncontained by white society?

American society presents itself as a melting pot of ethnic and racial difference; however, contemporary popular cinema gives little screen consideration to the nonwhite experience, and when it does, representations are often problematic (Gates 1). All too often, in what has proven to be suitable for mainstream consumption, African Americans are cast as a subcultural group, social outcasts, and "Others" (Campbell 15, 37, 59, 69; hooks, *Black Looks* 21–39) inhabiting and existing in a small, controlled, dingy, inner-city environment that is contained and structured to fit the context of contrived ideological themes, plots, and characterizations represented as the norm. These stereotypical representations (Hall, *Representation: Cultural* 258–89; Lipmann 81) are thus framed in such a way to show consensus and acceptance within the victimized group (African Americans) and also among others (mainstream white Americans) in Hollywood's myopic representation of this group, which is overwhelmingly presented as existing on the peripheral, on the outskirts of guarded politically and socially correct white society: the American norm. Too often African Americans are featured in Hollywood films in shadowy, crime-ridden, drug-infested settings where crack-addicted mothers rely on welfare with their illegitimate children who rarely know their fathers and where black men are represented either as missing in action or solely as frightening, dangerous, symbolically dark, shady, gritty, one-dimensional, hard-core criminals—"thugs in the hood" who are depleted of a proper home base, void of family and a respectable station in life, without a legitimate job or formal education, and lacking in ethical and moral codes that are needed to sustain themselves, family, and community. Such portrayals have become a dominant representation of African Americans (Strother-Adams 70–91).

However, members of the dominant culture are often portrayed as problem solvers and problem-free: void of social and political baggage that is of any real consequence for the disenfranchised minority. As part of the preservation and spread of the dominant cultural ideology, whites are represented as Christians: saviors of those who, in reality, the hegemonic system that they (whites) serve, uphold, and are the benefactors of has left out. Thus race is often underplayed or turned into a lighthearted, laughable moment, thus representing white society and culture as the norm, the right way to be, and the group that is not only in charge but ordained to be.

It would be remiss to dismiss the fact that *The Blind Side* is based on a true story; thus it is necessary to explain that it is still important that we explore the types of films, whether based on fact or purely fiction, that "Hollywood chooses to produce," particularly the characters and themes that are emphasized. Representations of African Americans are especially important because they support and help maintain the dominant culture's ideology.

The literature reveals that major problems continue to exist in Hollywood's representations of African Americans. First, the African American community has been criminalized disproportionately, giving the impression that criminal behavior is the norm (Campbell 69; Hall, *Representation: Cultural* 251; Lule 124) and thus innate to this group (Hall, *Representation: Cultural* 239–42), whose representation, many suggest, "possess[es]" a hunger "not guided by normal perceptions of good and evil" (Lule 124). This is particularly characteristic of the representation of African American males (Hall, *Representation: Cultural* 251), who are often shown in both news and entertainment media in "handcuffs" or "posed in mug shots" (Campbell 69). However, Hollywood has extended this criminality to the black female, often marginalizing her in roles where she is associated with drugs, prostitution, and child abuse and neglect (Jones 35–39; Ladson-Billings 89). Jones offers that "historically, the overwhelming majority of portrayals of African American women in American cinema have perpetuated stereotypical ideas" (36). According to Jones, black women are often presented as "decentralized, marginalized, and un-empowered individuals, thus, reinforcing the racial, class, and gender hierarchies which position women of color as socially and politically disenfranchised" (36).

Background

In early films, such as *Imitation of Life* (1934/1959) and *Gone with the Wind* (1939), black women were cast as maids, often in the guise of the traditional *mammy* (Bogle, *Toms* 10). Despite her oppression, the maid/mammy was extremely loyal, always jolly, and typically unattractive by Hollywood's standards, as she was noticeably overweight and dark complexioned. A central aspect of her character was that she was asexual, living only to service the master, mistress, and their children, an aspect immortalized in that iconic image of black womanhood, "Aunt Jemima" (Ladson-Billings 89). In the 1970s, a replica or likeness of the archetypal *sapphire* emerged. This archetype, whose origin is deeply rooted in the image of her namesake, the character "Sapphire" (played by Ernestine Ward), the wife of the "King Fish" in *The Amos and Andy Show* (1950s), took center stage as black women in film borrowed heavily from this archetype. Thus, in the 1970s, black women enjoyed character roles as action heroines during what has come to be known as the blaxploitation era; such films as *Get Kristy Love* (1974), *Cleopatra Jones* (1973), *Foxy Brown* (1974), and *Coffy* (1973) featured black women, such as Pam Grier, as strong, smart, defiant, confident, controlling, and in charge. Jones offers that these films were a model of liberation in their focus on assertive (yet strikingly beautiful) African American women, an image that was appealing to (white) feminists (36). Freydberg argues that such films also offered a kind of "soft porn" (2335). Ironically, white females have now taken on this role as the female superhero, or *saffire*, in "buddy films," which traditionally featured white males in the lead with black males as their sidekicks; examples are such films as *48 Hours* (1982) with Nick Nolte and Eddie Murphy and *Lethal Weapon* (1987) with Mel Gibson and Danny Glover. As a historical note, the black male as buddy to a white lead hero dates back beyond cinema. Leslie Fiedler offers that the representation of the black male as the archetypal dark-skinned noble savage as buddy to the white male, a refugee from civilization, dates back to classics such as *The Adventures of Huckleberry Finn* and *Moby Dick* (15). The new trend, however, is to feature white females in these roles as tough, hard-hitting sidekicks (*sapphires*) to leading black men, such as megastars Morgan Freeman and Denzel Washington, in films such as *Along Came a Spider*(2001), *Kiss the Girls*(1997), *Pelican Brief* (1993), and *The Bone Collector* (1999). This is important because, initially, the black male sidekick was the *savage*; however, as Ames explains, later a shift occurred, and the white male lead became the savage, uncivilized animal, capable of surviving in the wilderness, be it literal or the metaphorical inner-city "jungle." Gibson in *Lethal Weapon* is an example. On the other hand, the black sidekick became the civilized family man and devoted husband and father: calm, void of action, and out of touch with his "savage masculinity" (53); Glover in *Lethal Weapon* is an example. The white female in this role is the new savage. We see the white female cast as the *mammy/ good mother* in *The Blind Side*, and she also takes on characteristics of the *savage*, which is akin to the *sapphire*; more important, the white female takes over, emerging as the stronger character when cast opposite both the black male and female. Buddy films featuring the white female as a sidekick to the black male are also important because there is a noticeable absence of the black female in these films. She would seem to be the logical buddy for the black male, given society's continued taboos concerning any hint of interracial relations and also given the shortage of viable roles for black females. Ironically, as more black male stars have evolved to the lead, demanding megamillions, the white female has seized his old role, taking her seat alongside the black male as partner and "buddy," thus appropriating this position for herself and leaving the black female out once more. Not only did the white female confiscate the 1970s superwoman role once held by the black female, but she also combined the superwoman/*sapphire* with the *mammy*, thus taking on the image of the stereotypical black mama, which is personified by actor and director Tyler Perry's well-known character "Madea." Madea is typical of the mythological black woman joked about by many black comedians as one who gathers superstrength and courage to protect her family, especially her children. This we see with Mrs. Tuohy, for example, as she takes on "thugs in the hood" to protect Oher.

The 1980s and 1990s saw Hollywood productions of films written by African Americans, such as Alice Walker's *The Color Purple* (1985). As Bogle offers, in the past, the women of *The Color Purple* would have been maids, "comic servants," not to be thought about twice (*Blacks in American Films* 61). However, Bogle adds that director Steven Spielberg's camera treated these black women with respect and concern. The visual statement, Bogle says, "moves and affects us, even as we are disappointed in other areas" (*Blacks in American Films* 61). Jones offers that Terry McMillan's *Waiting to Exhale* (1995) fails to adequately explore the real problems of social and economic injustice that African American women face (37). Similarly, hooks offers that the film took the novelistic images of professional black women concerned with issues of racial uplift and gender equality and turned them into a progression of racist, sexist stereotypes that feature "happy darkies who are all singing, dancing, f—, and having a merry old time even in the midst of sad times and tragic moments" (hooks, *Reel to Real* 54), while Toni Morrison's *Beloved* (1998), produced by Oprah Winfrey, remained true to its literary genius. A work of great complexity and importance in the scheme of the American narrative, the Pulitzer Prize– and Nobel Prize–winning novel presented a reality Winfrey was conscious enough not to depart from in the film version, as it demonstrated on many levels the pain of slavery and the depth of motherly love, in which a mother would rather see her children dead than have them suffer at the hands of the oppressor. The film stayed true to Morrison's objective, which was to show how a people, African Americans, have suffered irreparably. Thus it did not fit Hollywood's prescription for how African Americans should be presented in cinema and did not enjoy the commercial success enjoyed by *Waiting to Exhale*.

However, there is a regression back to the traditional black *mammy* in *The Help* (2011). Set in Mississippi in the 1960s, *The Help*, based on the book by the same name by Kathryn Stockett, is a period piece, featuring black females as servants caring for prominent white families: a sure winner among mainstream American audiences. However, it is important to note that black women in *The Help*, as was true in the early films of the 1930s, are the nurturers, the mother figures, and the caregivers for white children while struggling to keep their own families afloat. In these early portrayals, the white female, though inept and lacking as a mother and homemaker, remains in both fiction and reality the supreme force, the boss, "the Missus," solidly planted in white society, while, poor, politically and socially powerless black females, though shown in such films to be responsible, strong, hardworking, and morally good, are framed within a context that leaves them to appear comical and childlike, definitely not to be taken seriously, though they impart wisdom, give comfort, and provide protection to their white mistresses and particularly to the white mistresses' children. This portrayal of the black female as *mammy*, though subservient, is a strong indication of a historical realism that, though replete with stereotypes in its representation, provides some evidence of black females playing a pivotal role in the care and lives of Southern whites, particularly in the upbringing of white children. Further, Hollywood's black *mammy* has little life of her own, and any hint of life beyond white life is generally negative, such as the abusive, drunken, lazy, unemployed husband (as demonstrated in *The Help*). However, to refuse to work for the white woman was often not acceptable, as was demonstrated through the character Sophia, played by Oprah Winfrey in *The Color Purple* (1985), who is beaten, blinded in one eye, and sentenced to jail time only to have as part of her sentence upon release from jail a requirement of working for her white accuser, thus being stuck with her for life. As is the case in *The Help*, the black maid's cooking is preferred over that of the white mistress. This idea of the Southern white woman as inept in the household and especially in the kitchen is widespread in literature and also in black culture and lore. The white female was not thought to be capable of taking care of anyone—her husband, her children, or even herself. The black woman became her "help." It is a throwback to William Faulkner's novel *The Sound and the Fury* (1929), where the maid, Dilsey, gets sick and the white mistress, Mrs. Compson, offers to do the cooking in her place. Dilsey asks her who's going to eat her mess (see chapter 1). Such a reaction speaks volumes about the respect the black female was given for her skill in the kitchen, and when Mrs. Compson tells her son, Jason, that she wishes she could do the housework, his response is that they would live in a fine pigsty. Similarly, in the made-for-television movie *Long Walk Home* (1990), a 1950s period piece, we see the story of the Montgomery bus boycott of 1955, starring Whoopi Goldberg as a maid and Sissy Spacek as her white mistress, who says "you" have been the real mother to "my" child. This becomes very important as we explore Hollywood's shift in the portrayal of white females as mothers and housewives and the black female as "bad."

More Background: Evolution of the Black Woman as "Bad"

The 1990s ushered in a noticeable string of films featuring black women as "bad," oversexed, unfit mothers, and unsuitable mates; the archetypal *jezebel* and *sapphire* often combined to form a disturbing ideological symphony. Ladson-Billings (88) argues such negative constructions of the image of black women makes them appear unfit as mothers and teachers. Ladson-Billings maintains that the irony is that these stereotypes sometimes operate simultaneously, and what black women cannot be are innocent victims, engendering sympathy or support in literature, art, film, or social policy (89). Often the jezebel's image is intertwined with that of the tragic mulatto (Ladson-Billings 89), played by Dorothy Dandridge, Lena Horne, and, more recently, Hallie Berry in *Losing Isaiah* (1995), *Introducing Dorothy Dandridge* (1999), and *Monster's Ball* (2001).

Berry was cast as Khaila Richards, a crack addict who abandons her baby in a trash dump, in director Stephen Gyllenhaal's *Losing Isaiah* (1995). The baby is saved and eventually adopted by a white social worker, Margaret Lewin (Jessica

Lange), and her husband, Charles Lewin (David Strathairn), who raise him with their daughter in a loving home, but years later, Richards discovers that the child is alive and wages a fierce court battle to get him back and wins. The made-for-television film opens to a classic ghetto scene, the "Other world," with sounds of a baby crying and a woman smoking crack and then abandoning a baby in a garbage dump. Blacks are linked with crime, drugs, and absence. Lewin is represented as Christian, redemptive, and forgiving. Quoting the Bible, she says, "Isaiah, he shall be called wonderful" and gives the abandoned baby a biblical name. She sings a song to Isaiah that she calls her grandmother's song, sharing and establishing strong roots, family ties, and bonding as mother with the infant. She is warm and loving, the "*good mother*," a modern day white *mammy*: nurturing, self-sacrificial, strong and capable, willing and able, and caring for her own family while extending herself to an abandoned child, foreshadowing the character of the white female protagonist in *The Blind Side* (to be discussed later). Richards and other addicts are referred to as "pill poppin, alcoholic asses," and one addict says to another, "Like your kids don't know that you're turning tricks," prompting Richards to admit she only "did it" (sold sex) to obtain drugs. Though Richards is awarded custody of Isaiah, in the end, it is Lewin that he refers to as his real "mommy." This is akin to the white mistress in *Long Walk Home* telling the black maid that she realizes she (the black maid) has been the real mother to her child. One important scene in the film is when the Lewins' daughter asks Isaiah what is different about their hands, and Isaiah says his are smaller. He does not see color as a difference. The scene represents Hollywood's way of saying that race is not a problem. In the end, Lewin's words to Richards are very telling. Giving birth, she says, does not mean you are a mother—an animal can give birth. Richards gets it and asks if Lewin is calling her an "animal." Thus Hollywood's referencing the black female in the same context or sentence with an animal proved prophetic, as the black female is rarely represented as a *good mother* in Hollywood, where such an image is a dying breed. She is instead oversexed, drugged out, on welfare, and having babies out of control.

Berry won an Oscar for her controversial performance in director Marc Forster's *Monster's Ball* (2001), which marks the second time a black woman received the award, the first being Hattie McDaniels as Mammy in *Gone with the Wind* (1939). Rebecca Wanzo (136) offers that Berry is the first black woman to win best actress for a role that fits a "set of stereotypes about black women as bad mothers and oversexualized whores." Ladson-Billings says, "Indeed [Berry's] academy award was given for such a role in *Monster's Ball*" (89). Berry's character represents a combination of the *jezebel* and *sapphire* archetypes. The film centers, in part, on Leticia Musgrove (Hallie Berry) and her obese son, Tyrell (Coronji Calhoun). Musgrove is the "unfit" mother who verbally and physically abuses her son, beating him and referring to him as a "little piggy." After he is tragically killed in a hit and run, during a grief-stricken moment, she comments that whenever she bought Popeye's chicken, he would eat the whole thing ("eat his ass off")—thus presenting the fried chicken stereotype. Hollywood goes overboard to showcase Berry's beauty in all films wherein she appears. As a rule, as is the case in *Losing Isaiah*, her looks are a part of the script. In *Monster's Ball*, Musgrove's husband, Lawrence (Sean Puffy Combs), compliments her even as he prepares to be executed—very contrived. Further, by this constant acknowledgment of Berry as beautiful (the tragic mulatto), the sexy temptress stereotype is always maintained. Hollywood, however, is uncomfortable with representing brown- and dark-skinned women as beautiful. We can only deduce that Berry's looks are close enough so as to not be threatening to the standard "beauty"—a title bestowed upon white women only by Hollywood. To recognize women such as Angela Bassett (*What's Love Got to Do with It?* [1993]) as beautiful might call into question what true beauty means and challenge the legitimacy of the white standard. However, the sex scene in *Monster's Ball* between Musgrove and Hank Grotowski (Billy Bob Thornton) is easily one of the most controversial interracial unions known to modern cinema. Critics offer that a black woman had to go to extremes and degrade herself, becoming a *jezebel*, to win an Oscar. Grieving, Musgrove begs, "Make me feel real good." She is aggressive, a sex-starved "temptress," tugging at Grotowski's body, while he is portrayed as innocent, as if he is not sure what to do. When it ends, he vomits, announcing it has nothing to do with her, as she looks on in bewilderment; but very conveniently for Hollywood, the audience is left wondering—for this serves to pacify mainstream viewers who are uncomfortable with interracial relations. It is a way of contextualizing the act, of leaving room for doubt that a white man could be serious about a black woman. In another scene, Musgrove brings Grotowski a gift: a hat. His father, Buck Grotowski (Peter Boyle), an acknowledged racist, insults her, saying that in his prime he had a thing for "'nigger' juice." "You ain't a man till you split dark open," he tells her. Hence the black woman as *jezebel* is a stereotype that began with slavery; even though the black woman was victimized by the white master, a widespread myth is that the black woman somehow tricked the white man into having sex with her, thus giving the white man a pass for his savage criminal behavior—a pass that still holds today. Moreover, hooks offers that it is widely assumed among white males that sex with a black female, "the Other," is a way of "making themselves over, of leaving white innocence . . . and entering the world of experience" (*Black Looks* 21–25). Further, hooks argues whites were confident that people of color had more life experience and were more sensual, sexual (*Black Looks* 23). Thus these insulting, disrespectful comments also help put some in the mainstream at ease because they degrade the black woman, implying that sex with her is an act deplete of love and affection, placing it on the level of sex with a prostitute—nothing of any real significance. It also serves to maintain white female beauty standards by calling into question the character and alleged promiscuous sexual behavior of black women (Ladson-Billings 88). It was no surprise when it was widely reported that Don Imus, conservative radio talk-show host, referred to black girls on the Rutgers University women's basketball team as "nappy headed 'ho's,'" even though these were hard-working, good student athletes who attended one of the nation's best schools. A black female's social or educational status does not guarantee respect. Consequently, it was no surprise when news reports surfaced indicating that XM Radio shock jocks "Opie and

Anthony" joked about raping then Secretary of State Condoleezza Rice. During the broadcast, the two speculated about how Rice would react as she was being held down, raped, and even punched in the face by her assailant, a streetwise, vulgar "guest" who appeared on their show.

In a similar vein, in keeping with Hollywood's traditional stereotype of the black male as criminal—the *savage/trickster* archetype—in *Monster's Ball*, Musgrove's husband sits on death row awaiting execution after committing heinous crimes. He tells his son, "I'm a bad man. You ain't me." In the tradition of the *sapphire* archetype, Musgrove shows him no love, no sympathy, no forgiveness. He dies a horrible death befitting a *savage* animal, literally cooking, with smoke coming from his head.

Precious (2011), directed by Marc Forster and based on the novel *Push* (1996) by Sapphire, takes place in Harlem and is the story of Precious (Gabourey Sidibe), an overweight, abused, illiterate, African American teenage girl who lives with her abusive, welfare-dependent mother, Mary (Mo'Nique), who has allowed her boyfriend, who is also Precious's father, to have sex with Precious and impregnate her twice. Pregnant with her second child, Precious gets a second chance when she is invited to attend an alternative school. Groundbreaking in many respects, the film earned Jeffrey Fletcher, an African American writer, his first Oscar for best screenplay adaptation and actress-comedian Mo'Nique an Oscar for best supporting role.

Precious has Hollywood's rubber stamp, as it represents an abundance of derogatory stereotypes associated with African Americans. Taking the archetypal *jezebel*, *sapphire*, and *mammy* and throwing them together in one gigantic, shocking ball makes the film a sure winner for mainstream acceptance. The lead character, Precious, is in denial about her real looks, reinforcing negative stereotypes and images of black female looks in the eyes of white mainstream America. An overweight, dark-skinned, traditional Hollywood mammy type, Precious says she wants to be on the cover of a magazine and dance on BET. Her mother, Mary, the archetypal sapphire/jezebel, yells out, "Nobody wants to see your big ass dancing!" Precious has a crush on her white teacher and entertains thoughts of him leaving his white wife. Mary blames Precious for her own victimization even though Precious was an infant when her father began molesting her. This, for some, might serve to reinforce the idea of the black female as innately bad. As is the case in the majority of films discussed here, the black male is either absent, criminal, or a combination of these—a *savage/trickster*. Though we do not see him physically, Precious's father, also the father of her children, is represented as an animal, having no social morals. The film, however, ends on a hopeful note, with Precious, though HIV positive, emerging strong and literate, leaving her mother with her two children in tow, one with Down syndrome.

Methods: A Qualitative Approach

In this work, qualitative semiotic textual analysis is used to analyze *The Blind Side*'s film text. Semiotic analysis involves the interrogation of language, signs, and symbols within text. It is a way of looking at and analyzing language in the form of myth, stereotypes, and metaphors in *The Blind Side* in order to derive cultural meaning. In semiotics, words and images function as symbols of meaning as well as other cultural objects (Hall, *Representation: Cultural* 36–37), such as social position, socioeconomic status, and character. In *The Blind Side*, semiotic analysis becomes crucial as a way of examining systemic, strategically positioned representations of characters.

Theoretical Framework

In order to explore Hollywood's representation of African Americans in films that are acceptable to the mainstream, special attention must be given to Hollywood's representation of principal white characters, because therein lies the real objective or ideological lean that Hollywood wishes to achieve and thus fix in the psyche of viewers as reality, or the norm. Richard Dyer (44) argues that mainstream cinema is predominately an articulation of white experience and that whiteness secures its dominance by appearing to be nothing at all. Hall (*Media and Representation*) offers that media are linked with power, and the groups who "wield" power influence the dominant images. The objective of ideology, Hall maintains, is to "fix"; thus, when we are immersed in these images (the white female as the new *good mother/mammy*, the black female as *jezebel/sapphire*, and the black male as the *tom*, the *victim*, and the *savage/trickster*), like a fish in water, we do not question but instead come to accept this as the norm and are therefore less likely to interrogate these images for deeper ideological meaning (Hall, *Media and Representation*). Thus *The Blind Side* promotes the idea of white society as the norm and the adoption and embracing of white middle-class values, culture, ideals, and lifestyles as the answer to the social problems that African Americans face. Gates (28) offers that Hollywood's vision is essentially middle class, consumerist, and American, and the working class becomes a space for the exotic. In *The Blind Side*, the major overarching conflict that has ideological consequences is the shift in the character positioning of the white and black females. The white female—typically pampered, coddled, and taken care of by everyone, especially the black female as maid or *mammy*—is cast as the archetypal *good mother/mammy*, while the black female—traditionally cast as the *mammy*—is portrayed as the archetypal *jezebel/sapphire* rolled into one. In order to understand the reframing of the white female as *good mother/mammy*, it is important to understand the historical journey of the black female in film, since the white female's new image is at least a partial appropriation of the black female's past image. It is also important to identify archetypal images of the African American male that are the mainstay in Hollywood and serve to paint the black male as the criminal other, in conflict with mainstream white society. Hall further argues that "ideas and values are articulated through the construction, maintenance, and perpetuation of stereotypes, over generalized beliefs that seize the few simple, vivid, memorable widely recognized characteristics about a person, reducing everything about the person to those traits, exaggerating and simplifying them, and fixing them without change or development to eternity" (*Representation: Cultural* 58). These stereotypes, which exist in the culture, are transferred through popular media (Hall, *Representation: Cultural* 251).

Consequently, we accept and view this myth—the *mammy, sapphire,* and *jezebel* and the *victim* and *savage/trickster*—as the norm and see no other way (Hall, *Representation: Cultural* 249–51; Hall, *Media and Representation*). Further, as Diawara offers, whites occupy the center of the narrative space in popular media such as film, and blacks occupy the periphery, which is constructed only in relation to the white protagonists (12). Space, Diawara argues, is related to power, and those at the center (whites) have power, and those on the periphery (blacks), the other, do not (12). Consequently, in *The Blind Side*, we see only unempowered blacks who occupy highly fixed, media-contextualized, marginalized spaces as they are positioned deliberately around the dominant white cast. Hollywood producers, directors, and script writers have as their primary goal in *The Blind Side* the presentation of and preservation of white culture, society, and ideals. Several myths are central in *The Blind Side*. At the center of the film stands the character of the white female protagonist, Tuohy, as a symbol and protector of white middle-class values, to which the male protagonist, Oher, must aspire if he is to exist and survive in a white world. Several myths are operative in the film. The most prominent is the myth of the *good mother/mammy*, which shows itself best functioning at the center of the other myths. The myths that revolve around this myth and give it its potency are the myth of the *jezebel/sapphire* and the myths of the *victim, tom,* and *savage/trickster*.

Thus we begin with the archetypal *good mother*, represented by Tuohy. Lule (106) offers that the *good mother* emanates with the first deep bonds that develop between an infant and an adult, though not always a mother. The "*good mother* offers maternal comfort and protection" (Lule 23), representing goodness and kindness, and is often hailed above others as the Christian crusader, a Mother Theresa, and a savior of the world and especially black children, a modern-day version of the *mammy*. Ladson-Billings (89) offers that the *mammy* is bossy, nonsexual, an older black woman, dark skinned, and devoted to the white family she cares for, especially the children. The fact that she is an older woman, nonsexual, and considered unattractive makes her safe. This representation of the black *mammy* is common in American media, even in early novels such as William Faulkner's *The Sound and the Fury* (1929), in which the maid Dilsey is described as once being a large woman who adorns herself in men's clothing: a man's hat and an army coat. However, the white woman as *mammy* is highly sensual, attractive (according to the white standard), bossy, and devoted not only to her own family but to the care of others, like the traditional *mammy*. Thus the two— *good mother and mammy*—combine in the character of Tuohy to form the *new mammy*, which will simply be referred to as the *mammy* in this work. However, the white *mammy* in *The Blind Side* is in direct conflict with the black female as *jezebel/sapphire*. Ladson-Billings (89) offers that the "*jezebel* is synonymous with sexual promiscuity, an insatiable sexual appetite, someone who uses treachery and trickery to get her way, a temptress, generally in the tradition of the tragic

Mulatto. The *sapphire*, on the other hand, is stubborn, 'bitchy,' bossy and hateful" (Ladson-Billings 89). Just as important are the archetypal caricatures that have historically followed the African American male. In *The Blind Side*, there is the myth of the black male as a *victim*, hapless, in need of saving (Lule 43–44); as the *tom* (*Uncle Tom*), effeminate, protector to white females and children, safe (Bogle, *Toms* 6); and finally the *savage/trickster*. The savage is an inhuman beast, a brute, an animal, unfit for civilized society, crude, and sex-obsessed, one who can barely control his animal instincts or criminal tendencies—for he is a boundary crosser, a rule breaker who does not respect social barriers. He is animal in his approach and behavior (Lule 124).

Results/Analysis: *The Blind Side*

The Blind Side is a showcase of mythological, archetypal characters positioned to perpetuate systemic ideological stereotypes that maintain dominant culture ideology.

Hollywood's New White Mammy/Mythical Good Mother

We see at least a partial role reversal: a flip in the ideological script in the way Hollywood film makers represent the white and black female and, consequently, the way Hollywood *wants* America and the world to view the two. Thus Tuohy, as the white *mammy*, is the standard white beauty—thin, blond, feminine, sexy, superwoman—and unlike the black *mammy*, who is often absent from or in conflict with her family (if her family is featured at all), Tuohy in *The Blind Side* effortlessly cares for her white family, who are featured in a warm, loving, supportive home, complete with an economically well-off husband who owns more than one hundred Taco Bell restaurants. Like the *good mother*, she is Christian. Oher's mother tells her, "You're a fine Christian lady." This *mammy* is Bullock in *The Blind Side*, the ultimate in white beauty, ranked with Marilyn Monroe, the "white goddess of beauty." Written and directed by John Lee Hancock, and based on the 2006 book *The Blind Side: Evolution of a Game* by Michael Lewis, *The Blind Side*, the film, features Tuohy as a well-to-do Republican white woman who, guided by Christian charity, takes in and eventually adopts Oher (Quintin Aaron), a homeless teenager whose mother is a "crack addict." The film is advertised on television as a "fascinating true story, a strange and wonderful mother/ son story." The announcer says that something was missing in the Tuohy family until "Michael" showed up, which made the family complete, and that "Michael" has no idea who his father is and that his mother is a "crack-cocaine addict." Oher is said to have little formal education and "few skills to help him learn," implying that he received very little from his absent mother. Thus Tuohy takes charge, which is her nature, and ensures that he has every opportunity. She goes all out to help Oher, including giving the football coach ideas on how best to use his skills and hiring a tutor to help him qualify for an NCAA Division I athletic scholarship to Ole Miss, where he inevitably becomes the first-round pick of the Baltimore Ravens in the 2009 NFL draft. Thus the white female's role as *mammy* contributes to the marginalization of the black female, leaving her, historically, naked, hollow, and unfit as a mother and caretaker of children, especially her own, while the white female is elevated to a fictionalized status as the supreme mother. Keeping with tradition, Tuohy, like the black *mammy*, is a "strong willed Southern matriarch, most content when bossing others" (Bunch). When she first spots Oher, she asks where he is going, and before he answers, she boldly orders "Don't you lie to me!"—a gutsy move, given that she does not know him. Her husband, Sean, comments he has seen that look many times: "She's about to get her way," letting viewers know just how fierce, pushy, and in charge Tuohy is. During a football game, she marches across the field to "dispense her cultured pearls of wisdom . . . feisty . . . [At another instance] taking on a crack dealer and his pals . . . Hard to imagine these guys not laughing" as she "channels Charlton Heston" (Puig). In short, Tuohy is a "pistol toting mama," a real bad white mama, as she takes on "ghetto thugs" to protect her son. She is the image of Tyler Perry's Madea, akin to the "angry black woman," a stereotypical metaphor now associated with black women by some white conservatives. She also takes on characteristics of the archetypal *savage* mentioned earlier in reference to white females in buddy films with African American males. She is an "animal," capable of surviving in the inner city, symbolic of the other world, the wilderness, the jungle. When confronted by a "thug" who threatens Oher, telling her to warn him to "sleep with one eye open," Tuohy says, "You threaten my son, you threaten me . . . Ah'm a member of the NRA and Ah'm always packing," she threatens, patting a pistol in her "gilded handbag" (Puig), the archetypal *saffire* of the blaxploitation era of the 1970s. First, this scene establishes Tuohy as a tough, protective *mammy*, but it also communicates to viewers that she has become Oher's mother. She refers to him as "my son," a term of endearment. At one point, Oher tells her he never had a bed before, and she says, "Well, you have one now." Further, Tuohy is "Momzilla": bossy, opinionated, unstoppable, and complaining when she is asked to wait in line when she goes to inquire about adopting Oher, prompting the attendant to say she feels sorry for the child Tuohy wants to adopt. Her husband pays for everything, but she runs the show (Muir 14). Perhaps one of the most memorable yet insulting scenes is when Tuohy sidles up to the coach and informs him that Oher scored in the 98th percentile in "protective instincts," suggesting the coach should use this to motivate Oher. Here Hollywood asks us to see a mother who knows "her child," as is generally the case. This is a hard sell, however, given that Oher is a teen when the family adopts him. It comes off as being a bit contrived. More important, Tuohy seems to suggest the coach tap into Oher's instinctive side, as in his "animal instincts," often associated with blacks and black athletes in particular. Some critics have cited Bullock's role as comical and unrealistic, prompting one to label it a "surprisingly humorous film" ("Movie Review: *The Blind Side*"). However, Hollywood's portrayal of Tuohy as a new *mammy* is no laughing matter. Richard Dyer argues that whiteness secures its dominance by seeming to be nothing in particular (44). In essence, the white *mammy* has replaced the black *mammy*, who, barring negative stereotypes, was perceived as strong, trusting, capable, and dependable—the real mother figure in the lives of many Southern white children, sometimes suckling at her breasts. She was the saint and the savior on whom all could depend. Mama Flora in Alex Haley's *Mama Flora's Family* (1998) said to a young white man who threatened her as she tried to buy a cup of coffee from a local white-owned restaurant that it was her "milk" that gave his father life and was, therefore, responsible for him having life. Even more important, the black woman has historically contributed greatly to the sustaining of the black family and community, caring for her children and providing undying support to the black man. Given this, the shift in the role of the white woman who has now taken on this banner of the *mammy* (and, in many instances in film, partner and support to the black man) has deeper ideological meaning as Hollywood rewrites history for the good of the white woman, thus contributing to, maintaining, and, more important, enhancing her role as the dominant female in American culture as queen mother, a position she did not hold in the past; this repositioning is thus to the detriment of the black female, downplaying and denying the role that she has played historically and continues to play, much like Rosa Lynn Sinclair in *Down in the Delta*, who risks the family's prized heirloom to save her family. Finally, one of the most important scenes in the film occurs when Tuohy reads a children's story, *Ferdinand the Bull*, to Oher that she read to her children when they were younger. It is important that the mother bond with the child in the infant stages. This act allows Tuohy to fulfill this important characteristic of the *good mother* archetype. It is after this act—along with the separation from the inner city, after a fight with thugs, and his failure to locate his mother—that Oher refers to Tuohy as "Mama."

The Black Woman as Jezebel/Sapphire; Harmful to Black Children

Hollywood's representation of the black woman paints a picture of a creature with little or no moral fiber or direction: a lost soul, an empty vessel, with little or no value to society or to anyone. Such stereotypical constructions leave the black female unfit to serve as either a mother figure or a role model in any real capacity. Unfortunately, such images carry over to the real world, where many black women find it difficult when they are often forced to prove themselves and create more positive real-life images: images that are few and far between on the big screen for the black woman. For example, "rarely do we find depictions of black women as model mothers" (Ladson-Billings 89). Further, Ladson-Billings offers discussion and representation of the construction of black women as a central strategy for organizing a truth around motherhood and the care and education of children (88). Thus film has played a significant role in how black women are perceived in our culture. In *The Blind Side*, the issue of race is replaced with the issue of class and maybe attitude and background. Focusing on class instead of race allows for the degrading of the black female—for she is treated as if it is her class, not race, that contributes to her downfall and that the choices she has made (taking drugs, dropping out of school, having too many children with different fathers) have landed her in a particular class (welfare dependent) or caused her to remain low class or in poverty. Hall (*Media and Representation*) suggests that media "re-presents" people and place, assigning meaning through a deliberate use of systemic ideology that is positioned or set in place through the use of discourse. Without discourse, Hall argues, there is no meaning (*Media and Representation*). The discourse that defines the principal black female character, Oher's mother, Denise Oher (Adriane Lenox), is an image of poverty, welfare, drugs, a ghetto existence, illegitimate children, and low class. She is a resident of Hurt Village in the inner city. One of Tuohy's high-society friends says she grew up in Hurt Village but does not mind work, and this is why she is where she is, eating in a restaurant that charges $18 for a salad. The implication is that the poor and disenfranchised such as Oher's mother are where they are because they are lazy and do not want to work. In short, they have caused their own demise. It is widely asserted that the stereotype of the black woman as the "welfare queen," made popular in the 1980s during the Reagan administration, helped establish the welfare mother as a deviant social creature who is irresponsible, unwilling to work, sexually promiscuous, and defiantly has children with different fathers. Thus it is assumed she will not transfer decent morals to her offspring or others in society (and is a *jezebel*). Bobo offers, "Fictionalized creations of black women are not innocent; they do not lack the effect of ideological force in the lives of those represented in that black women are rendered as objects and useful commodities in a very serious power struggle" (36). An interesting sidenote comes to mind as we view this in terms of power and ideology. In the cinematic production *Queens of Comedy* (2001), directed by Steve Purcell, actor-comedian Mo'Nique (*Precious* 2011), as part of her stand-up act, scolds "skinny black women" for "dissing . . . fat black women." She says that "fat women" are now in vogue, in style, and that "skinny women" are now jealous. This gets great laughter, of course. In another instance, she says, "I'm most proud of being a sister," adding, "regardless of the size, black women are special, and if you look around, every sister in here is so pretty and we age so gracefully. You never know how old a black woman is." This is important because at one point it was difficult to locate this section from the monologue (declaring black women as "beautiful") on the Internet. However, the section that focused on "fat" versus "skinny" women was more easily assessable on the Internet. One might deduce from this that there is a deliberate attempt to censor declarations of black women as beautiful to prevent its reaching the masses and thus affecting how black women are viewed in society. Even though black women traditionally sport full lips and shapely buttocks, rarely are they recognized positively in mainstream cinema for possessing these attributes—features now sought after by many in the dominant culture. This prompted comedian Paul Mooney (*Paul Mooney: The Godfather*) to ask why black features are considered ugly on black women but beautiful and sensual on white women.

Three black women are portrayed in *The Blind Side*: the most prominent is Oher's mother, Denise Oher (Adriane Lenox). She is physically a shadow, the picture of impending death, with dark bulging eyes; the stereotypical crack addict, she licks her dry lips and says she has a little health problem. She is the mother of at least 12 children, all with different fathers, and she does not know where her children are. She is said to be on that "crack pipe." She tells Tuohy that "Mike" (Oher) is a runner and will not stay in any one place and that he always "slips out and comes to take care" of her, thus giving the impression that a child who has nothing is more responsible than his irresponsible, unfit mother—a direct contrast to Tuohy, who tells Denise Oher that she gets no money for taking care of Oher. Showing Denise Oher asking about money makes for controversial messaging. On one hand, viewers may sense that she wants to ask Tuohy to share any money that she might receive with her; on the on the other hand, it may be assumed that she is suggesting that Tuohy is being well paid for what she does for Oher and therefore is benefitting herself financially. Even worse, she cannot remember who her son's father is and gives Tuohy the wrong name, then corrects herself; crying, she says she had forgotten who the boy's father is. Including this in the film helps secure the widespread stereotype of the black woman as sexually promiscuous, a *jezebel*, engaging in sex with multiple partners and unfit as a mother. Unfortunately, African Americans unknowingly help perpetuate such stereotypes. Comedian Steve Harvey does a skit in his video *Steve Harvey: Still Tripping* (2009) about an alleged niece he says is "ghetto," 25 years old with 5 children, all with different daddies. Moreover, Denise Oher is said to be in and out of jail for drug possession and other acts (hints of prostitution) and will not want trouble with the authorities; further degrading Denise Oher, a social worker advises Tuohy that she will not be required to contact her prior to adopting Oher, since she no longer has custody. In another scene, Tuohy takes her children, including Oher, to the library. She and her children reminisce about books they have read together. She asks Oher if his mother ever read any of those books to him. Of course, his answer is "No." This scene appears to be thrown in for shock effect and serves to further establish Denise Oher as a bad mother who did not nurture her son properly. She does not have good habits and therefore cannot pass them on to her offspring, thus establishing that she is the cause of her son's poor academic performance while suggesting on a larger scale that the black mother is detrimental to her children's well-being and that she, like Richards in *Losing Isaiah* and Mary in *Precious*, is at fault for the continual revolving door of poverty that is too common in the black community. Nathalie Augustine offers that the perception of poverty plays an important role in the lives of disenfranchised African American women and thus contributes to this group's social reality. Augustine further offers that the African American female is often characterized as able bodied but lazy and unwilling to work and instead is comfortable relying on the state and prolonging her dependent status as she continues to have children out of wedlock. Augustine offers, finally, that the African American female lacks the educational skills and motivation to get ahead, is her own worst enemy, and is the root of her family's intergenerational poverty and related social ills; moreover, having no morals of her own, she is not equipped to pass on good morals to her children, and she is black (144). Thus, as Ladson-Billings argues, black womanhood is routinely debased and denigrated, and this helps construct black women as unfit and unworthy as mothers (88). The irony here is that there are no reasons why such situations exist. No real background information is included on Oher's mother that would help the audience understand what brought her to her plight. No attention is given to the historical role of race and/or socioeconomic conditions that exist for many such as Denise and Michael Oher, who find themselves caught up in a cycle of drugs and poverty. Audiences are left with the idea that this is the world of the black Other, especially the black female. To add fuel to this idea of the promiscuous black female who has illegitimate children spread out everywhere, Oher is seen talking to a young black man. It turns out it is his brother. He tells Tuohy the last time he saw him was when he was little. The second image of a black woman in the film is that of a woman we only hear as she yells to Big Tony, "Let someone else do the Christian thing" in terms of helping Oher—an interesting line to include, given that the film is big on Tuohy as a Christian. Big Tony's girlfriend also complains about the food that Oher eats and selfishly argues that she is unable to spend time with Big Tony because of Oher. As a result, Big Tony reluctantly kicks Oher out on the streets. Big Tony's girlfriend is a class *saffire*, cold and uncaring, and though her role is minor, she represents the bad black female. Finally, there is the black female investigator who questions Oher about his college choice. She again stands opposite to Tuohy, who remarks to her husband, Sean, that this woman is "tough"; *cold* might also be an appropriate description, a *saffire* who exudes no warmth, no concern for the family. Sporting a short, masculine haircut and wearing a suit with an open-shirt look that bears no femininity, the investigator pounds away at Oher, causing him to bolt from the room and head off to find his mother, who never shows. In the end, Tuohy comes to his rescue, assuring him he will be safe from a "thug" whom he physically assaulted. She gives him the courage to go back and tell the investigator that he chose Ole Miss because his family, the Tuohy's, went to school there. Thus Oher is hard pressed to find affection from any black female in *The Blind Side* and so are viewers.

The Black Male as Victim, Tom, and Trickster

The Black Male as Victim

Gates (21, 28, 29) offers that the presence of African Americans on the screen can be seen as a positive; however, such images are offered only when they can be contained and regulated by specific cinematic codes of representation (2). Two dominant portraits of Oher emerge—the archetypal *victim* and the *tom*. The *victim* will be discussed here. According to Lule, the *victim* falls prey to terrible social circumstances and is generally saved or almost saved by members of the dominant class. Oher is literally pulled in off the street, rescued by the Tuohy family who spot him walking, cold, hungry, and dressed inappropriately for the weather, in the tradition of the fallen hero in a Shakespearean tragedy, "wandering, naked in the wilderness." He is literally and figuratively naked, having very few possessions—"a T-shirt and a pair of shorts"—and no real family. He has been in and out of seven institutions, there is no record of his whereabouts for several months, and his grade point average is a zero. Comparing Oher to "Pip," the protagonist in Charles Dickens's *Great Expectations*(1861), Oher's tutor tells him that he, like Pip, was poor and an orphan that was found and taken in and that he should be able to relate to that. Flashbacks reveal that Oher, as an infant, was exposed to his mother doing crack and being arrested for drug abuse,

and we hear babies crying, calling out to their mother as they are being separated. A wealthy friend asks Tuohy if she has taken Oher in because of feelings
of guilt. Oher's home, Hurt Village, is represented as a vile place, a prison, a
jungle, the Other world. Confirming this, Tuohy asks Oher, "How did you get
out, Mike?" Visiting Hurt Village, Tuohy threatens a "thug," telling him that he
better not cross over to uptown, her world, white society. When Tuohy enters
Oher's mother's apartment, it resembles a dark hole. In another scene, a teacher
reads questions to Oher from a test, and he doesn't know the answers. He can
barely read. The coach praises him, saying he's brave to come to a better school
to get the education denied him in the poor-quality schools he's attended. We are
given the impression that he is the victim of a poor-quality school in the black
community. There is no indication of the reasons why certain schools are not as
good as others, no mention of the lack of money and resources allotted to the
poorer areas. Thus Oher reveals in a note that he has never done homework and
does not understand what the teachers are saying. One teacher asks, "How's the
spelling?" They look for something that indicates Oher is intelligent. However,
the note further establishes how far outside of their world, the standard norm,
he is. To add to all this, Oher, who does not know his father, learns of his father's
death from a school official. He is told that his father fell off an overpass and died
and that police found Oher's name in a registry. When he is asked when he last
saw him, he answers, "I don't know."

Hollywood's Archetypal Young Tom: The Protector

Gates (8–9) argues that mainstream cinema features blacks on screen without
addressing race or ethnic issues or placing them in situations where race is a factor
that is outside of the black community, without a black context. *The Blind Side*
begins with Bullock as Tuohy sharing how the left tackle evolved to be the ultimate "protector" of the quarterback's "blind side," which symbolically comes to
represent anyone that needs looking out for (the family) and, as mentioned earlier, represents the ability to blot out, to forget. The symbol of the protector,
however, becomes a metaphor that runs through the film, particularly in reference to Oher, who is both symbolically and literally a left tackle, guarding and
protecting. Tuohy describes what is perhaps the most horrific sports injury caught
on camera: the Washington Redskins' legendary quarterback Joe Theismann, she
explains, received a life-altering injury when New York Giants' lineman Lawrence
Taylor tackled him, making the left tackle on the defensive line the second most
important play position as the protector of the quarterback's blind side. Thus that
Oher scores in the 98 percentile for "protective instinct" becomes significant in
the framing of the story. Protective instincts are defined as natural, inborn,
innate, and more toward nature or animal, as in "animal instincts." Thus the
implication is that he has more of this than anything else, more one way (instinctive, natural, animal) than the other (possessing of intellect, having the ability to
pass tests, to compete academically). Consequently, when Oher answers several
questions read to him from a test, the teacher announces, "Big Mike is not
'dumb.'" They are surprised he understands the simplest of things, which helps

maintain the idea that blacks are not intelligent and more brawn than brain, thus feeding a long-held stereotype and giving the impression that it is the norm for blacks to be deficient and inferior (Other), while it is the exception, a surprise, when intellect is displayed. Thus present-day images of blacks are filtered through media lenses; consequently, the problems that blacks face are historical; black men are commonly portrayed and thus seen as thugs, pimps, and not as intelligent and articulate. However, protective instincts also hint of mothering qualities, connected to the nature exhibited in the archetypal *tom* (*Uncle Tom*), the faithful, happy, submissive servant. Oher wanders around, as Tuohy says, "like a fly in milk," highly visible, captured, contained (Guerrero "Black Man" 237), out of place, outside of his natural environment. Oher is in a totally white world (he writes in a note that everything is white). He is an oddity, a gentle giant, "a big black bear," as he is labeled by a "redneck" spectator during a football game, used to elicit a response from the other characters. Valerie Smith argues that by placing black characters within white mainstream definitions of middle-class values, lifestyle, and profession, they are made more familiar, identifiable, and unthreatening (217). One of Tuohy's friends comments on the Tuohy family's Christmas card photograph, which features Oher, telling Tuohy that she looks so "teeny-tiny" next to Oher, reminding her of "King Kong and Jessica Lange." Kong takes on a protective, even romantic, role with Lange's character in the film *King Kong*; however, the comparison is problematic for other obvious reasons: "The Bullock as Barbie look allows the director . . . to contrast the tiny blond woman [Tuohy] and the friendly bear of a black man [Oher] . . . [He] is a defender. His position at football is symbolic of the role that mainstream audiences are comfortable seeing a black male play. Films that place blacks in the center of the narrative use a variety of strategies of containment suppressing any threat that black masculinity might seem to imply" (Guerrero, "Black Image" 237), thus creating an effeminate *tom*-like figure. Oher is established as a protector, palatable to white society, safe, nonsexual, and nonthreatening—the archetypal *tom*. When Tuohy asks him if he will protect her, he says, "I got your back." When Oher and SJ (Jae Head), the Tuohys' young son, are involved in a car crash, Oher uses his arm to protect SJ from permanent damage or maybe death; when Tuohy asks him what happened to his arm, he says, "I stopped it," referring to the air bag. When "thugs" make misogynistic comments about Tuohy and her daughter Collins (Lily Collins), Oher risks life and limb to protect their honor. Collins observes Oher gently pushing a little girl on a swing in a playground. As the child giggles, asking him to push her higher, Collins looks on, circling Oher, studying him, cautiously, through a metal fence, which might be interpreted as being symbolic of a cage or metal bars. Prior to this scene, Tuohy asks Collins if she is comfortable having Oher in the house, which comes on the heels of Tuohy's friend asking if she had concerns about having a "large black boy" sleeping under the same roof with her daughter. Thus having black males play with white children is a common technique used by Hollywood to relieve white fears and establish the black male as protector. It is also a source of containment, assuring that the black male is safe, harmless. However, one of the most offensive scenes in the film for black viewers comes at the end, when Tuohy tells Oher that if he gets a girl pregnant at college, she will come and cut off his "penis." Given the historical implications, one would think Hollywood would have avoided this line. It gets a laugh but leaves an eerie feel about the historical threat of castration/mutilation of the black males' sexual organs, and it is a sad reality that such a threat, though used in a humorous way, remains acceptable as a source of containment of the black male's body—as a way of getting the mainstream audience to laugh to stave off feelings of uneasiness about black male sexuality. Thus to "cut off" the penis is to make effeminate, again a characteristic of the archetypal *tom*. This provides a great segue to the coach saying, during a disappointing practice, that Oher looks like Tarzan and plays like Jane. Gates argues that the black male's body is offered as heroic only when it is contained by a lack of sexuality or action, isolation from a black community (Oher outside of and in conflict with the black community), or class. When the coaches visit from various universities to recruit Oher, SJ takes over as negotiator and Oher sits quietly, yawning, getting a laugh and putting audiences at ease. This is a common trend in Hollywood in both film and commercials—the pairing of black male athletes with white children as buddies. Athletes such as Michael Jordan and Shaquille O'Neal have been featured in movies and commercials with white children. Finally, there is the scene where Oher's team is losing and Tuohy asks him if he will protect the family, which is his "family." Oher picks up an opponent and carries him off the field. Fed up with the trash talking, Oher says to the coach, "It's time for this kid to . . . go home." Since Oher, "the 6 ft. 4in., . . . delivering the line is portrayed as almost painfully shy and reticent, it's a guarantee laugh" (Rogers 14). Displacement of the black character into isolation in a white middle-class community is a strategy of containment that maintains "positioning of the black male hero . . . [placing] the black male's body in protective custody" (Guerrero, "Black Image" 239). Guerrero argues that such positioning places the black male in conformity with the mainstream white sensibilities and expectations of what blacks should be ("Black Image" 239). Such positioning, Guerrero offers, appeals to black audiences by offering subjectivity while appealing to white audiences by providing a point of reference by offering a token liberalism ("Black Image" 240). Moreover, this containment also assures that the *savage/trickster* archetypes, often represented by black male characters in film, are abated and thus allowing the *tom* archetype to stand in opposition to any threat of the *savage/trickster* archetypes displayed in other characters—stereotypes that are also mentioned, by some, in reference to Oher.

Savage/Trickster

Guerrero argues that the black male image in commercial cinema is a paradoxical mix of stereotype and adoration driven by a "defined yet complexly contradictory formula" ("Black Image" 395). In short, the black male is, in many respects, admired and emulated for the very image that media, on the other hand, portrays as a threatening, dangerous, and alien other. Comedian Paul Mooney, in his video *It's the End of the World* (2010), offers that the black man is the most imitated of all around the world: "Everybody wants to be black, but nobody wants to be a black." To be black, in essence, is to be "cool." As hooks explains, "the desire is to become the other," wherein the "primitive," dark, and exciting is thought to exist—the "savage," the "nasty" (*Black Looks* 21–26). *The Blind Side* begins with Bullock as Tuohy describing the classic left tackle (Oher): "big, wide in the butt, massive in the thighs, long arms, feet as quick as a hiccup," a rare combination, she adds. In 1988, Jimmy the Greek Snyder said blacks were bred to be athletes and that their "big thighs" helped make them superior. The profile also harkens back to the Southern auctioning block, where black males were advertised naked as "bucks" and sold to the highest bidder. Similarly, sports team ownership of black athletes has been compared with slavery. *New York Times* sports columnist William Rhoden refers to black athletes as a "lost tribe—wandering" with no real power. Tuohy's referencing of the common phrase "One Mississippi, two Mississippi" adds insult to injury, even though it references Ole Miss, as Mississippi is considered the "Southernmost state" from a racial ideological perspective, given its history with slavery and race problems involving blacks, including heinous acts such as the lynching of 14-year-old Emmett Till in 1955—a tragedy that, in part, sparked the civil rights movement of the 1960s. Thus the physical portrait of the left tackle is a common caricature of the *savage* black male, the *buck*, imposing in size, with long, lanky limbs, massive feet and thighs, and protruding buttocks, with animal speed. Such is reminiscent of sportscaster Howard Cosell's comment about an African American Redskins' NFL player, "That little monkey gets loose, doesn't he?"

Thus a final portrait that emerges in *The Blind Side* is that of the black male as *savage/trickster* combined. Black male masculinity traditionally depicted in mainstream Hollywood cinema represents an archetypal type that has evolved over time from a cast of controversial and colorful characters, both fictional and factual, to become the composite stereotypical criminal, the thug, the gangsta, the drug dealer, the addict (Strother-Adams 70–71). Whether this image is presented within a serious or humorous context, whether the tone is light or dark, audiences are continually "blindsided" with this stereotype, which has become a common belief, as demonstrated by Oher's coach, who is disappointed that he is not more aggressive, claiming that most kids from bad neighborhoods can't wait to be violent. When the coach is first introduced to Oher, he says, "Mother of Jesus." On the football field, a spectator refers to Oher as a "big black [circus] bear." When he stays the night at the Tuohys', Leigh Anne asks her husband, "You don't think he'll steal anything, do you?" She adds, "If you hear a scream, call the insurance adjuster." Thus these stereotypes cause the audience to laugh, as black males are perceived as natural criminals, *savage/tricksters*; these images are constantly reinforced, an indication of how deeply ingrained in the culture these stereotypes are. Such scenes, however, serve to remind the audience of these stereotypes. When Tuohy and Oher go to the 'hood, to Hurt Village, a "thug" refers to her as "snow flake" and says, "They [white women] always go for the wink." A "thug" also asks Oher if he has "tapped that," meaning had sex with Tuohy. He then tells Oher he would like a little mother/daughter action (sex) with Tuohy and her daughter (*savage*). Thus he is a *savage/trickster*, totally out of step with decent, common morals: a boundary crosser, lusting after white women, operating outside the law, selling drugs, and engaging in other illegal activity, including ruining the lives of young men. For example, one of Oher's old friends, once an accomplished basketball player, now works for the thug selling drugs. He also tells Oher he has a job for him. When Oher asks his friend why he dropped out of school, he says he was tired of people telling him what to do and tired of rules—an indication of a desire to live outside of society in a lawless world that Oher must escape to be accepted by white society. Oher says his mother taught him to close his eyes when she was "doing drugs and other bad things." Sean Tuohy says Oher's strength is his ability to forget the past, to not hold grudges, to forgive. Oher says he learned to "blot out the bad; thus, he literally has a 'blind side.'" There are positives and negatives here. The positive, of course, is his ability to forgive; however, to forget can also mean shedding his beginnings, history, roots, black family, community, and black identity. A display of black masculinity is viewed as a threat to mainstream white culture (Gates 21). Thus Hollywood cinema finds it necessary to contain black male masculinity and sexuality to avoid offending mainstream white audiences (Gates 22). Consequently, using Oher as a protector to Tuohy and her daughter serves to contain any gesture of sex or attraction that the thug expresses. However, it's deeper than this, because the thug's expression of his desire to offend white women reinforces the idea that black men want to rape white women. Thus Oher, by protecting white female sanctity, is adopted not only into the Tuohy family but also into white society. Further, Hollywood's portrayal of the black male as infatuated with the white female is a throwback to D. W. Griffith's *The Birth of a Nation* (1915), where black males are depicted as rapists, lusting after white females. Since the creation of *The Birth of a Nation*, Hollywood has wrestled with the archetypal *buck*, sexually on the prowl, a rapist, a *savage*. As far back as the 1800s, mainstream media have promoted the idea of the white female as the standard and the object of the American male's desire. In *The Birth of a Nation*, the black males are stereotyped as "beast rapists," a term made popular by Southern white newspaper editors (Raper). When Tuohy's friend cautions her about having a large black boy stay in the house with her daughter, we later see Collins watching Oher as he pushes a little girl innocently on a swing. Collins's reaction reinforces the notion that black males are dangerous in general and should be approached with caution. That this scene is included in the film makes it appear acceptable that Oher and other black males are viewed in this way, as potential rapists, and in the case of Oher, what seems to be suggested is that he is an exception.

Discussion

The Blind Side, which was well received by mainstream America, is quite complicated and controversial in its social, political, and psychological implications. The film does not stray from the surface and is a parade of a "series of kind acts by . . . [the Tuohy's], but never delving into the ramifications of their actions nor exploring more complicated socioeconomic and racial issues that are glossed over for the purpose of greater mass consumption" (Puig 4D).

Representations of African Americans rely heavily on stereotypes, myths, and archetypes that are rooted in slavery and white Southern tradition. Unfortunately, Hollywood's projection of the African American male and female reflects society's tendency to view this group as alien other, outside the white norm—a permanent refugee in need of being saved by white society while contained under siege and suspicion. Further, if the black male cannot prove his devotion and willingness to defend and protect white women, children, and white society, he is not accepted in white society. Black women are represented as a "despised other," much more than an other, that is "dangerous to the society—morally, culturally, politically, and economically" (Ladson-Billings 96). The female protagonist in *The Blind Side* becomes a symbol of the perpetuation of the myth of the white female as the new Christian savior, the good mother, the new mammy. The irony of this concept is that it appropriates—thus denying a historical fact associated with black women. As the poet Langston Hughes says, "You done taken my blues and gone." Such appropriation of history from African Americans is much too common with serious implications and rarely without purpose.

Works Cited

Ames, Christopher. "Restoring the Black Man's Lethal Weapon: Race and Sexuality in Contemporary Cop Films." *Journal of Popular Film and Television* 20.3 (Fall 1992): 52–60. Print.

Augustine, Nathalie. "Learnfare and Black Motherhood: The Social Construction of Deviance." *Critical Race Feminism: A Reader*. Ed. Adrien Katherine Wing. New York: New York UP, 1997. 144–45. Print.

Barthes, Roland. *Criticism and Truth*. Trans. and ed. Katrine Pilcher Keuneman. Minneapolis: U of Minnesota P, 1987. Print.

———. *Elements of Semiology*. Trans. Annette Lavers and Colin Smith. London: Cape, 1968. Print.

———. *Mythologies*. Trans. Jonathan Cape Ltd. 1972. New York: Hill and Wang, 1957. Print.

Bell, Derrick. *Faces at the Bottom of the Well: The Permanence of Racism*. New York: Basic Books, 1992. Print.

The Blind Side. Dir. John Lee Hancock. Perf. Sandra Bullock, Tim McGraw, and Quinton Aaron. Broderick Johnson, Andrew Kosov, and Gil Netter, 2009. Film.

Bobo, Jacqueline. *Black Women as Cultural Readers*. New York: Columbia UP, 1995. Print.

Bogle, Donald. *Blacks in American Films and Television*. New York: Simon and Schuster, 1988. Print.

———. *Toms, Coons, Mulattoes, Mammies, and Bucks: An Interpretive History of Blacks in American Films*. 2nd. ed. New York: Continuum, 1989. Print.

Bunch, Sonny. "Blind Look at Sports, Race: Tale of Football and Love without Much Kick." Rev. of *Blind Side*, dir. John Lee Hancock. *The Washington Times*, November 20, 2009, Section B, Show: 3. Print.

Campbell, Christopher P. *Race Myth and News*. Thousand Oaks, CA: Sage, 1995. Print.

The Color Purple. Dir. Steven Spielberg. Perf. Whoopi Goldberg, Danny Glover, and Oprah Winfrey. Steven Spielberg, Quincy Jones, Kathleen Kennedy, and Frank Marshall, 1985. Film.

Diawara, Mathia. "Black American Cinema: The New Racism." *Black American Cinema*. Ed. Manthia Diawara. AFI Film Readers. New York: Routledge, 1993. 3–26. Print.

Dyer, Richard. "*White.*" *Screen* 29.4 (Autumn 1988): 44–65. Print.

Faulkner, William. *The Sound and the Fury*. New York: J. Cape and H. Smith, 1929. Print.

Fiedler, Leslie. *What Was Literature: Class Culture and Mass Society*. New York: Simon and Schuster, 1982. Print.

Foucault, Michel. *The Archaeology of Knowledge*. Trans. R. Swyer. London: Tavistock, 1972. Print.

Freydberg, Elzabeth Hadley. *Sapphires, Spitfires, Sluts and Super Bitches: African Americans and Latinas in Contemporary American Film*. Ed. Kim Marie Vaz. Black Women in America. London: Sage, 1995. Print.

Gates, Philippa. "Always a Partner in Crime." *Journal of Popular Film and Television* 32.1 (Spring 2004): 20–29. Print.

Guerrero, Ed. "The Black Image in Protective Custody: Hollywood's Biracial Buddy Films of the Eighties." *Black American Cinema*. Ed. Manthia Diawara. AFI Film Readers. New York: Routledge, 1993. 237–246. Print.

———. "The Black Man on Our Screens and the Empty Space in Representation." *Callaloo* 18.2 (1995): 395–400. Print.

Hall, Stuart. "Culture, Media, and the Ideological Effect." *Mass Communications and Society*. Ed. James Curran, Michael Gurevitch, and Janet Woollacott. Beverly Hills: Sage, 1976. 313–48. Print.

———. *Media and Representation*. Dir. Sut Jhally. Prod. Sut Jhally. Presenter: Stuart Hall. Media Education Foundation Video/Film, 1997. Film.

———. *Representation: Cultural Representations and Signifying Practices*. London: Sage, 1998. Print.

The Help. Dir. Tate Taylor. Perf. Emma Stone, Viola Davis, Bryce Dallas Howard, and Octavia Spencer. DreamWorks, 2011. Film.

hooks, bell. *Black Looks: Race and Representation*. Boston: South End Press, 1992. Print.

———. *Reel to Real: Race, Sex, and Class at the Movies*. New York: Routledge, 1996. Print.

Jones, Sharon L. "From Margin to Centre? Images of African-American Women in Film." *Social Alternatives* 17.4 (October 1998): 35–39. Print.

Kaplan, E. Ann. *Looking for the Other: Feminism, Film and the Imperial Gaze*. New York: Routledge, 1997. Print.

Ladson-Billings, Gloria. "Who You Callin' Nappy-Headed? A Critical Race Theory Look at the Construction of Black Women." *Race Ethnicity and Education* 12.1 (March 2009): 87–99. Print.

Lewis, Michael. *The Blind Side: Evolution of a Game*. New York: W. W. Norton, 2007. Print.

Lippmann, Walter. *Public Opinion*. New York: Harcourt Brace, 1922. Print.

Long Walk Home. Dir. Richard Pierce. Perf. Whoopi Goldberg and Sissy Spacek. Dave Bell, 1990. Film.

Losing Isaiah. Dir. Stephen Gyllenhaal. Perf. Hallie Berry, Jessica Lange, David Strathairn, and Cuba Gooding, Jr. Paramount Pictures, 1995. Film.

Lule, Jack. *Daily News Eternal Stories*. New York: Guilford Press, 2001. Print.

Monster's Ball. Dir. Marc Forster. Perf. Hallie Berry, Billy Bob Thornton, Heath Ledger, and Peter Boyle. Lion's Gate Entertainment and Lee Daniels' Entertainment, 2001. Film.

Mooney, Paul. *The Godfather of Comedy*. Dir. Paul Mooney, Debbie Allen, Michael Blackson. Prod. Paul Mooney, Henry Petty Jr., Chet Brewster. Perf. Paul Mooney. Atlanta: DavenStar Productions, 2012. Film.

———. *It's the End of the World*. Dir. Paul Mooney, Mary Pelloni. Perf. Paul Mooney. Prod. Paul Mooney, Mary Pelloni, Helene Shaw, Andy Streitfeld. Dallas, Texas: The Lodge. 2010. Film.

"Movie Review: The *Blind Side*." Rev. of *The Blind Side*, dir. John Lee Hancock. *The New Zealand* Herald, May 6, 2010, General News Section. Print.

Muir, Kate. "Christian Charity Is Not Colour Blind." Rev. of *Blind Side*, dir. John Lee Hancock. *The Times London*. National ed. 1st ed. 26 March 2010: 14. Print.

Precious. Dir. Lee Daniels. Perf. Mo'Nique and Gabourey Sidibe. Tyler Perry Studios and Lee Daniels' Entertainment, 2009. Film.

Puig, Claudia. "*Blind Side*, Side Steps Issues: Strong Acting Can't Outrun Shallow Tale." Rev. of *Blind Side*, dir. John Lee Hancock. *USA Today*. Life Section. Final ed. 20 November 2009: 4D. Print.

The Queens of Comedy. Dir. Steve Purcell. Perf. Mo'Nique, Adele Givens, Laura Hayes, and Simmore. Latham Entertainment and Paramount Pictures, 2001. Film.

Raper, Arthur F. *The Tragedy of Lynching*. Montclair, NJ: Patterson Smith, 1969. Print.

Rhoden, William. *Forty Million Dollar Slaves: The Rise, Fall and Redemption of the Black Athlete*. New York: Random House, 2010. Print.

Rogers, Mark. "The Lineman Straight out of Tinseltown: A Fairytale First NFL Campaign for Michael Oher Could yet Have the Perfect Ending." Rev. of *Blind Side*. *The Sunday Times (London)*. National ed. 1st ed. 10 January 2010: 14. Print.

Sapphire. *Push*. New York: Knopf Doubleday, 1996. Print.

Smith, Valerie. *Not Just Race, Not Just Gender: Black Feminist Readings*. New York: Routledge, 1998. Print.

Strother-Adams. "Black Male Masculinity in Cinema: De-sexed, Feminized, and Absent." *Journal of Black Masculinity* 1.2 (Spring 2011): 70–91. Print.

Tolnay, Stewart E., and E. M. Beck. *A Festival of Violence: An Analysis of Southern Lynching, 1882–1930*. Chicago: U of Illinois P, 1995. Print.

Wanzo, Rebecca. "Beyond a Just Syntax: Black Actresses, Hollywood and Complex Personhood." *Journal of Feminist Theory* 16.1 (March 2006): 135–152. Print.

CHAPTER 13

Blindsided by Racism

A Critical Racial Analysis of *The Blind Side*

Charise Pimentel and Sarah Santíllanes

Many people have been captivated by the story of National Football League (NFL) player Michael Oher. Oher was born and raised in severe poverty in Memphis, Tennessee, to an absent and then later deceased father and a drug-addicted and mostly absent mother. He lived most of his life in the projects, where he was often left alone to fend for himself and his eleven siblings. He then found himself in various foster care homes, was homeless from time to time, and throughout all these experiences, suffered greatly in school. Oher was able to turn all this around by focusing on sports—namely, basketball and football. During his senior year of high school, he made up several years of schooling so he could be eligible to play college football; then he attended the University of Mississippi on a football scholarship, was a first-round draft pick in the NFL, and ultimately won a Super Bowl ring when his team, the Baltimore Ravens, won the 2013 Super Bowl. Oher's story became widely known when Michael Lewis wrote the *New York Times* bestseller *The Blind Side* and then subsequently when John Lee Hancock set the book to screenplay and produced the movie *The Blind Side*, both of which center on Oher's life. Even though these white-authored narratives garnered much public attention and acclaim, Oher takes offense to and has contested both narratives. In response, Oher wrote an autobiography, *I Beat the Odds: From Homelessness, to* The Blind Side *and Beyond*, where he sets out to write a more complete story and "separate fact from fiction."

In reference to Lewis's book, *The Blind Side*, Oher states that he was never consulted and that Lewis had almost completed the book before he ever had a conversation with Oher. In his autobiography, Oher writes, "He [referring to

Lewis] was just wrapping up his writing of the book, so the timing worked out well. After a couple of discussions, he felt he had the story he needed to help bring a human face to the position of left tackle" (203). Oher was no less offended by the movie version of his life. Oher explains that the movie is largely embellished and omits key people and events from his life. Oher points out that the Tuohys (the white family who adopted him when he was in high school) were not the only influential family in his life. In truth, Oher met the Tuohys during his senior year of high school. College scouts had already taken an interest in him and were already attending his high school games regularly. By his own admission, the Tuohys were most helpful to him as he struggled with National Collegiate Athletic Association (NCAA) eligibility due to his grades (128).

Perhaps most upsetting to Oher is how the movie portrayed his character as someone who is slow and childlike with no athletic ability whatsoever. Oher states, "I could not figure out why the director [of the film] chose to show me as someone who had to be taught the game of football. Whether it was SJ moving around ketchup bottles or Leigh Anne explaining to me what blocking is about, I watched these scenes thinking, 'No, that's not me at all! I have been studying—really studying—the game since I was a little kid!'" (206). Rightly so, Oher is upset about how the white-authored narratives fail to represent who he is. In this chapter, we build on Oher's critique of the movie. Beyond the impact the movie has had on Oher, we make the case that the film narrative has far-reaching social implications. In our analysis, we argue that the movie is produced and consumed as a colorblind text that dismisses race, resulting in the (re)production of white supremacy as the social norm. In what follows, we situate the film within the particular racial context in which it was produced, in which it continues to be consumed and contested in, and that which it ultimately (re)produces.

The Racial Context

A year before *The Blind Side* was released in theaters, Barack Obama was elected to his first term of presidency, and almost immediately a national rhetoric confirmed what many had already believed for quite some time: the United States was indeed postracial. As it turns out, Obama's election to the presidency was neither a reflection of nor an impetus to a postracial society. This postracial rhetoric would be challenged in the media over and over again. The same year President Obama was first elected to office, black comedians Chris Rock and Dave Chappell made light of what they considered the absurdity of a postracial society. In his stand-up routine, Rock stated, "There ain't no white man in this room that will change places with me—and I'm rich. That's how good it is to be white. There is a one-legged busboy in here right now that's going: 'I don't want to change. I'm gonna ride this white thing out and see where it takes me'" (see "Bigger and Blacker"). Also in 2008, Chappell detailed a fictional scenario that was reminiscent of Derrick Bell's parable "The Space Traders." Chappell detailed a scenario of "Terrorists on a Plane," claiming that "one time racism saved my life" (see "Terrorists on a Plane"). In what was to be an attempted plane hostage situation,

Chappell and one other Nigerian black man came to the realization that their safety was assured, as "terrorists don't take black hostages because black people are bad bargaining chips."

In 2012, Obama's second bid for the White House was visually marred by racism. There was actor Clint Eastwood's monologue with the "empty chair" at the 2012 GOP Convention; subsequently, "No-Bama" empty-chair lynchings were spotted in cities including Austin and Centreville (see Eng). Mitt Romney's son Tagg relayed that the presidential debates fueled a desire for him to "jump out of [his] seat . . . rush down the stage and take a swing at him [referring to President Obama]." Tagg's comments were later referred to as a "joke" and not a potential federal crime (Sirota). Eventually, most conservatives, such as Fox News's Bill O'Reilly, came to the conclusion that the 2012 elections were a "wake-up call" in a "new America" where the "white establishment is the minority" (see Rich).

In 2013, the topic of race continually made national news as the US population and eventually a jury of six women had to consider why George Zimmerman would shoot and kill unarmed black teenager Trayvon Martin, who was walking home at night with a bag of Skittles and a bottle of iced tea in his pockets. A similar but much less publicized case occurred when 45-year-old white male Michael Dunn murdered black teenager Jordan Davis in November 2012 because he felt "threatened" by Davis's loud rap music at a Florida gas station (see Maddox). Both of these cases served as prompts for the US population to consider how the black male body is racialized as "threatening," even when the victims in both cases were unarmed teenage boys.

Racism was also a repeated topic in entertainment news. Paula Deen, a celebrity cook on the Food Network, lost her contract on the television network due to her use of racial slurs. Also making entertainment news were the several white cast members of the 2013 unscripted summer hit show *Big Brother*, who launched so many racist remarks that the show eventually decided to post a disclaimer at the beginning of each show, some of which states, "Houseguests may reveal prejudices and other beliefs that CBS does not condone" and "Viewer discretion is advised." Also, when General Mills aired an innocent enough 30-second commercial for Cheerios cereal, featuring a fictitious interracial couple with a biracial child, racist slurs abounded on the YouTube video of the commercial—so much so that YouTube decided to eliminate those comments and disable any future comments on the YouTube website.

These media spots focusing on instances of individuals expressing and acting on their racist beliefs publicly challenge the notion of a postracial society. And these accounts do not even take into consideration the everyday institutional and discursive forms of racism that do not get reported, and arguably do not even register on society's perceptual field, yet continue to structure inequities. In this chapter, we argue that the United States is still defined by racism; however, this reality is rarely captured in the production of mainstream Hollywood movies, such as *The Blind Side*. In most of the highly consumed and thus culturally influential movies, race is treated as a nonissue as audience members are entertained with storylines that downplay race at the same time they reify racial constructs with images and storylines that paint whites as the desired norm that people of color often deviate from. *The Blind Side* can be considered a colorblind text because the narrative serves as a testimonial of sorts to the racial transcendence and/or colorblindness our country has achieved. The movie, after all, demonstrates that this country has come to a point in history whereby blacks can live under the same roof as whites, not as housemaids or servants, but as part of a loving and functional family. This movie illustrates how a black adolescent can assimilate from an all-black environment to a white home, neighborhood, and school with apparently no need to talk about race and without any racial discord whatsoever. It is also colorblind to the extent that it displays vast disparities in wealth, education, employment, drug use, and many other criminal activities between blacks and whites without any attempt to contextualize these disparities in historical and ongoing manifestations of racism. In this chapter, we analyze the movie *The Blind Side*, finding that it is at once colorblind and racist. Within this analysis, we posit that colorblind film discourse is a manifestation of the white ideological frame that produces and reproduces the erroneous notion that race no longer matters at the same time it (re)produces white supremacy.

Colorblind Racial Ideology

To examine the ideological "film talk" utilized throughout *The Blind Side*, we utilize Bonilla-Silva's theoretical framework on colorblind racial ideology as presented in his book *Racism without Racists: Color-Blind Racism and the Persistence of Racial Inequality in the United States*. As a racial ideology, colorblindness is invested in the normalcy of white supremacy. This ideology denies the history and lived experiences of people of color by diminishing everyday instances of racism and maintaining that contemporary racism is solely the act of irrational individuals. Bonilla-Silva argues that modern racism is less about coercion and violence and instead manifests in an invisible normalcy—a "racial grammar" that produces a racial order as just the way things are (Bonilla-Silva, *Invisible Weight of Whiteness* 174). He explains that the modern conception of "racial domination necessitates something like a grammar to normalize the standards of white supremacy as *the* standards for all sorts of everyday transactions rendering domination almost invisible" (Bonilla-Silva, *Invisible Weight of Whiteness* 174). Ultimately, colorblindness serves to dismiss everyday racism by creating the illusion that issues of race no longer matter.

While colorblind racial ideology is a distortion that maintains white supremacy, it must be actively gained, maintained, and perpetuated via discourse. Ideology and racial reproduction works via a "discourse as dominance" with and through social constructions such as race. Scholars such as Leonardo and Bonilla-Silva argue that the effects of these discourses are not only ideologically problematic but yield material affects within our schools and society. As an example, empirical studies find that urban students of color fare worse in terms of their academic achievement (see Solorzano and Yosso). Wage, wealth, and health disparities reflect America's color line, where whites fare the best and blacks fare the worst (see Leonardo). Distorted racial constructions also manifest psychologically, whether this is via a sense of inferiority or feelings of superiority; this is what W. E. B. Du Bois termed the "psychological and material wages of whiteness." Du Bois recognized the power of whiteness and argued that it "operated as an opportunity structure," solidifying the white race together at the expense of others who did not qualify as white (see Allen).

As stated previously, *The Blind Side* is a good example of a colorblind text because it never takes up race in a significant or critical manner. The Tuohy family does not see Oher as a black adolescent or understand his circumstances as emanating from a racialized context, much less their own social positions. Quite simply, they see an individual in need of help, and they are in a position to offer their help. As Leigh Anne Tuohy states in a *20/20* interview ("The Blind Side— The Real Story behind the Movie"), this story has never been about race. It has been about seeing a child in need and doing something about it. As we explain in this chapter, not only does the film reinforce colorblind ideologies, but it simultaneously reinforces ideologies of white supremacy by creating a narrative that produces concepts of black and white as opposing constructs on a binary. We also introduce the concept of the white cinematic lens, which refers to how the physical aspects of the film conform to the racial ideologies of colorblindness and white supremacy. Thus the white cinematic lens is an ideological frame that shapes the physical production of the film, including such aspects as the camera lens, script, voiceovers, timeline, storyline, character development, settings, and positioning of the camera.

The White-Authored Narrative

In a colorblind narrative such as *The Blind Side*, the characters, including Oher, are presented as raceless, and because of this, the people narrating Oher's story are easily and unproblematically transferred from Oher to white writers, producers, and cast members. Much like dominant historical and fictional narratives that gain credibility because of their white authorship, Oher's story may have gained currency in its social reception and in ticket sales because of its white authorship. In the visual text and written script, we find that Oher rarely speaks; he often looks down or into space when adults talk to him; and he is unlikely to respond to questions directed to him. What audience members do learn about Oher is through white people—characters who represent real people but who only knew him for a brief amount of time.

The movie opens with a voiceover by Sandra Bullock, the actress playing Leigh Anne Tuohy, explaining the importance and physical attributes of a left tackle as images of Oher's physique are displayed on the big screen. Audience members continue to learn about who Oher is through Leigh Anne Tuohy, her family members, and a whole host of other white people. Several white teachers read off his academic record, his intelligence score, assessments of his academic progress and potential, and other documentation attesting to his identity (or lack thereof) as a student. White coaches and white spectators size up his athletic ability in the game of football. When audience members finally gain some insight into Oher's perspective on his own life, we hear about these feelings, not from Oher himself, but from one of Oher's white teachers. She reads his words from a white page—a poem he wrote titled "White Walls," about being surrounded by whiteness. From this poem, it becomes clear that Oher has much to say, especially in regard to his transition to an all-white family and school.

The problematic nature of the white people writing and narrating Oher's life stems from their limited knowledge of Oher's life, their failure to consult with him in the construction of the story, and their limited knowledge of the sociopolitical context in which he was raised. The Tuohys, who are the primary source of information for the film, are a white, Christian, upper-class, Southern family who have lived racially isolated and privileged lives. Leigh Anne Tuohy admits that despite living in Memphis her whole life, she had never been to "that" side of town (where Oher is from) prior to meeting Oher. Later in the film, the Tuohys boast about the magnitude of diversity they have been exposed to, making light of the fact that they actually got to know a black person (Oher) before they got to know a Democrat (Oher's tutor). By eliminating Oher's voice, *The Blind Side* reinforces race relations whereby white people speak on behalf of black people—a historically racist practice whereby white knowledge circumvents black knowledge and undermines black agency.

The (Under)development of Characters and Scenes

Given the particular white authorship of this film, many physical aspects of the film (the white cinematic lens) conform to these white authors' sensibilities, including the development of characters and scenes. As the movie delves into Oher's path to the NFL, audience members are introduced to Oher, not as a young child, but as a teenager who is already a few years into high school. Thus audience members' journey toward getting to know Oher starts when the Tuohys got to know him. By starting at this point in Oher's life (which is only a couple years before he is recruited to play college football), the audience is denied Oher's full life story. In the entire film, Oher's life prior to meeting the Tuohys is reduced to only a few traumatic flashbacks lasting no longer than ten seconds. As a result, audience members know very little about what Oher thinks and feels about major aspects of his life, such as his upbringing, his schooling, his adoption, football, peer pressure, love interests, or exchanging the all-black community of Hurt Village for his new, white, upper-class family.

Not only does Oher's story supposedly begin when the Tuohys met him, but most of the screen time and settings are dedicated to the character development of the Tuohys, not Oher. A majority of the screen time, settings, and shots, for example, center on the Tuohys' surroundings, including their home, the school their children attend, their car, and the restaurants their family and friends frequent. Due to the skewed screen time and settings, Oher's character development in comparison to that of the Tuohys' is very limited. Whereas the Tuohys are shown in complex, well-developed shots, Oher is seen in decontextualized and fragmented shots. For example, in the contested shot of Oher walking down the street in the cold rain, we see him as the Tuohys see him—in a fragmented and decontextualized perspective. We only know he is walking down the street. We do not know where he is coming from, where he is going, why he is walking out in the cold rain without a jacket, and so on. Unlike these underdeveloped and decontextualized shots of Oher, in the same scenes, we get a much richer, more detailed story of the Tuohys. We know, for example, that they are on their way home from SJ's (the Tuohys' son) Thanksgiving pageant at his middle school that started at 7 p.m., that SJ has a crush on his classmate Kenzie, that the Tuohys are amid a family conversation in the car in which Leigh Anne affirms SJ's performance as "Indian #3" in the pageant, and that SJ actually tried out for the role of "Indian Chief" in the play, but the role went to a Chinese student instead, which SJ claims might have been due to some kind of casting bias. These well-developed shots of the Tuohys occur throughout the movie, producing full-bodied white narratives and characters at the same time the movie takes a reductionist stance in developing the black narratives and characters.

The Spectator's Gaze

The failure to develop characters and scenes that center on Oher's life—and the lives of all black characters in the film, for that matter—effectively renders black experiences as unfamiliar and marginal, again downplaying the importance of black experiences while situating whiteness as the norm. When we look at physical aspects of the film, such as cutaway and over-the-shoulder camera shots, we find that these camera shots align with the Tuohy's gaze, creating a spectator's gaze of black life. Essentially, audience members find themselves looking at Oher, not with Oher. Through these camera shots, audience members get to know Oher in the way the Tuohys got to know Oher—through their own point of view as outsiders looking in. For example, when Oher picks up popcorn that has been left behind in the bleachers after a volleyball game, audience members do not see what Oher sees. Rather, the camera shots of Oher are aligned with Mr. Tuohy's point of view, not as a close-up of Oher, but from a distance. So audience members join with Mr. Tuohy to observe Oher from afar as though he is someone other than the subject of the film. In scene after scene, the audience is introduced to new aspects of Oher from this distant and unfamiliar spectator's gaze. Another example occurs when Oher runs into his brother Marcus (whom he has not seen since he was a young child) at a restaurant. The cutaway shot of this reunion is from outside the restaurant and through a window, aligned with the Tuohys' point of view. Physically aligned with the Tuohys through camera shots and a written script, audience members are left not knowing to whom Oher is talking and are unable to hear what they are saying.

In a similar fashion, when audience members are first introduced to Hurt Village, they observe as outsiders who gaze through the car windows of Leigh Anne's car. When audience members are first introduced to Oher's biological mother, Denise Oher, they are introduced as guests. The audience's visual field is constrained to the outside of her apartment alongside Leigh Anne, where we wait for Denise to answer so that we can enter and gaze on her and her surroundings. Even when the Tuohys are not part of a scene, the movie does not break from this distant spectator lens in which audience members look at Oher instead of with Oher. For example, while Oher waits for his shirt to dry at a laundromat, where he steals dryer time from another customer, audience members look from outside and through a window via a cutaway shot, watching and trying to make sense of his life circumstances.

By the constant use of cutaway, over-the-shoulder, and selective point-of-view camera shots, audience members are invited to join in a two-hour journey with the Tuohys to experience Oher as they experienced him—the unfamiliar, decontextualized, and curious life of a young black man. As audience members join in this journey with the Tuohys, they get to see and make sense of Oher's life from the observances and sensibilities of the Tuohys, not Oher. Consistent with Bonilla-Silva's colorblind racial ideology, whiteness works through this film as the unstated norm to which racial "others"—in this case, blacks—are deemed unfamiliar and incomprehensible. Thus this movie carries on with the project of race in which whites are presented in well-developed, "familiar" narratives and blacks are presented in hollowed-out, decontextualized, and "unfamiliar" narratives. As a colorblind text, it is assumed that the audience can identify with and comprehend the white cinematic lens, which renders white experiences as normal and black experiences as distant, fragmented, and unfamiliar. The white cinematic lens from which audience members see and understand the life of Oher assumes, without explicitly stating so, that the audience can identify with and comprehend the lens from which this story is told. As we expand our analysis to Hurt Village and the white Memphis suburb of Briarcrest, and their corresponding inhabitants, we see that colorblind racial ideology shapes how these communities are presented and understood.

Colorblind Conceptions of Hurt Village and the White Suburbs

In Oher's autobiography, he devotes part of his narrative to the sociohistorical underpinnings of Hurt Village and acknowledges that "the history of public housing in Memphis has always been pretty bad" (Oher 6). Oher goes on to explain that "after World War II, the city put up a couple of different neighborhoods just for black people to live in . . . The goal was to keep black families away from white ones, so the poor white housing projects were completely separate" (7). He also refers to racial segregation, stating that "there were still laws that restricted where in the city black people could live . . . Many discrimination laws were still in place, which meant a lot of black families literally had no where to go" (7). Oher even goes on to discuss the advent of "white flight" in Memphis and informs his readers that "Hurt Village started out as one of those housing projects that was originally built for poor white people in the 1950s. But that changed as Memphis did . . . By the 1970s there wasn't a white person to be seen in Hurt Village" (7–8).

In contrast to Oher's sociohistorical and racial contextualization of Hurt Village, *The Blind Side* portrays binary images of Hurt Village and the white Memphis suburb of Briarcrest, where the Tuohys live, as just the way things are. Decontextualized from race, the scenes that focus on these two neighborhoods are oversimplified and give further life to white supremacy, which works to sustain the inequitable opportunities and living conditions that audience members see manifested in these two communities. There is no arguing that Memphis, like most US urban centers, is segregated by race and socioeconomic status, whereby people experience different life outcomes in terms of educational achievement, occupations, and socioeconomic status along these racial and socioeconomic lines. As a colorblind text, however, the rationale for this segregation and differentiation in life outcomes in *The Blind Side* is deemed natural and merit based. Within the film, there is no reference or historical background to the racial, socioeconomic, and overall power relations that create and sustain the physical and conceptual boundaries that exist in cities like Memphis. As a result, the audience is likely to deduce from these decontextualized scenes that the varying life circumstances stem from individual agency.

Essentially, audience members get a sense that the Tuohys live in Briarcrest because they are hardworking and family oriented, whereas the community members of Hurt Village are lazy, corrupt, and negligent of their family responsibilities. Therefore the segregation and contrasting living conditions in Memphis are self-inflicted and warranted. Indeed, a white upper-class woman who goes out to lunch with Leigh Anne claims she is from Hurt Village. During lunch she states, "I didn't mind hard work and look where I am now." This upper-class white woman reinforces the notion of individual agency that is embodied in the rhetoric of the "American dream." Stripped from a racial lens, the American Dream ideology posits that it just takes hard work and dedication, and anyone can emerge from dire circumstances to achieve unlimited amounts of success academically, economically, and socially. If audience members buy into this myth, as this woman has prompted them to do, then they are left with only one conclusion in regard to the people who live in Hurt Village and those who live in the white suburb of Briarcrest. Put simply, people in Hurt Village are not hard workers, do not wish to improve their lot in life, and thus deserve their living conditions and life opportunities. People in the white suburb, in stark contrast, are hardworking and thus deserve the living conditions and material resources allotted to them because they have earned them.

The narrative and images in *The Blind Side* reinforce these dangerous, racially informed conceptions. In the film, Hurt Village, as the name implies, is a place of suffering. In the few scenes that take audience members into Hurt Village, we see young men throwing their lives away to drugs, violence, and other criminal activity. They are hypermasculine and even prone to raping white women. At one point in the movie, one of the men speaks with Oher about how he would have his way with Leigh Anne and Collins and would enjoy the mother/daughter action. The men in Hurt Village do not have jobs, which is illustrated in the several scenes that show them in the middle of the day sitting on their door stoops, chatting about strippers, drinking beer from brown paper bags, and playing card games. The women in Hurt Village are not much different. They do not have jobs, as evidenced by their walking around outside in the middle of the day in bathrobes and slippers. They are also drug addicts, promiscuous, and negligent to their children. The living spaces in Hurt Village are unkempt and even unsanitary. The only scene in Ms. Oher's apartment, for example, is careful to show its disarray. The camera's wide shot of Ms. Oher's apartment details the empty beer cans and wine bottles, dirty dishes piled high, a mattress on the floor, and dirty clothing strewn across the apartment.

These scenes at Hurt Village are in sharp contrast to the scenes in the white Memphis suburb of Briarcrest, where the Tuohys live. In the initial scenes of Briarcrest, we see images of white professionals on their way to work, a family playing baseball, a mother pushing her baby in a stroller, obsessively well-maintained yards and homes, and young children (as young as eight to ten years old) selling lemonade from a homemade stand. From these images, we get a sense that white folks are hardworking, family oriented, and as evidenced by the lemonade stand, industrious and entrepreneurial, even at a young age.

The notion of an innate work ethic is reinforced by the film's emphasis on Leigh Anne's job as an interior home decorator. Needless to say, Leigh Anne is consumed with the lives and activities of two teenage children, as well as her younger son. Financially, the Tuohys are well off, and Leigh Anne does not have to work in order to pay the bills or put food on the table. However, even though there is no real need or desperation, the movie is careful to point out in several scenes that Leigh Anne works nonetheless. Audience members are led to believe that Leigh Anne finds joy and fulfillment in the simple act of working. In this sense, the act of working is portrayed as a characteristic shared by all functional members of society, whether they need to work or not.

The binary conceptions of Hurt Village and Briarcrest extend to the idea of family as well. Whereas the audience members see several instances of child neglect and abandonment in Hurt Village, the Tuohys are a loyal, peaceful, caring, and charitable family with two doting parents (especially Leigh Anne). We see the Tuohys attending their kids' sporting events and school performances, driving their kids to school, reading books to their kids, watching football games together, and taking Christmas family portraits in their home. Their love and caring is without boundaries, and that is why they all come together very effortlessly to bring a homeless teenager into their home. In addition to the love and care that can be found in the Tuohy home, there is also a sense of tranquility and calmness to each of the Tuohy family members and how they interact with each other. They never have disagreements, bicker, or argue. While Oher's biological mother seemingly struggles daily to maintain emotional and physical order in her life, the Tuohys accomplish this almost effortlessly. Even in the most horrifying moments in the film, such as when Oher gets into a car accident that nearly kills SJ, the Tuohys still maintain their cool with no outbursts or expressions of anger.

The simplified binary portraits of Hurt Village and the white suburb of Briarcrest within *The Blind Side* are not only stereotypical images of what white and black racial conceptions have signified historically in this country but lack a larger context to make sense of the ongoing implications of a racialized society and how that affects communities such as Hurt Village and Briarcrest. An example of this decontextualization is the Tuohys' lifestyle and material resources. The Tuohys' upper socioeconomic status is the result of their ownership of not one but eighty-five Taco Bell, Kentucky Fried Chicken, and Long John Silver restaurants. Even though these restaurants are the source of the Tuohys' extravagant income and lifestyle, we never once see these restaurants up close. We do not see the daily operations, the restaurant workers, or much less any of the Tuohy family members working at these restaurants. The omission of these aspects of the restaurant business never allows audience members to complicate the economic and race relations in Memphis. We are never prompted to question the low wages that workers are paid at Taco Bell (or any other fast-food restaurant). Further, we are never prompted to question the labor relations of the larger food industry wherein landowners, managers, and restaurant owners are largely white and upper class, while the underpaid, labor-intensive jobs—including those of field workers, food processors, poultry and beef workers, truck drivers, cooks, preparers, and servers—are largely held by poor to working-class people and people of color. The labor of these people—people who likely live at Hurt Village or other similar poor housing—is the labor the Tuohys profit from. Because we do not delve into these economic and race relations, we are left with oversimplified and disillusioned images of these two communities—one in which whites are hardworking individuals who deserve their allotted material resources and educational opportunities and one in which blacks (and other people of color) do not work hard and are lazy and delinquent and thus deserve their living conditions and lack of opportunities.

Conclusion

With little doubt, there is a broad appeal for the rags-to-riches narrative presented in *The Blind Side*. The movie took in more than $250 million nationally and $309 million globally from ticket sales and has earned an additional $102 million in DVD sales (Montez de Oca 133). According to the online book retailer Amazon.com, it was the eighth highest grossing movie of 2009 and number 63 of all-time highest grossing films at the Hollywood domestic box office. The film was nominated for two Academy Awards: Best Picture of the Year and Best Actress of the Year. Sandra Bullock won the coveted Oscar for Best Actress of the Year, as well as a Golden Globe, a Critics' Choice Award, a Screen Actors Guild Award, and a People's Choice Award (Montez de Oca 133).

Despite its strong social reception, our analysis reveals that the movie fails to capture Oher's story and is characterized by a lack of depth, omissions, and embellishments that render black life and experiences as having little importance. As a result of the colorblind ideological framing, audience members do not become privy to, among many things, Oher's meaningful relationships prior to meeting the Tuohys, his inner thoughts and fears, and his sense of dedication and resiliency. Even though Oher's early life experiences were underdeveloped in the movie, audiences find it compelling that Oher was able to overcome such drastic early-life circumstances (e.g., poverty, abandonment, lack of mentors, and the foster care system). In the larger social context, however, Oher's childhood experiences are by no means isolated. Delpit points out that African American males, more than any other subcategory in the US population, are likely to face a number of undesirable life circumstances. She states that African American males are consistently at the bottom in educational achievement; lead the nation in homicides, both as perpetrators and as victims; have the fastest growing rate of suicide; contract HIV/AIDS at a faster rate than any other segment of the population; are the only US population who are experiencing a decline in life expectancy; and are the least likely to be hired in the labor market and most likely to be unemployed. Specifically, in the area of school achievement, African American males are more likely to be suspended and expelled, less likely to enroll in college, more likely to be classified as mentally retarded or as having a learning or emotional disability, most likely to be placed in special education, and least likely to be placed in advanced placement and honors classes. Even in subject areas where males have traditionally performed strongly, including math and science, African American males are underperforming. In examining these unfortunate life circumstances, Delpit is careful to point out that none of these outcomes, as some researchers once thought or may even still think, are genetic or cultural. Rather, they are the result of historical and ongoing racial inequities that are embedded in everyday individual and institutional practices, including low teacher expectations.

The narrative communicated in *The Blind Side* fails to capture the effects of racism and instead obscures and eliminates from view the systems of oppression that create the outcomes Delpit speaks of and that we see documented in *The Blind Side*. Rather than illuminate the social relations of power that create and sustain racial inequities, the narrative in *The Blind Side* (re)produces a color-blind racial ideology that is ahistorical and devoid of a sociopolitical context. As such, the life outcomes we see in *The Blind Side*—including African Americans as drug addicts, gangsters, and uneducated and the contrasting images of whites as educated, hardworking, and wealthy—appear to be outcomes that simply and directly result from individual choice and responsibility.

Works Cited

Allen, Ricky. "What about the Poor White People?" *Handbook of Social Justice in Education*. Ed. William Ayers, Therese Quinn, and David Stovall. New York: Routledge, 2009. 209–230. Print.

Bell, Derrick. *Faces at the Bottom of the Well: The Permanence of Racism*. New York: Basic Books, 1992. Print.

"Bigger and Blacker." Writer and Producer Chris Rock. *Bigger and Blacker*. HBO Entertainment, 2008. Cable Television.

"The Blind Side—The Real Story behind the Movie." *20/20*. ABC News, 2010. DVD.

Bonilla-Silva, Eduardo. "The Invisible Weight of Whiteness: The Racial Grammar of Everyday Life in Contemporary America." *Ethnic and Racial Studies* 35.2 (2012): 173–194. Print.

———. *Racism without Racists: Color-Blind Racism and the Persistence of Racial Inequality in the United States.* Lanham: Rowman and Littlefield, 2014. Print.

Delpit, Lisa. *Multiplication Is for White People: Raising Expectations for Other People's Children.* New York: New Press, 2012. Print.

Du Bois, W. E. B. *The Souls of Black Folk.* New York: Tribeca Books, 1935. Print.

Eng, James. "Empty Chair 'Lynchings:' Anti-Obama Protest Gone Too Far?" NBC News Online, September 2012. Web. http://usnews.nbcnews.com.

Hancock, John Lee, dir. *The Blind Side.* United States, 2009. Film.

Leonardo, Zeus. *Race, Whiteness and Education.* New York: Routledge, 2009. Print.

Lewis, Michael. *The Blind Side.* New York: W. W. Norton, 2007. Print.

Maddox, Jack. "Florida Teen Dead after Brawl That Began with Loud-Music Complaints, Suspect Jailed." CNN News Online, November 2012. Web. http://cnn.com.

Montez de Oca, Jeffrey. "White Domestic Goddess on a Postmodern Plantation: Charity and Commodity Racism in *The Blind Side.*" *Sociology of Sport Journal* 29 (2012): 131–150. Print.

Oher, Michael. *I Beat the Odds: From Homelessness to* The Blind Side *and Beyond.* New York: Penguin, 2011. Print.

Rich, Benjamin. "Whites-Only GOP Meets Its Demographic Destiny." Stormfront-White Nationalist Community. n.d. Web. November 2012. http://stormfront.org.

Sirota, David. "Tagg Romney: Mr. White Privilege." n.d. *Salon.* Web. October 2012. http://salon.com.

Solórzano, Daniel, and Tara Yosso. "Toward a Critical Race Theory of Chicana and Chicano Education." *Charting New Terrains of Chicana(o)/Latina(o) Education.* Ed. Carlos Tejada, Corinne Martinez, and Zeus Leonardo. Creskill: Hampton Press, 2000. 35–65. Print.

"Terrorists on a Plane." Writer and performer Dave Chappelle. *Killing Me Softly.* Comedy Central Broadcasting, 2008. Cable Television.

Yosso, Tara. *Critical Race Counterstories along the Chicana/Chicano Education Pipeline.* Teaching Learning Social Justice Series. New York: Springer Press, 2006. Print.

CHAPTER 14

Django Unchained

An Analysis

Karen A. Johnson

*D*jango Unchained, the latest film written and directed by Quentin Tarantino, tells the story of a rescued enslaved person named Django (Jaime
Foxx) who teams up with his rescuer, a German-immigrant bounty
hunter named Dr. King Schultz (Christoph Waltz), in an effort to capture criminal fugitives "dead or alive" as a way of acquiring monetary awards. Django and
Schultz ultimately devise a scheme to liberate Django's enslaved wife, Broomhilda (Kerry Washington) from the brutal slaveholder Calvin Candie (Leonardo
DiCaprio). The film takes place in the South, in the time frame from 1858 to
1859. It is a film about revenge and redemption.

Although *Django Unchained* is supposedly a depiction of slavery, it is more
truly a part of the spaghetti Western genre, in every sense of the word. Even
the title, *Django*, is the same name of a 1960s spaghetti Western film made by
Italian filmmaker Sergio Corbucci. Tarantino's *Django* reflects Tarantino's typical derisively mocking, sardonic storyline motif, wherein the aestheticization
of violence is reverberated throughout the entire film and is carried out by the
main character, Django, and the other key supporting characters, such as Schultz
and Candie. According to one critic, "In true QT [Quentin Tarantino] stylistic
fashion, Django represents the antihero—a neo-noir personality type—who is
a tormented individual, due to the brutal horrors of slavery and to the separation of the love of his life, Broomhilda" (Johnson 1). She continues: "Django is
willing to engage in any type of revenge tactics necessary, albeit nihilistic acts
of violence, to rescue Broomhilda from Calvin Candie's plantation. One of the
redeeming aspects of the film is Django's unbridle love for Broomhilda and his

desire to travel to the bowels of the earth, if you will, in efforts to free her from the holocaust of enslavement. That type of commitment to black love is rare on Hollywood movie screens. It is a powerful story plot, indeed" (Johnson 1).

Django Unchained presents one of the rare depictions of a slave-genre Hollywood film wherein cinematic violence is front and center and the main enslaved character is a hero. Aside from the film's bloodstained, horrific, and sensational violence, it is a laudable cinematic piece for unveiling the brutal nature of slavery and for portraying a leading former enslaved character as a hero who engages in a vengeful act of resistance against his enslavement. Indeed, Tarantino's story is one that early twentieth-century slave-genre Hollywood films refused to truthfully unmask. Even the music that was chosen for *Django Unchained* signifies a departure from the types of music that were used in early twentieth-century films, such as *Gone with the Wind* or *The Birth of a Nation*. Unlike the sentimental African American music of the antebellum South, Tarantino utilized a variety of music genres, including hip-hop, in an effort to speak to Django's desire for freedom, revenge, and redemption; some music, such as "Freedom," by Anthony Hamilton and Elayna Boynton, among others, was composed specifically for the film.

Hence, taken as a whole, Tarantino's film provides a counterhegemonic cultural revisionist production of slavery by (a) creating a film that depicts the raw and in-your-face physical brutality that the enslaved endured in this nation; (b) depicting life on one of the two Southern plantation settings as being pathological as opposed to being idyllic, romantic, and nostalgic; and (c) presenting the lead enslaved character (Django) as an antihero who enacts retribution on one of the slaveholders and other white characters. As acknowledged by Tarantino in an interview with National Public Radio's (NPR) *Fresh Air* host Terry Gross, "What happened during slavery time is a thousand times worse than [what] I show" (qtd. in Gross, par. 3). Tarantino points out that he wanted to present two types of violence in *Django Unchained*: "the brutal reality that slaves lived under" for centuries and the "violence of Django's retribution" (qtd. in Gross, par. 4).

Indeed, Tarantino "is the only filmmaker who could pack theatres with multiracial audiences eager to see a Black hero murder a dizzying array of White slaveholders and overseers," notes historian Jelani Cobb (Cobb, par. 2). Yet in Tarantino's efforts to present graphic visual images of the vile abomination of slavery, he interjects lots of satirical humor as a way to make the horrors of slavery more palatable and acceptable. Nothing is humorous about human bondage and degradation. At the end of the film, in the predominantly white movie theater in which I viewed this film, I overheard audience members making comments such as, "That was a funny movie!" or "That was entertaining" (Johnson 2)! With these types of comments, what does that say about the (mis)representations of history in films regarding US slavery and race? Whose and what representational images are worth depicting accurately in film?

Additionally, it appears that Tarantino may not have fully utilized historical slave documents regarding slavery, such as slave narratives, United States Colored Troops' Civil War widows' pension testimonies, or any other reliable resources that could have provided support for his discursive structure or character depictions.

In subtle and not-so-subtle ways, *Django Unchained* draws on a gallery of stereo-typical popular depictions of the enslaved and their lived experiences on the old Southern plantation. These various depictions signify the idea that the enslaved were very docile or content with a life of oppressive servitude. In juxtaposition to the docile and content enslaved individuals, Django is presented as the exception to them—the exceptional black. Tarantino's creative venture begs the questions, How is *Django Unchained* worthwhile if it is mitigated by an ideological web of myths, stereotypes, and caricatures? In what ways could Tarantino have made the film a much more profound cultural critique of the exploitation of slavery and the resistance that the enslaved men and women engaged in?

Through a dialogue with history and the ideological contours of race and representation, this chapter examines how *Django Unchained* offers a reversed and alternative representation of slavery in a slave-genre Hollywood film, as well as how it reinscribes past ideological myths about slavery. This chapter begins by providing a discussion of the evolution of deep-seated racist beliefs in America and how such beliefs made their way into popular culture and into slave-genre Hollywood films. This section is followed by a brief discussion of race and how it is rooted and represented in cultural traditions and the mass media in this nation. After that, I provide a brief discussion of early slave-genre Hollywood films in an effort to put *Django Unchained* in the context of slave-genre Hollywood films.

Racist Depictions of Slavery in Hollywood Films

Understanding the Evolution of Deep-Seated Racist Beliefs in America

In order to understand the stereotypical depictions of slavery and the enslaved in slave-genre Hollywood films, one must understand the ideological contours of racism in the United States. Historically, the images and representations of Afri-can Americans in the US cinema have ranged from the obedient, passive, faith-ful, lazy, and buffoonish men, women, and children to angry, violent, aggressive, hypersexual people. As argued by cultural critic Karen Ross, "It is inescapably true that the position of black people in the image hierarchy has been framed historically by the ideological contours of race and representation" (xviii). The racist stereotypes and mediated images of African Americans in film do not exist in a vacuum but are tied to a long legacy of enslavement, institutionalized racism, white supremacy, and white cultural hegemony in the United States.

Historians have revealed that in the United States, during the nineteenth cen-tury, a proliferation of pseudoscientific racist ideologies emerged. These ideolo-gies reinforced developing and previously held notions of the inherent inferiority of African/black people and the superiority of whites. The Southern polygenists J. C. Nott and G. R. Gliddon drew on science to explore what made "Negros" scientifically different from whites—what made them subhuman. These polyg-enists' racist scientific assumptions effectively wrote blacks/Africans out of the human family as a way of justifying their human bondage. Pseudoscientific theo-ries of race were found in every intellectual and cultural center of the American social order. They were pervasive in the fields of anthropology, sociology, biology, theology, psychology, history, popular culture, and American literature (Boeck- mann; Gould; Frederickson).

Additionally, consumer products and advertisements, along with souvenirs, tourist items, postcards, advertising motifs, and household wares, depicted Afri- can Americans with distorted or grotesque features. These items were sold to the consumer public as a way of putting forth the idea that African Americans were less than human; hence they were individuals to be laughed at. As Goings explains, "By producing and using in advertising everyday items [that depicted blacks] as inferior, as objects worthy of torment and torture, manufacturers and consumers were giving a physical reality to the racist ideology" that was promul- gated during the nineteenth century (14). The pseudoscientific racist theories, along with the racist consumer ethnic products/collectibles, maligned African Americans and "affected the most influential early twentieth century conceptu- alizations of the entire African American historical experience" (Gutman 531). Pseudoscientific ideas became the lens through which this nation viewed issues of race, and they, in turn, gave rise to the political and social repression and sub- ordination of African Americans. These ideas found their way into slave-genre Hollywood films, particularly beginning with *The Birth of a Nation.*

Ideological Contours of Racism and Representation

Without a doubt, race is part of the American legacy, beginning with the near genocide of the American Indians and the holocaust of enslavement of Africans: "Created over four centuries, race has become an enduring narrative" (*Race: The Power of an Illusion*, episode 2). Race is an ideological system that is constructed by society to justify the political and social subordination of people of color. Racism is pervasive in this nation in that it is all-pervading and is intertwined through all societal establishments and influences every aspect of the American social order, including popular culture, film, and mass media. It is a system of oppression that denigrates and violates the human and civil rights of African Americans and other people of color in the US social order. It also operates through blatant bias, bigotry, and discrimination, as well as through the uncon- scious beliefs, ideologies, and behaviors that presume an unacknowledged but omnipresent and insidious white supremacist cultural norm (West; Bell; Omi and Winant; Tatum).

Additionally, racial images, depictions, representations, and beliefs are rooted in language and cultural traditions, which are imposed on the populace as a presumed norm. However, as Bell explains, "the alleged neutrality of social pat- terns, behaviors and assumptions in fact define and reinforce a form of cultural imperialism that supports white supremacy" (6–7). As a social and white cultural imperialist dimension, racism is very much reliant on modern discursive con- ventions and the effect of the explicit and subtle messages of the mass media. In fact, "no other social institution absorbed in the production and distribution of hegemonic discourses" argues Rocchio, has had the "pervasiveness and vol- ume of consumptions as the mass media" through which the common people in modern-day society obtain a large amount of their information "indirectly rather than through direct experience" (5).

The perpetuation of racial images, stereotypes, and myths in mediated texts cannot be disregarded without grasping its essential role in the way in which people come to understand their world. For example, Holtzman maintains that "when most Americans turn on the television, they want to be entertained . . . or simply anesthetized" (3). Rarely do they interrogate the subtle or covert messages about racist depictions of African Americans or other people of color that they are absorbing or their impact on their psyche or belief system. Hollywood films and other mediated texts socially construct binaries to provide an explanation of what it means to be male or female, white American or African American, powerful or powerless. In a racist and white supremacist nation such as the United States, African Americans are socially constructed as inferior, dangerous, dumb, lazy, and so on, and white Americans represent the epitome of what is good, normal, and human. In film, TV, and other mass media, the images and false depictions of African Americans have threatened and dehumanized the black community's image (Orbe 33, 45). As noted by Rocchio, "Precisely because racism remains a pervasive component of American society, the meanings about race that are disseminated by and through the [cinematic production and] mass media demand investigation as active participants" (5).

The Centrality of Race and Representation of Slavery in Hollywood Films

One can trace the cinema's negative and racist depictions of slavery and the enslaved person back to Hollywood's slave-genre films, particularly beginning with D. W. Griffith's *The Birth of a Nation* (1915). *The Birth of a Nation* is based on Thomas Dixon's racist, anti–African American novel *The Leopard's Spots* (1902). *The Leopard's Spots*, a white supremacist polemic, depicts African Americans during the postemancipation era as dangerous, evil, sexually aggressive, and immoral subhumans who are threats to American society and particularly to white women. In this novel and in the later film *The Birth of a Nation*, African Americans were depicted as being innately incapable of partaking fully, as citizens, in the white American social order and therefore had to be controlled by a white terrorist force such as the Ku Klux Klan (Leab). The enslaved were portrayed as content, loyal, childlike, and submissive in the film and novel. However, in freedom, they were juxtaposed as incapable of being mature, responsible, and independent adults. *The Birth of a Nation* incorporated a myriad of the stereotypes of African Americans that had been emerging in the movies since the late nineteenth century (Leab). It "established codes of narrative film practice and circulated as truth a range of black stereotypes for record-breaking audiences" (Smith 1). *The Birth of a Nation*, as a cinematic production, in effect defined African Americans in a manner that fit the movie industry's racist beliefs as well as US racist ideological assumptions (Leab).

The Birth of a Nation influenced the content of all films set in the slave South, such as *Jezebel* (1938) and *Gone with the Wind* (1939; Guerrero 17). In *Jezebel*, a stubborn and strong-willed antebellum Southern belle named Julie (Bette Davis) defies the cultural practices of her gender and class by wearing a red dress as opposed to the required white dress to a formal ball. Julie is compared to the biblical character Jezebel, who is considered a fallen and abandoned woman. However, toward the end of the film, Julie redeems herself when she decides to live on an island of lepers and yellow fever suffers in order to care for them. *Gone with the Wind* is an American period piece that was adapted from Margaret Mitchell's Pulitzer Prize–winning novel of the same name. It is a love story between Scarlett O'Hara (Vivien Leigh) and Rhett Butler (Clark Gable). The film takes place in the South during the Civil War and the Reconstruction era.

In both of these iconic slave-genre Hollywood films, representations of slavery, the enslaved, and the white aristocracy put forth a constructed mythology that portrays life on the pre–Civil War Southern plantations as idyllic, romantic, and happy for both the enslaved and the slaveholders. Both films contain filmic imageries and clichés, such as "white columned porticos, Mint Juleps, and white ladies in lavish formal gowns" who gossip and flirt at endless parties (Guerrero 11). As Guerrero points out, "nowhere do these slave-masters give much attention to what must have been a very demanding business—the punishment, torture, and exploitation involved in the day to day affairs of running a slave system" (21).

Problematically, these slave-genre Hollywood films not only continue to devaluate African Americans, but they render invisible the exploitative nature of the labor and capital wealth generated from the enslaved and hide the cruel reality of the system of human bondage. By masking the human denigration and economic exploitation of US enslavement in film, real-life political discussions about paying reparations to the ancestors of the enslaved or rendering an apology fall on deaf ears because the public (who, for the most part, receive their messages from the mass media) buy into the hegemonic notion that slavery was not a moral stain in US society.

Django Unchained: An Analysis

Portraying the Brutality of Slavery

In *Django Unchained*, we see that Tarantino has a strong commitment to portraying the violent ugliness of slavery. The opening scene in *Django Unchained* communicates to the viewing audience that they are being presented with a revisionist and alternate ideological portrayal of slavery in a Hollywood film. In the opening scene, the audience is introduced to Django and to the hellishness of slavery that he is forced to endure. Django and six other enslaved men, who have been recently sold on an auction block, are being taken to a slave plantation by two white male slave traders named the Speck brothers. A shoeless and shirtless Django is chained to the six men by leg-iron devices. During the day, the chained men struggle to walk in a hot desert/mountain region, which looks more like present-day northern Utah, Nevada, Idaho, or Wyoming than it does Mississippi. At night, these shirtless individuals shiver in the cold. No doubt, as black enslaved men, they are considered cattle—cattle to be bought and sold at will and for profit. Unlike *Jezebel* or *Gone with the Wind*, the aforementioned images in *Django Unchained* challenge and problematize previously held assumptions that African Americans are innately the "lesser race" and therefore justifiably suited for slavery and human degradation. In *Jezebel* or *Gone with the Wind*, the enslaved are characterized as happy, passive, and silent servants who are resigned to the fate of human bondage. In *Django Unchained*, these enslaved men's miserable and oppressive condition is exposed. We see that they are commodities or workhorses who will provide an economic benefit for the enslaver. In actuality, slavery was a backbreaking, coerced, and exploitative labor system that provided "raw materials, agricultural produce, and precious metals that created the modern capitalist economy" (Winant 26; Williams; Rodney 1981). Research reveals that "in the U.S.A., the enslaved African was profitable . . . as a commodity to be sold . . . an object of labor to be rented; and as a producer of cash products, such as cotton, tobacco, sugar, and rice" (Karenga 140). In early twentieth-century slave-genre Hollywood films, slavery was depicted as a munificent, paternalistic, and civilizing institution. With Tarantino's revisionist and alternate cinematic imagery, he flips the script by providing images that speak volumes about the exploitation Django and the other six enslaved men are forced to endure. These images visually communicate powerful ideas about the repulsiveness of slavery.

Later on in the opening scene, the viewing audience is exposed to the extensive welted scars that scourge Django's back. His scars were obviously administered by a slave driver's whip. Throughout the film, the audience views flashback scenes of Django and Broomhilda being viciously whipped by a slave-driver. Slave-drivers, overseers, and enslavers often used violent forms of punishment to coerce fear, submission, and docility on the part of the enslaved (Horton and Horton). The audience's exposure to Django's scarred back mirrors the infamous photo of the mutilated back of a real-life enslaved man named Gordon.[1] The scarring of the enslaved person's body played a pivotal role in controlling the black body. Scarring represented ownership as well as punishment through branding and/or whipping (Henderson). In *Django Unchained*, the scarred body of Django reveals the scathing indictment of slavery's brutality—an indictment that challenges the predominant belief that slavery was a benign tradition (Goodyear). Django's scarred back and the flashbacks to his and Broomhilda's whippings shatter the illusion that plantation life was a very loving and idyllic and nostalgic milieu. In the opening scenes, Tarantino does an excellent job in visually unmasking the notion that slavery was an institution that involved the exercise of power and oppressive violence toward African Americans.

The issue of the pathological enslaver or enslaved person represents another aspect of the cruelty of slavery in *Django Unchained*. In the film (unlike any other slave-genre Hollywood films), Tarantino reveals the complex and pathological relationship that the enslaver has with some of his enslaved. The character Calvin Candie is an excellent example of how slavery brings forth levels of psychopathology and delusional thinking and interactions. Candie operates under the myth that his slaves are content and grateful for their enslavement. He sees himself as a father figure to them and hence occasionally bestows special treats upon them.

For example, consider this scene: Candie hosts a small, private event wherein two enslaved man engage in a gory, bloodstained, vicious fight. Candie's slave wins the fight. To celebrate, he takes his domestic enslaved servant, Coco; his sexually exploited whore, Sheba; his bodyguard, Bartholomew; and Django and Schultz to the Cleopatra Club Restaurant in Greenville, Mississippi. Each enslaved person is eating a very expensive meal. In bragging to Schultz about his special dinner treat for his enslaved persons, Candie asks Schultz, "You spent a lot of time around niggers . . . ?" Schultz responds by saying no. Candie then states, "Well, if you did, you'd know what a treat this was for 'em'" (Tarantino 79). Candie proceeds by asking each of the enslaved if they felt special. With contentment on their faces, each responded, "Yes sir, Monsieur Candie," as they continued munching on their expensive meal (Tarantino 79).

I argue that the aforementioned scene in the restaurant indeed departs from the typical slave-genre Hollywood films. The scene suggests that the system of slavery in the United States contributed to an overall pathology on the part of the slaveholder and, to some extent, the enslaved. Candie is no doubt racist and delusional in his belief that the enslaved are subhuman beings; and for this reason, his expensive dinner treat is a civilizing force for them. In fact, in a much later scene in the film, Candie makes an argument that suggests that he strongly believes in the pseudoscience of phrenology—an argument/theory that suggests that blacks are inferior beings due to the shape and size of their brain and skull.

At any rate, Candie is happy that his little act of so-called kindness generates contentment on the part of the enslaved. But were Coco, Sheba, and Bartholomew really happy? Or were they pretending to be happy because they feared reprisal from Candie? Or were they pretending to be happy as a way to circumvent their oppressive condition? For the most part, historical research reveals that the enslaved knew their enslaver better than the enslaver knew himself and in turn used this to their advantage (Horton and Horton). Another question to be raised is, Were Coco, Sheba, and Bartholomew truly happy because they had internalized their own sense of oppression? Indeed, the system of slavery in the United States was not designed, by its very nature, to be a happy and munificent system for the enslaved—and certainly not one in which the enslaved would be blessed with a caring and loving father-like slaveholder figure. That is an oxymoron! It was, in fact, a system that was designed to break the spirit, free will, and agency of the enslaved in order to coerce him or her into a life of human bondage.

The uncritical viewer who buys into the ideological myth that the enslavers were kind and paternal may not grasp the idea that Candie is a complex and pathological character. Even though Candie is portrayed as a sadistic and masochistic slaveholder, he is simultaneously portrayed as someone who has tenderness in his heart for the wealth-generating human beings he owned—hence the complexity of his character. Yet the uncritical viewer who does not understand issues and assumptions about race and slavery may assume that this scene makes the cruelty and moral bankruptcy of slavery more palatable. He or she may view Candie as the white savior, and his act of kindness "soften[s] the historical reality of black folks' stolen labor" and masks the "parasitism of the master class" (Guerrero 20–21). Still, Tarantino, by portraying Candie as pathological, departs from the assumption that the Southern enslaver was a normal and rational person in his beliefs and interactions with his enslaved "property."

Django: Unpacking His "Exceptionalism"

The character Django is a different and interesting enslaved person from the racist slave-genre characters of the past. The only other Hollywood enslaved character that represented a departure from the past slave-genre racist tropes is Mandingo, a character in a film called *Mandingo*, which debuted in 1975.

In the opening scene, Django is liberated from bondage by Schultz and soon after becomes Schultz's bounty-hunter apprentice. Schultz offers Django clothes and gives him a horse. With this proffer, Django has acquired some level of agency, albeit he is still subordinately tied to Schultz. Hence, early on, Django is marked as someone who is given certain opportunities (by his white savoir and emancipator) that set him on the path of being the exceptional slave (Tillet). Consequently, when juxtaposed against the other minor enslaved characters in the film, the viewing audience sees Django as someone who is exceptional or different from the other enslaved individuals. He is free as opposed to being enslaved. He rides a horse when black men are not seen as people who ride horses. He carries a weapon when it forbidden for blacks to carry arms. Effectively, Django stands out *and* alone from the other enslaved people in that he is fearless, self-assured, intelligent, bitter, and vengeful.

Django's exceptionalism, particularly when juxtaposed against the other enslaved characters, operates as a central narrative in the film. It establishes the primacy of the racially coded meanings of exceptionalism, particularly the exceptional enslaved or freed slave, within the signifying operations of the film. As explained by Imani Perry, the concept of "racial exceptionalism is the practice of creating meaning out of the existence of people of color who don't fit our stereotypic or racial narrative based conceptions . . . The phenomenon of exceptionalism ultimately serves to support a general stereotyping of the larger populace . . . and justifies that stereotyping within a social context in which racial egalitarianism is proclaimed . . . when the normal state of people of color is assumed deficient, then the departure from that state puts one into a state of exception" (Perry 130–13).

In various scenes of the film, Django is described as being different, thereby he has the privilege to be granted certain opportunities befitting the exceptional black man. For example, one of the slaveholders, Spencer "Big Daddy" Bennett, describes Django as someone who is different because he is free; thus he ought not to be treated like all the other enslaved persons because "he ain't like these other niggers around here" (Tarantino 26). Instead, he is treated like the poor white boy who occasionally works on his plantation. In other words, Django is given an honorary poor-white class status. Candie also sees Django as exceptional because "he is a slaver," says Candie, and thus he allows Django to stay in the "Big House" (Tarantino 92).

In the following scene, we also see Django's exceptionalism more clearly, as he is juxtaposed in a binary oppositional position against Rodney, Chicken Charley, and Chester, the three enslaved Mandingos from Candie's plantation, Candyland. After Schultz and Candie later die in a shootout in Candie's home, Django is sold as a slave to the Lequint Dickey Australian Mining Company, along with Rodney, Chicken Charley and Chester. En route to the mining company, Django convinces the three Australian men that he is not a slave but a bounty hunter. In response to one of the men's statement, "You a slave," Django says, "I ain't no goddam slave. Do I sound like a [expletive word] slave? . . . I'm a bounty hunter!" (Tarantino 146). With this response, Django evokes his "exceptionalism"—his binary oppositional status as superior in the free/slave binary. Not only does he convince the Australians to free him due to his exceptional status as a non-enslaved person, but he is also able to convince them to give him a horse and gun so that he and the men can return to Candyland to hunt down a fugitive supposedly working on the plantation. After receiving the gun, Django shoots all three of the Australian men. Soon after, he walks over to the mining company's horse and unhooks it from the wagon. Django also walks over to the caged part of the wagon where Rodney, Chicken Charley, and Chester are imprisoned. Django asks one of them to hand him the dynamite. Rodney gives Django the dynamite, and immediately Django rides off into the dusty landscape.

What is interesting about this scene is that Django does not ask the men to help him liberate Broomhilda, nor do they offer. He has only one goal, and it is to liberate his wife and to hell with everyone else. Django has no sense of solidarity toward the other enslaved individuals. His goal of liberating his wife is a self-centered, one-man show. Perhaps the reason Django is self-centered is because he is hell-bent on revenge as opposed to having a revolutionary perspective about liberating the enslaved.

At any rate, Django would have been a more profound character had he had a progressive perspective of what it meant to be a free black person in a nation that federally supported, depended on, and defended slavery. It would have been powerful if he had to grapple with what types of responsibilities come with one's freedom, particularly in a region of the nation—the South—that was filled with enslaved men, women, and children. These were issues that real-life rebellious slaves, such as Denmark Vesey and Nat Turner, grappled with. They were committed to the abolishment of slavery. If Django had a sense of collective responsibility—similar to Vesey or Turner—to not only liberate Broomhilda but also to emancipate his enslaved brothers and sisters, then he would have clearly understood that the progress, freedom, self-determination, and overall political and economic success of the lives of African Americans (free or enslaved) are all interrelated. In the historical record, many of the enslaved who became free during the antebellum period felt compelled to engage in antislavery work. Many worked in *concert* with other enslaved or free blacks as well as with white abolitionists—rarely alone, as in the case of Django—to fight for their people's liberation (Douglass; Brent).

When Django rode off into the dust, Rodney, Chicken Charley, and Chester sat passively and flabbergasted. They had expressions of amazement on their faces as they watched Django ride in the direction of Candyland. It was as if they wanted to say, "Who is he? I've never seen a black man like him. He is indeed an exceptional black man!"

For the three enslaved men, Django did not fit the mythical narrative of what it meant to be an enslaved person. Rodney's, Chicken Charley's and Chester's behaviors are confusing in a film that is supposedly committed to depicting slavery differently from past Hollywood slave-genre films. In reality, the 1850s was a tumultuous and pivotal era in the United States as it pertained to the controversy over slavery. And it is important to note that African Americans (free and enslaved) were at the heart of it all in their struggle to put a death knell to the monstrous system of slavery.

Black and white abolitionists intensified their antislavery work largely due to the emergence of proslavery legal dictums. Also, John Brown's raid on Harper's Ferry and his subsequent execution took place in 1859. This is the same time frame that Django searches for Broomhilda. *The Weekly Anglo-African*, a nineteenth-century African American newspaper, "compared Brown's raid with Nat Turner's slave rebellion, touting it as one of the country's most effective attacks on slavery" (qtd. in Horton and Horton 166). Hence 1859 was a key turning point in the antislavery movement. Additionally, slave uprisings from previous decades, such as the large-scale one engaged by Nat Turner, "shaped a new era in American abolitionism" (Hine, Hine, and Harrold 157).

Therefore, why did Tarantino racially code Rodney, Chicken Charley, and Chester as passive and docile, particularly when the enslaved men and women during this time frame were resisting their bondage? History reveals that slavery did not work because of the various forms of resistance that the enslaved engaged in (Karenga; Franklin; Tobin, Dobard, and Wahlman). In fact, Gabriel Prosser's, Denmark Vesey's, and Nat Turner's rebellions (or, in the case of Prosser, his planned rebellion), as well as David Walker's *An Appeal to the Coloured Citizens of the World*,[2] influenced "radical black and white abolitionists in the North" and also influenced the enslaved's efforts to rebel, escape, and resist their enslavers (Hine, Hine, and Harrold 157). Additionally, the slave narratives of Frederick Douglass, Harriet Jacobs, and Sojourner Truth reveal a counternarrative of what it meant to be a slave in the antebellum South. Their narratives reveal their level of agency and strong desire to be free by any means necessary. By racially coding Rodney, Chicken Charley, and Chester as docile and frighten idiots, I argue it presents to the viewing audience a permanently fixed idea and an enduring myth that suggests enslaved people were waiting for the "Great Emancipator" to free them because they were too ignorant to take matters into their own hands! This ideological myth runs counter to what it actually meant to be a slave in this nation. If Tarantino had tapped into slave narratives and other sources, he would have learned that the enslaved went out of their way to undermine slavery.

Alas, unlike Rodney, Chicken Charley, and Chester, Django is angry at the exploitation and brutal oppression he has endured. And he is also tormented by the physical and emotional abuse his wife had been subjected to. In the film, the viewers see that Django had a resolute and determined will to liberate his wife, whereas Rodney, Chicken Charley, and Chester are very terrified and inept in helping Django liberate his wife as well as themselves. Hence all these depictions make Django's character stand out as an exceptional black man.

The idea that Django is an exceptional individual does not make sense in and of itself. Thus I argue that a binary oppositional stance helps unpack a clearer understanding of the meaning of difference or exceptionalism with regard to his character. And in this binary (fearless/fearful; self-agency/docility; intelligent/simpleminded), the viewing audience sees how Django is not only exceptional or different but fundamentally different from the other enslaved people. As an exceptional freed man, Django is cast against the grain (particularly with regards to the typical slave characters of past slave-genre Hollywood films) in that he is everything that the stereotypical Hollywood enslaved characters are not. In this filmic creation of Django, he transcends his supposedly inherent, inferior, former enslaved characteristics. Django's image insists on his agency—on his rightful place to engage in retribution for the crimes against Broomhilda and himself.

Nonetheless, the undergirding meaning of the idea that Django is an exceptional enslaved person reveals that this character is a reworking of the traditional Hollywood black male character stereotypes. It is in fact a reimagined character that is simply "dressed in new garb to look . . . hip, provocative, and politically relevant" (Bogle 232). Django, the character and the film, links back to 1970s black exploitation films such as *Shaft* (1971) and *Super Fly* (1972), with their "thematic emphasis on black confrontation, with or victory over white oppression" (Guerrero 31; Bogle). Indeed, Django, as an antihero character who enacts forms of violence against the enslavers, can be viewed as a major significant shift from how Hollywood cinematic productions previously portrayed African American enslaved characters. However, Django, as an exceptional freedman, sustains long-established racial assumptions of the larger enslaved populace.

Stephen: An Enigma

Stephen, Candie's loyal slave, is the exact opposite of Django. And he is Django's archenemy. He is spiteful and malicious. In fact, it appears that skin of the actor who plays Stephen (Samuel L. Jackson) is intentionally darkened with custom makeup for the purpose of racially producing the effect of evilness. Black or dark, in the Western discursive hegemony, is evil. In the film, Stephen's facial expressions are grimacing, his tone projects anger, and he walks with a limp. Stephen is "the Basil Rathbone of House Niggers," writes Tarantino (Tarantino 91). He is "scheming . . . [and] always trying to influence and manipulate power for his own self-interest" (Tarantino 91). Sadly, Stephen provides comic relief to the viewing audience. And what is even sadder is that Django's final bloody and violent showdown for his and Broomhilda's liberation is between Django (the freedman) and Stephen (the enslaved) as opposed to between Django and Candie (the enslaver).

Stephen's loyalty is an enigma, especially after Candie dies in the film. In the film, the only so-called power that he has is the opportunity to terrorize the other enslaved people. He also has the privilege to drink alcohol and smoke tobacco on a so-called man-to-man level with Candie. Why was Stephen not given the opportunity to take his freedom the first chance he got after Candie was murdered? Why was he made to remain loyal even in Candie's death?

For the most part, the historical record reveals that the enslaved always longed for their freedom and resisted their enslavement. If they exhibited any form of loyalty, it was a way to circumvent their oppression. John and Eliza Quitman, real-life enslavers, were delusional in their belief that their enslaved servants were loyal. When they took their slave John, their most "kind, attentive, and faithful [servant]," to Boston for a vacation, he ran away the first chance he got (Horton and Horton 121). The Quitmans were convinced that he was kidnapped by abolitionists. They refused to believe that he was a free-thinking human being who was willing to exercise his own self-agency for freedom. With regards to Stephen, it would have been more powerful if Tarantino had him pretend that he was loyal and, upon Candie's murder by Schultz, had him join forces with Django to help liberate all the enslaved persons on the plantation. If Tarantino had created that type of twist in the storyline, then it would have been a revolutionary reversal from previous slave-genre Hollywood films. Alas, Stephen's character links back to nineteenth-century racial assumptions about the faithful black slave or servant. Still, in this sense, Tarantino does not depart from these ideological myths but instead reinscribes them.

Summary

Quentin Tarantino's *Django Unchained* provides a revisionist depiction of slavery. In this revisionist depiction, he presents the harsh, gory, and brutal reality of the holocaust of enslavement. His main character, Django, is a heroic former enslaved man who engages in bloody acts of violence and revenge in an effort to liberate his enslaved wife from the ownership of a ruthless enslaver. In many respects, *Django Unchained* can be commended for providing a reversed and complex portrayal of slavery in the American South. This film truly departs from early nineteenth-century slave-genre Hollywood films such as *The Birth of a Nation*, *Jezebel*, and *Gone with the Wind*. Yet there were also many aspects of the film that did not diminish or challenge Western and racist assumptions about the historical experience of the enslaved individual in this nation. Instead, I argue, Tarantino draws on past racist tropes and ideological myths and assumptions about the enslaved person's lived experiences in such a way that it constructs the enslaved person as one who is docile, passive, and inept. By depicting the enslaved blacks in this manner, it invalidates or delegitimizes the legacy of liberatory struggle of enslaved and free blacks in this nation. In this manner, Tarantino falls short on this film.

So many years after the Civil War and the Emancipation Proclamation, at what point will this nation seriously come to grips with its ugly past? While

Tarantino falls into the trap of reifying past slave-genre tropes, he simultaneously puts forth a serious effort to unpack the truth about the brutality of slavery. It would be great if Tarantino created a *Django Unchained 2* in which Django and Broomhilda are made into badass revolutionary liberators on the level of Nat Turner and Harriet Tubman. That type of slave-genre Hollywood film would be groundbreaking indeed! And Tarantino is one major US Hollywood blockbuster filmmaker who could get the financial backing to produce such a project. It is time for that type of film!

Notes

1. Gordon was an enslaved man who received a severe whipping from one of his slave drivers. After Gordon ran away from the plantation, he joined the Union Army. The surgeon of the army who examined Gordon made a photo of his back. Later mass photocopies of Gordon's back were circulated and used as part of the antislavery literature for abolitionists because it was emblematic of the horrors of human bondage.
2. David Walker (1796–1830) was an eighteenth-century African American antislavery abolitionist. In 1829, he wrote *An Appeal to the Coloured Citizens of the World*, which was a call for enslaved blacks to engage in forceful acts of struggle to gain their liberation from slavery. His *Appeal* radically shaped the antislavery abolitionist movement.

Works Cited

Bell, Lee. "Theoretical Foundations for Social Justice." *Teaching for Diversity and Social Justice*. Ed. Maurianne Adams, Lee Anne Bell, and Pat Griffin. New York: Routledge, 2007. 1–14. Print.

Boeckmann, Catherine A. *A Question of Character: Scientific Racism and the Genres of American Fiction, 1892–1912*. Tuscaloosa: U of Alabama P, 2000. Print.

Bogle, Donald. *Blacks in American Films and Television: An Encyclopedia*. New York: Garland, 1988. Print.

Brent, Linda. *Incidents in the Life of a Slave Girl*. 1861. Charleston: Create Space Independent Publishing Platform, 2012. Print.

Cobb, Jelani. "How Accurate Is Quentin Tarantino's Portrayal of Slavery in *Django Unchained*?" January 2, 2013. Web. January 10, 2013. http://www.newyorker.com/online/blogs/culture/2013/01/how-accurate-is-quentin-tarantinos-portrayal-of-slavery-in-django-unchained.html.

Douglass, Frederick. *Narrative of the Life of Frederick Douglass*. Cheswold, DE: Prestwick House Literary Touchstone Press, 2004. Print.

Franklin, John H. *From Slavery to Freedom: A History of African Americans*. New York: McGraw-Hill, 2000. Print.

Frederickson, George. *The Black Image in the White Mind: The Debate on Afro-American Character and Destiny, 1817–1914*. Middleton, CT: Wesleyan UP, 1987. Print.

Goings, Kenneth W. *Mammy and Uncle Moses: Black Collectibles and American Stereotyping*. Bloomington: Indiana UP, 1994. Print.

Goodyear, Frank H. "Photography Changes the Way We Record and Respond to Social Issues." n.d. Web. July 15, 2013. http://click.si.edu/Story.aspx?story=297, 2011.

Gould, Stephen J. *The Mismeasure of Man*. New York: W. W. Norton, 1996. Print.

Gross, Terry. "Quentin Tarantino, Unchained and Unruly." *Fresh Air*, January 2, 2013. Web. January 5, 2013. http://www.npr.org/2013/01/02/168200139/quentin -tarantino-unchained-and-unruly.

Guerrero, Ed. *Framing Blackness: The African American Image in Film*. Philadelphia: Temple UP, 1993. Print.

Gutman, Herbert G. *The Black Family in Slavery and Freedom, 1750–1925*. New York: Vintage, 1976. Print.

Henderson, Carol E. *Scarring the Black Body: Race and Representation in African American Literature*. Columbia: U of Missouri P, 2002. Print.

Hine, Darlene C., William C. Hine, and Stanley Harrold. *African Americans: A Concise History*. Upper Saddle River, NJ: Pearson Prentice-Hall, 2006. Print.

Holtzman, Linda. *Media Messages: What Film, Television, and Popular Music Teach Us about Race, Class, Gender, and Sexual Orientation*. Armonk, NY: M. E. Sharpe, 2000. Print.

Horton, James O., and Lois E. Horton. *Slavery and the Making of America*. New York: Oxford UP, 2005. Print.

Johnson, Karen A. "Django Unchained: Historical Inaccuracies and Racial Tropes Abound." December 29, 2012. Web. http://www.politeonsociety.com/2012/12/29/ django-unchained-historical-inaccuracies-and-racial-tropes-abound.

Karenga, Maulana. *Introduction to Black Studies*. Los Angeles, CA: U of Sankore P, 2002. Print.

Leab, Daniel J. *From Sambo to Superspade: The Black Experience in Motion Pictures*. Boston: Houghton Mifflin, 1975. Print.

Omi, Michael, and Howard Winant. "Racial Formation." *Racial Formation in the United States from the 1960s to the 1980s*. Ed. Michael Omi and Howard Winant. New York: Routledge, 1986. 57–69. Print.

Orbe, Mark. "Constructions of Reality on MTV's *The Real World*: An Analysis of the Restrictive Coding of Black Masculinity." *Southern Communication Journal* 64.1 (1998): 32–47. Print.

Perry, Imani. *More Beautiful and More Terrible: The Embrace and Transcendence of Racial Inequality in the United States*. New York: New York UP, 2011. Print.

Race: The Power of an Illusion. California Newsreel, Executive Producer Larry Adelman, DVD, 2003. Film.

Rocchio, Vincent F. *Reel Racism: Confronting Hollywood's Construction of Afro-American Culture*. Boulder, CO: Westview Press, 2000. Print.

Rodney, Walter. *How Europe Underdeveloped Africa*. Washington, DC: Howard UP, 1981. Print.

Ross, Karen. *Black and White Media: Black Images in Popular Film and Television*. Cambridge: Polity Press, 1996. Print.

Smith, Valerie. "Introduction." *Representing Blackness: Issues in Film and Video*. Ed. Valerie Smith. New Brunswick, NJ: Rutgers UP, 1997. 1–12. Print.

Tarantino, Quentin. *Django Unchained, Best Original Screenplay*. New York: Weinstein Company, 2012. Print.

Tatum, Beverly. *Why Are All the Black Kids Sitting Together in the Cafeteria?: And Other Conversations about Race*. New York: Basic Books, 1997. Print.

Tillet, Salamishah. "Quentin Tarantino Creates an Exceptional Slave." *In America*, December 25, 2012. Web. December 26, 2012. http://inamerica.blogs.cnn.com/ 2012/12/25/quentin-tarantino-creates-an-exceptional-slave.

Tobin, Jacqueline, Raymond Dobard, and Maude Wahlman. *Hidden in Plain View: A Secret Story of Quilts and the Underground Railroad*. New York: Anchor Books, 2000. Print.

West, Cornel. *Race Matters*. New York: Vintage, 1994. Print.

Williams, Eric. *Capitalism and Slavery*. Chapel Hill: U of North Carolina P, 1994. Print.

Winant, Howard. *The World Is a Ghetto: Race and Democracy Since World War II*. New York: Basic Books, 2001. Print.

CHAPTER 15

Are the Kids All Right?

A Look at Postracial Presentations in *The Kids Are All Right*

Jenise Hudson

Introduction

On May 9, 2012, one day after North Carolina voters dealt a blow to the nation's same-sex marriage movement by passing its controversial Amendment One ban on domestic partnerships, President Barack Obama announced his support of same-sex marriage; the next day, *Newsweek* magazine's cover proclaimed that the nation had welcomed its first "gay" president into office. This provocative analogy of the nation's social striving toward civil rights progress across race and gender lines was intended, arguably, as a celebratory illumination of the cooperative means by which achievements in the racial justice movement have served as touchstones for subsequent gender-related legislation. Yet, as Andrew Sullivan's commentary in *Newsweek* would show, the headline also signaled the appeal of a discourse of interchangeability between African American and same-sex platforms that likened the advocacy of white gay rights proponents to the long since imagined completion of racial projects for socioeconomic and political equity. Reflecting on Obama's political volleying between "marriage equality" and "civil union" during the early years of his campaign, Sullivan questioned the apparent eth(n)ical irony of the soon-to-be-president's reticence to acknowledge same-sex marriage: "Was this obviously humane African-American advocating a 'separate but equal' solution—a form of marital segregation like the one that made his own parents' marriage a felony in many states when he was born" (Sullivan)? Couched in an otherwise nuanced

analysis of the campaign's strategic courting of the LGBT vote was Sullivan's presumably postracially influenced allusion to Obama's obligation, as a raced ben-
eficiary of twentieth-century civil rights legislation, to ensure the progression of
federal protections for LGBT communities who were next in line as the nation's
most disenfranchised group.

Sullivan's appeal to a purely linear narrative of "race, then gender rights" signifies the discursive complications of ideological approaches that overdetermine the
sequential nature of civil and human rights progress.[1] As scholars such as Siobhan
Somerville have argued, the absence of intersectional perspectives in such "like
race" dialogues has often resulted in a stilted analysis of ongoing race-related
advocacy. When African American and same-sex platforms are tethered together
strategically to advocate for (and, in recent years, to achieve) legal recognition
of the latter group's civil rights—mainly because "like race" analogies have been
"more [judicially] appealing because of the distinctive argumentative power of
race in federal constitutional reasoning" (Somerville 343, 345)—a residual effect,
at times, is the oversimplification both of the intersectional identities of African
Americans identifying with LGBT communities and of the racially and socioeconomically advantaged positionalities of white nonheterosexual individuals: "Such
a view tends to rely on an optimistic reading of the history of civil rights in the
twentieth-century United States, a reading . . . in which all individuals have equal
opportunities to inhabit the roles, rights, and responsibilities of citizens [. . . and
in which] the rights gained by one group establish a precedent for another group's
entitlement to the same rights" (Somerville 335). While these approaches aim to
"elevat[e] sexual orientation to the level of judicial review . . . that race currently
receives" (Somerville 345), they tend to "enact a kind of amnesia" (336) that
overlooks the missteps of social advancement that, many times, have required
a circling back to, and amendment of, state and federal laws that have failed to
enforce and protect oppressed groups' legal rights.

Within the public arena, particularly, the mitigating tenor of such postracial
discourses has eschewed the presence of racism at the center of some gay rights
platforms purportedly founded on "colorblind" (Bonilla-Silva) systems of inclu-
sion. Smuggled in the false bottom of these decidedly "neoliberal" (Whitehead)
arguments is a trenchant narrative of disparity, which—by way of an intersectional reliance on race and class privilege—obsequiously upholds and "justif[ies
the] racial status quo" (Bonilla-Silva 210) through a "structure [. . .] of practices,
mechanisms, and institutions that maintain systemic white privilege" (Bonilla-
Silva 221). This discursive trend toward assimilationist politics in the Obama
era is evidenced in Judy Rohrer's essay "Black Presidents, Gay Marriages, and
Hawaiian Sovereignty: Reimagining Citizenship in the Age of Obama," which
exposes conservative gay rights advocates' hijacking of postracial narratives in
the wake of California's 2008 passing of Proposition 8. Revealing these media
pundits' efforts to shame black voters they characterized as uncommitted to their
political agenda—and whom they erroneously blamed for the bill's passing—
she writes, "The media picked up the story and broadcast it nationwide with
storylines that were all variations on a theme: how could a community that had

fought so hard for civil rights and had finally been 'given' a Black president turn around and deny rights to another oppressed community" (Rohrer 116–17). Rohrer's interrogation of the political spin placed on "like race" analogies by gay rights leaders not only throws into relief pundits' denial of black voters' agency in the election; importantly, it exposes the racism and class privilege engrafted onto some gay rights groups' ostensibly culminating narratives of equity.

The Kids Are All Right: Analysis

It is with an understanding of the evolving tensions that underwrite discourses of raced and same-sex cultural rites, legal rights, and legislative writings that this chapter endeavors to enter into the ongoing conversation about what happens when white writes black in the 2010 independent film The Kids Are All Right, directed by Lisa Cholodenko. Set in Los Angeles during an unspecified time period that paradoxically acknowledges California's sanctioning of same-sex marriage without rendering legible any of the state's political upheaval over Proposition 8, *Kids* imagines a different California: one in which not only is same-sex marriage legalized, accepted, and normative but all traces of the nation's firestorm of debates over gay and lesbian marriage recognition are illegible.[2] The film centers on the lives of lesbian spouses Nic and Jules (actresses Annette Benning and Julianne Moore) as they work to save their marriage in the wake of infidelity and raise their two children, Laser and Joni. Nic, a medical doctor, and Jules, a burgeoning landscape architect, encourage their children's academic and personal achievement in a manner that demonstrates compliance with conventional middle-class values. Daughter Joni (whose name is a tribute to Nic's favorite singer, Joni Mitchell) is a college-bound National Merit Scholar, while son Laser (whose name aptly reflects his parents' open-mindedness) is a responsible, sensitive (yet masculine), multitalented high school athlete.

Idealized, law-abiding, nonthreatening examples of sanitized homosexuality that adhere to rigid heteronormative standards of normalcy,[3] the entire family registers as a palatable version of the "everyday American" nuclear same-sex household. Sociologist Jay Cee Whitehead's analysis of what he terms "gay and lesbian neoliberalism" helps illuminate the political capital of Nic and Jules's posturing within such a framework. Whitehead asserts, "Neo-liberal technologies aim to bring individuals' concepts of freedom and morality in line with projects for reducing the state's fiscal responsibility for population-level problems" (7). In the case of Nic and Jules, their marriage offers the economic benefit of health care and insurance, as well as the sharing of household responsibilities that fall in line with conventional expectations of American heterosexual families. As such, their union solidifies "developments in historical sociology, governmentality, and feminist political theory [that] have paved the way to reframe the case of marriage equality in terms of the dwindling American welfare state" (Whitehead 12). The couple's duplication of nuclear family values to approximate largely conventional middle-class value systems is underscored, and a contrast is made between Nic and Jules's values and the values of Joni and Laser's biological father (i.e., donor),

Paul, who enters their life after Joni reaches out to him on her brother's behalf.[4] In a scene where Paul comes to Nic and Jules's home to have a barbeque with the family, Nic interrogates him about his occupation and about his marital status: "Are you married, divorced, dating?" The conversation reveals that Nic's traditional standards of monogamy align with a traditional, middle-class lifestyle. In comparison, Paul, who is a local food producer and restaurateur, comes across as being irresponsible and unsettled despite his heterosexual identity.[5]

Yet, at the same moment that Nic and Jules's conventional, nuclear parenting strategies bear out the film's claim of homosexual and heterosexual common ground (and hence the right of gay and lesbian couples to legislative enforcement of that common ground), their investment in the infrastructural value systems that foster the idea of the nuclear family implicates them as vested participants in entrenched systems of racism and classism. Consider, for example, an early scene that demonstrates the couple's penchant for cultural voyeurism. In the scene, Nic and Jules are watching an episode of the National Geographic Channel's television series *Lockup: Abroad*. The image that projects from their plasma flat screen television shows a white man in an extreme close-up angle yelling frantically at a tribally dressed black man. The man screams repeatedly, "I want my knife!" while the black man patronizingly sneers in pauses, "Do . . . you . . . want . . . to . . . die?!" Amused by the spectacle, Nic turns to Jules, who is sitting beside her on their plush living room sofa. "Remind me never to do drugs in Morocco or Uganda," she states with mocking urgency. Jules, smirking, complies with the joke: "I hate it when that happens."[6] The scene figuratively displays the unbalanced power dynamics of white, Western imperialism in nonwhite, third-world nations: as Nic and Jules sit on their couch watching *Lockup: Abroad*, their "seat of privilege" is both materially and metaphorically manifested. In a blatant contrast of Nick and Jules to the culturally "othered" backdrop of the National Geographic program, viewers are encouraged to see the women as unquestionably American, irrespective of their sexual orientations (because at least they aren't like *those* people). Viewers are prompted to laugh at the sarcasm of Nic and Jules's banter rather than question the subtle racism or the long-reaching consequences of their voyeuristic, socioeconomically and racially exploitative engagement of the television program.[7]

Further evidence of the film's tendency to soft-pedal glaring issues of racialized cultural exploitation appears in Jules's dehumanizing, paternalistic treatment of her Latino gardener, Luis. In a move that is highly racist, Jules fires Luis to cover up the fact that she has been repeatedly having sex with Paul on the jobsite where he has hired her to landscape his local vegetable garden. Jules fabricates a narrative that Luis is unreliable and potentially drug addicted in order to justify his termination: to this end, she relies on maligning stereotypes that portray the Latino/a community as shiftless and irresponsible.[8] Luis, who functions primarily to verify Jules's power as a white employer[9] over classes of working poor, receives virtually no opportunity to rebut his employer's defamatory claims. Rather, he becomes the silenced scapegoat for Jules's improprieties.[10] Jules's behavior in the scene of Luis's firing exposes the trenchant nature of her investment in such privilege even as viewers are encouraged to believe that her easygoing, hipster image precludes her from racially hegemonic outlooks.[11] In the scene, Jules becomes flustered when she sees that Luis, whom she has sent to the local Home Depot for supplies, has returned to the jobsite early. Jules has just finished having sex with Paul, and she immediately is defensive when she finds Luis standing in the yard:

> **JULES:** Did you go to Home Depot?
> **LUIS:** Yep, just got back.
> **JULES:** That was fast.
> **LUIS:** Yeah, no lines. (He smiles broadly.)
> **JULES:** What's that look you're giving me?
> **LUIS:** What look?
> **JULES:** The look that you're giving me right now?
> **LUIS:** No. That's no look. That's my face?
> **JULES:** Yeah, no, I'm not going to play this game. You can keep your judgments to yourself.
> **LUIS:** I didn't give no look, Senora.
> **JULES:** I didn't ask why you blow your nose all the time. If you have a drug problem, that's your business!
> **LUIS:** (Emphatically) I don't have no drug problem. I have allergies.
> **JULES:** Then why are you a gardener!?
> **LUIS:** (Stutters, confounded) Because I love the flowers.
> **JULES:** You know, this is not going to work. I'm going to pay you through the end of the day and then we're through.
> **LUIS:** Senora . . .
> **JULES:** (Retreating quickly to the house) Thank you very much . . . thanks . . . thank you.
> **LUIS:** Can we talk about this?
> **JULES:** No, we can't. You know why? Because there's nothing to talk about. I think you know.

Jules's infantilizing and paternalistic demand to know what Luis is staring at, as well as her blatantly racist suggestion that Luis "knows" why he is being fired, is outrageous. Not only do her statements invoke trenchant narratives of racial policing,[12] but they force this viewer to the larger interrogation of why the film never rectifies the grossly privileged tenor of Jules's (or Nic's) words and actions. Prior to Luis's firing, there are other scenes in which Jules lashes out at the gardener because she fears he will expose her affair. In a similar jobsite scene, for instance, Jules is in the midst of having sex with Paul when she hears Luis calling for her outside. In her rush to get dressed, she forgets to put her shoes back on. Jules immediately redirects the attention to Luis when she sees him staring at her bare feet. Patronizingly, she asks, "What? I was using the bathroom. Do . . . you . . . have . . . to . . . use . . . the . . . bathroom?" Viewers are encouraged to laugh at her pathetic attempts to conceal her affair rather than question the highly racist nature of her statements, even as Jules erects a racist narrative to suggest that Luis's confused expression is the consequence of his poor knowledge of the English language.

Kids also encourages viewers to believe that Jules's guilt over firing Luis is an equal trade for his lost wages and maligned character. To wit, though, Jules's regret is more about her guilt and less about the negative material consequences of her actions on Luis. In a scene where she again has slept with Paul, Jules bemoans the choice to fire Luis. She wonders aloud, "Jesus what is wrong with me? I shouldn't have fired Luis like that. I was so wrong. I am so fucked up." Yet Jules's statements of guilt are stifled quickly by her selfish desire to keep Nic from uncovering her infidelity. When Nic comes to the jobsite and inquires about Luis's whereabouts, Jules immediately lies and defames Luis:

> **JULES:** I had to fire him.
> **NIC:** Oh, no!
> **JULES:** Yeah, he had a drug problem.
> **NIC:** No! What drug?
> **JULES:** Blow, I think.

Ostensibly, this exchange between Nic and Jules is meant to add comic light-heartedness to a tense moment. However, the danger of viewing Jules's actions humorously lies in the ability of such a perspective to obfuscate material conflicts surrounding Luis's employment prospects. The film's characterization of Luis as a nonnative English speaker without a written work contract suggests that his livelihood is impacted hugely by her decision to fire him.[13] To this end, the film's dismissive treatment of Luis's wrongful firing works against the civil rights efforts of advocates seeking to improve the material conditions of racially marginalized communities.

That *The Kids Are All Right* shies away from shedding light on the parallels that exist between Luis's disenfranchisement and that of gay and lesbians is especially curious, since the film's geographical setting of California marks a hotbed of controversy in terms of its extension of civil rights protections to both same sex couples and illegal immigrants.[14] Arguably, this is an oversight that has the unanticipated effect of exposing the contradictory political stances of characters such as Jules and Nic, as well as the negative effects of their stances on the material conditions of those persons they objectify. To this end, even as *The Kids Are All Right* positively exposes the humanity and success of same-sex households, close critique of its neoliberal obfuscation, or overwriting, of intersectional race and class privilege ultimately reveals both the danger of presuming that one is precluded from participation in oppressive systems of classism, racism, or sexism if (s)he ostensibly is liberal minded and/or socially progressive and the ineffectiveness of sentimental discourse where there needs be infrastructural change.[15]

Notes

1. In her article "The Kids are All Right but the Lesbians Aren't: Queer Kinship in US Culture," Suzanna Danuta Walters discusses the pervasiveness of similar narratives within popular culture discourses of gay visibility. She states, "The trajectory of gay visibility is neither a singular and linear narrative of progress and victory, nor a simple story of no movement at all. The (liberal) celebratory progress narrative may be delusional and dangerous but the (more radical) two-steps back and no steps forward tale is similarly dismissive and short-sighted" (918).

2. *Kids* is a work that Cholodenko in the past has hesitated to label as political in press junkets for the film's release. For instance, in a 2010 interview for *Cineaste*, Cholodenko credited the film's absence of overt political engagement to her high artistic disposition. Speaking to Cynthia Lucia and Richard Porton, she confessed that she is not an "overly political person." Yet, as this chapter posits, the film's rendering of an "idealized," "normative" (i.e., universally relatable), "modern" American same-sex family that conforms to standards of heteronormativity is highly political. Specifically, the film's leveraging of Nic and Jules's sexual marginalization with intersectional race and class privilege that is predicated on the on-screen oppression of otherwise marginalized black and brown communities signifies a trenchant and troubling narrative of hegemonic neoliberalism at work even in postracial gay rights platforms. It is with an eye toward rendering visible the inextricable links between Cholodenko's film and these politicized discourses that this chapter examines several instances in which *Kids*'s appropriation of dominant, honorarily heteronormative discourses whitewashes and overwrites (or overrites or overrights) the oppression of other marginalized characters.

3. Without overtly invoking the negative stereotypes of sexual deviance purported by conservative, heteronormative, and religious sects, Nic and Jules's children's academic success and well-adjusted natures refute homophobic claims that same-sex parents are incapable of providing the same quality of healthy upbringing to young, impressionable children as heterosexual families.

4. In the film, Laser prompts his sister to contact Paul because, as an 18-year-old, she is able to do so. The film suggests that while he loves his "momses," he yearns to have a relationship with a father figure as well.

5. He is also painted as very new age or hipster. His employee is a black woman played by the model Yaya, who is reminiscent of Foxy Brown. In fact when he sees her, he says, "Hey Foxy."

6. It might be significant to note that the white man in the scene is likely imprisoned for attempted drug trafficking. If this is so, the irony becomes that Nic and Jules are indulging in a show about another white person who has sought to capitalize on the economy of the racially oppressed.

7. Importantly, the film includes more than one scene where Nic and Jules, along with Joni and Laser, are watching the National Geographic program.

8. Viewers first witness Jules's disrespectful treatment toward Luis in a scene where Luis interrupts a conversation Jules is having with Paul to announce that he has completed his shift for the day. Arriving at the kitchen door where Jules and Paul are discussing the blueprints for his outdoor living space, Luis knocks on the door and gestures that it is quitting time. "Senora, five o'clock," he says. Jules replies dismissively, "OK, thanks." The gardener turns to go but doubles back. He calls, "Same time tomorrow?" and smiles. Jules, who is perturbed that Luis has disrupted her twice, hastily looks up. "Yep, same time tomorrow," she answers. Once more, Luis

calls to her. "Goodnight," he says, waving a friendly good-bye. Jules is frazzled by Luis's talkativeness and impatiently stutters, "Goodnight!"

9. In the first scene where Jules has sex with Paul, she does not hesitate to go through with the act because of any remorse where Nic is concerned. Rather, she pauses because she does not want to endanger her position of authority as Luis's employer. She briefly stops Paul, stating, "I can't . . . I have a guy outside." Jules's concern with her ability to maintain an image of power where Luis is concerned exposes her deep investment in hegemony.

10. Despite the film's attempt to establish Luis in a comic manner, viewers should not overlook the oppressive conditions under which he works or the racism he is forced to endure from ostensibly open-minded characters.

11. Jules perpetuates the stereotype that gay and lesbian individuals are more culturally sensitive when she jokes with Laser that she wishes he was gay so he'd be more sensitive. She overlooks that this is a stereotype and that maliciousness and heteronormative behavior abounds even among gay men.

12. Recall that earlier in the film, Luis finds it necessary to ask Jules if he should report for work at the "same time tomorrow." His uncertainty about his day-to-day work schedule as Jules's gardener suggests he is working as a noncontracted employee.

13. In this vein, Rohrer asserts of the efforts of California Republicans to get support against Prop 8, "Californians, they encouraged us to think, are 'better than that' (except, of course, for our hardcore discrimination against migrants/immigrants, our anti-affirmative action policies, our astronomical incarceration of people of color and so forth)" (117).

14. The film fails to reconcile the disconnect that exists between gay and lesbian queer advocacy groups and racially, socioeconomically impoverished groups that struggle for similar societal gains.

15. Addendum: Since beginning this project in summer 2012, many historic judicial moments have occurred to effect positive movement on these issues of gay marriage rights. Simultaneously, federal actions such as Attorney General Eric Holder's investigation into racial profiling, the Supreme Court's invalidation of portions of the Voting Rights Act, and the nation's debates over immigration reform have served as reminders that the time and space for race and gay rights platforms are overlapping. My hope is that where *Kids* shies away from shedding light on the parallels that exist between racial and gendered disenfranchisement, examinations such as this will keep us vigilantly aware of crucial matters of intersectionality.

Works Cited

Bonilla-Silva, Eduardo. *Racism without Racists: Color-Blind Racism and the Persistence of Racial Inequality in the United States*. 3rd ed. Lanham: Rowman and Littlefield, 2010. Print.

Cholodenko, Lisa, dir. *The Kids Are All Right*. Focus Features, 2010. Film.

Lucia, Cynthia, and Richard Porton. "Gay Family Values: An Interview with Lisa Cholodenko." *Cineaste* 35.4 (Fall 2010): 14. Print.

Rohrer, Judith. "Black Presidents, Gay Marriages, and Hawaiian Sovereignty: Reimagining Citizenship in the Age of Obama." *American Studies* 50.3/4 (Fall/Winter 2009). Print.

Somerville, Siobhan. "Queer Loving." *GLQ: A Journal of Lesbian and Gay Studies* 11.3 (2005) 335–70. Print.

Sullivan, Andrew. "The President of the United States Shifted the Mainstream in One Interview." *Newsweek*, May 12, 2012, 22. Print.

Walters, Suzanna Danuta. "The Kids Are All Right but the Lesbians Aren't: Queer Kinship in US Culture." *Sexualities* 15.8 (December 2012): 917–933. Print.

Whitehead, Jay Cee. *The Nuptial Deal: Same-Sex Marriage and Neo-Liberal Governance.* Chicago: U of Chicago P, 2011. Print.

Manufactured Maids, Mammies, and Falsified History

No White Help Wanted or Needed

Maulana Karenga

The issue of the white assumption of the right and requisite experience and expertise to speak African Americans' cultural truth as persons and a people in life, literature, the media, the academy, and various other venues raises necessary and useful questions, not only about the movie *The Help*, but also about the larger issues of cultural and political hegemony. The hegemonic posture, practice, and resultant problem bring to the surface a set of interrelated issues, and central among these is the social and cultural definition and construction of reality and the relentless cultivating of a consciousness receptive to its acceptance in passive silence or eager approbation, in spite of its negative impact and effect. Indeed, one of the greatest powers of an oppressive society is its capacity to define reality and make others accept it, even when it's to their disadvantage. And one of its major tools to accomplish this is the media in all its forms, both corporate and social, for in each, the interest and ideas of the ruling race and class reign in spite of self-congratulatory conversation of openness and free space and calculated traces and trial-balloons concerning diversity.

Thus a constant concern of ours in this regard—indeed, the hub and hinge on which our consensus of concerns turn—is the principle and practice of self-determination. By this I mean our right and responsibility as persons and a people to speak our own special cultural truth—the truth of our lives, work, struggles, hope, pain, and oppression and all the other experiences, initiatives, and aspirations—that makes us who we are and are constantly becoming as we strive to come into the fullness of ourselves. Or put another way, as the second principle of the *Nguzo Saba* (The Seven Principles), *Kujichagulia* (Self-Determination), states, self-determination is the right and responsibility "to define ourselves, name ourselves, create for ourselves and speak for ourselves" (Karenga 50). And in the exercise of this most fundamental right, we need *no help* from others, no matter how well-meaning their stated intentions and aspirations are.

This principle and stance is even more morally and culturally compelling in the context of racial oppression as a historical fact and a current and continuing reality, for racism by definition is a system of denial, deformation, and destruction of a people's history, humanity, and human rights based exclusively or primarily on the specious concept of race. And race stripped of all its pseudoscientific mystification is essentially a sociobiological construction employed to assign human worth and social status using whites as the paradigm. Far from racial prejudice, hatred, and hostility directed toward different racialized peoples, racism is the capacity and action of turning that hatred and hostility into public policy and socially sanctioned practice. Indeed, racism expresses itself in three basic aggressive ways: as imposition of both physical and psychic violence; ideology that justifies the imposition, claiming superiority of the dominant group and inferiority of the dominated; and institutional arrangements that promote and perpetuate the imposition and ideology. And the media (especially, in this case, movies) is a key institution in the promotion of this imposition and ideology.

Moreover, regardless of postracial fantasies and accompanying self-deluding conversations, racism as plantation paternalism (and maternalism) still informs so much of what is written, thought, spoken, and practiced in this society. Thus, with all due respect to our beloved, beleaguered and still-believing president, cotton-land consciousness and practices are still with us in life and literature, at sites of work and worship, and at places of higher learning and lower pleasures. And it is played out in scenes of racist and racialized understandings and interactions, even at the movies. Certainly, the movie *The Help*—with its manufactured maids, mammies, and falsified history—is a classic example of this, once again turning black oppression, perceived pathology, and undeserved suffering into a central source of white entertainment and profit and providing, as a result, parallel and self-congratulatory illusions of whites having saved blacks and redeemed them from the awesome indictment the evidence of history offers.

And make no easily achieved mistake: this racism is not simply a product of the sinister and slow-to-learn South but also a reflection of a pervasive conception of black and white and the unequal human worth and social status assumed and enforced for each. Clearly, this is a white American story with manufactured maids and mammies used for local and living color and for nursing their soon-racialized infants and racial egos. It is the white woman who is the celebrated and reputedly sensitive writer, the would-be insightful reader of the "Negro" mind, the redeemer of the pawned and oppressed black soul, and the real racial heroine as Hollywood's racial protocol, established order, practice, and white sensibilities would have it. Thus even though it is black women's stories, experiences, voices, ideas, and writings that are the material out of which the central contents of the movie are made, these women are not allowed and presumed to be unable to write or present these narratives themselves. They are made out to be classically dependent creatures with obvious racial disadvantages and derived relevance, needing a white hand and mind to lead them into the light of their own limited self-realization. And this is not to mention their men, who are portrayed as irresponsibly absent and abusively present.

There is, in this template of cinematic racial remembrance and reality construction, a toxic and terribly dizzying mixture of white acute denial and self-delusion, the deformation of black humanity, and the shameless falsification of our history. The story takes place in the era of segregation, yet it strives hard to hide the horror and savagery of segregation history. Segregation, by its very nature, is a violent process and practice—physically, psychically, politically, and economically. Thus to pretend with the author and moviemakers that the central focus should be on the issue of dual toilets, unkind and intemperate words, and bad attitudes is to be complicit in the cover-up of the systemic violence that was a daily part of the lives of black maids—that is, rape, sexual harassment, assaults, and other daily degradations of various forms. Also, we must not forget or put aside for cinematic sake the larger context of violence against black families and black people as a whole, for racism is by definition and design a violent imposition and savage practice of domination, deprivation, and degradation. And by any name and honest measure, segregation, Jim Crowism, or apartheid were and are systems of racism in some of their rawest and most brutal and savage forms.

At the heart of segregation was its signature weapon of white terrorism: lynching. Thus to leave this barbaric practice out of any story of this period is self-deceptive at best and, at worst, dishonest and dismissive of the horrific violence meted out to black people with ruthless and relentless regularity. In spite of the cinematic techniques used to elicit laughter, tears, heart-tugs, hugs, and contrived harmony, it is clear that this movie trivializes the tragedy, terror, and suffering of black oppression as well as the resilience and resourcefulness of black maids and black people. Even the police beating of a black woman is quickly taken off camera to reduce the depiction of the raw violence endemic to a racist, segregated society. And the history of the civil rights movement is summed up in a broadcast announcement of Medgar Evers's assassination and martyrdom—given little more than a honorable mention and definitely not placed in the context of white supremacy and violence as a racial, religious, economic, and political way of life.

Furthermore, black resistance is reduced to a passive, quiet dignity of a sort; self-discipline under the backbreaking burden of undeserved suffering and humiliation; various expressions of impotence, like eye-rolling or talking on the side-and-sly; and putting feces and other filth in the oppressor's and abuser's food. This is not the material out of which heroes and heroines are made, and it is more the action of alienated, abused, and frustrated waitresses than conscious witnesses and midwives of history, which many of the maids and other black women were with black men in the black freedom movement, as well as those who struggled in their own way before the movement.

There are obvious lessons communicated to a black audience by this film. First, it reminds us of Paul Robeson's message to writers, artists, and intellectuals seeking to escape the imminence and urgency of struggle. He says to them, then, and to us now, "The battlefront is everywhere; there is no sheltered rear." Second, it reminds us of the Kawaida contention that the battle we are constantly fighting is the battle to win the hearts and minds of our people, to speak our own special cultural truth, and to make our own unique contribution to how this society and the world are reconceived and reconstructed in the interest of human dignity, freedom, and flourishing. Moreover, it is to recognize the constant efforts of the dominant society to define reality in its own image and interests and make us accept it. It thus tends to cultivate the craving in some for any small gesture of "help," or human caring from even oppressors or their limitedly "rebellious" off-spring. Thus those affected, even unconsciously, dance to their own degradation or applaud their own humiliation in music, movies, and books peddled as portraits of "real" black life—that is, deformed, deficient, and patently pathological.

Also, the movie seeks to reinforce a falsification of black history that is an inaccurate, reductive, insensitive, dignity-denying violation of the memories of those whose suffering, sacrifice, and life-and-death struggles paved the path and opened the horizon of history and possibility for us. Perhaps nothing is more pernicious and pathetic in these movies and books of unwanted white "help" and presumption of right and expertise than their attempts to push the liberal line of moral and social equivalence of black oppression and liberation struggle with white liberal discomfort with superficial aspects of our oppression and their efforts to ease, but not end, our oppression.

Thus the main white character is bothered by bathroom bigotry, not the codi-fied brutality of the system as a whole—by the sick silliness of the segregationist bigot, not the system's savagery, terrorism, and daily violence of various kinds. And we cannot miss or mistake the fact that the whites' solution is always a spe-cious spiritual conversion requiring more from the oppressed than the oppressor and suggesting that righteous anger is wrong and robust resistance is suicidal. The logic of the situation leads us to the conclusion that ultimately we must depend on the questionable "kindness" of our oppressors. But as Malcolm notes, the logic of the oppressed cannot and must not be the logic of the oppressor if the aim and upward thrust of the oppressed is toward liberation. As the character Preacher Green says in the movie, "If you can love your enemy, you already have victory." This means loving them, not their loving us, or any other "enemy" they might teach and tell us to hate.

In the end, the white men's violence is camouflaged and the white women's collaboration and lack of moral courage are excused with the bromide from the film version of *The Help*: "Sometimes courage skips a generation." Thus they are generous without giving justice, sympathetic without serious and sustained engagement, and personally humane without an equitable and systemic sharing of wealth, power, or status. The solution here seems simple: don't buy books or attend and applaud movies that deny our dignity, usurp our right and responsi-bility to speak our own special cultural truth, and make caricatures and cost-free liberal causes out of our lives; in a word, we should not collaborate in our own oppression in any form. On the contrary, the moral and cultural imperative is to practice and promote the principle of self-determination and to retrieve and relate our sacred narrative in the dignity-affirming and life-enhancing collective and personal ways it deserves and demands, and through this and righteous and relentless emancipatory struggle, we must pose and pursue a new world and way of relating as humans in the world.

Work Cited

Karenga, Maulana. *Kwanzaa, A Celebration of Family, Community and Culture*. Los Angeles: University of Sankore Press, 2008. Print.

Index

146; self-alignment with South Central LA, 148; statement of intentions, 149

semiotics, 179–80

Semple, Kirk, 112

sexual violence, experienced by black women working in white households, 71n1

Shaft (film), 222

Shakur, Sanyika: *Monster,* 143, 146, 149, 151–52

Shanks, Ruth, 160

Shields, David, 144

Sidibe, Gabourey, 6, 99, 179

signifying, 28–30

Simone, Nina, 164

Simpson, O. J., issue of N-word in trial of, 140

Skove Nevels, Cynthia, 103

slave auction, 191

slave-genre films, 212, 216, 217, 223

slave narratives, 153, 212, 221

slavery: holocaust of, 214; pathological relation of enslaver with enslaved, 217–19; scarring as representation of ownership, 217

slaves, escaped, risk of sharing their history with white audience, 21

slave uprisings, 221

Smiley, Tavis, 6, 97–98

Smith, Valerie, 189

Smith Act of 1940, 121n35

Snyder, Jimmy the Greek, 191

Social Security Act of 1935, denied Social Security to domestic workers and farmworkers, 112–13

Somerville, Siobhan, 228

Soul Sister (Grace Halsell), 4, 8; comparison with *The Help,* 167–68; experimental blackness, 159–68. *See also* Halsell, Grace, and *Soul Sister*

South African apartheid, 109

Southern belle fantasy trope, 102, 118; among white women participating in Bronx Slave Market, 108; cannot exist without antithetical black mammy trope, 114; contention that all white women stem from Southern planter class, 104–5; and cult of true womanhood trope, 104; overlooks white supremacist brutality of Southern belle, 104

Southern Literary Messenger, 59

Spacek, Sissy, 176

spaghetti Western genre, 211

Spanish heritage fantasy, 105

Spencer, Octavia, 6, 71n2, 97–98

Spielberg, Steven, 175

Starr, Kevin, 151

Steve Harvey: Still Tripping, 186

Stiller, Ben, 6

Stockett, Kathryn, and *The Help:* apprehension in using voices of black domestic workers, 25–26; capitalization on secondhand terror, 168; condescending skepticism toward tales of black maid, 33–34; initial trouble in publishing *The Help,* 5–6; insistence on her intimacy with childhood black maid, 35, 110, 111–12; motivation for writing *The Help,* 27; note to Cooper denying relationship between Cooper and her fictional character, 26–27; novel as expiation of white guilt over failure to ask childhood mammy about her life, 166–67, 168; personal nostalgia for old South and black mammies, 7, 68–69; similarities to Eudora Welty, 44; situation of self outside the world of the black community, 33; "Too Little, Too Late," 26, 107. *See also The Help* (film); *The Help* (novel and film)

Stolar, Robert, 161, 163

Stone, Emma, 95

Stone, Ruthie, 102, 117

Stowe, Harriet Beecher: *Uncle Tom's Cabin: Life Among the Lowly,* 2, 4, 7, 8, 43; comparison with Stockett's *The Help,* 61–71; influence on image of the mammy in popular culture, 62; project to expose racial injustices by showing pious nature of blacks, 61; and race representation, 150

Strathairn, David, 177

Streep, Meryl, 6

street gang memoirs, 143, 145–46, 152, 153, 154

Stringer, Vickie, 153

Styron, William Styron. See *The Confessions of Nat Turner* (William Styron)

Suite 101 website, 145, 147

Sullivan, Andrew, 227–28

CPSIA information can be obtained
at www.ICGtesting.com
Printed in the USA
LVHW082328301018
595433LV00005B/81/P

9 781137 446251